THE STRAIGHT MIND IN CORINTH

SEMEIA STUDIES

Number 88

THE STRAIGHT MIND IN CORINTH

Queer Readings across 1 Corinthians 11:2–16

Gillian Townsley

SBL PRESS

Atlanta

Copyright © 2017 by Gillian Townsley

Library of Congress Cataloging-in-Publication Data

Names: Townsley, Gillian, author.
Title: The straight mind in Corinth : queer readings across 1 Corinthians 11:2–16 / by Gillian Townsley.
Description: Atlanta : SBL Press, 2017. | Series: Semeia studies ; number 88 | Includes bibliographical references.
Identifiers: LCCN 2016056511 (print) | LCCN 2016057450 (ebook) | ISBN 9781628371475 (paperback) | ISBN 9780884141761 (hardcover) | ISBN 9780884141754 (ebook)
Subjects: LCSH: Bible. Corinthians, 1st, XI, 2-16--Criticism, interpretation, etc. | Bible—Gay interpretations.
Classification: LCC BS2545.H63 T68 2017 (print) | LCC BS2545.H63 (ebook) | DDC 227/.20608664—dc23
LC record available at https://lccn.loc.gov/2016056511

Printed on acid-free paper.

Contents

Abbreviations

Primary Sources

Ab urbe cond.	Livy, *Ab urbe condita*
Acts Andr.	Acts of Andrew
Acts Paul	Acts of Paul
Aen.	Virgil, *Aeneid*
b.	Babylonian Talmud
Bacch.	Euripides, *Bacchae*
Bib. hist.	Diodorus Siculus, *Bibliotheca historica*
Contempl. Life	Philo, *On the Contemplative Life*
Cult. fem.	Tertullian, *De cultu feminarum*
Dial. meretr.	Lucian, *Dialogi meretricii*
Diatr.	Epictetus, *Diatribai* (*Discourses*)
Diatr.	Musonius Rufus, *Diatribai* (Discourses)
Epod.	Horace, *Epodi*
Gen. an.	Aristotle, *De generatione animalium*
Gos. Thom.	Gospel of Thomas
Is. Os.	Plutarch, *Isis and Osiris*
Metam.	Apuleius, *Metamorphoses*
Metaph.	Aristotle, *Metaphysica*
Od.	Homer, *Odyssey*
Pol.	Aristotle, *Politica*
QE	Philo, *Questions and Answers on Exodus*
Quaest. gr.	Plutarch, *Quaestiones graece*
Rewards	Philo, *On Rewards and Punishments*
Shabb.	Shabbat
Sat.	Juvenal, *Satires*
Spec. Laws	Philo, *On the Special Laws*

Secondary Sources

AB	Anchor Bible
ABR	*Australian Biblical Review*
AFS	*Australian Feminist Studies Journal*
AGJU	Arbeiten zur Geschichte des antiken Judentums und des Urchristentums
ANTC	Abingdon New Testament Commentaries
ASNU	Acta Seminarii Neotestamentici Upsaliensis
ATR	*Australasian Theological Review*
BA	*Biblical Archaeologist*
BECNT	Baker Exegetical Commentary on the New Testament
BETL	Bibliotheca Ephemeridum Theologicarum Lovaniensium
BibInt	*Biblical Interpretation*
BibInt	Biblical Interpretation Series
BJS	Brown Judaic Studies
BNTC	Black's New Testament Commentaries
BR	*Biblical Research*
BSac	*Bibliotheca sacra*
BSNA	Biblical Scholarship in North America
BTB	*Biblical Theology Bulletin*
CBC	Cambridge Bible Commentary
CBQ	*Catholic Biblical Quarterly*
CD	Barth, Karl. 1936–1977. *Church Dogmatics*. Translated by G. T. Thomson et al. Edited by G. W. Bromiley and T. F. Torrance. 4 vols. in 14. Edinburgh: T&T Clark.
CEV	Contemporary English Version
EKKNT	Evangelisch-katholischer Kommentar zum Neuen Testament
ESEC	Emory Studies in Early Christianity
EvQ	*Evangelical Quarterly*
EvT	*Evangelische Theologie*
ExpTim	*Expository Times*
FCNTECW	Feminist Companion to the New Testament and Early Christian Writings
FS	*Feminist Studies*
GLQ	*GLQ: Journal of Lesbian and Gay Studies*
GNB	Good News Bible
GPBS	Global Perspectives on Biblical Scholarship

GW	God's Word Translation
HDR	Harvard Dissertations in Religion
HR	*History of Religions*
HTR	*Harvard Theological Review*
HTS	Harvard Theological Studies
IBC	Interpretation: A Bible Commentary for Teaching and Preaching
ICC	International Critical Commentary
IJBS	*International Journal of Baudrillard Studies*
Int	*Interpretation*
JAAR	*Journal of the American Academy of Religion*
JAARSup	Journal of the American Academy of Religion Supplements
JAC	*Jahrbuch für Antike und Christentum*
JBL	*Journal of Biblical Literature*
JETS	*Journal of the Evangelical Theological Society*
JHebS	*Journal of Hebrew Scriptures*
JFSR	*Journal of Feminist Studies in Religion*
JRS	*Journal of Roman Studies*
JSNT	*Journal for the Study of the New Testament*
JSNTSup	Journal for the Study of the New Testament Supplement Series
JSOTSup	Journal for the Study of the Old Testament Supplement Series
JSSR	*Journal for the Scientific Study of Religion*
JTS	*Journal of Theological Studies*
KD	Barth, Karl. 1932–1970. *Die kirchliche Dogmatik.* 4 vols. in 14. Zurich: EVZ.
KEK	Kritisch-exegetischer Kommentar über das Neuen Testament
KJV	King James Version
LB	Living Bible
LCL	Loeb Classical Library
LHBOTS	Library of Hebrew Bible/Old Testament Studies
LNTS	Library of New Testament Studies
MNTC	Moffatt New Testament Commentary
NAB	New American Bible
NASB	New American Standard Bible
NCBC	New Century Bible Commentary

NEB	New English Bible
NIBCNT	New International Biblical Commentary on the New Testament
NIGTC	New International Greek Testament Commentary
NIRV	New International Reader's Version
NIV	New International Version
NJB	New Jerusalem Bible
NKJV	New King James Version
NLT	New Living Translation
NovT	*Novum Testamentum*
NovTSup	Supplements to Novum Testamentum
NRSV	New Revised Standard Version
NTAbh	Neutestamentliche Abhandlungen
NTG	New Testament Guides
NTS	*New Testament Studies*
OBT	Overtures to Biblical Theology
Phillips	*The New Testament in Modern English,* J. B. Phillips
PMLA	*Proceedings of the Modern Language Association*
PRSt	*Perspectives in Religious Studies*
RefR	*Reformed Review*
RSV	Revised Standard Version
SAC	Studies in Antiquity and Christianity
SBEC	Studies in the Bible and Early Christianity
SBLSP	Society of Biblical Literature Seminar Papers
SBLStBL	Society of Biblical Literature Studies in Biblical Literature
SCJ	*Stone-Campbell Journal*
SemeiaSt	Semeia Studies
SNTSMS	Society for New Testament Studies Monograph Series
SNTW	Studies of the New Testament and Its World
SP	Sacra Pagina
ST	*Studia Theologica*
STDJ	Studies on the Texts of the Desert of Judah
STS	Studies in Theology and Sexuality
SVTP	Studia in Veteris Testamenti Pseudepigrapha
Sup	Supplement
T&S	*Trouble and Strife*
TBN	Themes in Biblical Narrative
TDNT	Kittel, Gerhard, and Gerhard Friedrich, eds. *Theologi-*

	cal Dictionary of the New Testament. Translated by G. W. Bromiley. 10 vols. Grand Rapids: Eerdmans, 1964–2006.
TNTC	Tyndale New Testament Commentaries
TQ	*Theologische Quartalschrift*
TynBul	*Tyndale Bulletin*
USQR	*Union Seminary Quarterly Review*
Virg.	Tertullian, *De virginibus velandis*
WTJ	*Westminster Theological Journal*
WUNT	Wissenschaftliche Untersuchungen zum Neuen Testament
ZAW	*Zeitschrift für die alttestamentliche Wissenschaft*
ZNW	*Zeitschrift für die neutestamentliche Wissenschaft*

Acknowledgments

This book has been in the making for far too long. My daughter Isabel was born a few months after I began my research, and she has just now celebrated her fourteenth birthday. A journey of this sort, therefore, cannot be possible without the support and encouragement of many.

Paul Trebilco and James Harding, who always had faith in me and who gave me the freedom to explore. My editor, Fiona Black, whose advice and encouragement enabled me to turn this project into a book, particularly when I felt that the task was impossible, and whose book, *The Artifice of Love* (2009), continues to be influential. Other key scholars whose belief in this project enabled me to persevere with it include Joseph Marchal, Christina Petterson, and Roland Boer. In particular, I mention my friend and mentor Judith McKinlay, who has always provided encouragement and wisdom.

My friends and family—without their practical help and emotional support this project would not have been possible. I make special mention of Chris Caradus, who formatted the original version of the last chapter with columns of changing width, and David Lupton, whose discussions and photography were inspirational. There are many more friends I could mention whose support and interest have buoyed me throughout this long process.

Thank you. You are all the *sine qua non* of this book.

And, of course, I dedicate this to Isabel.

Introduction: Ideological Inter(sex)ions

Whatever it was that the Corinthians were doing with their hair or head coverings while praying and prophesying during public worship, it was something that appears to have disconcerted Paul. In 1 Cor 11:2–16 Paul addresses this issue, creating a text that while presumably intended to be clear to the Corinthians has confused and confounded its readers ever since. The result has been the spawning of countless articles, chapters, theses, and books, with scholars divided on virtually every issue. Yet, despite the lack of both historical and exegetical clarity, this passage has been fundamental to understandings of gender and sexuality in many Christian traditions. In particular, although it has been used to bolster a variety of gender models, from the strictly hierarchical and patriarchal through to those that emphasize the equality of the sexes, with regard to the issue of sexuality there is almost always an assumption of heteronormativity.[1]

While many studies on 1 Cor 11:2–16 concentrate on the multitude of exegetical and historical issues presented by the text, this one focuses instead on the ideologies that lie behind these models of gender and sexuality. Given that these models, arising from various readings of this and other biblical texts, have been instrumental in reinforcing certain relational structures in Western societies, from the level of personal identity through to familial, ecclesial, and societal formations, these models of gender and sexuality are profoundly political.[2] While heteronormative relational models tend to be viewed as normal or natural (or God-ordained) and are thus positioned at the privileged center of society, other models are deemed as abnormal or unnatural and are pushed to the disadvantaged margins. Binary/oppositional relations are favored, which at best emphasize the mutuality and interdependence of the sexes; but given that misogynist and homophobic currents still run deep in Western societies, it seems clear that an androcentric, heteropatriarchal model nevertheless predominates. That 1 Cor 11:2–16 can be read as supporting such a model highlights the importance of examining the ideologies of gender and sexuality reflected in this text as well as the politics and power relations that lie behind both the text itself and the various interpretations and utilizations of it.

I propose that an engagement with queer theory enables such a critical examination. Queer theory reveals models of gender and sexuality as ideological constructs—as social constructs maintained through systems of power relations. But it goes further than this and challenges these models by both exposing the instabilities of the supposedly normal (androcentric heteropatriarchal) model and also presenting alternative models of gendered and sexed being. One of the originators of queer theory, Eve Kosofsky Sedgwick (1994, xii), observes that the word *queer* has its origins in the Indo-European root -*twerkw* meaning "across," which she states "also yields the German *quer* (transverse)" and thus has a sense of being "transitive—multiply transitive." In other words, that which is queer is that which cuts across various ideologies of gender and sexuality and transverses the terrain of the supposedly normal. As key queer theorists Michael Warner and Teresa de Lauretis both explain, "'queer' is also a way of cutting against mandatory gender divisions" (Warner 1993, xxvi) and a way "to avoid all of these fine distinctions in our discursive protocols … to both transgress and transcend them" (de Lauretis 1991, v).

More broadly, Sarah Cooper (2000, 18) suggests that queer theory also places these issues of gender and sexuality "at points of intersection with other critical discourses on identity" and thus invites a methodological approach that crosses traditional disciplinary boundaries.[3] One result of this process of intersection according to Cooper is that "queer theory is seen to trouble compartmentalized kinds of academic theorizing" (18). Warner (1993, xxvi) also notes this aspect of "queer": "For both academics and activists, 'queer' gets a critical edge by defining itself against the normal rather than the heterosexual, and normal includes normal business in the academy."

My intention in this project therefore is to enable various biblical, theological, and queer lines of inquiry to intersect *across* 1 Cor 11:2–16 and consider the various ideologies of gender and sexuality that are revealed by the resulting connections and collisions. I do not, therefore, take a traditional historical-critical approach that either looks *into* the passage, seeking to pull *out* of it the supposed meaning of specific words or phrases, or that looks *behind* the text in order to build the most plausible reconstruction *around* it. While at times I consider particular words or historical backgrounds, the purpose is not to determine the correct meaning or sociocultural context, but to consider and critique the various ideologies of gender and sexuality that inform the interpretations of the text on those issues.

Stephen Moore (2007, 10) has noted that queer theory "has the capacity to shift the increasingly tired debates on biblical texts that apparently deal with homosexuality [and, he adds later, heterosexuality] into a radically different register." It is into this particular space, then, that I situate this project. Rather than rehashing the "increasingly tired debates" on the various exegetical and historical issues that occupy much of the scholarship on this passage, I aim to shift the discussion on 1 Cor 11:2–16 into "a radically different register" whereby various lines of inquiry will intersect across this passage—traversing, troubling, transgressing, and even transcending the normal.

My approach will therefore be queer in that it not only cuts across these traditional attempts to examine this passage but also raises issues of gender, sexuality, and power in ways that are troubling to the androcentric heteropatriarchal norm that continues to dominate the field of biblical studies. By intersecting biblical studies and queer theory, this project creates a marginal zone of critical inquiry, something that theorist Judith Butler (1999, xxxii) reminds us is required when examining the complex issues of gender and sexuality. The creation of this zone of inquiry out of the "transgressive juxtapositions of things normally kept apart" (Stone 2001b, 31)—in this instance biblical studies and queer theory—might be resisted or rejected by some, as something "abject" and alien to both these fields;[4] but my suspicion is that the fruit of such a supposedly unnatural pairing enables a new que(e)rying of 1 Cor 11:2–16.

I begin in chapter 1 with an investigation into the "queer" (troubling, strange, questionable) state of current research on this passage. While historical-critical approaches have often resulted in greater insight into and awareness of its context and content, not only has little consensus emerged on these issues but also little attention has been paid to issues of gender and sexuality. When we take into account an understanding of gender and sexuality that views these as ideological constructs, it becomes clear that a heteronormative (if not heteropatriarchal) model tends to dominate the various ways biblical scholars have interpreted 1 Cor 11:2–16. In this chapter I also situate queer theory in relation to its poststructuralist context as well as in relation to the history of gay and lesbian studies. Within this section I also situate myself, given the contested matter of *who* can *do* queer theory. Finally, I consider the particular subfield of queer biblical studies, discussing the development of this coupling of two fields often perceived as diametrically opposed.

In chapter 2, I seek to respond to the challenge posed by French feminist lesbian philosopher Monique Wittig (1992c, 87) to "systematically particularize" the masculine gender. The persistent focus by historical-critical scholars on the "problematic women" of Corinth (M. MacDonald 1990, 164) betrays an androcentric framework whereby women are seen as specific—gendered—objects and men are deemed universal subjects, thus rendered invisible and able to avoid scrutiny. This has meant scholars have tended to either ignore the role of the Corinthian men in Paul's argument or have deemed their behavior hypothetical. By exploring the possibility that the "problematic" men of Corinth are also involved in behavior that Paul wishes to correct, I render these men highly visible and specific. In this process, one scenario for the men's behavior emerges that needs close scrutiny: the suggestion that behind Paul's argumentation lies a "horror of homosexualism" (Barrett 1971, 257). This is an oft-cited but seldom justified explanation, but a consideration of the sex-gender ideologies of the first-century Mediterranean world reveals that the biblical commentators have not adequately understood the complex relationships between effeminacy, masculinity, and sexual relations that emerge from a careful reading of the first-century data. This exploration also reveals how this passage is currently being used to bolster heteronormative models of gender and sexuality.

The materialist lesbian theory of Wittig provides a strong avenue of exploration regarding ideologies of gender and sexuality and therefore provides the theoretical basis for discussion in the rest of this project. Wittig's work was brought to the attention of academic feminist circles in the West through Butler's reading (and critique) of her theory, and so in chapter 3 I not only outline Wittig's theory but also examine Butler's concerns. However, many Wittig scholars argue that Butler's critique of Wittig's theory is a *mis*reading. Daniel Boyarin (2003, 14) uses Wittig's theory to explore early Christian formulations of gender (such as found in 1 Cor 11:2–16) in light of a discussion on the "dominant fiction" of the phallus in Western ideologies of gender. But as his reading of 1 Cor 11:2–16 is dependent on Butler's *mis*reading of Wittig, in this chapter I offer a *re*reading of this passage in light of a *re*reading of Wittig's theory. While Boyarin focuses on the dominant voices of Butler and Paul (and the phallus) and considers the behavior of only the Corinthian women, I offer a *re*reading of this passage that seeks to hear the subdominant voices of Wittig and the Corinthians (and Wittig's lesbian figure), focusing on the behavior of the men. In this way I take up Wittig's (1992c, 87; 2005b, 47) challenge to "les-bianize the men" and present the possibility that the "problematic" men in the Corinthian congregation may be comparable to Wittig's theoretical lesbian figure.

Wittig also challenges us not only to "attack the order of heterosexual-ity in texts" (1992c, 87; 2005b, 47) but also to "produce a political transfor-mation of the key concepts" (1992i, 30). In chapters 4, 5, and 6, I explore three key concepts from 1 Cor 11:2–16, seeking to reveal and challenge the ideologies of gender and sexuality that lie behind traditional inter-pretations of these problematic verses by intersecting these with Wittig's theory: κεφαλή ("head") from verse 3, the *imago Dei* from verse 7, and ἡ φύσις ("nature") from verses 14–15. I introduce each of these chapters with a short vignette (a "scene") that will play, albeit in a serious way, with these concepts. The intent of these scenes is twofold. First, they serve to remind the reader that debates about gender and sexuality are not just academic or theoretical but are fundamental to issues of personal identity formation within broader relations of power and desire. Second, they highlight how that which is queer troubles the academic and theoretical by also being creative and sensual, engaging not just the rational but also the imagina-tive and visual.

In chapter 4, I examine the first key concept, the term κεφαλή ("head") from 1 Cor 11:3. This term has been the subject of heated debate, espe-cially within evangelical circles in the United States, with the traditional metaphorical meaning for κεφαλή, *authority over*, pitted against the mean-ing *source, origin*. I examine both views in this chapter through an explo-ration of two evangelical organizations: the Council for Biblical Manhood and Womanhood (CBMW) and Christians for Biblical Equality (CBE). While they hold opposing views on issues of gender, both organizations subscribe to a heteronormative ideology of sexuality, which ultimately serves a capitalist political ideology. I also consider an alternative under-standing of this highly controversial word—as *prominent, foremost, pre-eminent*—although it proves to be no less problematic than the previous options. In this chapter, I also examine the hierarchy that Paul outlines in this verse by placing it alongside that found in Rom 1:18–32—a passage with many connections to 1 Cor 11:2–16—in particular exploring three of the ambiguous ontologies positioned within this framework, that of "human," "female," and "Christ."

In chapter 5, I focus on 1 Cor 11:7 and in particular explore the binary pairing of ὁ ἀνήρ and ἡ γυνή ("man" and "woman") as asymmetrically related to each other and to God through the notion of the *imago Dei*. Marcella Althaus-Reid (2005, 267) critiques what she calls the "patriarchal heterosexual order" of much Christian theology, which I would also equate with the "whole conglomerate of sciences and disciplines" that Wittig (1992i, 29) describes as "the straight mind." Perhaps no better example of this can be found than in the influential work of theologian Karl Barth (*CD* 3.1:184, 288), who argues that the *imago Dei* is seen most clearly in the fundamental "I-Thou" relationship of "the unequal duality" of the heterosexual married couple. Because such a view finds support in 1 Cor 11:7, I reveal and challenge the ways in which Barth's theology on "Man and Woman" reflects androcentric and patriarchal ideologies. His affirmation of this "natural dualism" of man and woman is also linked with a rejection of what he describes as the "malady called homosexuality," thus also revealing a heterosexist ideology (3.4:121, 166). Barth's understanding of Jesus as the *imago Dei* also finds support in 1 Cor 11:7 in that Jesus is not to be thought of as an isolated figure but as the "Husband," an "I" paired with a "Thou," both as Israel's Christ and as Christ with his bride, the church (3.2:303). Yet Barth elsewhere speaks of Jesus as "Real" and "Whole," a "One" who is "a true and absolute Counterpart" for all people (3.2:134). Consequently, I conclude this chapter by contrasting Barth's vision of the *imago Dei*, the "unequal duality" of the "I-Thou," with Wittig's vision of the ungendered, universal, whole lesbian "I," whom I argue is mirrored in Barth's "Real" and "Whole" Jesus.

Finally, in chapter 6, I focus on 1 Cor 11:14–15a, where Paul turns to an argument from "nature itself" (ἡ φύσις αὐτή). Arguments over what is "natural" (and "unnatural") are common in contemporary political and religious debates in the West (particularly in the United States) concerning gender and sexuality, and particularly over issues of sexual orientation and same-sex marriage. I begin this chapter by briefly examining some of the Stoic philosophical rhetoric that parallels Paul's statement in this verse, showing that appeals to "nature" in the first century were part of a potent ideological discourse aimed at shaping both the individual and sociopolitical body. This rhetoric is also evident in some contemporary evangelical arguments concerning "proper" understandings and expressions of gender and sexuality that are seen as part of "God's design in creation."

At the center of the evangelical notion of "God's design in creation," with its emphasis on sexual differentiation, is the view that heterosexual intercourse is "natural" and same-sex intercourse is "unnatural." What is "natural" becomes equated with the anatomical, and thus reproductive "complementarity" becomes determinative for ethics regarding sexual behavior. Robert Gagnon is currently the leading spokesman for those who subscribe to the complementarity argument against homosexuality, and in chapter 6 I proceed to examine his arguments in detail. Underlying his "natural" view of gender and sexuality is an androcentric heteropatriarchal ideology that is not only also infused with a conservative capitalist view of society but also utilizes a rhetoric of fear and shame in order to promote androcentric heterosexuality as normative behavior.

In order to que(e)ry the androcentric heteropatriarchal construct of gender and sexuality found in Gagnon's book, *The Bible and Homosexual Practice*, I also explore in chapter 6 Wittig's fictional writings, in particular her third text, *The Lesbian Body*. Both these books include a barrage of anatomical detail, but whereas Gagnon (2001, 70–71) consistently rejects same-sex erotic behavior as "inherently degrading" and "destructive," Wittig deliberately adopts these qualities in the form of the "monstrous lesbian" in order to transgress conventional categories of sex, gender, genre, and even language (Scanlon 1998, 73; see also Whatling 1997, 238–40). Because both of these texts place an emphasis on the physical body, the discussion on these two texts is undertaken in a physical form that plays with the positions of the material on the page. The discussion on *The Bible and Homosexual Practice* begins as the dominant piece on the page, since the androcentric heteropatriarchal construct of gender and sexuality is the dominant ideology in society, while the discussion on *The Lesbian Body* is positioned beneath this, as the subdominant voice. However, the material on *The Lesbian Body* slowly but surely physically pushes up against the space on the page dedicated to Gagnon's work, diminishing the presence and power of the androcentric heteropatriarchal ideology and increasing that of the queer view. By the end of the chapter, *The Lesbian Body* forcibly removes the discussion on *The Bible and Homosexual Practice* from the page altogether in an appropriate stylistic gesture of critique.

By intersecting queer theory and biblical studies, I offer a new exploration of this passage. In my view, far more is at stake in a study of this passage than the exegetical or contextual issues (of headgear and hairstyles, or what Paul meant by his reference to "the angels," for example) that are often the concern of traditional historical-critical approaches. Indeed, while this passage has now elicited much important feminist work in the area of gender, a queer approach enables us to do more than this and to examine not only the critical issues of gender *and* sexuality, but also the deeply embedded issues of politics and power that pervade the scholarship on this passage. In particular, this approach reveals that models of gendered and sexed being are ideological constructs, be they the androcentric hierarchical ideologies of the Mediterranean context or the androcentric heteropatriarchal ideologies presumed by many contemporary readers of the text. Finally, this approach enables the imaginative exploration of alternative models of gendered and sexed being, thus affirming Wittig's (1992e, 19–20) proposal that "a new personal and subjective definition for all humankind can only be found beyond the categories of sex (woman and man)."

Notes

1. This term, and the terms *gender* and *sexuality*, will be discussed in more detail in ch. 1.

2. I would also suggest, therefore, that this may also be the case in societies that have been subject to Western colonialism and the influence of the various Christianities that have subsequently been imported (Punt 2007). I use the problematic term *Western* precisely because of the hegemonic connotations of the term and not as part of "an interested desire to conserve the subject of the West" (Spivak 1988, 271).

3. See Voss (2000, 184), for example, who considers the intersections and connections between archaeology, feminism, and queer theory.

4. I discuss this notion of the "abject" in more detail in ch. 1; see also Kristeva 1982, 1–4; Butler 1999, 169–70.

1

Que(e)rying 1 Corinthians 11:2–16

Historically Critically Queer

queer *adjective and noun*
 adjective 1. Strange, odd, eccentric; of questionable character, suspicious.
 2. Bad; worthless.
 3. Out of sorts; giddy, faint, ill.
 4. Esp. of a man: homosexual.
queer *verb, trans.*
 1. Ridicule; puzzle; swindle, cheat.
 2. Spoil, put out of order; spoil the reputation or chances of (a person).
 3. Upset, disconcert; make (a person) feel queer.
      — Shorter Oxford English Dictionary

Most current biblical scholars who examine 1 Cor 11:2–16 agree on little else other than that it is difficult, if not "notoriously difficult."[1] Indeed, many suggest that this is one of the most difficult of all the Pauline passages to decipher, if not one of the most difficult of the entire New Testament.[2] Some scholars describe Paul's argument, at best, as showing "complexity, subtlety, and care" (Thiselton 2000, 848), while, at worst, Paul is criticized for being "inarticulate, incomprehensible and inconsistent" (Bassler 1998, 417). Other scholars fall somewhere in between, stating, for example, that this passage is "obscure" and "convoluted" or just simply "curious" and "strange."[3] In his commentary, Hans Conzelmann (1975, 182) even comments that this passage "is probably a piece that was first talked over and sketched out in the schoolroom, if indeed it was not entirely composed there." Perhaps most colorfully, Dennis Ronald MacDonald (1987, 72, 89) describes this passage as both a "linguistic labyrinth rivalling Daedalus's and befuddling a host of would-be Theseuses" and "an exegetical Rorschach test [where] the responses to Paul's ink blots have revealed little more than the imaginative powers and penchants of the interpreter."

MacDonald's comment concerning the role of the interpreter in this process is important. Although many commentators on this passage begin their discussions by noting the difficulty or obscurity of the text, Caroline Vander Stichele and Todd Penner (2005, 287) have observed the tendency for scholars then to proceed to offer their own particular explanation, which supposedly renders the text "perfectly comprehensible." Indeed, commentators on this text (either as a whole or with regard to a specific verse) often describe it as a "puzzle" in need of solving or something "cryptic" that could be solved if only we just had the right clue (Carlé 1998, 32; Wire 1990, 121; D'Angelo 1995, 133; Webb 2001, 188; Demirer and Duran 2004, 452; Calef 2009, 22). Ed Christian (1999, 291) perhaps exemplifies this attitude most clearly in the opening sentence of his article: "1 Corinthians 11:1–16 is a challenging passage, and breaking the code is deeply satisfying."

In their analysis, Vander Stichele and Penner give the example of Bruce Winter's (2003b, 77) discussion on the "'new' wives" of Roman Corinth, a first-century sociocultural phenomenon that he suggests "throws important light on the issue of veiling in 1 Corinthians 11:2–16."[4] Like the commentators mentioned above, Winter acknowledges the difficulties that this passage presents and in particular likens the difficulty in understanding Paul's reference to the angels in verse 10 "to the struggle to untie the Gordian knot" (89).[5] He examines various Roman "ancient literary, legal, and non-literary sources" regarding this phenomenon, arguing that they can "illuminate the New Testament texts by securing their social setting with a greater certainty" (xi, xiii). Vander Stichele and Penner (2005, 287) suggest that the desire "to make sense" of Paul's otherwise strange arguments, frequently through an historical reconstruction of the situation at Corinth, "coheres well with the commitment of historical criticism to explain the context and language of a particular text so as to render it sensible and comprehensible to modern readers."

The example of Winter is just one of many that could be given. I myself have previously considered the passage in this way, attempting to make sense of it through proposing a particular historical reconstruction and noting that its apparent perplexity "could be taken as an indicator that the usual approach to this passage has been misguided" (Townsley 2003, 36). Utilizing D. MacDonald's analogy, I suggested:

The pathway through this "linguistic labyrinth" may become easier to follow if the behaviour of the men is also taken into account ... and thus the way may be opened up for a greater understanding of this "problem passage." Ariadne's thread may have been waiting there for us all along, if only we opened our eyes, and Paul himself may even be rescued from an image some hold of him as the Minotaur! (36)

Troy Martin's work on this passage provides another recent example of this historical-critical strategy. He begins his discussion by noting how "Paul's notorious argument ... is frequently criticized for being logically convoluted and confused" and that "the argument from nature in vv. 13–15 is particularly problematic" (2004, 75, 76). But he then suggests the "key for explaining" Paul's argument lies in appreciating the linguistic and physiological associations made in Greco-Roman literature between female hair and male testicles with regard to the term περιβόλαιον in 11:15b (traditionally translated as "a covering") (76). He concludes, "The problem with Paul's argument from nature for the veiling of women in public worship arises not from Paul's convoluted logic or flawed argumentation but from the philological confusion of modern interpreters who fail to understand the ancient physiological conception of hair (κόμη) and confuse a testicle (περιβόλαιον) with a head covering" (84).

Such confident assertions are indicative of the positivism of the historical-critical approach, but the result for readers of this passage is a confusing array of incompatible possibilities. Here then we discover a flaw in the historical-critical methodology, namely, an ideological commitment to determining a single authoritative meaning of the text. Using Martin's analogy of a "key," we find that while each scholar confidently presents his or her key as that which will finally illuminate and clarify the passage, readers are left in the dark when it comes to knowing which key is the right one. In addition, there is little if any dialogue among historical-critical scholars about this situation. Other than dismissing other scholars' keys as "misguided" or as arising from their own "confusion," there appears to be little awareness shown by scholars of the way in which this insistence on finding the one correct key renders the historical-critical approach suspect to increasingly disconcerted readers.

Lest it appear that I see no value in this kind of historical-critical process, whereby scholars provide an explanation in order "to make sense" of Paul's statements, it is important to note that the critical investigation into the various historical (or anthropological or archaeological, for example) backgrounds of the Pauline material has without doubt been an informative and productive development in biblical studies. A plethora of material now exists from sociological, feminist, and rhetorical perspectives that can enable more accurate insights into the complex and diverse ancient Mediterranean world and thus into the similarly complex and diverse world of the New Testament.[6] In this regard, I would agree with postcolonial biblical scholars who argue that the traditional historical-critical approach can be described as one of the "master's tools," so to speak, in that there is also both a level of indebtedness to this methodology as well as a level of complicity that is almost unavoidable in any engagement with biblical studies (Penner and Vander Stichele 2005, 27–28).[7] However, such acknowledgment of this value does not alleviate the flaws in this approach outlined above that do not seem to be addressed by its proponents.

Two recent responses to Martin's explanation are indicative of the troubled state of historical-critical scholarship on this passage. Like Martin, Joseph Fitzmyer (2008, 405) strongly rejects the notion that Paul's argument is obscure or unintelligible, and he sets out "to clear the air about some of the details." Nevertheless, he forcefully rejects Martin's explanation, dismissing it as "completely far-fetched" (421). Christopher Mount (2005, 313), on the other hand, notes the difficulties surrounding the interpretation of this passage, suggesting that our knowledge of the situation being addressed "was lost long ago" and that the situation itself "can no longer be reconstructed with any certainty." But, regarding 11:15b, he finds that Martin has "persuasively argued" his case (333). In the end, however, Mount becomes the latest of a small but persistent group of scholars who suggest that the entire passage is an interpolation (315–16). On the contrary, like the majority of scholars, Fitzmyer (2008, 407) suggests that the interpolation option is "too easy a way to get rid of a complicated passage" (see appendix 1 below for more detail on this option).

This example of contradictory yet confidently asserted stances on the various interpretive matters surrounding 1 Cor 11:2–16 is common. While it is widely agreed that the issue being addressed by Paul concerns behavior during the activities of praying and prophesying, virtually every other aspect of this passage is either vigorously debated or simply assumed. Even the seemingly basic question of which verse begins this pericope is problematic; many scholars do not debate this but presuppose that this section starts at either verse 1, 2, or even 3. Other questions that arise include— but are certainly not limited to—asking if the context is that of private or public worship. Is Paul dealing with the behavior of both the men and women or just the women?[8] Does the situation in Corinth center on the issue of head coverings (be this a veil or a toga), or is Paul's concern with the Corinthians' hair (be this lengths or styles)? Should emphasis be given to a Greek, Roman, or Jewish milieu, or a Mediterranean combination of all three? With regard to exegetical matters, should the word κεφαλή ("head," 11:3) mean "source" or "authority," or something else altogether?[9] Finally, perhaps causing more anxiety and confusion than any other verse in this passage, what does Paul mean when he states, διὰ τοῦτο ὀφείλει ἡ γυνὴ ἐξουσίαν ἔχειν ἐπὶ τῆς κεφαλῆς διὰ τοὺς ἀγγέλους ("Because of this the woman ought to have authority on her head because of the angels"; 11:10)?[10] (See appendix 1 for responses to these questions.)

Gwen Ince (2000, 59) observes, "If all the possible permutations and combinations of points of view that may be taken were tested, many millions of interpretations would be produced." With the myriad options available, widely divergent yet arguably plausible scenarios emerge; and while each scholar who presents their "key" is confident that theirs is the only one that unlocks the passage and that other keys are misguided, readers committed to the historical-critical approach are left confused and anxious with regard to which key they should choose.

A quick comparison of four more recent commentaries on just two matters serves as a final example of the conflicting yet confident stances taken on these matters, whether the issue concerns both men and women, or just women, and whether the issue concerns head coverings or hairstyles. Indeed, "all the possible permutations and combinations" are produced. Ben Witherington III (1995, 238, 231–32) states that it is "very believable" that the issue involved both the men and the women and that it is "clearly" about head coverings; discussions about hair and hairstyles "are quite beside the point." On the other hand, Richard Hays (1997, 185) equally forcefully declares that Paul's comments about the men "are purely hypothetical" and that to view the issue as being about hairstyles "makes excellent sense for a number of reasons." Alan Johnson (2004, 189, 182) acknowledges the lack of consensus on this passage but agrees with Hays that "a quite convincing case" can be made for the issue being about hairstyles; however, he simply comments without further discussion that "both men and women were involved in this practice." On the other hand, Fitzmyer (2008, 405–6) decisively states, "The problem is not that Corinthian men were praying or prophesying with covered heads"; rather it "is about a woman wearing a head-covering or her failure to do so," and "has nothing to do with" hairstyles.

Such is the current state of historical-critical research on this passage; not surprisingly, perhaps, it is no less convoluted and confusing than the passage itself. Indeed, 1 Cor 11:2–16 is a passage that continues to defy explanation. Despite multiple attempts to "break the code" and the confidence and satisfaction with which scholars present their solutions, this text refuses to conform to expectations and seems to actively resist any attempt "to render it sensible." As for the student who approaches the "bulky dossier of literature on the passage" (Engberg-Pedersen 1991, 679) or the lay reader who relies on the commentators, it is enough to make even the bravest feel giddy, faint, or even ill. I suggest therefore that it is possible to describe both this text and the state of historical-critical scholarship on this text as "queer." According to their observers, some of the Corinthians were behaving in ways that were questionable, perhaps even odd or eccentric. Paul was upset or at least disconcerted by their behavior and their spoiled reputation, and readers have subsequently found his written response to be puzzling, out of order, strange, and even out of sorts with the rest of the letter. Yet this passage is also deeply relational, dealing as it does with the ways in which Paul expects men and women to relate to each other and to God. Some scholars have even suggested that the Corinthians were in fact "queer," or at least behaving in ways that blurred the distinctions between the genders.[11] But I am getting ahead of myself here and am playing with the multiple ways in which the term *queer* can be understood. In fact, far from being queer—"*whatever* is at odds with the normal, the legitimate, the dominant" (Halperin 1995, 62)[12]—this passage has been used to bolster models of gender and sexuality that are strictly heteronormative, if not heteropatriarchal.

Que(e)rying Sex, Gender, and Sexuality

Queer means to fuck with gender.
— Cherry Smyth, *Lesbians Talk Queer Notions*[13]

Despite this rather "queer" state of affairs regarding the background and meaning of this passage, 1 Cor 11:2–16 has nevertheless often been fundamental to understandings of gender and sexuality throughout the history of Christianity, although seldom are these topics given the depth of analysis accorded to the exegetical and sociohistorical matters. As Jorunn Økland (2002, 137) astutely observes, the "checklist questions" (such as I outlined above) often "seem to be used as 'emergency exits,' so that in discussions one does not have to deal with the implications of what is after all seen to be the main message of the text."[14] Or to rephrase this point, while topics such as οἱ ἄγγελοι or head coverings are examined in minute detail, issues of gender and sexuality are often ignored or are subject to numerous unexplored assumptions. In particular, scholars frequently focus upon the notions of headship and/or sexual differentiation that emerge from this text, noting the way in which Paul's pronouncements about men and women are placed within a theocentric framework, and thus view these as crucial components in some form of divine ordering of gender relations (in the home, the church and also, for some, in society). Even for those scholars who prefer to focus on the creation account (Gen 1–3) when considering the topic "man and woman," or on Rom 1 when considering "homosexuality," references to 1 Cor 11:2–16 still frequently figure in their discussions.[15]

However, New Testament scholarship has not always recognized that concepts such as sex, gender, and sexuality, and thus also homosexuality and heterosexuality, are modern notions that become problematic if anachronistically placed onto first-century data. All of these terms can appear to be self-explanatory, and yet the way in which they are used often reveals that they are, rather, deeply ideological. Indeed, the very fact that these terms are often viewed as so obviously "natural" and fundamental to the concept of being human that they need no comment indicates the importance of examining the deeper ideological frameworks in which they are embedded.

It is a commonly held view that *sex* refers to the biological makeup of an individual so that a person is either naturally *male* or *female,* and thus sex is treated as "an unanalyzable given" (Winkler 1990, 3).[16] *Gender* is then understood to refer to the way in which that person's sex is expressed in their society, as a set of behaviors and characteristics that are viewed as being indicative of *masculinity* or *femininity* and that, when coupled with the biological state of male or female, enable someone to be recognized as a *man* or *woman* (J. Weeks 2003, 4). In this view, gender flows naturally from the biological; gender is thus viewed as "a set of innate social traits that naturally accompany biological sex ... the universal and essential social correlative of binary biological differentiation" (Tolbert 2000b, 99).[17] Certain sectors of Christianity hold firmly to the notion that masculine and feminine roles and behavior flow from the biological and are thus God-given and exemplified in the biblical material. For example, some Christian groups emphasize that leadership is a naturally masculine characteristic while submission is a naturally feminine one and that both of these innate traits are affirmed in the Bible as part of God's design for what it means to be male and female.[18]

The work of feminists since the mid-twentieth century, however, has challenged this modernist view and revealed that gender is instead "a socially constructed set of behaviors with deep political roots, and rather than being universal, it is enacted in multiple and different ways in each historical and local setting" (Tolbert 2000b, 99).[19] With such roots, gender is therefore not only a social construct but also, more profoundly, an ideological construct. In other words, the ways in which various components of masculine or feminine gender are formulated and assigned are neither natural nor neutral but are implicated in various systems of power relations.

While this view of gender as an ideological construct recognizes that behavior labeled as masculine or feminine does not arise naturally from anatomical difference, one can also argue that sex too is an ideological construct and not merely a natural phenomenon.[20] Despite its deceptive simplicity, as something so basic that it needs no analysis, sex is a concept imbued with ambiguity and complexity. Jeffrey Weeks (2003, 4) notes that this point can be observed by the fact that sex has multiple meanings; sex "refers both to an act and to a category of person, to a practice and a gender" (see also Sedgwick 1994, 6–7). Perhaps more influential than any other theorist on these issues, Butler explains that rather than viewing sex as a natural and/or neutral surface upon which gender is imposed and inscribed by culture, the various discourses of gender that operate within society also shape the way in which sex (and thus the body) are understood. In particular, they produce the very notion of sex as something natural and/or neutral.

> Gender ought not to be conceived merely as the cultural inscription of meaning on a pregiven sex (a juridical conception); gender must also designate the very apparatus of production whereby the sexes themselves are established. As a result, gender is not to culture as sex is to nature; gender is also the discursive/cultural means by which "sexed nature" or "a natural sex" is produced and established as "prediscursive," prior to culture, a politically neutral surface on which culture acts....
>
> Gender is the repeated stylization of the body, a set of repeated acts within a highly rigid regulatory frame that congeal over time to produce the appearance of substance, of a natural sort of being. (1999, 11, 43–44)[21]

With regard to sexuality, a modernist viewpoint views sexuality as a combination of behaviors, desires, and/or orientations that, like gender, are also linked to biological sex. Thus a strongly bifurcated notion of identity as either male or female becomes attached to a supposedly natural expression of this in reproductive heterosexuality. As with gender, this is a view endorsed in certain Christian circles as a God-ordained—and thus fundamental and natural—aspect of human identity. Feminists such as Gayle Rubin (1984, 308), however, have argued that "it is essential to separate gender and sexuality analytically to more accurately reflect their separate social existence."[22] Theorists in the fields of history and gender studies have contested the stability and givenness not only of anatomical sex but also of sexuality, viewing it, like gender, as an ideological construct.[23] In particular, Michel Foucault (1990a) argued that the commonly understood concept of sexuality today—as an innate aspect of each person's identity, influencing their erotic choices, orientations, and behaviors—is the specific product of late-nineteenth-century medical, legal, and religious discourses in Western society. He makes clear this understanding of sexuality in the following statement:

> Sexuality must not be thought of as a kind of natural given which power tries to hold in check, or as an obscure domain which knowledge tries gradually to uncover. It is the name that can be given to a historical construct: not a furtive reality that is difficult to grasp, but a great surface network in which the stimulation of bodies, the intensification of pleasures, the incitement to discourse, the formation of special knowledges, the strengthening of controls and resistances, are linked to one another, in accordance with a few major strategies of knowledge and power. (1990a, 105–6)

Sexuality, then, is not something so natural and universal as to be beyond scrutiny, especially those expressions of sexuality deemed to be supposedly normal or natural. While individuals experience desire and emotions, and engage in relationships, Foucault is arguing that the ways in which these experiences are actually understood by those individuals is shaped by the societies in which they live. Or to explain it another way, Foucault (1990b, 3) was not engaging in a *social history* that would reveal what individuals experienced in their erotic encounters, but in a *discursive analysis* of the ways in which sexual behavior is defined, regulated, and produced in different societies (see also Halperin 2002c, 26–38). As Ken Stone (2000a, 235) remarks, "biological and physiological processes associated with sexuality, though unquestionably real, do not contain inherent meanings but rather obtain meaning and impact experience through sociocultural organization and interpretation."

Analyzing the different discourses that have shaped and determined the various public constructions of sexuality within different societies from different periods of history thus becomes a viable task for the historian. David Halperin explains:

> To discover and write the history of sexuality has long seemed to many a sufficiently radical undertaking in itself, inasmuch as its effect (if not always the intention behind it) is to call into question the very naturalness of what we currently take to be essential to our individual natures.... We must acknowledge that "sexuality" is a cultural production ... and we must struggle to discern in what we currently regard as our most precious, unique, original, and spontaneous impulses the traces of a previously rehearsed and socially encoded ideological script.... We must, in short, be willing to admit that what seem to be our most inward, authentic, and private experiences are actually, in Adrienne Rich's admirable phrase, "shared, unnecessary and political." (1990, 39–40)[24]

An examination of both modern and ancient Mediterranean constructs of sexuality, as undertaken initially by Foucault (1990a), reveals that the category of homosexuality and the concept of a homosexual identity (as well as heterosexuality and a heterosexual identity) are strictly modern inventions, and are therefore *not* part of the conceptual framework of the first century. To put it somewhat simplistically, in the first century sexual *acts* were categorized, not *people* (J. Weeks 1981, 81; Halperin 1990, 26; Winkler 1990, 45–46; Walters 1993, 25). Robert Padgug (1989, 60) elaborates on this point and explains, "'Homosexual' and 'heterosexual' *behavior* may be universal; homosexual and heterosexual *identity and consciousness* are modern realities.... To 'commit' a homosexual act is one thing; to *be* a homosexual is something entirely different."[25]

While 1 Cor 11:2–16 belongs to a cultural and historical era where discourses surrounding sexual behavior differ profoundly from those of twentieth- and twenty-first-century Western societies, the pairing (and opposition) of "man" and "woman" in this passage is often assumed by interpreters to affirm a biblical basis for a heterosexual model of sexuality. As Lauren Berlant and Michael Warner (1998, 548 n. 2) explain, this assumption and privileging of heterosexuality—or heteronormativity— can be understood as "the institutions, structures of understanding, and practical orientations that make heterosexuality seem not only coherent—that is, organized as a sexuality—but also privileged."[26] Warner (1991, 8), who originally coined the term *heteronormativity*, explains this privileging by suggesting that it "lies in heterosexual culture's exclusive ability to interpret itself as society."[27] In other words, "Het culture thinks of itself as the elemental form of human association, as the very model of intergender relations, as the indivisible basis of all community, and the means of reproduction without which society wouldn't exist" (1993, xxi; see also 1991, 9–10). Warner acknowledges that the precursor to the idea of heteronormativity is found in the work of Wittig (1993, xxi), and it is her theories of gender and sexuality that form the basis of much of this project.[28] Wittig states:

> to live in society is to live in heterosexuality.... [Heterosexuality is] a nonexistent object, a fetish, an ideological form which cannot be grasped in reality, except through its effects, whose existence lies in the mind of people, but in a way that affects their whole life, the way they act, the way they move, the way they think.... We cannot think outside of the mental categories of heterosexuality. Heterosexuality is always already there within all mental categories. (1992d, 40–43)[29]

Heterosexuality, then, is accorded an "invisible, tacit, society-founding rightness" and frequently "marked as a natural state" (Berlant and Warner 1998, 548 n. 2). But more than this, as Wittig (1992d, 43, 45) shows, heterosexuality is a "political regime."[30] This hegemonic political and ideological process by which heterosexuality is privileged is summed up by the term *heteronormativity*. This comprehensive structuring of sex, sexuality, and gender—with all their desires, emotions, pleasures, and articulations—as naturally heterosexual, is a fundamental discourse in the twentieth- and twenty-first-century West.

Philip Culbertson (2008, 50) is more specific, however, and describes heteronormativity as "the privileging of the standards of white, heterosexual, educated, married, middle-class, powerful males."[31] There is an ideology at work in society that normalizes and privileges not just heterosexuality but also white, middle-class, hierarchically, androcentrically gendered relations. Consequently, this is an ideological framework that can be described as heteropatriarchy.[32] Lisa Isherwood (2006, 1) describes this as "a system that while incorporating heterosexuality goes far beyond the binary opposites of gender into the binary, hierarchical and elitist divisions evident in our world." This connection with issues of class, politics,

and economics is an essential component of heteropatriarchy; as Isherwood also notes, capitalism can be described as "that beast of heteropatriarchy" (122).

Accepting that gender, sex, and sexuality are ideological constructs
is an important recognition that biblical scholars ought to bring to their
work on the various passages in the New Testament that deal with matters
of gender and sexuality, particularly given the heated ecclesial debates on
the issue of homosexuality; yet this is only slowly happening. While there
has been considerable historical-critical work on 1 Cor 11:2–16, as discussed above, theoretical reflection on the concepts of gender or sexuality
has been virtually nonexistent, despite the deeply polemical and political
debates that have arisen over the way this passage has been interpreted.[33]

With regard to 1 Cor 11:2–16 and the issue of gender, to begin with,
opinions are clearly divided on both the model of gender relations that
Paul is expounding and the authoritative status of the passage for gender
relations today. On one side of the debate are the "hierarchicalists"[34] who
argue both that Paul teaches a hierarchical relationship between men and
women, where the man is the "head" of the woman and thus has authority over her, and that this is the only valid gender model for today.[35] In a
survey of evangelical scholarship on this passage, Michael Lakey (2010, 19)
notes that while "male leadership" is central to those who are hierarchicalists, they do have "different viewpoints regarding where, and if so how,
male leadership ought to be acknowledged in the form of restricted access
to office-bearing roles." Indeed, some scholars who accept the validity of
a hierarchical model have attempted to soften this stance somewhat.[36]
Craig Blomberg (1994, 217) even goes so far as to argue that the themes of
mutuality and interdependence in 1 Cor 11:11–12 "radically redefine that
hierarchy in ways that should render it unobjectionable" (and, indeed, it is
"not only innocuous but wonderful"), while still arguing that male headship means that leadership roles in ministry ought to be restricted to men,
albeit a leadership that "is one of empowering others … rather than 'lord-
ing it over' them" (129).[37]

Despite these attempts to ameliorate or redefine the notion of hierarchy, those in this camp still view leadership and authority as male pre-
rogatives that are sanctioned by this Pauline text. The hierarchical gender
model that Paul outlines in this text is seen as not only valid but also vital
for gender relations (in the home, church, and, by some, society) today.
This model is thus not viewed as an ideological construct peculiar to Paul's
ancient Mediterranean sociopolitical environment but as an eternal prin-

ciple outlined in Scripture that therefore is not only natural but also ought to be universally normal.

On the other side of the debate are the egalitarians. This position is more complex than the hierarchicalist position as there is a diverse range of responses to the text. Some argue that the text presents a hierarchical gender model, but they do not find this authoritative for today.[38] In apologetic fashion, some view the text as indicative of the problem Paul has in being consistent with either his own practices (such as accepting female coworkers without qualms; Rom 16:1–15; 1 Cor 1:11; Phil 4:2–3; etc.) and/or his own views expressed elsewhere (such as Gal 3:28).[39] In a decidedly unapologetic vein, however, Lone Fatum (1995, 67) accepts Paul's views in this passage as an expression of his desire to reinforce "male sexual control" and his acceptance of "the hierarchic arrangement of patriarchal society." Fatum (1995, 79) unflinchingly argues that there are no redeeming features in either this text or in other Pauline texts (including Gal 3:28) as Paul has "an altogether negative attitude to women and sexuality."[40]

Alternatively, although less frequently these days, in order to dismiss the relevance of this particular passage (or certain verses within the passage), Paul is sometimes said to be revealing his Jewish heritage as opposed to his Christian viewpoint in his argument. Thomas Shoemaker (1987, 61) succinctly explains this perspective, saying that "it is an unfortunate case of Paul the rabbi proving victorious over Paul the apostle, and as such, Paul and this text are to be rejected."[41] For some this rejection of 1 Cor 11:2–16 (and other passages in the New Testament that are viewed as supporting male dominance and female subordination, most commonly 1 Cor 14:33b–36[42]) is because such passages are viewed as non-Pauline interpolations. For example, William Walker (1983, 104) states that such texts "represent one aspect of a post-Pauline reaction against what can be termed the 'radical egalitarianism' of Paul himself" (see also Trompf 1980, 196–97; Shoemaker 1987, 61).

By contrast, some in the egalitarian camp argue that the "'radical egalitarianism' of Paul himself" is indeed present in the text, and thus they view the text as authoritative. In this approach there is more of a desire to view Paul himself in a positive light, as affirmative of an egalitarian gender model. For example, Robin Scroggs (1972, 283) confidently states that "it is time, indeed past time, to say loudly and clearly that Paul is, so far from being a chauvinist, the only certain and consistent spokesman for the liberation and equality of women in the New Testament." These scholars attempt what can be called a "recuperative" or "revisionist" reading of the text, an approach often associated with evangelical feminism (Bible and Culture Collective 1995, 245; Schüssler Fiorenza 1992, 21–24; Osiek 1985, 100–101; Boyarin 1990, 31).[43] Here the hermeneutical task becomes one of *re*reading the text in such a way as "to remove the layers of centuries of androcentric interpretation that cover up the supposed original meaning of the biblical text," and thus restore both Paul as one in favor of egalitarian gender relationships, and the text as liberating (Schüssler Fiorenza 1992, 23).

In particular, with regard to 1 Cor 11:3, there has been a strong attempt to challenge the traditional meaning of κεφαλή as *authority over* with the supposedly more egalitarian meaning of *source, origin*.[44] Alternatively, the mutuality and interdependence between the sexes that is expressed in 11:11–12 is touted as the "theological climax of the whole argument" (Scroggs 1972, 302). At the very least it is often stated that "the whole discussion is based on the assumption that women will lead" (Polaski 2005, 56). For those in this wing of the egalitarian camp, Paul is outlining an egalitarian gender model, and therefore—just as for the hierarchicalists—this is both valid and vital for gender relations (in the home, church, and society) today. While the hierarchical model is sometimes said to have come about as a result of the fall, and is thus pervasive in society, it is the created order's "loving harmony between the man and the woman" that is natural and ought to be normal (Hess 2004, 90). As with the hierarchicalists, there is no recognition of the constructed nature of this gender model.

Two key scholars whose work on 1 Cor 11:2–16 ought to be considered in detail at this point are Elisabeth Schüssler Fiorenza and Antoinette Clark Wire. While both of these scholars can be situated within the egalitarian camp, they have challenged the usual framework whereby Paul and his text are dominant and have instead shifted the focus to a consideration of the Corinthians (in particular the Corinthian women) and to their behaviors and possible viewpoints. This will be important for my approach in chapter 3, where I also focus on the subdominant voices of the Corinthians (but, in particular, the Corinthian men).

Schüssler Fiorenza (1983, 56–60, 108–9) developed a feminist critical approach using a "hermeneutics of suspicion," which assumes that "biblical texts and their interpretations are androcentric and serve patriarchal functions" (1984, 15).[45] In relation to 1 Corinthians, Schüssler Fiorenza (1983, 213, 240–42) proposes an historical reconstruction of the early Christian community, which she describes as a "discipleship of equals"—an "egalitarian" movement engaged in "implicitly subverting economic or patriarchal-androcentric structures" and based on the baptismal formula of Gal 3:28. In the context of their worship practices, Schüssler Fiorenza suggests that the women were letting their hair "flow freely" in the manner common to "the ecstatic worship of oriental divinities" (227). She explains that "the Corinthian pneumatics presumably took over such a fashion because they understood their equality in the community and their devotion to Sophia-Spirit by analogy to the worship of Isis, since Isis was also said to have made the power of women equal to men" (227–28). Schüssler Fiorenza goes on to argue that, although Paul held a theological position that affirms equality, as indicated elsewhere in the letter (1 Cor 7), at this point he "is bent on curbing the pneumatic frenzy" of the women's worship for the sake of order (228).[46]

Utilizing rhetorical analysis, Wire has also proposed a reconstruction of the situation at Corinth. She argues that Paul's rivals were a group of women prophets who interpreted the pre-Pauline baptismal formula of Gal 3:28 to mean they are "a new creation in Christ, made in God's image"; thus they remove their head coverings and "practice gifts of prayer and prophecy without regard to gender" (1990, 126). According to Wire, Paul responded in 1 Cor 11:2–16 by rejecting both this practice and the theology behind it, although 11:16 indicates that he clearly expected opposition to his argument. Wire argues that Paul's desire is that "woman must be covered to ensure the exclusive praise of God in worship," an argument that "seems to be predicated on a male experience of tension between self-glory associated with woman's uncovered head and God's glory associated with undistracted worship" (132).

In comparing these reconstructions, Økland (2004, 10) notes that Schüssler Fiorenza "tried to show that biblical texts, including Paul, may leave room for both affirmation and liberation of women." But she suggests that Wire's scenario, while also "open to the possibility of gender equality in the early Christian groups," reveals an approach more akin to the position taken by Fatum, in that Wire also views Paul "as non-affirmative of the women in the congregation" (11).[47]

One must acknowledge that many of these hermeneutical approaches are not mutually exclusive and often overlap. While discussing the strands of what he calls thematic and strategic feminist theories, Boyarin (1990, 41) makes a comment that could be applied to the broad sweep of approaches just discussed: "these dichotomies and their intersection with each other prove very slippery when read closely." In all of this, what emerges is that different scholars have read 1 Cor 11:2–16 in differing ways, and yet have tended to find (or affirm) two predominant models of gender, either a hierarchical model or an egalitarian model. For those who find a hierarchical model, this is either affirmed or rejected as authoritative (in the home, in the church, and/or on a societal level). For those who find an egalitarian model, this is usually affirmed; I have yet to discover an example of a reading that finds and yet rejects an egalitarian model.[48]

But in either case, in relation to the issue of sexuality, there is almost always an assumption of heteronormativity. As noted earlier, the oppositional pairing of "man and woman" in this text lead scholars of both camps to affirm (or, more often, to assume) a heterosexual model of sexuality. The understandings of gender and sexuality that scholars derive from their readings of 1 Cor 11:2–16 are foundational to notions of personal, group, societal, and cultural identity and thus to the power relations within those structures; whether or not individual scholars tend toward an egalitarian or hierarchical gender model, these models are therefore inevitably profoundly political. In particular, certain configurations of family life and of masculine and feminine roles and behaviors tend to be posited as properly Christian, and yet on examination they emerge as typical expressions of the Western middle-class nuclear family so central to capitalism. These heteronormative relational models are portrayed as normal or natural (or God-ordained) and are positioned at the privileged center of society, while other models are deemed abnormal or unnatural and are pushed to the disadvantaged margins.[49] Binary/oppositional relations are favored, which at best emphasize the mutuality and equality of the sexes, but given that misogynist and homophobic currents still run deep in Western societies, it seems clear that an androcentric heteropatriarchal model nevertheless predominates, privileging not only heterosexuality but also—more often than not—middle-class values. That 1 Cor 11:2–16 can be read as supporting such a model highlights the importance of examining the sex and gender ideologies reflected in this text as well as the issues of politics and power relations that lie behind both the text itself and the various interpretations and utilizations of it.

What (and Who) Is This Thing Called Queer?[50]

Queer is a continuing moment, movement, motive—recurrent, eddying, *troublant*. The word "queer" itself means *across*—it comes from the Indo-European root *-twerkw*, which also yields the German *quer* (transverse), Latin *torquere* (to twist), English *athwart*.... [It] is transitive—multiply transitive. The immemorial current that *queer* represents is antiseparatist as it is antiassimilationist. Keenly, it is relational, and strange.

— Eve Kosofsky Sedgwick, *Tendencies*

Work done in the field of New Testament studies has been slowly awakening over the last few decades to a consideration of gender and sexuality. But while feminist approaches to 1 Cor 11:2–16 abound,[51] I am unaware of any study that goes beyond an association of gender with feminism and considers the ideologies of masculinity that lie behind not only this text but also various interpretations or utilizations of it. This may partly be explained, I suspect, by the lack of recognition by the majority of scholars that the Corinthian men are involved in the problem Paul is addressing, a matter I consider in the next chapter. In addition, masculinity studies is a developing area in the field of biblical studies (Anderson and Moore 2003; Moore 2007, 12–13, esp. 12 n. 28; A. Wilson 2006; Conway 2008; Huber 2008; Swancutt 2010; Thurman 2010; Myles 2010), and only a handful of studies have explored masculinity in relation to the Corinthian correspondence or in an examination of Paul the man (Moxnes 2003; Clines 2003; Larson 2004; Glancy 2004; Ivarsson 2007; Mayordomo-Marín 2008). But to go further and examine either the ideologies of gender and sexuality behind 1 Cor 11:2–16, or behind various interpretations or utilizations of the text, is an important area yet to be explored not least because related questions of politics and power are often unrecognized or ignored in relation to this passage.[52]

Consequently, I am proposing that an engagement with queer theory (a continuing moment, movement, motive) is needed in order to examine critically these intertwined (twisted) issues of gender and sexuality, as well as the deeply embedded issues of politics and power, both in terms of the content of Paul's argument and also in terms of the ideological positions taken by scholars. Queer theory not only reveals these models of gender and sexuality as ideological constructs, but goes further and challenges (troubles) these models, both by exposing the instabilities of the supposedly normal model and by presenting alternative (relational and strange) models of gendered and sexed being.[53]

Queer theory has its parentage in the field of gender studies, the "(unisex) umbrella" that currently "offers shelter to lesbian and gay studies, and its obstreperous offshoot, queer theory," as well as feminist criticism and masculinity studies (Moore 2001, 12).[54] Moore notes that while feminist and masculinity studies have "succeeded in making *gender* a viable subject for academic research," it is sometimes said that "queer theory has succeeded in making *sex* and *sexuality*" equally legitimate subjects (2001, 13).[55] But such a territorial view of scholarly investigation has been strongly critiqued by Butler, one of the key theorists in queer theory, as being unhelpful and incorrect. Butler (1994, 6) even goes so far as to see this as "a mundane sort of violence," commenting that "what passes as a benign, even respectful, analogy with feminism is the means by which the fields are separated, where that separation requires the desexualization of the feminist project and the appropriation of sexuality as the 'proper' object of lesbian/gay studies."[56]

This raises the issue of the distinction between queer theory and lesbian and gay studies. Are these synonymous terms, or, if not, in what ways is queer theory the "obstreperous offshoot" of lesbian and gay studies? To begin with, it has been noted that queer theory has a tendency "to install itself retrospectively" into lesbian and gay studies (Jagose 1996, 4–5). Annemarie Jagose wryly comments: "In a movement simultaneously forwards and backwards, queer is designated as not only the evolutionary extension of a more conventional lesbian and gay studies but also its bent progenitor" (4–5).[57] It is also important to note that the term *queer* is often used as "a convenient shorthand" for the multifarious identities indicated by the conglomerate term *LesGayBiTrans* (LGBT) (Jagose 1996, 97). As Gabriel Rotello, editor of the then newly established *Outweek* magazine, explains to Alessandra Stanley (1991, 24) in an article for the *New York Times*, part of the appeal of the word is simply journalistic expedience: "When you're trying to describe the community, and you have to list gays, lesbians, bisexuals, drag queens, transsexuals (post-op and pre), it gets unwieldy. Queer says it all" (see Goldman 1996, 173). This utilization of the term *queer* may be convenient, but it is also problematic. Gloria Anzaldúa (2009, 164) explains: "Queer is used as a false unifying umbrella which all 'queers' of all races, ethnicities and classes are shoved under. At times we need this umbrella to solidify our ranks against outsiders. But even when we seek shelter under it we must not forget that it homogenizes, erases our differences" (see also Berlant and Warner 1995, 344; R. Boer 1999, 14).

Nevertheless, if we bear these points in mind, it is possible (and important) to trace some differences in the origins and objectives between queer theory and lesbian and gay studies. A survey of the history of lesbian and gay studies dates the rise of the gay liberation movement to the Stonewall riots of 1969.[58] Gay liberation, with its emphasis on "coming out" and consciousness-raising, sought not only recognition of homosexuality as a legitimate identity for a minority population but also to "free the homosexual in everyone" (Wittman 1972, 341; see also Duggan 1992, 15; Smyth 1992, 24–25; N. Sullivan 2003, 31). Over time, the focal point shifted from transforming universal social structures to the assimilationist strategy of securing specific rights as a minority group, but this process of stabilization disenfranchised others who did not fit so neatly into the two categories of lesbian and gay (Duggan 1992, 13–15; Smyth 1992, 19–20; N. Sullivan 2003, 22–36). For some, this led to a demand for equal recognition of non-normative categories of identity (hence the term *LGBTQIA*); the notion of a unitary gay identity was challenged, not just in terms of sexuality but also in relation to issues of class, race, gender, and disability; and thus the labels became more complex in their attempts to capture this diversity (Duggan 1992, 17–22; Smyth 1992, 28–35; Butler 1993, 227; Jagose 1996, 58–71; N. Sullivan 2003, 37–39.).[59] For others, according to Jagose (1996, 71), "this developed into a dissatisfaction with the categories of identification themselves and a questioning of their efficacy in political intervention." Ultimately, Jagose (1996, 74) suggests, it is out of such "constructionist problematising" of these allegedly universal identity categories that the concept of queer emerges.

This shift in both terminology and thinking around the notion of identity can also be seen as characteristic of the development of postmodernism in the 1970s (Morton 1996, 10–12; Moore 2007, 3–10; Aichele, Miscall, and Walsh 2009; Moore and Sherwood, 2011). If queer theory was conceived through a disillusionment with identity politics, then it is the poststructuralist theories of intellectuals such as Foucault that have provided the context out of which queer theory was born (Sarup 1993, 1–4; Weedon 1997, 12–41; Fuss 1989a, 77). Foucault has been touted as "the most important intellectual catalyst of queer theory" (Spargo 1999, 8), and certainly his three-volume *History of Sexuality* is widely regarded as "the charter document" of queer theory (Moore 2001, 14; see also Goss 1993, 181–90; Halperin 1995, 15–125; Jobling, Pippin, and Schleifer 2001, 8–12; Halperin 2002b; Huffer 2010, 44–83). Moore (2001, 14) descriptively notes that this work "deftly unhooked sexuality from its presumed attachment of 'nature' and left it dangling, naked and shivering, from the peg marked 'culture' instead." However, it is important to make clear that as Foucault's interest lay in the broad areas of knowledge, power, and discourse (Mills 2003, 81–95; Huffer 2010, 40), he is "not the origin of queer theory, nor is queer theory the destination of Foucault's thinking" (Spargo 1999, 10).[60]

Given the phenomenon that Esther Fuchs (2003, 104–6) calls the "paternity of postmodern theories"—the predominance of the "male-authored theories" of Foucault, Jacques Derrida, and others such as Roland Barthes and Jacques Lacan (see also Marcus 1982; Schor 1987; Wolfe and Penelope 1993, 5)—it is also important to note the point made by William Turner (2000, 34) that "the originators of queer theory are all feminist scholars." Mention must be made of three key scholars, beginning with Sedgwick. Called by Moore (2001, 13) the "doyenne of queer theory," her groundbreaking study *Between Men* (1985) is described by Jagose (1996, 119) as "the point of origin of queer studies."[61] Sedgwick's subsequent work, *Epistemology of the Closet*, is an equally pioneering critique of the "homo/heterosexual definition" that she suggests structures (and fractures) "many of the major nodes of thought and knowledge in twentieth-century Western culture as a whole" (1990, 1).[62]

In the same year that Sedgwick published *Epistemology of the Closet*, Butler published her landmark work, *Gender Trouble*. Butler's work, including the follow-up publication *Bodies That Matter* (1993), has also been central to the development of queer theory, and she too has been called "the doyenne of contemporary queer theory" (Hughes 2002, 991). Jagose (1996, 83) states that Butler is "the theorist who has done most to unpack the risks and limits of identity," while Sedgwick (1994, 1) herself states in regard to *Gender Trouble* that one "couldn't help being awed by the productive impact this dense and even imposing work has had on the recent development of queer theory and reading."[63]

However, it was de Lauretis who coined the actual term *queer theory* in the effort, she explains, "to avoid all of these fine distinctions in our discursive protocols, not to adhere to any one of the given terms, not to assume their ideological liabilities, but instead to both transgress and transcend them—or at the very least problematize them" (1991, v). She makes the additional point: "My 'queer,' however, had no relation to the Queer Nation group, of whose existence I was ignorant at the time.... There is in fact very little in common between Queer Nation and this queer theory" (1991, xvii n. 2).[64]

Queer Nation was one of many political groups that emerged during the early 1990s, symbolizing the new defiant style of political activism that rejected the liberal assimilationist strategies of the gay liberation movement, as they made clear in their popular saying, "We're Here, We're Queer—Get Used To It!"[65] Tamsin Spargo makes the observation, "In popular culture, queer meant sexier, more transgressive, a deliberate show of difference which didn't want to be assimilated or tolerated" (1999, 38).[66] This new development was partly in response to the AIDS epidemic in the 1980s when a more defiant attitude was needed (Berlant and Warner 1995, 345; Schneider 2000, 207). However, queer theory is not just the academic underpinning of this cultural movement, as is made clear in the statement by de Lauretis above. As intimated already, it arises from different understandings of identity and power: "If queer culture has reclaimed 'queer' as an adjective that contrasts with the relative respectability of 'gay' and 'lesbian,' then queer theory could be seen as mobilising 'queer' as a verb that unsettles assumptions about sexed and sexual being and doing" (Spargo 1999, 40). Or as Cooper (2000, 20) simply puts it: "Queer theory is what queer theory does."

This brings me to the issue of *who* can *do* queer theory; does one have to *be* queer to *do* queer? While many scholars who do queer theory openly identify as gay, lesbian, or queer, Cooper (2000, 12 n. 4) notes that those queer theorists who identify as straight (or even bisexual) tend not to specify their sexual orientation and consequently "place themselves in a more difficult relation to queer theory than if they were to classify their erotic investments as lesbian, gay, or queer." For myself, as a straight-identified scholar, this is a deeply pertinent issue. Alex Hughes (2002, 991) articulates the anxiety that I have personally felt: "those of us who [enact] queer theoretical exegesis from a straight-identified position, are regularly assailed by doubts as to the ethics of our 'touristic' critical activities." Questions of identity/identification and the authority of personal experience arise; for those who have no personal experience of what it might be like to *be* queer—in other words, who operate from within the heteronormative paradigm of society and thus experience some of its privileges—are they able to *do* queer scholarship and offer something of value to the field, or would this be a "colonizing move" whereby they appropriate an identity that is not theirs (Cooper 2000, 27)?[67] These questions are not easily answered, as Cooper explains:

> While queer theory may not always be *about* dissident sexuality, the critiques and readings performed by queer theorists are intended to function in a queer-affirmative manner and do something *for* queers, lesbians, and gays. Can straights and bisexuals ever be in a position to do such queer-affirmative queer theoretical work?… The term "queer" might have become a recognized category of self-definition for some lesbians, gays, and sexual dissidents and for a theoretical area concerned primarily with sexuality, but the issue of who can use the term "queer,"

and how they use it, and in what context, is by no means clear-cut.
(2000, 24)

However, queer theory questions the naturalness and normative
value of identity categories and recognizes the problematic nature of the
very concept of identity. It is still important to acknowledge the various
aspects of our identities—such as race or class, for example—so as to
avoid the hegemonic presumptions that can otherwise occur; as Nikki
Sullivan (2003, 48) notes, queer theory "has been accused of being,
among other things, male-centered, anti-feminist, and race-blind."[68] But
narrowing the concept of identity to the single strand of one's sexuality
(or sexual orientation), so that one is only identified as either straight or
queer, for example, is hardly consistent with a queer approach as it over-
simplifies distinctions among people by resorting to a dichotomous and
essentialist logic. That which is queer is akin to a "zone of possibilities"
(Edelman 1994, 114) that refuses to stake its claim, preferring indetermi-
nacy, elasticity, and nonspecificity; or, in the words of Sedgwick (1994, 7),
it is "the open mesh of possibilities, gaps, overlaps, dissonances and reso-
nances, lapses and excesses of meaning where the constituent elements
of anyone's gender, of anyone's sexuality aren't made (or *can't* be made) to
signify monolithically."

If one accepts that people have many differing elements that intersect in various ways to form their identities, then it is also possible to
recognize that "numerous systems of oppression interact to regulate
and police the lives of most people" (Cohen 1997, 441). While I might
experience some of the privileges of race and class, other aspects of my
identity, such as my gender, marital status, and socioeconomic status, all
function to disadvantage and marginalize me in the heteronormative (if
not heteropatriarchal) society within which I live. Cathy Cohen (1997,
442) addresses this issue in her quest for a "broadened understanding
of queerness." She asks, "how would queer activists understand politically the lives of women—in particular women of colour—on welfare,
who may fit into the category of heterosexual, but whose sexual choices
are not perceived as normal, moral, or worthy of state support?" (442).
An identification as straight does not unconditionally award someone
with an exemption from oppression. Indeed, as Cohen notes, given the
portrayal of the bourgeois nuclear family as an ideal in society, to live
outside this arrangement is also to find oneself "on the outside of heteronormative privilege" (455). Cohen suggests that a queer approach engage

in what she calls an "intersectional analysis" as this leads to the recognition that all identities are "invested with varying degrees of normative power" and thus challenges the "assumption of a uniform heteronormativity from which all heterosexuals benefit" (442, 452). Thus while not wanting to erase the stigmatization experienced by those who do identify as gay or lesbian (or bisexual or transgendered or queer, etc.), I would argue that *doing* queer theory as a straight-identified, queer-affirming, privileged-yet-oppressed *being* has credibility.[69]

A related perspective comes from Adrienne Rich's (1980, 648) notion of a "lesbian continuum" by which she meant "to include a range—through each woman's life and throughout history—of woman-identified experience; not simply the fact that a woman has had or consciously desired genital sexual experience with another woman." Deryn Guest (2005, 24–25) explains that one therefore "does not have to be biologically wired to undertake a lesbian perspective, but can be adopting a strategic position of choice." Any straight-identified woman who is prepared to engage critically with her own personal experiences of heterosexuality and with the ways in which heteronormativity has been upheld and maintained in society could therefore be said to be adopting a lesbian position.

However, some lesbians have criticized this notion for downplaying the notion of desire and erotic behavior between women, with the consequence that Rich (1993, 249) added an afterword to a reprinting of her original essay, in which she made the point, "My own problem with the phrase [lesbian continuum] is that it can be, is, used by women ... as a safe way to describe their felt connections with women, without having to share in the risks and threats of lesbian existence." Guest (2005, 35) also makes the point that another problem with the idea of a lesbian continuum "lies in its unreserved commitment to the category of woman."[70] This is a matter addressed by Wittig and her notion of the lesbian as someone who has escaped the regime of heteronormativity; as she so provocatively puts it, "Lesbians are not women" (1992i, 32).

This challenge by Wittig to the identity categories of both "lesbian" and "woman" is indicative of queer theory's quest to expose and destabilize the ideologically constructed foundations of sexed and gendered identity categories. This desire to unsettle, to destabilize, to question, and to queer taken-for-granted understandings and assumptions, particularly those of heteronormativity—but of whatever is "the normal, the legitimate, the dominant"—is descriptive (but never definitive) of queer theory (Halperin 1995, 62). It is also the approach to 1 Cor 11:2–16 that I wish to take.

Biblically Queer

The suspicion soon arises that queer theory and the New Testament are
already having an affair behind our backs.
                                        — Stephen Moore, *God's Beauty Parlor*

Of course, not all biblical scholars accept that an engagement with post-
structuralism or postmodernism—let alone something as transgressive
as queer theory—is an appropriate or proper way to approach the New
Testament. As Elizabeth Castelli (1991b, 37) noted when she pioneered
a Foucauldian analysis of power in an examination of Paul's call to imitation, "The field of New Testament studies has often eschewed theoretical considerations. Some would avoid theory on the basis of its alleged
irrelevancy.... There are also some critics who see theory as dangerous,
as a threat to the uniqueness of Christianity." Writing ten years later on
the value of bringing queer politics into the area of biblical interpretation,
Stone (2001b, 11) acknowledges that some readers will find this association "dubious," while others "have tried to ignore the changing shape of
biblical scholarship, and others ... have expressed critical reservations."[71]
Writing more recently, Moore (2007, 2) notes that "historical criticism's
hegemony in the international field of biblical studies has not diminished
significantly during the past two decades."[72] But he also adds that while
New Testament literary criticism was initially slow to take up deconstruction and poststructuralism, the major developments of the 1990s, such as
cultural studies, postcolonial studies, queer theory, masculinity studies,
and autobiographical studies, "had all been taken up in New Testament
studies even before that decade had come to an end" (3). Yet, in considering the developments of the 2000s, Moore also notes that while each of
these fields "constitutes a considerable resource for New Testament studies
... each has barely begun to be engaged by New Testament scholars" (10;
see also Stone 2005, 17; Punt 2007, 385, 389).[73]

    Given that queer theory investigates and problematizes the very con-
cepts of sexuality and gender, and specifically challenges the heteropatriarchal models that are often presented by conservative biblical scholars
as natural and God-given, it is perhaps not surprising that there has been
some resistance to queer approaches to the New Testament. Robert Myles
(2010, 67) points out, "Like many reading strategies that go against the
grain of traditional interpretation, a queer hermeneutic expects to be met
with suspicion and distrust." Some of this resistance can be explained

simply by the decision to intersect queer theory and biblical studies, two fields of inquiry that many perceive to be diametrically opposed. On a personal level, Alison Webster (1998, 30) poignantly discusses the difficulty of identifying as both lesbian and Christian, noting the pressure from each community to "come down on one side or the other." She explains that "there are the pressures from the secular gay and lesbian and feminist communities [that] share an assumption that there is something a little odd, if not masochistic, about a Christian affiliation.… On the other hand, there is, of course, the more obvious pressure from within the Christian community [to] give up lesbianism" (29–30).

On a more theoretical level, Webster notes that the Kristevan term *abject* is an apposite descriptor of a Christian-lesbian positionality in that each community wishes to expel and exclude the "other" from its presence in order to maintain its boundaries and sense of clear identity, but in doing so constructs the possibility of a new (albeit abject) subject (29). Some feminist scholars contest the usefulness of this concept, arguing not only that it has been overused but also, more importantly, that it tends to reproduce a disgust of the maternal rather than challenging it, and thus serves a patriarchal center (Krauss 1997, 235; Tyler 2009, 77–98). However, other feminists have seen the connection between this Kristevan concept and Wittig's work (M. Walker 1998, 80 n. 34), and given my exploration of ambiguous ontologies in chapter 4 and the discussion of Wittig's "monstrous lesbian" in chapter 6, I would argue for its usefulness in this project. Julia Kristeva's description of the process of abjection is visceral and powerful, and I cite this description in full here:

> Food loathing is perhaps the most elementary and most archaic form of abjection. When the eyes see or the lips touch that skin on the surface of milk—harmless, thin as a sheet of cigarette paper, pitiful as a nail paring—I experience a gagging sensation and, still farther down, spasms in the stomach, the belly; and all the organs shrivel up the body, provoke tears and bile, increase heartbeat, cause forehead and hands to perspire. Along with sight-clouding dizziness, *nausea* makes me balk at that milk cream, separates me from the mother and father who proffer it. "I" want none of that element, sign of their desire; "I" do not want to listen. "I" do not assimilate it, "I" expel it. But since the food is not an "other" for "me," who am only in their desire, I expel *myself*, I spit *myself* out, I abject *myself* within the same motion through which "I" claim to establish myself.… During that course in which "I" become, I give birth to myself amid the violence of sobs, of vomit. Mute protest of the symptom, shat-

tering violence of a convulsion that, to be sure, is inscribed in a symbolic system, but in which, without either wanting to or being able to become integrated in order to answer to it, it reacts, it abreacts. It abjects....

It is thus not lack of cleanliness or health that causes abjection but what disturbs identity, system, order. What does not respect borders, positions, rules. The in-between, the ambiguous, the composite. (1982, 2–4)[74]

I suggest that the notion of "abject" is also an apt descriptor of the intersection of biblical studies and queer theory despite the contested nature of this concept. Stone (2001b, 29, 31) observes that queer biblical commentary can lead to some "strange, and sometimes disturbing, couplings," not least because the notion of queer "continues to call to mind unorthodox combinations and transgressive juxtapositions of things normally kept apart."[75] The new alien subject that is established through the coupling of two fields "normally kept apart" might be resisted or rejected by some, but I suggest that it also creates a marginal zone of critical inquiry, which Butler (1999, xxxii) reminds us is required when examining the complex issues of sexuality and gender. My suspicion is that the fruit of such a supposedly unnatural pairing—as "abject" as it might be to some—enables a new que(e)rying of 1 Cor 11:2–16, one that both challenges notions of stable (hierarchical, heteronormative) identity and resists the imposition of traditional rules and borders regarding academic inquiry.[76]

Perhaps more than the work of any other biblical scholar, Moore's work reveals the (abject) fruit of queer biblical studies. In a prose style that tends to polarize his readers,[77] Moore explores what he describes as "queer spaces in and around the Bible."[78] He (2007, 10) suggests that the intersection between queer theory and biblical studies "has the capacity to shift the increasingly tired debates on biblical texts that apparently deal with homosexuality into a radically different register." By creating a marginal zone of critical inquiry in which ideologies of gender and sexuality can be exposed and challenged, my aim is to also shift the "increasingly tired debates" on the various exegetical and historical issues that occupy an historical-critical approach to 1 Cor 11:2–16 into a "radically different register." In fact, rather than rehashing these debates or proposing yet another possible reconstruction of the situation in Corinth, I will come at this passage from oblique angles, so that the normal—that which is expected in terms of content and even presentation—might be unsettled.

Moore specifically mentions the debates on the issue of homosexuality, and while 1 Cor 11:2–16 is not one of the obvious biblical texts used in this debate—unlike Rom 1:18–32, for example—it is a text used to bolster a heteronormative model of gender and sexuality, and therefore I suggest that we *must* consider it in this debate. Moore (2007, 11) also notes this important point in the expansion of his comment above: "to limit queer biblical commentary ... to the tiny handful of biblical texts that explicitly touch on homoeroticism would be to miss a major contribution of queer theory.... For heterosexuality has been queer theory's object of investigation as much as homosexuality."[79] By focusing on homosexuality as an object of study, Stone (2001a, 114) argues that that this leaves "unproblematized sexual relations between women and men and [contributes] to the impression that those relations, in contrast to homoerotic relations, have maintained stable forms and meanings from biblical times to the present" (see Halperin 1995, 61; D. Martin 1995b). By revealing and challenging the ideologies of sex and gender that not only lie behind 1 Cor 11:2–16 but are also apparent in the ways in which this passage has been interpreted by modern scholars to reinforce heteronormativity (if not heteropatriarchy), I will seek to do something queer with this passage; something abject, something "at odds with the normal, the legitimate, the dominant" (Halperin 1995, 62).

However, it is precisely this preoccupation of queer theory with homosexuality and heterosexuality that causes Moore to question its ability to cope with cultures, such as those out of which the New Testament arises, that do not possess the heterosexual/homosexual divide. The ideologies of the first-century Mediterranean world do not overlap exactly with those of the twentieth- and twenty-first-century West. Moore answers his own question, however, and explains that it is not only possible to utilize queer theory to examine ancient cultures but also important:

> If life in contemporary Western culture (sexual life especially) is regulated by regimes of the normal, life in ancient Mediterranean culture (sexual life especially) was regulated by regimes of the natural ... and the natural, no less than the normal, demands close critical scrutiny—all the more since "their" natural was the progenitor of "our" normal—and queer theory, although a critical sensibility more than a methodology, eminently equips us to scrutinize it. (2001, 17–18)

It is perhaps this level of "close critical scrutiny" of "'their' natural" and the "'our' normal" that differentiates queer biblical studies from what can be called LGBT biblical studies. In many ways these two approaches to the

Bible parallel both the development of and the differences between queer theory and gay and lesbian studies.[80] In particular, an LGBT approach tends to be apologetic in nature, grounding a quest for liberation and justice in both a confident identity politics and a positive view of the Bible as a "friend" (Comstock 1993, 11), and as a "text that 'does no harm'" (M. West 1999, 35; see also N. Wilson 1995, 73; Boyarin 1997, xvii; Goss and West 2000a, 5; Goss 2002, 214–17, 256; Stuart 2003, 10).[81] Scripture can therefore be approached with the assumption that gay, lesbian, and bisexual people have always been hidden in the text, and one's aim should be to liberate these characters and stories from their ancient closets.[82] Other LGBT biblical studies examine the "texts of terror" (e.g., Lev 18:22; 20:13; Rom 1:26–27; and 1 Cor 6:9) with the aim of seeking and affirming interpretations that have been obscured by traditional (often homophobic) approaches (Trible 1984, 1–7; see also Comstock 1993, 61–78; Goss 1993, 90–94; 2002, 185–203; Goss and West 2000a, 3).[83]

Queer biblical studies moves beyond these strategies, however, not least because it finds problematic statements such Mona West's (1999, 35) assertion that the text "does no harm." Such a statement not only overlooks the centrality of the interpreter in the process of determining how the text is both understood and used,[84] but it also neglects the way in which ideologies have shaped the text in the first place. Queer theory provides a framework for revealing these ideologies and as such can "illuminate texts and traditions in helpful if sometimes unsettling ways" (Schneider 2000, 211). For example, those doing LGBT biblical studies might examine the "texts of terror" in a way that seeks to redeem them, to make them friendly.[85] By contrast, a queer theorist engaging the same texts "will be more interested in their perceived necessity and the dynamics of power that they reveal than in any culturally transcendent moral claims that they can possibly make" (208).[86]

As cited at the outset of this section, Moore (2001, 18) suggests that queer theory and the New Testament are "already having an affair behind our backs." So far, however, the majority of queer biblical studies have been done on the Hebrew Bible, while work on the New Testament has tended to concentrate on the gospels. Of the seventeen essays in the seminal collection *Take Back the Word* (Goss and West 2000b), for example, twelve of these concern the Hebrew Scriptures while four of the five that concern the New Testament have to do with the gospels; only one essay examines the epistles (Bohache 2000).[87] While the *Queer Commentary and the Hebrew Bible* was published in 2001 (Stone 2001c), no equivalent has been produced for the New Testament, although *The Queer Bible Commentary* was published in 2006 (Guest et al. 2006). Perhaps it is the draw of narrative that attracts scholars to these parts of the Bible, coupled with the fact that it is the New Testament epistles that contain the "texts of terror" (Rom 1:26–28; 1 Cor 6:9; 1 Tim 1:18), but only a handful of material has been produced on the epistles.[88]

Moore's work on Rom 1:18–32 in *God's Beauty Parlor*, however, is an excellent example of a queer reading of a Pauline text and provides a useful rationale for my project. He both reveals the "hyperheteronormativity" of the Greco-Roman sex-gender system and considers the ways in which Pauline theologies of human-human and human-divine relations might be reconfigured once one realizes that Paul's soteriology was produced within such a "phallofixated" system (2001, 170). In concluding his essay, Moore suggests that the "trick" for radically reforming these relations "would be to take that which is farthest outside the camp in Romans, that which is most anathemized—sex between women …—and usher it into the center, into the tabernacle itself" (172). One of the consistent critiques aimed at queer theory has been its tendency to render lesbians and lesbian issues invisible, as happened in the gay liberation movement.[89] Indeed, there is an anxiety that "queer will not be gender neutral but will install a new universal masculinity at its heart" (Guest 2005, 46; see also Schneider 2000, 212–18; Myles 2010, 69, 80). My intent with this project is precisely to bring "that which is most anathemized"—that which is most abject—to the center of an examination of 1 Cor 11:2–16. I suggest that Wittig's materialist feminist lesbianism ought to do the trick since Wittig is a devastating critic of heteronormativity and 1 Cor 11:2–16 is a text used to bolster a heteronormative model of gender and sexuality.[90] Thus I will employ Wittig's theories of gender and sexuality to examine some of the ways in which contemporary commentators have interpreted this text. In particular I will focus on Wittig's concept of the lesbian, a theoretical figure that I will introduce in more detail in chapter 3.

Through her writing, Wittig seeks to universalize the particular, to make central that which is on the fringes (or invisible, anathematized, deemed monstrous, or abject), and thus to reappropriate the universal subject position for the minority point of view.[91] For a text such as 1 Cor 11:2–16, its explicit mention of women has had the result that the Corinthian men have often been rendered invisible. Stone (2001b, 26) suggests that "a critical gender analysis needs to be extended not only to biblical representations of women (which have understandably been at the centre of most feminist studies) but also to biblical representations of men and of 'masculinity.' "[92] I suggest that another potentially abject coupling is taking place here, not only between biblical studies and queer theory, but also between Wittig's materialist lesbianism and explorations of both ancient and contemporary constructs of masculinity, most specifically, between Wittig's lesbian and the Corinthian men.

One last point to discuss here is that of methodology. Some queer theorists have suggested that the notion of "commentary" is more aptly suited to this approach than the notion of "theory" (Berlant and Warner 1995, 343–44). Indeed, the very fact that this term has a long association with historical-critical biblical studies makes it a subversively appealing choice (Stone 2001b, 13–14). I view the historical-critical approach to this passage as somewhat queer in any case,[93] and so in many ways these descriptors—both *queer* and *commentary*—play nicely into the framework of my project. In a way that resonates with my approach, Stone (2001b, 33) concludes that "queer commentary on the Bible" can be understood as "a range of approaches to biblical interpretation that take as their point of departure a critical interrogation and active contestation of the many ways in which the Bible is and has been read to support heteronormative and normalizing configurations of sexual practices and sexual identities." I would only add that queer commentary can also interrogate and contest the ways in which the Bible has been read to support "normalizing configurations" of gender practices and gender identities.

"Queer commentary" involves a *re*reading of the biblical material in a way that is queer, not only in that heteronormative ideologies of gender and sexuality are revealed and traditional readings are challenged, but also in ways that are experimental and unconventional—and thus potentially abject (R. Boer 1999, 15; Myles 2010, 67). This then leads to a consideration of "the possible shape(s) of queer writing" (Stone 2001b, 30). In relation to several essays in the volume *Queer Commentary and the Hebrew Bible*, Stone (2001b, 30) comments that "assumptions about the proper boundaries between, and roles of, academic and literary writing are no less susceptible to a queer destabilizing than are assumptions about proper boundaries and roles in sexual activity" (see also Warner 1993, xxvi). Moore's work particularly exemplifies this resistance to the normal, and it is also an issue discussed by Wittig in her political essays and actualized in her works of fiction. As Namascar Shaktini (2005a, 158) states of Wittig's work, the act of writing is always a political act "of unwriting and rewriting."[94]

I hope, then, that the material presented in this book might also be of an experimental nature that resists "normalization" as it also challenges "normal" readings of 1 Cor 11:2–16—as it "disturbs identity, system, order [and] does not respect borders, positions, rules" (Kristeva 1982, 4). This will be initially evident in the way that I intersect a diverse range of scholars, theologians, and writers across this biblical passage. The simple juxtaposition of these in the bibliography testifies to the making of some unlikely and uneasy bedfellows who may well "gag" and "convulse" at the thought of touching so intimately (Kristeva 1982, 2–3), from Barth and Butler to Gagnon and Guest; from Schreiner and Stone to Watson and Wittig. The "scenes" that introduce each of chapters 4, 5, and 6 are also of an experimental nature and play with both the boundaries of academic writing and the sensual/visual dimensions of gender and sexuality, power and desire. Finally, this will be especially evident in chapter 6 when I juxtapose Gagnon's *Bible and Homosexual Practice* (2001) with Wittig's *Lesbian Body* (1976) through the play of the material on the page.[95]

Notes

1. These two words are common descriptors of this passage or of specific issues within the text (see, e.g., Fee 1987, 492; Witherington 1995, 231; Horsley 1998, 153; Soards 1999, 224; Keener 2005, 94).

2. See, e.g., Schirrmacher 1993, 47; Blomberg 1994, 214; A. Johnson 2004, 195. Schreiner (2006a, 124) goes so far as to say that 1 Cor 11:2–16 is "one of the most difficult and controversial passages in the Bible."

3. Scroggs's (1972, 297) frequently cited comments about this passage are worth quoting in full: "In its present form this is hardly one of Paul's happier compositions. The logic is obscure at best and contradictory at worst. The word choice is peculiar; the tone peevish." Like Scroggs, Schüssler Fiorenza (1983, 219, 228) is also often cited on this point, stating that Paul's argument "is very convoluted and far from being intelligible even today" and that this is "a very convoluted argument which can no longer be unravelled completely." For "curious," see, e.g., Glen 1965, 131; Jewett 1979, 67; Winandy 1992, 621; J. D. Miller 2009, 65. For "strange," see e.g., Gordon Clark 1991, 170, 176; Engberg-Pedersen 1991, 681; Amjad-Ali 1995, 207.

4. By " 'new' wives" Winter (2003b, 21–38) is referring to the emergence in the first century of elite women who were financially independent and experienced a degree of freedom in their lives hitherto unheard of among married women.

5. See appendix 1 for further discussion on this verse.

6. While these are too numerous to cite comprehensively, mention must be made of at least the following book-length studies: Theissen 1982; Meeks 1983; Schüssler Fiorenza 1983; Wire 1990; Mitchell 1993; D. Martin 1995b; Horrell 1996; Welborn

1997; Meggitt 1998; Winter 2001; Økland 2004; Osiek and MacDonald 2006. See also the collections of essays in Horsley 2000; Schowalter and Frisen 2005, 2010.

7. Penner and Vander Stichele have taken the imagery of "the master's tools" from the poet Audre Lorde (1983, 98–99), who is referring specifically to "the tools of racist patriarchy." For more on historical-critical methodology as a modern enterprise and the clash with postmodern biblical methodologies, see Aichele, Miscall, and Walsh 2009; Van Seters 2009; Horrell and Adams 2004; Dunn 2004.

8. Incidentally, I have yet to come across anyone who argues that Paul is concerned with the behavior of only the men, although Thiselton (2000, 825) does make the significant point that "the *first concern of 11:2–16 is about men, not about women.*" As this is a minority view, but one that I feel is of ideological importance, I will examine it in more detail in ch. 2.

9. Given the intense nature of the debate over the interpretation of κεφαλή and the ideological issues that this entails, I will examine this issue in more detail in ch. 4.

10. Unless otherwise stated, all biblical translations are my own.

11. In ch. 2 I will explore in more detail the suggestion that there were "male homosexuals presiding at the liturgy" (Murphy-O'Connor 1996, 279).

12. As I will discuss in more detail below, however, that which is queer is also that which resists definition.

13. Smyth cites an anonymous "Queer Power Now" leaflet circulating in London in 1991.

14. Perhaps the most comprehensive list of checklist questions is that given by D. MacDonald 1987, 72–81.

15. I will examine the scholarship and discussion of these issues in more detail in later chapters, but with regard to "man and woman" it is often εἰκών ("image") that links Gen 1:26–27 and 1 Cor 11:7–9; with regard to "homosexuality" it is often φύσις ("nature") that links Rom 1:18–32 with 1 Cor 11:13–15.

16. Winkler (1990, 3) does not accept this view, but is describing the way in which sex is generally treated in the social sciences, as "the province of biology or perhaps psychology, but not subject to cultural investigation."

17. Tolbert (2000b, 99) does not agree but is describing the views of those who hold this "modernist perspective."

18. This is clearly evident in the material produced by the CBMW that I will examine in more detail in ch. 4.

19. This understanding of gender raises the "essentialism/constructionism impasse" that has dogged feminist theory and politics since the 1980s. See the overviews in Edwards 1989; G. Lloyd 1989; D. Thompson 1989; Schor 1992; Szesnat 1997, 336–42; Haraway 2001, 52–58; Donadey and Lionnet 2007, 230–31; Culbertson 2008, 44–46.

20. Boyarin (1998, 117) also notes the dangers of a simplistic sex/gender opposition, stating that it "invokes the terms of the nature/culture opposition upon which so much of Western misogyny is based."

21. In this regard, Butler (1999, xxviii–xxix) argues that gender is a "cultural performance." I will return to Butler's work in more detail in ch. 3.

22. Rubin (1984, 307–8) explains here that in her earlier essay, "The Traffic of

Women," she did not distinguish between "lust and gender … gender and desire" and that she has now changed her argument.

23. The work of Foucault in the 1970s and 1980s on *The History of Sexuality* was groundbreaking, as was that of Dover and Veyne, both of whom influenced Foucault; see Foucault 1990a, 1990b, 1988; Dover 1978; Veyne 1978. In addition, the year 1990 was significant in this field and not only saw the publication of Butler's *Gender Trouble*, but also Laqueur's *Making Sex*, Winkler's *Constraints of Desire*, Halperin's *One Hundred Years of Homosexuality*, and the collection of essays edited by Halperin, Winkler, and Zeitlin, *Before Sexuality*.

24. See also Jeffrey Henderson 1988, 1250; Winkler 1990, 17–18, 40; Padgug 1989, 54–57. Halperin's citation is from Rich's poem "Translations," lines 32–33 (1973, 41). A similarly pithy saying by anthropologist Godelier (1981, 17) is also often cited on this issue: "it is not sexuality that haunts society, but society which haunts the body's sexuality."

25. There is a debate, however, between a constructionist and essentialist view of sexuality, coupled with the way in which scholars have responded to the work of Foucault. See the work of Boswell 1980; 1997, 118–19; Davidson 2007; Richlin 1991, 16–18; 1993; Halperin 2002a, 235–59; 2002c; Sedgwick 1990, 44–48. For more on these differing approaches and the complex issues surrounding the development of sexuality as a domain of inquiry, see also J. Weeks 1981, 77–103; 2002; 2003, 11–40.

26. Berlant and Warner (1998, 553–54) go on to state, "Heterosexual culture achieves much of its metacultural intelligibility through the ideologies and institutions of intimacy.… This privatized sexual culture bestows on its sexual practices a tacit sense of rightness and normalcy. This sense of rightness—embedded in things and not just in sex—is what we call heteronormativity."

27. Although Warner uses the term *heteronormativity* in this earlier article, scholars usually point to his later essay (1993, xxi–xxv) for the origin of the term. See the discussion in Chambers and Carver 2008, 144.

28. Wittig's theories will be discussed in more detail in ch. 3.

29. Wittig's presentation of her paper "The Straight Mind" in 1978 at the Modern Language Association's annual conference in New York, where she infamously suggested that "lesbians are not women," was the beginning of this challenge to view heterosexuality as an ideological construct; see the discussion in Turcotte 1992, viii.

30. This point is also made by Rich 1973, 41; 1980, 648; Rubin 1984, 267, 280–81, 309. See also Butler's phrase *heterosexual matrix*, used throughout *Gender Trouble* (1999). Butler (1999, 194 n. 6) notes that she has adapted this term from Wittig's notion of the heterosexual contract and also Rich's notion of compulsory heterosexuality. Butler (1999, 24; 1993, 91) also uses the term *heterosexualization*. Butler later dropped the phrase *heterosexual matrix* (see Chambers and Carver 2008, 144).

31. Warner (1993, xxi–iii) suggests as much in his consideration of Carl Sagan's infamous portrayal of "humanity" in cartoon form etched onto the side of NASA's *Pioneer 10* spacecraft. A report from NASA states that *Pioneer 10* is "carrying a gold plaque that describes what *we* look like.… The physical makeup of the man and woman were determined from results of a computerized analysis of *the average person* in *our* civilization" (NASA 2007a; 2007b; emphasis added). Of course it must be noted that

this image of "humanity" on the *Pioneer 10* probe was produced in the early 1970s and was criticized at the time, according to Squeri (2004, 483–84), both by "moralists" who "accused NASA of promoting smut," by "feminists" who "complained that the woman on the plaque was subservient," and "still others [who] criticized the couple for being white." Consequently, when NASA launched *Voyagers I* and *II* in 1977, the project intentionally emphasized diversity, and the diagram of male and female was radically different from the earlier version; see http://tinyurl.com/SBL0685z. This image is a vast improvement on the earlier portrayal of "humanity," but heterosexual reproduction is still privileged as representative of what it means to be human.

32. The term *heteropatriarchy* was first coined by Penelope (1983, 19), although she does not define it.

33. I will consider this issue in more detail in ch. 4 when I examine the dispute between two key evangelical groups in the United States, the CBMW and CBE, over the meaning of κεφαλή in 1 Cor 11:3. Lakey (2010, 10, 22) argues that the debate within evangelicalism in the United States over 1 Cor 11:2–16 "can hardly be ignored" when considering issues of gender and is "now largely managed" by these two "rival organizations."

34. The issue of nomenclature is complex and has to a large extent been determined by the prolific debate within evangelical circles in the United States on gender roles. To begin with, it needs to be noted that self-designations differ from the labels that are given by those on the opposing side. Those who argue that equality between men and women is biblical frequently call themselves *egalitarian*, although more recently they also lay claim to the descriptor *complementarian*. However, *complementarian* is generally the favored self-description of those who argue for both a hierarchical model of relationships between men and women and gender-specific leadership roles. Egalitarians are often labeled as feminist or liberal by complementarians, while complementarians are labeled as traditionalist or patriarchalist by egalitarians. For a moderating view, and the one that I will follow, see Beck and Blomberg (2005a, 16–17), who conclude that *egalitarian* and *hierarchicalist* are the best descriptors for these two groups. For a discussion on the issue of nomenclature within this debate from an egalitarian perspective, see Groothuis 2004, 303–4; from a hierarchicalist perspective, see Grudem 2006a, 13–16. See also Linda Mercadante's (1978, 75–153) classic overview of scholarship on 1 Cor 11:2–16 from the time of Calvin through to the late 1970s; she divides scholars into the categories of "traditional" and "non-traditional."

35. See, e.g., Schreiner (2006a, 122, 129), who argues that in this passage "a hierarchy is definitely established.... God has ordained that men have the responsibility to lead, while women have a complementary and supportive role [and they] should pray and prophesy in a manner that makes it clear that they submit to male leadership."

36. See, e.g., Theissen's (1982, 107) explanation of what he calls "love patriarchalism." See Horrell (1996, 126–29) for a discussion of those who found this concept useful and others who had criticisms.

37. Blomberg (2007, 1–3, 13) has subsequently stated that he "would like to be an egalitarian" but acknowledges that he is "moderately hierarchalist" and thus tentatively labels himself as "a hyper-ultra-soft patriarchalist," a play on the label of "ultra-

soft patriarchalist" given to him by Webb (2001, 242–43). Blomberg notes that Beck, with whom he edited the book *Two Views* (2005b), thinks that Blomberg has "forged a third, mediating position," although Blomberg's chapter in this book falls under the complementarian view. Blomberg (2007, 2) states that the publishers were not convinced that there ought to be a third section to the book.

38. For example, Engberg-Pedersen (1991, 681–82) states that the underlying idea of Paul's argument is that "there is a certain ontological hierarchy with God at the top and with men being closer to Christ and (through him) to God than women, who are one step further down in the hierarchy." But he also says, "I do not find it in any way binding on us" (680).

39. See, e.g., Moloney 1984, 26; Heine 1987, 82–105; Witherington 1988, 104–17, 125–27; Trebilco 1990; M. MacDonald 1999, 199, 218; Polaski 2005, 43–46; Osiek and MacDonald 2006, 225–29. While Gal 3:28 is frequently read as an expression of egalitarianism, this interpretation is problematic; for more on this verse and the way it has been used apologetically, see Fatum 1995, 51–65.

40. For more on the contribution of Fatum to feminist hermeneutics and her unapologetic stance, which Fatum called *elendighedsforskning*, meaning "misery research," as opposed to an apologetic *værdighedsforskning*, or "dignity research," see Økland 2002, 144–46; 2004, 10.

41. For similar views see Craig 1953, 124; Simon 1959, 113; Glen 1965, 130–35; Chakkalakal 1997, 194; Freed 2005, 151. Castelli (1999, 231–32) discusses the tendency of Christian interpreters to create "a negative backdrop" of Judaism against which they then "project a utopian and preconceived notion of 'Christian freedom.'" See also the detailed discussions in Plaskow 1993; Boyarin 1994; Rehmann 2000, 12–18; Ehrensperger 2004, 16–27.

42. The case for rejecting 1 Cor 14:33b–36 is complex and involves both manuscript evidence and the possible contradiction with 11:5, where Paul accepts that women are "praying and prophesying" in public worship and thus clearly not being "silent" as in 14:33b–34. See the detailed discussions in Fee 1987, 699–708; Thiselton 2000, 1147–52.

43. For more on the general development of feminist readings and approaches in New Testament studies, see Brooten 1980; Castelli 1994; Rehmann 2000. However, the label *feminist* is problematic for some scholars in this category, particularly those who identify as evangelical. See the discussion on nomenclature above in n. 34 and the discussion in Pierce 2004, 60. Grudem is perhaps the most prolific writer against what he calls "evangelical feminism"; beyond the initial 1991 publication of *Recovering Biblical Manhood and Womanhood* (and its 2006 and online editions), which he coedited (Piper and Grudem 2006b), see Grudem 2004, 2006a, 2006b. From both a New Zealand and a North American evangelical feminist point of view, see the discussion in Hoggard Creegan and Pohl 2005, 12–13, 178–80.

44. As noted above, I will this issue in more detail in ch. 4.

45. To describe this critical approach in another way, Spivak (1993, 284) notes that "favorite sons and daughters who refuse to sanctify their father's house have their uses. Persistently to critique a structure that one cannot *not* (wish to) inhabit is the deconstructive stance" (emphasis added).

46. For more on the contribution of Schüssler Fiorenza to feminist biblical criticism, see the discussions in Økland 2002, 141–44; Castelli 2004, 36–52.

47. For more discussion on the contribution of Wire to feminist hermeneutics, see Økland 2002, 146–48; Kittredge 2000, 103–9.

48. Lakey (2010, 17–18) concurs with Grudem (2004, 518–24) that there are four main responses to egalitarianism: "two-point complementarian," where male headship is affirmed in both home and church; "one-point complementarian," where male headship is only affirmed in the home; "uncommitted," where there is "no official stance towards gender roles in either family or church"; and "egalitarian," where equality is affirmed in both home and church. Despite the variety of these practical positions, however, it is clear that they derive from the hierarchical and egalitarian models I have discussed. I suspect that Lakey's third model, those of an "uncommitted" stance, will reveal an unofficial mode of actual practice that leans toward one of these models as there are likely to be political reasons why certain congregations or groups of people have no official stance.

49. As Klesse (2007, 10) notes, reminding the reader of the personal implications of this ideological framework, "Heteronormativity stands for a complex regime of moral assumptions and cultural practices, which have the potential to instil a sense of rightness in some individuals and a devastating feeling of shame in others."

50. To echo Smyth 1992, 17.

51. As discussed in the previous section. See Schüssler Fiorenza 1983, 226–30; Wire 1990; Fatum 1995, 65–75; D'Angelo 1995, 132–42; Økland 2004; Penner and Vander Stichele 2005; Vander Stichele and Penner 2005.

52. The pioneering work of Castelli must be noted at this point; although not examining 1 Cor 11:2–16, Castelli (1991b, 98–115) used a Foucauldian analysis of power in Paul's call for his readers to imitate him, which therefore included a study of 1:4, 16, and 11:1.

53. One must recognize, however, that queer theory is not so much a methodology as a "critical sensibility, an encompassing angle of vision that … brings previously unperceived or disavowed data into focus" (Moore 2007, 23). It is "a horizon of possibility whose precise extent and heterogeneous scope cannot in principle be delimited in advance" (Halperin 1995, 62).

54. See also the similar "potted history" by Hayes (1994, 14) that culminates in the description of "the shotgun marriage of lesbian and gay politics" whose "child is Queer, and a problem child it surely is."

55. This is an observation first made by the editors of *The Lesbian and Gay Studies Reader* regarding the difference between lesbian and gay studies and women's studies (Abelove, Barale, and Halperin 1993, xv).

56. This issue has been contentious within the fields of feminist, gender, gay/lesbian, and queer studies; see de Lauretis 1991, vii–viii; Smyth 1992, 26–27; B. Martin 1994; Jagose 1996, 44–57, 128; Schneider 2000, 210; Jeffreys 2003, 32–56; N. Sullivan 2003, 32–35; Huffer 2010, 44–47. See also the collection of essays in Weed and Schor 1997.

57. Jagose notes this "slippage" in the differences between the first and second editions of Sedgwick's important work, *Between Men: English Literature and Male Homosocial Desire* (1985 and 1992).

58. For an account of the event itself and of the subsequent rise of the gay libera-tion movement, see D'Emilio 1998; Duberman 1994; Carter 2004; Halperin and Traub 2009, 3.

59. Duggan (1992, 18–19) cites a report by Sloan in the *San Francisco Bay Guard-ian* on the Second Annual Lesbian and Gay Writers' Conference (February 1991) in which she describes the meeting of "cross-sections of the human multiverse" and "the oxymoronic community of difference" that makes up "the queer community." For more on the "endless and fruitless debates over terminology," see Smyth 1992, 20–22; Halperin 1995, 63; Jagose 1996, 72–75, 101–15, 125–26.

60. Although one could be forgiven for thinking otherwise given the way Fou-cault is venerated in queer academic circles; the publication of Halperin's *Saint Fou-cault* (1995) alludes to such thinking with its title, especially as the book cover incor-porates an equals sign in the title: *Saint = Foucault*. See further discussion in Huffer 2010, 46–47.

61. Indicative of the difficulty in separating the genealogy of lesbian and gay stud-ies from queer theory, however, Smith (1992, 9 n. 17) states that *Between Men* "is generally thought to have inaugurated a theoretically informed body of lesbian and gay studies."

62. Also significant is Sedgwick's subsequent book *Tendencies* (1994), from which the opening quote of this section was taken. For more on the influence of Sedgwick see Jagose 1996, 18–19; Schneider 2000, 209; N. Sullivan 2003, 38.

63. Named by *The Face* magazine as one of the most influential thinkers of the late twentieth century (McMillen 1997, A14), Butler has had such a phenomenal impact on gender and queer studies that it would be impossible to cite a comprehensive account of those who have discussed this impact, let alone those who have utilized her theories; the following works provide some sense of overview, however: Salih 2002; Breen and Blumenfeld 2005; Kirby 2006, 129–43; M. Lloyd 2007; Jagger 2008. For an attempt at reading 1 Cor 11:2–16 in light of Butler's theory of performativity, see Townsley 2006.

64. It is of interest to note, however, that three years later de Lauretis (1994, 297) abandoned the phrase *queer theory*, commenting that it had "quickly become a con-ceptually vacuous creature of the publishing industry." See also Berlant and Warner 1995, 343; Moore 2001, 10–12.

65. For the history of the Queer Nation (based in the United States) see Smyth 1992, 17–27; Gross 1993, 82–86.

66. One of the criticisms of queer theory has been its "vogueishness" and the sense that at times it has been more about "style rather than substance" (Jagose 1996, 109).

67. At times within feminist circles a similar question arises regarding men who are engaged in feminism; can men *do* feminism or *be* feminist? See Jardine and Smith 1987; Fuss 1989.

68. The issue of race in relation to queer theory is contested; see de Lauretis 1991, viii–xi; Goldman 1996, 172–75; N. Sullivan 2003, 57–80.

69. For more on this issue, see the discussion on Halperin's concept of "an eccen-tric positionality" in Stone 2005, 15. Halperin (1995, 62) humorously makes the point that this eccentric positionality "is not restricted to lesbians and gays but is in fact

available to anyone who is or who feels marginalized because of her or his sexual practices: it could include some married couples without children, for example, or even
(who knows?) some married couples *with* children—with, perhaps, *very naughty* children." Or even, I would add, divorced solo parents with *very good* children. See also
Bohache 2000, 236 n. 1; Stone 2001b, 28; Goss 2002, 224–25, 234; Myles 2010, 69, 80.

70. Guest (2005, 46–58) ultimately resists the idea of a "queer hermeneutic," arguing for the notion of a "lesbian-identified hermeneutic"; she recognizes the difficulties
the retention of the term *lesbian* presents with regard to issues of identity formation
and representation, but argues that the addition of "-identified" indicates that the term
"is not a fixed state, but a perpetually unclear signifier that carries a diversity of different identifications."

71. Stone cites Barr (2000) as an example of the latter, especially ch. 6 on postmodernism.

72. To illustrate this point, an international conference on "Saint Paul and the
Corinthian Correspondence" held in Corinth in 2007 included ninety-six presenta-
tions, which covered a variety of theological, philological, historical, philosophical,
and sociopolitical approaches; nevertheless, only two papers considered issues of
gender and none examined issues of sexuality (Papadópoulos, Mpelezos, and Despotis 2009).

73. As an example, we could point to Goulder (2001, 268–73), who adds an
appendix to his work on Corinth in which he describes "new critical approaches"; he
notes, "The last two decades have seen a blooming of nontraditional lines of study"
(268). But the "new" and "nontraditonal" approaches Goulder outlines are simply
sociohistorical and rhetorical criticism.

74. See also Grosz 1989, 71–78; Butler 1999, 169.

75. Stone proceeds to cite E. White's (1999, 81) metaphor regarding the "heat"
of "creative energy" that can be "generated when two genres are rubbed against each
other to form something entirely new."

76. Scholars engaging in this coupling of queer and biblical studies also note
the "fruitful" potential of this interaction (Stone 1997, 140; 2001a, 108; Punt 2007,
383). Although preferring a lesbian-identified hermeneutic to a queer approach, as
discussed above, Guest (2005, 43) suggests that the "application of such theory within
biblical studies does herald new insights" and produces "interesting effects."

77. Stone (2003, 706) describes Moore's work as "engaging, frequently humorous
… [and] clever." F. Watson (2002, 109), on the other hand, disapproves of Moore's
"endless rhetorical artifice … freedom from conventional inhibition … and carefully
crafted jokes and provocations." F. Watson notes that his reservations are not just
with Moore but with those he describes (more than a little disparagingly, I suggest) as
"Moore's sect," who hold certain "dogmatic convictions," such as "gender differences
are always socially constructed and never simply 'given'" (109–11).

78. This is the subtitle to *God's Beauty Parlor* (2001).

79. Stone (2001a, 113–14) has also made this point in his discussion of Nissinen's
work, *Homoeroticism in the Biblical World*, and Nissinen's (1998, 123) recognition of a
"heterosexist bias" that can be manifested in attempts to discover "what the Bible really
says about homosexuality." See also Halperin 1995, 43–48; Stone 2000, 57; 2001b, 23.

80. Stone (2005, 16 n. 11) notes these are "arguably distinct" approaches; see also Schneider 2000, 208. For a history of the development of gay and lesbian theology, see Goss 2002, 239–50; Stuart 2003, 7–10; Guest 2005, 59–62; Lowe 2009, 49–50.

81. M. West describes her approach as queer, however, highlighting one of the difficulties in discerning the differences between queer and LGBT approaches.

82. Jonathan and David, Ruth and Naomi, Jesus and the beloved disciple are all "outed"; even the story of Queen Vashti is turned around in such a way that she becomes a role model and an encouragement to those in LGBTQIA communities (Comstock 1993, 49–60). In this process, speculation and imagination are acceptable, and no claim is made to be infallible (N. Wilson 1995, 112–13).

83. Other biblical studies that consider these texts (but which do not specifically come under an LGBTQIA umbrella) include Scroggs 1983; Brooten 1996, 195–302; Nissinen 1998, 37–55, 103–22; Countryman 2007, 21–33, 99–118; Loader 2010.

84. Tolbert (2000a, ix) puts this more bluntly: "Of course, the Bible itself does not kill people; groups of readers of the Bible do that in its name."

85. Kader's confidently entitled book, *Openly Gay, Openly Christian: How the Bible Really Is Gay Friendly* (1999), is a prime example of this approach. Guest (2001, 66) considers the debate on homosexuality in the church and compares Kader's book with D. Wold's book *Out of Order* (1998), which opposes homosexuality; she notes, "The battle rages around the interpretation of familiar texts as both men seek to convince their readers that the Bible really *does* condemn homosexual activity, or really does *not*."

86. It is still vitally important to address biblical texts that are interpreted as referring to same-sex behavior; see Brooten 1996; Olyan 1997; Stone 2000, 57; D. Martin 2006, 37–64.

87. I see Bohache's (2000) essay as another example of work that fits better into LGBT studies than queer criticism, however, given his concern over the "texts of terror" and his statement that there is a need for "the Pauline corpus to be redeemed for queer Christians" (227).

88. Overlapping in many ways with feminist approaches, early works include D'Angelo 1990; Boyarin 1995; Brooten 1996; Sawyer 2002. More explicitly associated with a queer approach are Hornsby 2005; D. Martin 2006; Hearon 2006; Swancutt 2003, 2006, 2010.

89. See the discussions in the previous section on the fraught relationships between feminism and queer theory, as well as on the use of the term *queer* as an umbrella term. See also Stone 2001b, 20–21.

90. Another scholar who has effectively used Wittig to critique heteronormativity is Stone (2000), who applies queer criticism to the so-called heterosexual contract in the garden of Eden story.

91. These ideas will be discussed in more detail in chs. 2 and 3, but see Wittig 1992b, 55–58; 1992e, 11–16; 1992f.

92. See also Sawyer (2002, 15), who comments, "the gender games apparent in biblical literature apply as much to constructed masculinity as to femininity."

93. See the first section of this chapter.

94. See also Epps and Katz (2007, 432–33), who argue for an understanding

of "queer" that emphasizes "the act of saying and unsaying, of writing, erasing, and rewriting."

95. I was inspired by Moore's (2001, 146–69) use of two columns, although I have gone further in using sections of changing "weight" or height.

2

Que(e)rying the Corinthian Men

*In a new version the masculine gender must be more systematically par-
ticularized.... The masculine must not appear under they but only under
man, he, his, in analogy with what has been done for so long to the feminine gender (woman, she, her).*

— Monique Wittig, "The Mark of Gender"

Introduction

Throughout the history of interpretation of 1 Cor 11:2–16, it has been the
Corinthian women who have come under the scrutinizing gaze of predominantly male commentators and scholars. Given that this passage is
one of the few in the Pauline epistles that specifically mentions women, it
is perhaps not surprising that Margaret MacDonald (1990, 164) can state,
"First-century Corinth is indeed renowned among New Testament scholars
... for housing problematic women."[1] In the early twentieth century these
"problematic" women were described rather chauvinistically as having "ill-
timed and dangerous lusts for emancipation" (Tischleder 1923, 156; see
also Héring 1949, 90–91; Leipoldt 1954, 172); and although such comments
are rare these days, contemporary scholars still concentrate their gaze primarily on the women, noting, for example, that "some women in Corinth"
were expressing a sense of "evangelical emancipation in the assembly," a
"disorderly" practice that Paul "seeks to redress" (Gorman 2004, 264–65).

For feminist biblical scholars the presence of these "problematic women"
has enabled the reclamation of women's voices and the recognition of the
influence of powerful women in early Christianity, as attested to in the works
of Schüssler Fiorenza and Wire.[2] As Boyarin (1990, 40) notes, such a shift
from these traditional (and often derisive) views of the Corinthian women
as disorderly, sexually loose, insubordinate, disobedient, and even dangerous, toward a view that reads *"for* the female subject-positions" within the

text—seeing them positively as prophetically gifted and capable women in leadership positions, as Wire does—shows "how the reception history of the text has closed off subject-positions and ideological voices within the text."

But such attention on the women in this passage, be it negative or positive, has also had the result that the Corinthian men are rendered invisible.[3] Indeed, to utilize Boyarin's analysis, one may suggest that the reception history of this passage has "closed off" any awareness that the men also occupy "subject-positions" within this text. Schüssler Fiorenza questions the ideologies that lie behind the attention given to the women in various Pauline texts, and her observations are important to note:

> Insofar as scholars single out the "role of women" as a special problem they reflect our own cultural, androcentric perspective according to which male existence is the standard expression of human existence and Christian history. In such an androcentric paradigm *only the role of women becomes a special historical problem* while the androcentric presuppositions of such a historiography remain unexamined.... In analyzing 1 Cor 11:2–16 and 14:33–36 exegetes neglect to place these texts into their historical situation and their immediate context. Instead scholars presume that *only these texts speak about women*, whereas the rest of chapters 11–14 deals with male prophets and enthusiasts. (1978, 154, emphasis added)

A further corollary of Schüssler Fiorenza's argument is that in such an androcentric paradigm, scholars presume that such texts speak *only* about women. In such a paradigm, male existence is deemed the universal standard of human existence, and it is only women who become a special historical problem; as Wittig (1992f, 60–61) states, "There is only one [gender]: the feminine, the 'masculine' not being a gender. For the masculine is not the masculine but the general" (see also Butler 2007, 522–26). Thus scholars frequently overlook the possibility that the Corinthian men might also constitute specific subjects with their own concrete problems. A feminist analysis rightly restores the place and subject position of women in the rest of 1 Cor 11–14, for example, so that specific mention is no longer required before one can assume that women were involved in whatever issue is being addressed. In other words, a feminist analysis engages in what Wittig (1992k, 74) describes as the "vital and strategic" task of universalizing the point of view of minority subjects, of those who are otherwise objectified as specific and particular.

But "a critical gender analysis" as called for by Stone (2001b, 26), which extends its purview to "biblical representations of men and of 'masculinity,'" might equally remove men from their universal subject position, rendering them highly visible and specific. Wittig (1992c, 87) puts it plainly: "the masculine gender must be more systematically particularized." In this chapter, therefore, I will first explore the possibility that the "problematic" men of Corinth are also involved in behavior that Paul wishes to correct in 1 Cor 11:2–16. This is not intended as a way of determining *the* correct background to the situation in Corinth, but to provide a corrective not only to the many androcentric readings of this passage but also to what Økland (2004, 1) describes, in accord with Wittig, as "the false, but dominant notion that only women are gender."

Second, if it is accepted that the behavior of the men in this passage could have been actual, and not dismissed as hypothetical, then one scenario that needs to be explored is the possibility that behind Paul's argumentation lies—in the words of C. K. Barrett (1971, 257)—a "horror of homosexualism." In other words, that Paul is dealing not merely with the surface matters of headcoverings or hairstyles but with the supposedly more deeply disturbing issue of "male homosexuals presiding at the liturgy" (Murphy-O'Connor 1996, 279). A consideration of the sex-gender ideologies of the first-century Mediterranean world reveals, however, that biblical commentators have not adequately understood the complex relationship between effeminacy, masculinity, and sexual practices that emerge from a careful reading of the first-century data. As a result, it will become evident that the issue in Corinth is not likely to have been "male homosexuals presiding at the liturgy" primarily because the categorization of people according to sexual orientation was not part of the first-century Mediterranean sex-gender mentality. Paul's issue (as proposed in this scenario) is not therefore with "homosexuality" but with certain representations of masculinity. Diane Griffin Crowder (2005, 82) notes that it is not just women who have been viewed as specific historical problems by (predominantly) male scholars, but "the nonstraight" have also been "minoritized" and particularized as the object of study (see also Halperin 1995, 61). By shifting the focus from the specific issue of "male homosexuals presiding at the liturgy" to a consideration of the often overlooked yet deeply ideological constructs of masculinity in general, I will be rendering not just the *men* but also *masculinity* highly visible and specific.

Hypothetical or Actual Behavior?

In the previous chapter I noted that one of the many questions about 1 Cor 11:2–16 is whether the issue at stake involves both the Corinthian men and women. While many modern translations of this passage use headings that sidestep any decision on this matter, throughout the history of interpretation most commentators have determined that the problem Paul is addressing here concerns the women alone, and the men are only mentioned so that Paul can make his point by way of a contrast.[4] Jason BeDuhn (1999, 296) probes a little deeper into why it might be that women are causing such anxiety and, in accord with Wittig's argument that it is the feminine gender that is marked while the masculine is universalized, suggests that although Paul is "not exclusively concerned with either women or men … [he] gives slightly more attention to the women in his reply because in Paul's culture, as in so many others, it is their difference from the male norm that must bear the burden of being marked."[5]

By far the majority of scholars simply avoid or overlook any discussion on the behavior of the men, or their role in Paul's communication to the congregation, and focus entirely on the issues surrounding the women. Scholars simply state that the passage is about the conduct or behavior of women in worship, usually regarding their veiling or covering, but sometimes regarding the issue of women's place or role in the church, and at times specifically their subordinate position in the church and home.[6] So common is this view that Mount (2005, 313–14) can state, "Perhaps the only consensus that has emerged about this passage is that the 'I' is Paul and the [issue] has something to do with women."

The predominance of this particular approach causes Richard Oster Jr. (1988, 483) to wonder, "Is it a masculine bias that focuses on Paul's injunction for women and assumes that the injunction for men had no occasion?" (see also 1995, 262). I would answer in the affirmative and suggest that the ease with which scholars ignore the presence of the men in this passage indicates the strength of an androcentric ideology; not only are the men deemed as "the abstract form, the general, the universal," and therefore easily rendered hypothetical or even invisible, but the women are deemed specific, problematic, and therefore subject to scrutiny and injunction (Wittig 1992c, 79–80). As Wittig (80) predicts, "gender by enforcing upon women a particular category represents a measure of domination."

A few scholars, however, do endeavor to provide an interpretation that takes into account the behavior of both genders. In probably the most significant recent commentary published on 1 Corinthians, Anthony Thiselton (2000, 800, 805) states at the very outset of his discussion on this passage that the issue involves both men and women: "most writers insist that this passage concerns the clothing (or hairstyle) of *women* rather than (as 11:4 makes clear) of *men and women*.... 11:2–16 is not simply about 'the head covering of women,' but about *men* and women." In relation to his discussion on the possible backgrounds behind the phrase κατὰ κεφαλῆς ἔχων (11:4), he states, "The most important point of all, however, can too easily be overlooked. *This recent research proves conclusively that 11:4 does not present a merely hypothetical case ... the first concern of 11:2–16 is about men, not about women*" (825, emphasis original). Thiselton's position on this issue is therefore completely at odds with the majority of Corinthian scholars. So what is this research that "proves conclusively" that the men were involved in the situation Paul addresses in 1 Cor 11:2–16?

With the renewed interest in the social history of early Christianity and the accompanying rise in the use of social-scientific methodologies that occurred in the latter part of the twentieth century in biblical studies, several scholars began suggesting reconstructions of the situation at Corinth based on a range of archaeological, literary, numismatic, and inscriptional sources. Such investigations into the ancient Mediterranean context within which the Corinthians lived and worshiped provide two main explanations for why the coiffure of the men could have been viewed as problematic in a Christian worship service. I will briefly outline each scenario, but I will also explore the way in which the ideologies and assumptions held by these scholars have also affected their treatment of this passage.

Jerome Murphy-O'Connor (1980, 483) was the first scholar to provide a sustained argument for viewing the problem at Corinth as something that "involved both sexes." In line with the historical-critical approach that I critiqued in chapter 1, Murphy-O'Connor (483) aims to show that Paul's argument was coherent, and he states at the outset that "to a great extent the failure to perceive the force of Paul's logic has been due to a misunderstanding of the problem he was facing." Murphy-O'Connor (489–90) proposes that the problem at Corinth centered on "elaborate ... unmasculine" long hair for men, and "disordered ... unfeminine" long hair for women, a practice that he suggests worried Paul because it "raised the disquieting question of homosexuality within the community." He bases this conclusion both on an examination of the vocabulary and structure of the passage, specifically on the "one clear hint" in the passage, the specific mention of κόμη in verse 14 (484), and on an examination of a series of texts from contemporaneous writers such as Pseudo-Phocylides, Philo, Juvenal, Epictetus, and Musonius Rufus, which he suggests confirm the "association of long hair with homosexuality" (486).[7]

Oster (1988, 482), in similar historical-critical fashion, argues that the "methodological disarray" in which studies of 1 Cor 11:2–16 find themselves is due to a neglect of both the urban Roman context of this passage and the behavior of the men in the Corinthian community. But, arguing against Murphy-O'Connor's position that the issue involved hairstyles, Oster (482) suggests that both "literary and artifactual evidence" points to the strong possibility that Roman devotional headcovering practices of *capite velato* lie behind Paul's injunction in 1 Cor 11:4.[8]

Both of these scholars have continued to argue for the validity and likelihood of the scenario they propose as part of an overall project to reconstruct a plausible background for the passage and the letter as a whole (Murphy-O'Connor 1982, 193–95; 1988; 1998, 112–17; Oster 1992; 1995, 260–64). Yet each scholar proposes a very different scenario and each argues that his proposal makes the best sense of the passage exegetically and in light of the archaeological evidence. With regard to 1 Cor 11:4, Murphy-O'Connor (1982, 194, emphasis added) states that it is "*most naturally* understood as referring to long hair," whereas Oster (1995, 264, emphasis added) equally emphatically states, "the words and idioms used by Paul *most naturally* refer to the Roman toga which would have covered the head of someone worshipping." As noted in the previous chapter, despite a desire for exegetical clarity and subsequent hermeneutical confidence—a clarity and confidence scholars frequently claim to offer—the conflicting viewpoints on this issue suggest that these are unrealistic goals. Indeed, in his discussion on 1 Cor 11:4, Thiselton (2000, 825) makes the observation that "the heat and apparent certainty with which each side seems to press its claims is surprising."

Penner and Vander Stichele (2005, 214) suggest that part of the impetus behind various attempts to reconstruct the situation at Corinth, and thus to decode Paul's argument, derives from a concern to determine Paul's views on the broader ideological issue of gender: "Central in the interpretation of its content has been the attempt to decipher the arguments Paul uses, evaluating them in terms of their implications for women, more specifically, whether or not they favor a more hierarchical or a more egalitarian view of the relation between females and males." That issues of ideology lurk in the background of exegesis and interpretation on this passage is perhaps why, as Thiselton (2000, 825) notes, "each side" presses its claims with such "heat and apparent certainty."

To probe a little deeper into this issue, and thus to discover why the clash of viewpoints is not as surprising as Thiselton suggests, Oster's comments on the value of archaeological and historical work in New Testament scholarship are important to consider. In a discussion on the way to avoid "ideology masquerading as exegesis," he (1992, 69, 73) suggests that scholars need to give greater attention to archaeological evidence so that "the current debate on Pauline attitudes toward issues of gender and culture will rest on firmer exegetical grounds." Oster implies that ideology is akin to the female monsters Scylla and Charybdis and implores the biblical scholar—the heroic Odysseus figure—to avoid "the fate" of presenting work that is likewise monstrous (Homer, *Od.* 12.73–110; Virgil, *Aen.* 3.410–432, 684–686). It might be tempting to dismiss Oster's (1995, 257) use of this particular imagery as harmless literary embellishment were it not for his discussion of "the dangers of feminist alchemy" in his section on 1 Cor 11:2–16 in his commentary. Oster (257) warns his readers of "the feminist interpreter" who "attempts to transmute ... Pauline words and theology into something deemed to be more desirable and precious than the original." He then immediately follows this caveat with the pronouncement, "There are far too many examples in current publications where *ideology is paraded about masquerading as exegesis*" (257, emphasis added).

While there is not the scope here to delve into detail regarding the symbolization of gender in Homeric (and other ancient) mythology and poetry, it is possible to say that widespread androcentric and misogynistic ideologies lie behind the portrayal of female figures as monstrous and thus as dangerous and/or alluring for (strong, heroic) men (see Eilberg-Schwartz 1995; Doniger 1995; Levine 1995). Oster's association of feminist interpretation with the imagery of alchemy and transmutation, and the perception of it as an enterprise deliberately hiding its ideological agendas behind a mask, reminds one of Circe—outwardly a "beautiful goddess" but in reality a powerful "sorceress"—who was responsible not only for the original transmutation of a beautiful nymph into the monstrous Scylla but also for advising Odysseus on the best way to pass between Scylla and Charybdis (Homer, *Od.* 8.448; 10.276, 289, 290–294, 394, 400, 455, 487, 549; 12.20, 36, 115, 143, 155). As perhaps the original femme fatale, Circe is described throughout *The Odyssey* as Κίρκη εὐπλόκαμος, δεινὴ θεὸς αὐδήεσσα ("fair-tressed Circe, dread goddess of human speech"; 10.136;

11.8; 12.150 [Murray-Dimock]). It is not only through her beauty—particularly her hair—but also through her way with words that makes Circe such a deceptive and powerful figure (Levine 1995, 91–95). Likewise, Oster is fearful that feminist interpretation will transmute Paul's words into something "more desirable," thus deceiving readers into viewing it as something that it is not, as exegesis when it is really ideology. Such fear-mongering regarding feminist exegesis not only reveals certain patriarchal representations of women (as deceptive and powerful), but also an acceptance of the myth of objectivity: a belief that exegesis can be free from ideology, agenda, or bias.

The clash of viewpoints is no less surprising when we realize that behind Murphy-O'Connor's (1982, 193) particular proposal lies a concern over the "widespread discrimination in the contemporary church … towards the active participation of women in the liturgy." He states, "the community has to examine itself as to the damage done" by such discrimination against women, and he argues that "since the Apostle [Paul] is often quoted in support of such discrimination, it is important to determine what his attitude to women really was" (193). Through his exegesis of 1 Cor 11:2–16, Murphy-O'Connor concludes that Paul "could not deny woman's rights. On the contrary, he explicitly defends them" (196; see also 1980, 498; 1988, 274; 1998, 116–17). It is not surprising, then, to discover that Murphy-O'Connor (1980, 491–93; 1982, 195; 1998, 111) proposes an exegesis of 11:3, for example, that emphasizes the mutuality and equality of the sexes, determining that its notoriously problematic key word κεφαλή ("head") ought to be understood as *source, origin,* and thus to have an egalitarian meaning.[9]

Oster (1995, 258–59), on the other hand, and no less surprisingly, prefers the traditional meaning of "leader" and the notion of "male 'headship'" to the *source, origin,* option; he adds that "the forceful impetus for promoting ['source'] typically comes from New Testament scholars … with strong feminist perspectives … with feminist-egalitarian commitments." That Oster can view one position on this exegetical debate as being the result of "forceful" promotion by those who have certain "perspectives" and "commitments," and the other position as being the result of an apparently objective examination of Paul's wording and argument, is a reminder that an androcentric perspective determines that male existence (and presuppositions) are deemed universal and thus remain unrecognized and unquestioned, while women (and feminist perspectives) are deemed specific and thus highlighted and questioned. The clash of views that Thiselton notes goes deeper, therefore, than a preference for a scenario based on hairstyles or headcoverings; competing ideologies of gender emerge as an unavoidable aspect of *any* exegetical enterprise, be it explicitly feminist or covertly "non-feminist."

Nevertheless, despite these differences in perspective on both the surface matters of hairstyles and headcoverings and the deeper issues of ideologies and agendas, at the very least one can say that the work of both Murphy-O'Connor and Oster, in providing different plausible historical scenarios, attests to the possibility that the Corinthian men were involved in a concrete and specific way in the issue Paul seeks to address in 1 Cor 11:2–16. If we also examine the structure and style of the passage, are there any indicators that both the men and women are being addressed in a way that would point to issues of actual behavior? Or, more specifically, are there indicators within the passage itself that suggest that the material concerning the men ought to be read as hypothetical but the material concerning the women ought to be understood as actual? I want to stress that it is not the determination of *the* actual historical situation or *the* correct interpretation of the text that concerns me. What interests me is the way in which scholars have determined that this text can (or ought to) be read as dealing with the actual behavior of women, but only hypothetically with regard to the men. Many argue this point on the basis of the structural and stylistic features of the passage, thus appearing to make an objective analysis of the text, and hence a decision based solely on supposedly ideologically untainted exegetical grounds. I propose, however, that it is difficult to find a clear difference between how Paul deals with the women and the men that would lead to an acceptance of the former being based on actual behavior and the latter functioning merely as hypothetical argument.

Leaving aside verse 3 for the moment, since it will be the main focus of chapter 4, verses 4 and 5a articulate the problem Paul is addressing and are the clearest indicator that the problem Paul is dealing with involved both men and women. Indeed, by using an argument from priority, whereby it is assumed that those being addressed (or spoken about) first are the main concern of the writer, as scholars do elsewhere in 1 Corinthians (Brooten 1988, 294–95; Thiselton 2000, 825), I could even posit that Paul views the men as the main cause of the problem. As noted above, Thiselton (2000, 825) recognizes that "*the first concern of 11:2–16 is about men, not about women.*" But given that this form of argument can be problematic,[10] at the very least it is possible to suggest that both the men and women are of concern to Paul, and certainly it is difficult to suggest from these two verses that the men are *not* of concern. There is no difference in Paul's language to indicate that the behavior of the men is hypothetical while that of the women is actual, since both statements use present participles, which indicate behavior that is ongoing, and there are no indicators of condition in the grammar, which one might expect if the behavior was hypothetical, despite some scholars' insistence that these are "if … then" statements (Padgett 1984, 70; Amjad-Ali 1995, 209):

11:4:   πᾶς ἀνὴρ προσευχόμενος ἢ προφητεύων κατὰ κεφαλῆς ἔχων
         καταισχύνει τὴν κεφαλὴν αὐτοῦ.
11:5a: πᾶσα δὲ γυνὴ προσευχομένη ἢ προφητεύουσα ἀκατακαλύπτῳ τῇ
         κεφαλῇ
         καταισχύνει τὴν κεφαλὴν αὐτῆς·

Indeed, these two statements appear to be deliberately constructed so as to emphasize the parallelism in Paul's mind about the behaviors of the men and the women. This makes the assertion by Noel Weeks (1972, 26) difficult to grasp: "Error in interpretation has arisen because vv. 4 and 5 have been taken as strictly parallel. A careful examination will show that while there is a similarity in thought there is a difference in structure because the point of each is different."[11] Weeks does not explain where the difference in structure lies; while the particular behaviors described are not the same—or at least are not described in identical terms—it is very difficult to suggest that these are anything other than parallel statements.

Confident assertions that the problem Paul is addressing concerns the women seem to depend not on verses 4 and 5a, therefore, but on the rest of the passage. Scholars tend to look at the overall balance of verses between the men and the women, and conclude that as several verses seem only to deal with the situation of the women, the entire issue therefore concerns the women, with the men only mentioned as part of Paul's attempt to influence the behavior of the women (Delobel 1986, 379–80; Wire 1990, 118; Horrell 1996, 170 n. 227; Horsley 1998, 154).[12] However, two points can be made against this argument.

First, it is somewhat extreme to argue that because *more* attention is given to the behavior of the women it means that the men are not involved *at all*. Rather, as noted above, BeDuhn (1999, 296) offers a plausible explanation for this imbalance, arguing that Paul "gives slightly more attention to the women in his reply because in Paul's culture, as in so many others, it is their difference from the male norm that must bear the burden of being marked." This would explain why Paul expands on his statement in verse 5a with an argument many scholars regard as a rhetorical reductio ad absurdum in verses 5b–6 (Soards 1999, 224; Thiselton 2000, 833).[13]

Second, while some scholars view verse 10 as one of the "recurring asides on the woman's conduct" (Wire 1990, 118), or even as the stand-alone center of the whole passage (Shoemaker 1987, 62; Terry 1995, 108), it is instead possible to view this verse as parallel with verse 7, where the argument concerns the behavior of the men. Both verses are statements of instruction concerning ἡ κεφαλή centering on the verb ὀφείλω. This is then followed with an explanation for that request with appeals to the broader cosmological order; in verse 7 it involves ὁ θεός, and in verse 10 it involves οἱ ἀγγέλοι. Then both appeals are followed by carefully structured formulations on the relationality of men and woman; in verses 8–9 Paul appears to draw on the creation accounts in Gen 1–2, while in verses 11–12 these are qualified by references to Christ (ἐν κυρίῳ) and God (τοῦ θεοῦ) (Murphy-O'Connor 1980, 495; Delobel 1986, 380; Fee 1987, 514; Jervis 1993, 242–43):[14]

11:7: Ἀνὴρ μὲν γὰρ οὐκ ὀφείλει κατακαλύπτεσθαι τὴν κεφαλὴν
εἰκὼν καὶ δόξα θεοῦ ὑπάρχων·
ἡ γυνὴ δὲ δόξα ἀνδρός ἐστιν.

11:8–9: οὐ γάρ ἐστιν ἀνὴρ ἐκ γυναικὸς
ἀλλὰ γυνὴ ἐξ ἀνδρός·
καὶ γὰρ οὐκ ἐκτίσθη ἀνὴρ διὰ τὴν γυναῖκα
ἀλλὰ γυνὴ διὰ τὸν ἄνδρα.

11:10: διὰ τοῦτο ὀφείλει ἡ γυνὴ ἐξουσίαν ἔχειν ἐπὶ τῆς κεφαλῆς
διὰ τοὺς ἀγγέλους.

11:11–12: πλὴν οὔτε γυνὴ χωρὶς ἀνδρὸς
οὔτε ἀνὴρ χωρὶς γυναικὸς
ἐν κυρίῳ·
ὥσπερ γὰρ ἡ γυνὴ ἐκ τοῦ ἀνδρός,
οὕτως καὶ ὁ ἀνὴρ διὰ τῆς γυναικός·
τὰ δὲ πάντα ἐκ τοῦ θεοῦ.

In the next section (vv. 13–15), it is without doubt that the argument focuses most clearly on the behavior of the women. Certainly for Joël Delobel (1986, 380), that verse 13 has no parallel is "the point of the whole story" (see also Fee 1987, 495–96; Collins 1999, 402). Thus it would seem that one unparalleled statement outweighs the evidence of the six equivalent pairs he lists—nine if we also count verses 3b, 8, and 9. But as Murphy-O'Connor (1988, 266) rightly challenges, "This is not sufficient to counter the weight of the number of references to men in the rest of the pericope…. Paul was interested only in getting his point across as clearly as possible, not in pure symmetry." There is undeniably an extra emphasis on the woman in this section, but this does not have to imply that Paul has *no* focus on the behavior of the men. In addition, as with verses 4–5, 7a–7b, 8–9, and 11–12, it is difficult to see that the comment concerning the man is to be understood in any way different to that of the woman; the μὲν … δέ structure with its perfectly balanced vocabulary at the center of this section seems to be deliberately mutual:

11:13:	Ἐν ὑμῖν αὐτοῖς κρίνατε·
		πρέπον ἐστὶν γυναῖκα ἀκατακάλυπτον τῷ θεῷ προσεύχεσθαι;
11:14:	οὐδὲ ἡ φύσις αὐτὴ διδάσκει ὑμᾶς ὅτι
		ἀνὴρ μὲν ἐὰν κομᾷ ἀτιμία αὐτῷ ἐστιν,
11:15:	γυνὴ δὲ ἐὰν κομᾷ δόξα αὐτῇ ἐστιν;
		ὅτι ἡ κόμη ἀντὶ περιβολαίου δέδοται (αὐτῇ).

While context provides the clue that the emphasis is on the women at this point, this does not diminish the possibility that the behavior of the men is actual. Judith Gundry-Volf (1997, 153 n. 8) notes how the grounding of the instruction to the man in the μέν clause in verse 7a shows that "Paul's concern about the man is secondary … but not for that reason hypothetical." In addition, there is nothing about the use of the μὲν … δέ structure at the center of this section to suggest that one clause is to be understood as actual while the other is not.[15] Thus although these verses do not help determine whether the behavior of the men is actual, at least it is difficult to declare that their behavior is hypothetical while that of the women is not.

The passage concludes with an appeal—possibly exasperated—to custom (συνήθειαν, v. 16). Exactly what custom Paul is referring to is debatable, however, either the tendency to be contentious (Engberg-Pedersen 1991, 684–86; Witherington 1995, 239) or the particular behavior of the Corinthians concerning their heads. Either way, depending on how one interprets the "we" in this verse (ἡμεῖς … οὐκ ἔχομεν), Paul appeals to the practices of himself and possibly also his coworkers (or the Pauline churches) as an example to finally persuade the Corinthians:

11:16:   Εἰ δέ τις δοκεῖ φιλόνεικος εἶναι,
         ἡμεῖς τοιαύτην συνήθειαν οὐκ ἔχομεν οὐδὲ αἱ ἐκκλησίαι τοῦ θεοῦ.

If Paul is referring to himself using the editorial or royal we (Barrett 1971, 258; K. Wilson 1991, 459), then it is difficult to understand his point if the issue at stake only involves women's attire or hairstyles. Gerd Theissen (1987, 160) sees the same problem, betraying a disconcerting belief that all Paul's coworkers must have been men: "One asks somewhat amazed where Paul and his collaborators would have had the opportunity to practice the disputed form of conduct; they certainly did not carry any specifically feminine articles of clothing in their baggage!"[16] Paul's point can be appreciated, however, if the circle is widened to include those women who certainly did work alongside Paul, or the Pauline churches in general, but on every level men are also included. This causes Wire (1990, 129) some difficulty, as her reconstruction for this passage involves suggesting that it is a powerful group of women prophets who want to oppose Paul on the issue of headcoverings. It may be that Paul sees the problem with the women as a problem for the whole church to resolve, or expects the men in the congregation to exert better control over "their women,"[17] hence his use of hypothetical references to the men as a way of drawing them into the issue and gaining their support. But as Murphy-O'Connor (1988, 266) says, "given Paul's awareness of the propensity of the Corinthians to misunderstand him (cf. 1 Cor 5:9–13; 2 Cor 1:13–14), it is highly unlikely that he would have complicated things by inventing a non-existent male custom."

In summary, this analysis of 1 Cor 11:2–16 demonstrates that Paul likely has the behavior of both the men and women in mind throughout his argument. In many instances Paul addresses the behavior of the men in an identical fashion to that of the women, and it is not clear how, on a strictly grammatical level, such parallel statements can be read so differently, allowing scholars to declare confidently that the references to the men's behavior are hypothetical. While it is not possible or even necessary to prove that the issue involves Roman devotional headcoverings or effeminate hairstyles or that the text *must* be read in a way that accepts the behavior of the men as actual, this same position must also be extended to the situation of the women. Apart from perhaps verses 5b–6 and 13, the passage reveals a deliberate mutuality that makes it difficult to distinguish between actual behavior and hypothetical argument with regard to either sex. In addition, the argument that *more* attention given to the behavior of the women indicates that the men are of *no* concern to Paul betrays a faulty logic.

The refusal of the majority of scholars even to acknowledge the presence of men in this passage also betrays an androcentric ideology that goes far deeper; the gaze of scholars renders the Corinthian women (and thus often women in contemporary congregations) highly visible and frequently problematic, while conversely rendering the men invisible and trouble free. Having reversed this tendency and "systematically particularized" the men (Wittig 1992c, 87), rendering them visible and problematic, one may then challenge the way in which the masculine so often functions "as the presumption of universality itself" (Butler 2007, 524). The Corinthian men are no more or less specific, gendered, concrete, and problematic than the women. An acceptance of the notion that the Corinthian men may have been engaged in actual behavior that Paul addresses—regardless of what that might have been, historically—provides a corrective to this androcentric tendency.

"Horror of Homosexualism"?

Another matter that needs closer scrutiny is Barrett's (1971, 257) suggestion that behind Paul's argumentation lies a "horror of homosexualism." While Barrett does not elaborate on this comment, Murphy-O'Connor explains the scenario in more detail. In describing the visit to the church at Corinth by Chloe's people, he says: "They participated in one of the liturgical assemblies and were shocked at the leading role taken by a man, who was apparently homosexual, and a very strange woman" (1996, 289). Their report back to Paul, while no doubt stressing the bizarre, "stunned him" because among other shocking behaviors there were "male homosexuals presiding at the liturgy" (279). Murphy-O'Connor (1980, 483) argues that Paul's response, in the form of 1 Cor 11:2–16, was therefore understandably convoluted. More recently, Kirk MacGregor (2009, 201–2) also proposes that one of the reasons why this has been such a misunderstood passage, and thus also so controversial, is because scholars "fail to grasp the central issue confronting Paul," namely, that both the men and women in the Corinthian congregation were "appearing and behaving in ways characteristic of the opposite sex which were indicative of homosexuality." Indeed, MacGregor (214) states more emphatically than any scholar since Murphy-O'Connor that an examination of "the Sitz im Leben disclosed by the remainder of the Corinthian correspondence ... proves that homosexuality was a major problem in the Corinthian church."[18]

This is an oft-cited but seldom justified explanation. Scholars tend to cite other scholars who have suggested this proposal, thus creating the appearance of a well-documented hypothesis (Evans 1983, 89, 93; Padgett 1984, 74, 84 n. 13; Byrne 1988, 36, 58 n. 66; Corrington 1991, 228–29, 229 n. 14; Chakkalakal 1997, 195). Other scholars simply suggest this scenario without any justification at all (Meier 1978, 219 n. 15, 223 n. 24; Snyder 1992, 154–55; N. Watson 1992, 111; Quast 1994, 68). Whether they agree with them or not, most scholars cite Barrett, Murphy-O'Connor, and/or Scroggs when discussing this possibility, so it is important to examine the work of these three scholars in detail.[19]

In addition, one of the issues that emerges from an examination of the way scholars discuss and/or dismiss this scenario is the matter of ideologies and politics in scholarship. As noted above, Scroggs is frequently cited regarding this possibility, and it is of interest to note that he states strongly that "it is not our purpose to explore that touchy subject here" (1972, 297). That homosexuality was a "touchy" subject when Scroggs was writing in the early 1970s is perhaps not surprising given the political and social climate of that time.[20] Scholars who have considered this scenario have continued to talk about "Paul's fears" and "concerns" about homosexuality (Meier 1978, 219 n. 15, 223 n. 24; MacHaffie 1992, 15), his "panic" (Theissen 1987, 168), and even "Paul's abhorrence of anything moving even slightly in the direction of homosexuality" (N. Watson 1992, 111). Those who have rejected this scenario have used strong language to dismiss it, saying, for example, that such a suggestion is "wholly gratuitous [and] an unnecessary distraction" (Fitzmyer 2008, 406, 412). Homosexuality has also continued to be a "touchy" subject in the twenty-first century as Christian communities in countries such as New Zealand have grappled with the issue of same-sex marriage (Townsley 2015). When Bishop Brian Tamaki, leader of the Destiny Church, organized a march to the New Zealand Parliament in August 2004 against the proposed Civil Union Bill, the marchers—predominantly men—intentionally dressed in black T-shirts and waved their fists while shouting the slogan, "Enough is enough."[21] The debate has continued in New Zealand with the passing of the Marriage Amendment Act in August 2013 that made it legal for same-sex couples to marry. Prior to the passing of this act, Anglicans were debating issues of same-sex marriage and the ordination of lesbians and gays at the General Synod in 2012, a debate that "at times included displays of raw emotion."[22]

That the issue of homosexuality can spark such strong reactions, from the personal sense of fear, concern, or even horror that scholars note with regard to this "touchy" subject, through to political debates at a national level, indicates the importance of closely examining the scholarship around this topic. In particular, it will be crucial to examine the sex-gender ideologies held not just by the Greco-Roman and Jewish writers whose material scholars cite, but also those of the scholars who are interacting with this material. I suggest that by examining this "horror of homosexualism" scenario in detail, it will become evident that sound theoretical reflection on issues of gender and sexuality is still required in New Testament studies.

Three key scholars are particularly significant: Barrett, Scroggs, and Murphy-O'Connor. I will examine each in turn and consider the merits of their proposals. But I will also discuss the recent work of Philip Payne and MacGregor to consider whether understandings of the sex-gender ideologies of the first-century Mediterranean have improved in biblical studies since the 1970s and 1980s and to examine the ways in which this passage is being used in current ecclesial debates on gender roles and the issue of homosexuality.

Barrett is frequently cited on this issue, presumably because he was the first to suggest it, but also I would guess because his phrase—"horror of homosexualism"—is so striking. The original comment in Barrett's 1971 commentary appears in brackets, as an aside to his main argument regarding verse 15. It is simply an idea he drops into the discussion without any further justification. Barrett's (1971, 257) complete thought is as follows: "(and it does seem probable that horror of homosexualism is behind a good deal of Paul's argument in this paragraph)." His suggestion appears in a discussion regarding what ἡ φύσις ("nature") teaches as appropriate for hairstyles. He makes a brief reference to the second-century CE satirist Lucian, suggesting that this text "outspokenly" illustrates that it is unnatural for a woman to shave her head (*Dial. meretr.* 257); like most scholars, his focus is on the Corinthian women. Barrett does not go into any further details, perhaps assuming that his readers are familiar with the story, or perhaps not wanting to disturb his readers' sensibilities, given the erotic nature of the dialogue.

In this account, Lucian tells the story of a woman named Megilla who—in making advances to a courtesan by the name of Leaena—removes her wig, revealing shaven (or short) hair (ἀποκεκαμένη) and is described several times as being δεινῶς ἀνδρική ("terribly like a man") and ἀνδρώδεις (manly) (*Dial. meretr.* 7.5.2–3 [§§290–291] [MacLeod]).[23] As reported by Leaena, Megilla describes herself as Μέγιλλος—the masculine form of Megilla—and as married to another woman, Demonassa from Corinth (7.5.1–3 [§§289–291]).[24] In commenting on her relationship with Megilla, Leaena says she is αἰσχύνομαι δέ, ἀλλόκοτον γάρ τί ἐστι ("ashamed, for it is unnatural" [MacLeod]). Perhaps Barrett wants to make the link with Paul's comments in 1 Cor 11:5 and 6, that it is shameful (κατασχύνει … αἰσχρόν) for a woman to shave her head. In his earlier discussion on those particular verses, he does cite Lucian, but it is with regard to the ways in which a woman who is an unworthy mother ought to be shorn (1971, 251–52; Lucian, *Syr. d.* 6). There is no mention by Barrett, at this earlier point in his commentary, of Lucian's *Dialogues*, or of any implications regarding same-sex behavior on the part of the Corinthians, or any anxiety about such behavior on the part of Paul.

Barrett (1971, 256) also refers to the Roman stoic philosopher Epictetus, whose comments on the value of τὰ ἔργα τῆς φύσεως ("the chief works of nature") he suggests provide "a good parallel" to Paul's at this point (Epictetus, *Diatr.* 1.16.9). Epictetus considers the τὰ πάρεργα (minor works) and argues that the hairs on the chin are a sign from nature that men and women are different (1.16.9–11). He says, διὰ τοῦτο ἔδει σῴζειν τὰ σύμβολα τοῦ θεοῦ, ἔδει αὐτὰ μὴ καταπροίεθαι, μὴ συγχεῖν ὅσον ἐφ' ἑαυτοῖς τὰ γένη τὰ διῃρημένα ("Wherefore, we ought to preserve the signs which God has given; we ought not to throw them away; we ought not, so far as in us lies, to confuse the sexes which have been distinguished in this fashion") (1.16.14–17 [Oldfather]). But one could not strictly take from this comment anything to connect it directly with issues concerning same-sex behaviors or "homosexualism." The key issue for Epictetus seems to be the maintenance of gender differences, a point that Barrett observes in his discussion: "The idea is [that] *Nature* (i.e., God) has made men and women different from each other" (1971, 256).[25]

Barrett's parenthetical comment gives no clear justification for seeing Paul's concern being with "homosexualism." The reasons behind a desire for the maintenance of gender differences in the second-century writers are perhaps more to do with particular views of women than they are about views on same-sex behavior, as I will discuss in more detail in the next section. Certainly nothing in the material Barrett cites could be taken as suggesting that Paul has *male* same-sex behaviors in mind. While some Greco-Roman sources characterize certain *female* same-sex behaviors as "mannish," based on the idea of a woman having a shaved head (or short hair),[26] Paul makes his comments in verses 5 and 6 as part of a rhetorical reductio ad absurdum, so it is uncertain that one could argue that he is responding to behaviors that were actually occurring in the congregation (Thiselton 2000, 833; Keener 2005, 92; see also Horsley 1998, 154; Collins 1999, 409). In any case, the link between activities that imply gender inversion (such as women having short or shaved hair) and "homosexualism" is not direct; Halperin (2002a, 249) suggests that Lucian's readers would have been familiar with "the stereotype of gender inversion, of sexual role reversal ... *not* homoeroticism *as such*" (see also Brooten 1985, 70; 1996, 53; 1998; Castelli et al. 1998; Halperin 2002c, 54–80, 172–78). Paul's rhetorical flourish in verses 5 and 6 or his comments in verses 14 and 15 appear to stem more from a concern over behaviors that blur gender distinctions than from a supposed "horror of homosexualism."

In "Paul and the Eschatological Woman," Scroggs (1972, 283) examines 1 Cor 11:2–16 as part of a valiant effort to rescue Paul from challenges of being "one of the great all-time chauvinists." With regard to this passage, he states bluntly that this is "hardly one of Paul's happier compositions. The logic is obscure at best and contradictory at worst. The word choice is peculiar, the tone, peevish" (297). Scroggs goes on to suggest, "All these difficulties point to some hidden agenda, hidden probably to the Apostle himself as well as his readers. If one had to guess what this might have been, as good an answer as any would be a fear of homosexuality"; and then he adds, as already noted: "but it is not our purpose to explore that touchy subject here" (297). He elaborates a little more in a footnote, however, making several comments worth considering.

To begin with, after noting that Barrett "also senses the homosexual undertones of this passage," Scroggs (1972, 297 n. 38) observes that elsewhere Paul is "extremely severe on homosexuals (Rom 1:26f, 1 Cor 6:9)" and on this matter "sounds more strident than his rabbinic peers." Scroggs refers to Derrick Sherwin Bailey's book, *Homosexuality and the Western Christian Tradition* (1955), which contains a discussion of the rabbinic views toward same-sex behavior. However, rather than supporting Scroggs's assertion, these views do sound rather severe. According to Bailey's account, only a passive minor (i.e., a boy under the age of nine—or three according to some rabbis) is exonerated from the law, the penalty otherwise was death by stoning (162–63).[27] In order to consider Paul's views as "extremely severe" by comparison, Scroggs may be referring specifically to Paul's inclusion of female same-sex behavior in Rom 1:26–27, as the Talmud regards such behavior only as, according to Bailey, "a mere obscenity" (61).[28] Scroggs further finds "a hint of this fear [of homosexuality] in verse 14f," regarding a man having long hair; he makes the connection that "Paul's emotional reaction" is akin to the "contemporary [i.e., 1970s] hysterical rejection of long hair for men," and that this "certainly" has something to do with "anxieties about one's own masculinity" (297 n. 38).

It is this link between effeminacy, homosexuality, and masculinity that is of particular interest to me. Scroggs is making the association—and assuming that Paul is making the association—between having long hair and homosexuality, while also noting that this involves "anxieties" about masculinity. Scroggs is probably correct that 1970s "establishment America" might have made this association, despite what the long-haired men themselves may have had to say about the meaning behind their behavior. Indeed, many conservative sectors of Western society may still feel this way about males who have long hair or who wear makeup or women's clothing—again, despite what the men themselves may have to say about their behavior—but one must ask whether this is a link that would have been made in a first-century Greco-Roman context. Barrett's comment, while also appearing amid his discussion of verse 15, was less explicit than that by Scroggs, but both assume that long hair equates with effeminacy, and that this equates with homosexuality.

Scroggs returns to his defense of Paul as a "truly seminal" figure in the history of women's liberation in "Paul and the Eschatological Woman: Revisited." While this is a brief article, Scroggs's (1974, 534) statement on the issue of homosexuality is important to consider: "I have suggested that the hidden agenda in Paul at this point [regarding 1 Cor 11:2–16] might be his fear of homosexuality. I am more convinced than ever that this is correct, although obviously incapable of proof." This is a tantalizing comment! What has made Scroggs "more convinced than ever"? Why does he feel so incapable of presenting any "proof"? Perhaps it might be reasonable to expect Scroggs to devote more space to this matter in his later book, *The New Testament and Homosexuality*. However, although Scroggs (1983, 99–122) considers various New Testament passages that he suggests concern homosexuality (1 Cor 6:9–10; Rom 1:26–27; 1 Tim 1:9–10), as well as references to Sodom that appear in the gospels, and other possible (but deemed unlikely) references to homosexuality in Revelation, Jude, and 2 Peter (100 nn. 1–3), he *nowhere* mentions 1 Cor 11:2–16 or refers to his previous articles where he discussed this issue. I have been unable to discover an explanation for this mystery—of both his initial confidence (and his incapability of proving such a strong opinion) and his later silence.[29]

I now turn to the scholar who has contributed the most to this debate so far. In his classic article "Sex and Logic in 1 Cor 11.2–16," Murphy-O'Connor (1980, 483) contends that scholars have failed to perceive the force of Paul's logic because they have misunderstood the problem he was facing. After arguing for the inclusion of the men in an analysis of the passage, Murphy-O'Connor proceeds to contend that the problem concerned hairstyles rather than headcoverings (primarily based on vv. 4 and 14). This is a point that both Barrett and Scroggs have not taken up; both consistently talk about veils and coverings, and mention hair (and homosexuality) only in regard to verses 14–15.

Murphy-O'Connor then considers why Paul might be so perturbed by long hair on the men. He examines comments on this issue by two hellenized Jews who were Paul's contemporaries, Pseudo-Phocylides and Philo, suggesting that the connection between long hair and homosexuality can be found here. Scholars frequently cite these writers on this issue, so it is important to take a closer look at them to see if this connection is as clear as they suppose.[30] I begin with lines 210–217 from Pseudo-Phocylides:

μὴ μὲν ἐπ' ἄρσενι παιδὶ τρέφειν πλοκάμους ἐπὶ χαίτης.
μὴ κορυφὴν πλέξῃς μήθ' ἄμματα λοξὰ κορύμβων.
ἄρσεσιν οὐκ ἐπέοικε κομᾶν, χλιδαναῖς δὲ γυναιξίν.
παιδὸς δ' εὐμόρφου φρουρεῖν νεοτήσιον ὥρην·
πολλοὶ γὰρ λυσσῶϊσι πρὸς ἄρσενα μεῖξιν ἔρωτος.
παρθενικὴν δὲ φύλασσε πολυκλείστοις θαλάμοισιν,
μὴ δέ μιν ἄχρι γάμων πρὸ δόμων ὀφθῆμεν ἐάσῃς.
κάλλος δυστήρητον ἔφυ παίδων τοκέεσσιν.

If a child is a boy, do not let locks grow on his head.
Braid not his crown nor make cross-knots at the top of his head.
Long hair is not fit for men, but for voluptuous women.
Guard the youthful beauty of a comely boy;
because many rage for intercourse with a man.
Guard a virgin in firmly locked rooms,
and let her not be seen before the house until her wedding-day.
The beauty of children is hard for their parents to guard.[31]

Pseudo-Phocylides is advising parents on various matters regarding the discipline and protection of their children, both girls and boys (a section

that begins earlier at line 207). Murphy-O'Connor (1980, 485) argues that
there is a connection of thought between these two sets of lines on the
basis that, "Not only is long hair effeminate, but the transition from vv.
207–12 (treatment of children) to vv. 213–17 (protection of children) is
intelligible only if, in the author's mind, long hair was associated with
homosexuality."[32] However, the link may still not be quite as clear as
Murphy-O'Connor would like. Long adorned hair may be associated with
effeminate beauty,[33] and boys who appear in this way may find themselves
being sought after by adult men with sexual intentions if their parents are
not careful; but what seems clear is both a concern to protect children
(both boys and girls) from the sexual advances of adults and a desire to
avoid effeminacy in men. It is important to note that effeminacy is also
associated here with excessive behavior and emotions, be that related to
luxurious hairstyles or excessive sensual emotions χλιδανός ... λυσσῶισι),
and thus Pseudo-Phocylides also appears to be concerned with the ways
in which masculinity ought *not* to be expressed.[34] The issue thus appears
to be men adopting the *adorned* hair and *elaborate* hairstyles, which were
associated both with women and with decadent self-indulgence.

Murphy-O'Connor (1980, 485) then cites Philo, *On the Special Laws*,
stating that this particular "tirade of emotionally charged invective" is
"directed against homosexuals." Following on from his equally strong
tirade directed against those ἐχθροὶ τῆς φύσεως ("enemies of nature")
who choose to marry women who are barren (3.34–36), Philo criticizes
μεῖζον κακόν, τὸ παιδεραστῖν ("another evil,... namely pederasty"; 3.37–42
[Colson]). This section is then followed by a condemnation of a behavior Philo describes as even worse: bestiality (3.43–45). Murphy-O'Connor
highlights the comment by Philo regarding τοῖς πάσχουσιν, οἳ νοσον θήλειαν
νοσεῖν ἐθιζόμενοι ... περιφανῶς οὕτως τὰς τῆς κεφαλῆς τρίχας ἀναπλεκόμενοι
καὶ διακοσμούμενοι ("the passive partners, who habituate themselves to
endure the disease of effemination ... [who] conspicuously braid and
adorn the hair of their heads"; 3.37 [Colson]). Murphy-O'Connor (486)
suggests that Philo's comment "must mean that homosexuals let their hair
grow longer than usual."

There seems to be a clear link here between long adorned hair and those
who engage in so-called passive same-sex behavior. Philo is strongly critical of such persons, about whom he says, καὶ τὴν ἄρρενα φύσιν ἐπιτηδεύσει
τεχνάζοντες εἰς θήλειαν μεταβάλλειν οὐκ ἐρυθριῶσι ("the transformation of
the male nature to the female is practised by them as an art and does not
raise a blush"; 3.37 [Colson]). He also states, τὸν ἀνδρόγυνον τὸ φύσεως

νόμισμα παρακόπτοντα νηποινεὶ τεθνάναι ("the man-woman who debases the sterling coin of nature should perish unavenged"; 3.38 [Colson]). Philo is also critical of the way in which τοὺς γοῦν ἀνδρογύνους ("these hybrids of man and woman"; 3.40 [Colson]) are involved in leading religious celebrations, for exhibiting ἀκρασίας ("licentiousness"; 3.40) [Colson]),[35] and for desiring to be μεταβολῆς τῆς εἰς γυναῖκας ("completely changed into women"; 3.41 [Colson]). Once again what emerges is the interrelation between effeminacy, masculinity, and views on women mixed in with views on same-sex behavior that is labeled as passive.

However, Philo is also critical of οἱ δράσαντες ("the active partners") because of their pursuit of τὴν παρὰ φύσιν ἡδονήν ("an unnatural pleasure"; 3.39 [Colson]) and lack of concern for procreation. This fits the overall literary context of this passage, since this is the main reason behind his condemnation of such acts as marrying a barren woman or engaging in bestiality. Philo is also critical of οἱ δράσαντες (also described in the singular as ὁ παιδεραστής; 3.39) because they teach the young men τῶν μεγίστων κακῶν, ἀνανδρίας καὶ μαλακίας ("the grievous vices of unmanliness and effeminacy"; 3.39 [Colson]) rather than training them in the more masculine virtues of ἀλκὴν καὶ ῥώμην ("strength and robustness"; 3.39 [Colson]). Again, issues concerning the definition of what constitutes masculinity appear crucial to Philo's discussion.

Murphy-O'Connor also cites several Latin sources in his aim to show this association of long hair with homosexuality. First of all, he cites Juvenal, who describes a participant at a ritual gathering of men to venerate the goddess Cotys (or Cotytto) as "reticulumque comis auratum ingentibus implet" ("[having] his substantial hairdo filling a golden hairnet"; *Sat.* 2.96 [Braund]). At first glance this quote on its own does not prove anything other than perhaps an association between hairstyles and religious behavior. However, Murphy-O'Connor is possibly assuming that his readers are familiar with this satire, which is a tirade against men of the upper classes who hypocritically deplore immorality while at the same time engaging in passive sexual behaviors. Reading the whole satire (particularly 2.83–98, 121–131, 155–163), it is clear that Juvenal is primarily concerned with effeminacy, and particularly that practiced by wealthy, well-born men who are therefore bringing disgrace to Rome and the virtuous, victorious masculinity that Juvenal thinks they ought to represent. Such men are described as being concerned with their appearances and clothing, and this would seem to include hair that has been carefully styled. But the description of such men goes well beyond their hairstyles and includes the way they walk, their use of makeup, and the wearing of jewelry.[36]

Murphy-O'Connor then cites Horace, who satirically states his love for a boy whose long hair is tied in a knot (*Epod.* 11.28). This may remind one of the lines from Pseudo-Phocylides above; once again there is a description of a beautiful youth with long styled hair who is an older man's object of desire. In the broader context of the poem, however, Horace cynically remarks, "amore percussum gravi, amore, qui me praeter omnis expetit mollibus in pueris aut in puellis urere" ("I am deeply smitten by Love—Love, who seeks me out beyond all others to set me on fire for tender boys or girls"; *Epod.* 11.2–4 [Rudd]). He then explains that from such love he cannot possibly be set free: "sed alius ardor aut puellae candidae aut teretis pueri longam renodantis comam" ("[unless it be] by another flame—either a pretty girl or a well-formed boy who ties back his long hair in a knot"; lines 27–28 [Rudd]). Again, while Murphy-O'Connor views this poem as an indicator that long hair is associated with homosexuality, what seems clearer is that both boys and girls are the objects of the poet's affections and that their attributes of beauty and tenderness indicate a construction of gender that separates active, adult males from passive, youthful others. Indeed, providing a further nuance to this complex dynamic, Ellen Oliensis (2007, 231) suggests that for Horace, "the axis of desirability is less 'virile versus feminine' than 'young versus old'" (see also Oliensis 2007, 221–34; John Henderson 1999, 93–113, 173–201; Woodman 2002).

Murphy-O'Connor then cites two Stoic philosophers, Musonius Rufus (a contemporary of Paul), and his disciple, Epictetus. Murphy-O'Connor (1980, 486) argues that in Musonius Rufus's discourse on hair cutting (*Diatr.* 21), the "association of long hair with homosexuality" is evident. Murphy-O'Connor cites various lines from this discourse and notes the objection by Musonius Rufus to the practice of some men who adopt carefully coiffed hairstyles because they are οἵ γε ἀνέχονται ἀνδρόγυνοι καὶ γυναικώδεις ὁρᾶσθαι ὄντες, ὅπερ ἔδει φεύγειν ἐξ ἅπαντος, εἰ δὴ τῷ ὄντι ἄνδρες ἦσαν ("men who can endure being seen as womanish creatures, hermaphrodites, something which real men would avoid at all costs"; *Diatr.* 21.33–35 [Lutz]).

However, again when reading the full discourse, it would seem that Musonius Rufus is not so much making the "association of long hair with homosexuality" as he is deploring men whose concern over their looks not only reveals them as being slaves to luxury but also reduces them to behaving like women. The link Murphy-O'Connor seeks is further weakened when it is also noted that Musonius Rufus describes these men as wanting to please *both* women and boys:

οἵ τε κειρόμενοι οὕτως ἄνδρες κατάδηλοί εἰσι δι' ἐπιθυμίαν τοῦ φαίνεσθαι καλοὶ οἷς βούλονται ἀρέσκειν τὰς μὲν τέλεον ἀφαιροῦντες τῶν τριχῶν, τὰς δὲ πλάττοντες οὕτως ὡς ἂν εὐοπτότατα ᾖ γυναιξί τε καὶ παισὶν ὑφ' ὧν ἐπαινεῖσθαι δέονται ... σαφῶς οὗτοι γε κατεαγότες ὑπὸ τῆς τρυφῆς καὶ ἐκνενευρισμένοι παντάπασιν, οἵ γε ἀνέχονται ἀνδρόγυνοι καὶ γυναικώδεις ὁρᾶσθαι ὄντες, ὅπερ ἔδει φεύγειν ἐξ ἅπαντος, εἰ δὴ τῷ ὄντι ἄνδρες ἦσαν.

So men who cut their hair are obviously doing it out of a desire to appear handsome to those whom they wish to please, and so some of their hair they cut off completely, some they arrange so as to be most pleasing to the women and boys by whom they want to be admired.... Clearly such men have become slaves of luxurious living and are completely enervated, men who can endure being seen as womanish creatures, hermaphrodites, something which real men would avoid at all costs. (21.28–35 [Lutz])

That such an indictment by Musonius Rufus has less to do with male same-sex behavior than with a concern over proper expressions of masculinity can also be seen in an earlier discourse (12), the topic of which is περὶ ἀφροδισίων ("on sexual indulgence"). It is the concern for excess, luxury, and self-indulgence that is central to Musonius Rufus's critique of men who engage in a variety of sexual behaviors with *both* other men and women beyond the bounds of marriage and childbearing. Both adultery and sex πρὸς ἄρρενας τοῖς ἄρρεσιν ("of men with men"; lines 9–10) are deemed παρὰ φύσιν ("contrary to nature"; line 10). Such behaviors are μεγάλα ἐγκλήματα ἀνθρώπου ἐστίν ("a grave indictment of manhood"; line 4), show lack of σωφροσύνης ("self-control"; line 13), are αἰσχρός ("a disgrace"; line 15), and ἐλπίδα παίδων οὐδενὸς διαφθείρει οὗτος ("destroy anyone's hope of children"; line 23). Men who have sexual relations with their female slaves are also put into this category (lines 30–40).[37] Musonius Rufus concludes his discourse on this matter by an attempt to shame men into better behavior by suggesting that πολὺ γὰρ κρείττονας εἶναι προσήκει τοὺς ἄνδρας, εἴπερ καὶ προεστάαι ἀξιοῦνται τῶν γυναικῶν ἂν μέντοι ἀκρατέστεροι φαίνωνται ὄντες, ⟨φανοῦνται ὄντες⟩ καὶ κακίονες ("it behoves men to be much better if they expect to be superior to women, for surely if they appear to be less self-controlled they will also be baser characters"; lines 1–4 [Lutz]). Again, it is masculinity and the way this is defined in

relation to gender distinctions—particularly in relation to self-control—
that is of central importance to Musonius Rufus, rather than issues of
male same-sex behavior per se.

Murphy-O'Connor then cites a discourse by Epictetus in which he
gives a lecture on personal adornment, sparked by the visit of a young
student περιεργότερον ἡρμοσμένου τὴν κόμην ("whose hair was somewhat
too elaborately dressed"; *Diatr.* 3.1.1 [Oldfather]). Murphy-O'Connor
(1980, 487) contends that in this discourse, "it becomes clear that for a
man to give exaggerated care to his appearance, particularly the hair of
his head and chin, is to blur nature's distinction between the sexes." This
is precisely the point that I have argued most of the sources Murphy-
O'Connor cites have also been making. The issue is *not* that long hair
is associated "with homosexuality," as Murphy-O'Connor usually insists,
but that hair that is "too elaborately dressed" is effeminate, reducing men
to the level of women, and is associated with excessive displays of luxury
and a lack of self-control.[38]

Murphy-O'Connor cites another section of Epictetus's discourse
regarding hair and adornment that also shows that he is concerned with
gender distinctions rather than male same-sex behavior (*Diatr.* 3.1.24–
31). It is clear from reading the whole discourse that effeminacy was unacceptable as it blurred the supposedly natural distinctions between the
sexes (Vander Stichele and Penner 2005, 302–6). More than this, however,
it also clearly indicates that for a man to blur those distinctions so that he
appears as a woman, and thus even "wishes to be a woman," is a "dreadful
spectacle" (*Diat.* 3.1.28 [Oldfather]; δείξω ὑμῖν ἄνδρα, ὃς θέλει μᾶλλον γυνὴ
εἶναι ἢ ἀνήρ. ὦ δεινοῦ θεάματος). Consequently, it is difficult to assume, as
Murphy-O'Connor does, that there is an obvious concern in this passage
with same-sex behavior. In fact, the lines following on immediately from
this section make clear that same-sex eroticism is *not* the issue:

τίνι θέλεις ἀρέσται; τοῖς γυναικαρίοις; ὡς ἀνὴρ αὐτοῖς ἄρεσον. "ναί· ἀλλὰ
τοῖς λείοις χαίρουσιν." οὐκ ἀπάγξῃ; καὶ εἰ τοῖς κιναίδοις ἔχαιρον, ἐγένου ἂν
κίναιδος; τοῦτό σοι τὸ ἔργον, ἐστιν, ἐπὶ τοῦτο ἐγεννήθης, ἵνα σοι αἱ γυναῖκες
αἱ ἀκόλαστοι χαίρθσιν; τοιοῦτόν σε θῶμεν πολίτην Κορινθίων, κἂν οὕτως
τύχῃ...; καλὸς πολίτης καὶ βουλευτὴς καὶ ῥήτωρ.

Whom do you wish to please? Frail womankind? Please them as a man.
"Yes, but they like smooth men." Oh, go hang! And if they liked sexual
perverts, would you have become such a pervert? Is this your business

in life, is this what you were born for, that licentious women should take
pleasure in you? Shall we make a man like you a citizen of Corinth, and
perchance a warden of the city...? A fine citizen and senator and orator!
(3.1.32–35 [Oldfather])[39]

In summary, the most that can be deduced from these citations is *not*
that long hair had a clear association with homosexuality, but that excessive adornment of hair as part of being an object of someone else's pleasure
had an association with being feminine and was therefore scorned because
the man was *not* being the active, self-controlled subject as was expected
of the ideal citizen. When Murphy-O'Connor (1980, 487) concludes his
discussion of these texts, he comes close to recognizing this point: "The
real issue was the way hair was dressed. The slightest exaggeration was
interpreted as a sign of effeminacy; it hinted at sexual ambiguity." However, such "ambiguity" was seen as an affront *not* so much because of
"homosexuality" as Murphy-O'Connor argues, but because wealthy, well-
born male citizens should not be trying to emulate women, either in their
passivity or in their appearance.[40]

Murphy-O'Connor (1982, 194) has continued to argue, "It is easy to
accumulate texts from 1st cent. A.D. Greek and Roman authors to show
that long hair was associated with homosexuality," and that this is a "well-
documented hypothesis" (1988, 268). As noted at the outset of this section,
Murphy-O'Connor (1996, 279) has fleshed out this hypothesis by suggesting that Chloe's people saw "male homosexuals presiding at the liturgy"
and that "the situation in the liturgical assemblies at Corinth, where the
men looked like women and the women looked awful, disturbed Paul ...
because he did not know whether homosexual appearances were associated with homosexual practices" (1998, 114). Murphy-O'Connor (1998,
115) suggests that Paul counters this behavior in 1 Cor 11:2–16 by emphasizing that "men should look like men and women like women," because
"the difference between [men and women] was intended by God and must
be respected."[41]

What is revealed by Murphy-O'Connor's comments is an emphasis
on *gender* rather than on *sexuality*, a concern to maintain gender distinctions rather than a concern over particular sexual practices. But Murphy-
O'Connor conflates these ideas so that it appears as if attempts to blur
these gender distinctions are symptomatic of certain sexual behaviors,
namely, for a man to have long hair not only makes him appear feminine
but it also therefore indicates the possibility of "homosexual practices." As

I have argued, this direct equation between long hair on men and homo-sexuality is inaccurate. Rather, long adorned hair was equated with effemi-nacy, and the reduction of men to the status of women. Masculinity (and the maintenance of clear boundaries between this and femininity) was of paramount concern, not same-sex eroticism.

Among those doing work in this area in recent time, Payne is a lead-ing spokesman and scholar in the egalitarian wing of evangelicalism in the United States, and he dedicates over a hundred pages to an examina-tion of 1 Cor 11:2–16 in *Man and Woman* (2009), providing one of the lengthier treatments of this passage. In typical historical-critical style, after noting the "notorious difficulty" of 1 Cor 11:2–16 (109), Payne (110; see also 2006, 9) attempts to explain this passage by proposing that Paul is objecting to the "long effeminate hair" of the men and the "loose" hair of the women. He suggests that this proposal "makes perfect sense" (2006, 15; 2009, 211) of the passage and "is the key to understanding the various puzzling expressions in this passage" (2006, 9; 2009, 110). In his earlier article, Payne (2006, 9) notes that long effeminate hair on men "was com-monly ridiculed as disgraceful because of its association with homosexu-ality," but in his later book (2009, 110) he amends this to an association with "effeminate homosexual relations." Payne seems to aim for a more nuanced appreciation of the interrelationships between gender and sexu-ality with his latter description, but his choice of phrase is still problem-atic, as will become clear.

Payne's book aims to make a contribution to the contentious issue within evangelical Christian circles (particularly in the United States) regarding the role of women in ministry and in the family. Like both Scroggs and Murphy-O'Connor, Payne (2009, 61) hopes to rescue Paul from his reputation "as a stone-faced misogynist with a particular dis-like for women." Payne states at the outset that he believes "in both iner-rancy and the equality of man and woman" and notes that this "may seem absurd to many on each side of the egalitarian/complementarian divide" (27). What emerges, therefore, is a careful balancing of the traditionally liberal idea of equality between men and women with the traditionally conservative idea of biblical authority.[42] In this current climate, therefore, a shift in the way in which this "horror of homosexualism" scenario is pre-sented becomes apparent. While Barrett, Scroggs, and Murphy-O'Connor are primarily occupied with showing that this passage does indeed deal with the situation of the men and that one possibility for the situation in Corinth might involve Paul dealing with the "touchy subject" of homosexuality (Scroggs), or more specifically with "homosexuals presiding at the liturgy" (Murphy-O'Connor), little was said regarding the consequences of this for any current application of the passage.

Payne develops the idea that the God-given differences between the sexes ought to be respected, and shifts the discussion to highlight heterosexual marriage as central to Paul's argument. For example, in his discussion on 1 Cor 11:4 and the meaning of κατὰ κεφαλῆς ἔχων, Payne (2009, 144) states, "Men wearing effeminate hair present themselves as women and so shame Christ by not accepting how he created them. This symbolism undermines marriage as ordained by God." Again, with regard to why this verse ought to be understood as referring to long effeminate hair hanging down from the head, as opposed to a head covering (*capite velato*), Payne states, "Hair advertising for homosexual relations fits Paul's argumentation in verses 7–9, where he advocates sexual differentiation and woman as man's sexual partner, the one in whom he glories" (145).[43] Payne views 11:7–10 and 11:11–12 as the "moral and theological basis" for Paul's argument and "the heart of Paul's concern" (175, 189). He draws out the link Paul makes in these verses to the account of creation in Genesis, and emphasizes:

> When husbands treat their wives as their glory, marriage is beautiful.
>
> Paul's appeal to woman as the glory of man affirms woman as the proper sexual partner for man. This exposes the error of effeminate hair, for in symbolizing homosexual relations it repudiates woman as man's sexual mate.... An ideal translation that captures Paul's argument is "woman, *not another man*, is the pride and joy of man."....
>
> Paul proves that he had God's purpose in mind by his concluding affirmation that woman was created "for the sake of man," to fulfill man's need for an intimate sexual partner. Effeminate display, however, symbolizes a man presenting himself as a sexual mate for other men and so opposes God's creation of woman to be man's mate. (179–81)

In the current evangelical climate, the emphasis is on the way Paul's argument can be used to bolster the importance of heterosexual marriage and reject the validity of same-sex relationships. For Payne, a key argument for giving heterosexual marriage such a central place is the issue of procreation. Payne (2009, 177) states that the image of God "entails creativity, and procreation expresses that creativity," and he comments, "Paul is clarifying that woman was made specifically *for* man in the Genesis sense of a partner in procreation corresponding to him" (197–98). As we saw in the writings of Philo and Musonius Rufus discussed above, procreation can play a part in some of the Greco-Roman arguments regarding sexual behavior, but this is not generally an argument Paul uses in his discussions on sex, marriage, or gender relations.[44]

So how does Payne suggest that this passage be applied today? He (2009, 214) states, "this passage should not be used to object to manly long hair today" because such a hairstyle—whatever "manly" long hair actually looks like—is not associated with homosexuality these days.[45] The problem therefore centers on the difference between *effeminate* and *manly* expressions of masculinity. For Payne, effeminate expressions of masculinity can be seen in "hairstyles, dress, or demeanor," with the key affront being that this amounts to "advertising for homosexual liaisons" (214). In line with the Greco-Roman material examined above, it is specifically effeminate portrayals of masculinity that are of concern. What Payne rejects is an image of passive, effeminate masculinity that he negatively associates with multiple sexual relations;[46] what he promotes is an active, heterosexual masculinity that announces its virility by the production (via monogamous marriage) of legitimate offspring (see Boyarin 1997, 97).

Ultimately Payne (2009, 214) suggests that the "most important application of this passage today" lies in recognizing that "men and women should show respect to each other, honoring the opposite sex as their source." Bravely countering the claims of those on the hierarchicalist side of the debate, Payne asserts that on the basis of this passage, "believers must affirm the equal rights and privileges of women and men in the Lord. Women as well as men may lead in public worship ... women who are gifted and called by God ought to be welcomed into ministry, just as men are" (215). In Payne's discussion, women are accorded "equal rights and privileges"; but in order to avoid the accusation of liberalism, there is no "approval of homosexuality" as feared by hierarchicalists such as Wayne Grudem (2004, 513). Yet, I would argue, it is not "homosexuality" as such that Payne portrays and condemns but a stereotyped image of "effeminate homosexual relations" that, in essence, is an image of masculinity that is not *manly* and thus not acceptable. The image that emerges is that of a gendered playing field, where both effeminate men and women in general—lesbians are ignored—are competing for an elevated status that would place them next to a manly man. The central figure in the discussion remains the active man, with effeminate men and women seen as competitors for fulfilling his sexual needs and as rivals for his affection. A man who presents himself as the object of sexual fulfilment *for* other men is viewed as antithetical to the man whose needs are met *by* a mate, who is his object of pride and joy. In this heteropatriarchal scenario, it is the woman who (apparently) "wins" and is put on the pedestal, but it is the manly man who is (always) already the winner.

MacGregor is the least well-known of the scholars I am considering here, but his article on 1 Cor 11:2–16 is a more recent advocate of the idea that the situation Paul is addressing in this passage concerns "homosexuality."[47] Acknowledging that his argument is "foreshadowed" by the work of Murphy-O'Connor and Payne,[48] MacGregor (2009, 214 and n. 32) is adamant that "homosexuality was a major problem in the Corinthian church," and he argues that both the *Sitz im Leben* of the Corinthian correspondence and the evidence from extrabiblical sources "proves" that this was the case. He is quick to note, however, that by "homosexuality" he is referring to "same-sex erotic behavior (and not to the modern concept of psychological orientation toward such behavior" (202 n. 3). He explains that the latter is a concept "with which the ancients would have been unacquainted," a point indicating the most nuanced understanding of the first-century situation seen in this discussion so far.[49]

In classic historical-critical style, MacGregor aims to rescue this passage from its reputation of being "one of the least understood and therefore most controversial passages in all of Scripture" (201). He refers to the "objective criteria of [the] grammatical-historical method," stating that these "prove" what the original author "most probably" intended to say to the original audience, and concludes that readers "should proceed to a straightforward application of the text which forbids homosexual practice, male effeminate and female masculine behavior, and dress indicative of the opposite sex" (216). Although MacGregor gives the impression of having an objective approach to this passage and its subject matter, the strength of his views on the topic of homosexuality can be seen in the following comment: "For Paul … when men with long hair and women with short hair performed religious duties, they committed the *monstrous blasphemy* of violating the sexual purpose for which they were naturally designed while standing in the immediate presence of their Designer" (213, emphasis added). Elsewhere MacGregor states that Paul expressed a "graphic admonition against the full range of homosexual behavior (6:9)" (203), yet a reading of this verse in its context—an admonition of believers who are taking each other to court—hardly justifies such a comment.[50] MacGregor's own description of "the monstrous blasphemy" is far more graphic than any of Paul's comments in 1 Corinthians. This is a classic example of how the issue of homosexuality can spark strong reactions. Despite the intention to approach this subject using the "objective criteria of [the] grammatical-historical method," feelings on matters than concern gender and sexuality—particularly those that concern expressions of masculinity—run deeply indeed.

Gender, Sexuality, and Power

Throughout this discussion, various issues of gender and sexuality have emerged. Primarily these have revolved around the interrelationship between effeminacy, masculinity, and same-sex behavior and the ways in which these have been entwined with certain views of women. Scholars have been quick to identify a concern with effeminacy in the Greco-Roman material and have generally equated this with a concern about homosexuality. Even when more recent scholars have used phrases that imply a clearer understanding of the first-century situation, they appear to make a direct link between homosexuality and effeminacy. Consequently, I suggest that a more nuanced consideration of the cultural construction of gender and sexuality in a first-century Mediterranean context is needed. This is illustrated by Dale Martin's (1995a, 33) blunt comment that cuts across the bulk of scholarly opinion outlined so far: "Contrary to modern heterosexist ideology, be it noted, *effeminacy has no relation to homosexuality*" (emphasis added).[51]

Martin's scenario-shattering statement is a reminder that it is anachronistic to use current constructions of gender and sexuality in describing first-century phenomena. Sexual behavior in the first-century Mediterranean context was not classified according to the twentieth-century framework of individual identity and an orientation toward individuals who are described as either the opposite or the same sex. According to the public discourse of first-century elite males, whose "idealizing and normative" writings are the only sources available to the twentieth- and twenty-first century scholar (Jeffrey Henderson 1988, 1249),[52] sexual behavior was classified according to the determinative factors of gender and social status. Free (citizen) adult males were able to choose both males and females as sexual objects as long as their own social status was maintained by both taking the active (penetrative/insertive) role and demonstrating the virtues of self-restraint and moderation. Women, boys, and slaves (male or female) would naturally be expected to take the passive (penetrated/receptive) role, as befitting their status in society.[53] Thus it was socially acceptable for a free adult male to engage in same-sex erotic behavior, as long as he was not being in any way effeminate, passive, or indulgent, and his partner was of a lower social status. In a sociosexual system that understood sex in terms of "phallic penetration" (Halperin 2002c, 147; see also Laqueur 1990, 11), the role of the active but restrained penetrator was essentially honorable and indicative of true masculinity. Indeed, penetration was thought of as "the manly act par excellence" (Foucault 1988, 24; see also 1990b, 215). The passive partner, however, if a free male, was open to ridicule and disapproval *not* because he was engaging in "homosexual" behavior, but because *as an adult male citizen* he ought to be taking the active, penetrative role in sexual matters and not the subordinate, inferior role of a woman (or boy or slave).

An examination of how sexual and gender relations were conceived in the ancient Mediterranean reveals that the adult male citizen was clearly the ideal being who was positioned at the pinnacle of the social hierarchy. This vertical "hierarchy of essence" (D. Martin 1995a, 15) was structured so that "men and women were arrayed according to their degree of metaphysical perfection ... along an axis whose telos was male" (Laqueur 1990, 5–6). Masculinity, therefore, is of central importance in determining identity. It was a "hard-won achievement," and those at the top were "always in peril of slipping into the servile or the feminine" (Winkler 1990, 50; see also Gleason 1990, 391–92). To be a man was a matter of status and hierarchy, not so much a matter of biology, as Jonathan Walters (1997, 31–32) pointedly states: "Not all males were men" (see also Laqueur 1990, 8; Gleason 1990, 390; Walters 1997, 29–30; Anderson and Moore 2003, 68–69). There were "real men" and then there were varying degrees of "otherness" that were defined in relation to that ideal (Horowitz 1976; Matthews 1986, 18; P. Allen 1997, 95–97).

Playing with the Latin and the English terms, one could say that this *vir* (a real or manly man) was defined by the upper class *virtues* of strength, mastery of self and others, moderation, honor, and *virility*.[54] Sexual behavior was incorporated into this ideological system with the result that the issue of engaging in same-sex erotic behavior as the so-called active partner was of little concern compared to the shame of becoming effeminate.[55] At its ideological heart, the ancient Mediterranean sexual system was all about *virility*—an elite androcentric configuration of gender, sexual behavior, and power relations. Effeminacy, therefore, was less about sexual behavior than about a departure from the norms of masculine behavior—

exemplified by the virtues of self-control and moderation—and an association with excesses of emotion, abandonment to lust, and self-indulgence with regard to food, wine, clothing, or other luxuries (Foucault 1990b, 44; C. Williams 1999, 125–59; D. Martin 2001, 90–96). Those adult male citizens who opted for a lifestyle that reflected a "slavish" or "womanish" desire for pleasure, lack of self-control, weakness, and softness may have also engaged in passive same-sex behavior, but this link is not a direct one; men notorious for womanizing could also be labeled as effeminate (C. Williams 1999, 143; see also C. Barton 1994, 88 n. 21). A man was therefore labeled effeminate not primarily because he was penetrated by others, but because he was a failure as a man. As Foucault (1990b, 19) notes, Greco-Roman literature delineates "a definite aversion to anything that might denote a deliberate renunciation of the signs and privileges of the masculine role."

This construction of masculinity "as the measure of virtue" therefore also "denigrates women's biology and constructs female gender negatively" (Moore and Anderson 2003, 269). Misogyny enabled effeminacy to be viewed as a negative masculine state and the labeling of a man as effeminate or "womanish" to be taken as an insult. As John Winkler (1990, 138) states, "Misogyny ... is a common trope of male discourse in Mediterranean cultures" (see also Richlin 1984; Braund 1992; Battisti 1994, 1–2, 68–108; Gold 1998; Butrica 2005, 236–38; D. Martin 2006, 47). Throughout the discussion above, it is clear that Greco-Roman writers deplored effeminacy precisely because it reduces men to the level of women and thus associates men with the shameful qualities of softness, passivity, self-indulgence, and excessive displays of emotion and behavior that were associated with women. The emphasis on maintaining the boundaries between the sexes, or not confusing the sexes, is therefore primarily about avoiding the "dreadful spectacle" of men being seen as effeminate (Epictetus, *Diatr.* 3.1.29 [Oldfather]).[56]

Foucault (1990b, 18) considers this stereotyped image of "the homosexual" as effeminate, noting that this "disparaging description" can be traced throughout the centuries and came to stand for homosexuality as a whole. He also argues that this stereotype reveals the difficulty societies have in dealing with the two phenomena of gender-role reversal and same-sex intercourse, a difficulty that indicates the link between misogyny and the modern phenomenon of homophobia. Beverley Harrison explains this rejection of homosexuality because of its association with the feminine in both the ancient Mediterranean and contemporary Western cultures:

It appears that some male homosexual activity came to be despised because one male was understood to play the passive role, that is, was penetrated. One stigma of homosexuality, then, was that it "reduced" some men to the role of females. Similarly, the intensity of much contemporary homophobia confirms this continuing element in the revulsion against male homosexuality. Homoerotic men are perceived as failed men, as no better than females. The widespread but empirically mistaken equation of male homosexuality with effeminacy is further evidence that the stigma of male homosexuality involves association with females and the "feminine." (1985, 140)

The interplay between gender, sexuality, and power briefly explored here reveals some of the complexity of the sex-gender ideological system of the first-century Mediterranean world. The relationship between effeminacy, masculinity, and sexual behavior is grounded in an ideology that accords greatest value to those elite male citizens defined as "impenetrable penetrators" and the least value to those who fall further down the social scale: noncitizens, women, slaves, and boys, who are defined as passive, receptive, and thus able to be penetrated (Walters 1997, 30–31). But "manly" or "real" men are also those who resist the path of luxury, self-indulgence, and excessive desire and emotion—qualities that are associated with the feminine and the slavish—preferring to practice (or at least value) the virtues of strength, self-control, and moderation. Effeminacy is thus incompatible with elite masculinity, and it is misleading to suggest that the modern construction of "homosexuality" has any direct relation to these Greco-Roman discourses.

While this reconfiguration of an understanding of gender and sexuality has spawned much research (and debate) in the fields of classical studies, anthropology, and history, it appears to have passed unnoticed by the majority of biblical scholars working on 1 Cor 11:2–16. For material produced either before or not long after the publication of Foucault's work during the 1970s and 1980s, and prior to the outpouring of work by Halperin and others in 1990, this is understandable. However, although scholars such as Boyarin (1993a, 2004), D. Martin (1995a), Brooten (1996), and Moore (2001) all demonstrate an awareness of the differences between the first and twenty-first centuries regarding ideologies of gender and sexuality, by far the majority of New Testament scholars producing work on 1 Cor 11:2–16 still assume that "homosexuality" is a phenomenon that crosses the borders of culture and history and that their research needs little or no methodological reflection on this issue.

To suggest that there were "male homosexuals presiding over the liturgy" at Corinth, then, or that "long hair is associated with homosexuality," is to demonstrate a serious lack of awareness about and understanding of ancient Mediterranean sex-gender ideologies. Long (adorned) hair on men was associated with effeminacy, but in the first century this says everything about gender, very little about sexual behavior, and *nothing* about "homosexuality." It was not the only, or even the central, indicator of effeminate behavior, but nonetheless a male with long carefully adorned hair would be seen as effeminate. Such effeminacy, if exhibited by an adult free male, was shameful. But it may not have been associated immediately with same-sex erotic behavior; it was also associated with living a life of excessive luxury and lack of self-restraint. Primarily, it was shameful because it indicated a male who was behaving like a woman, and that was "something which real men would avoid at all costs" (Musonius Rufus, *Diatr.* 21.34–35 [Lutz]).

My suspicion then, is that what 1 Cor 11:2–16 reveals is not so much a "horror of homosexualism" as a "fear of effeminacy" (C. Williams 1999, 217). Whatever the actual situation at Corinth may have been, Paul responds in a way that corresponds with first-century discourses and constructs of sex and gender, *not* in a way that reflects modern notions of sexual and gendered identity. It is thus not possible for Paul to be addressing modern issues of "homosexuality." He may well be insisting that the differences between the sexes be made clear in the Corinthians' worship practices, but this need for clear gender boundaries is likely to stem from a fundamental concern about representations of masculinity—in particular, the need for men to avoid being seen as womanish or effeminate—rather than from any perceived issues with same-sex behavior. However, even if same-sex behavior was of concern to Paul, this would not stem from a supposed "horror of homosexualism" but more likely from a "fear of effeminacy" in that some men may be passively being used as sexual objects, and thus may be deliberately renouncing their privileged and hard-won masculinity in favor of a despised and indulgent femininity.

Notes

1. In her revised version of this article, MacDonald (2004, 148) does not use this phrase but states, "the problem underlying the instructions about head attire in 1 Corinthians 11 is with women."

2. See the discussion in ch. 1. See also Schottroff 1993, 48–52.

3. In his investigation of Paul's masculinity, Clines (2003, 181) also concludes that this aspect of his identity has been overlooked by (male) scholars, and thus he describes Paul as "the invisible man."

4. Examples of modern headings include "Head Coverings" (NRSV, NKJV); "Propriety in Worship" (NIV); "Christian Order" (NASB); "Instructions for Public Worship" (NLT); "Rules for Worship" (CEV); "To Honor God" (The Message). For examples of commentators focusing on women, see Robertson and Plummer 1914, 229; Bruce 1971, 104; Conzelmann 1975, 181, 184 n. 35; Fee 1987, 495; Dunn 1995, 71; Hays 1997, 185; Bassler 1998, 416; Collins 1999, 400, 402; F. Watson 2000b, 45; Garland 2003, 506–7; Fitzmyer 2008, 405; Gundry 2010, 664.

5. Økland is more blunt, however, and states emphatically, "Paul here speaks to the men about women's dress … Paul does not address women directly…. Since Paul uses the men as mediators in his communication with the unveiled women, the women end up at the bottom of the message-hierarchy" (2004, 177; see also Fatum 1989, 72; 1995, 68, 101 n. 62).

6. For a focus on the conduct of women in worship, see, e.g., Craig 1953, 123; Thrall 1965, 78; Gillian Clark 1982, 259–60; Prior 1985, 179; Ellsworth 1995, 177; Bourne 2004, 80. For a focus on veiling or covering, see, e.g., Simon 1959, 110; Peifer 1960, 39; R. Brown 1970, 352; Orr and Walther 1976, 258; Morris 1985, 148; D. Martin 1995a, 229, 233–49; J. Barclay 2001, 1125; Crocker 2004, 153; Gundry 2010, 664. For the place of women in the church, see, e.g., Foreman 1962, 93; Mare 1976, 256; Linss 1985, 37–38; Vander Broek 1985, 229–31; Powers 2001, 18, 27; de Mingo 2004, 13–16; Hiigel 2005, 24–32. For the subordinate place of women in church and home, see, e.g., Thrall 1965, 77; Leske 1980, 12 n. 1, 14; Hurley 1981, 167; Lowery 1986, 156, 159; MacArthur 2007, 252.

7. Given the issues of gender and sexuality such a proposal raises, particularly in its anachronistic usage of the term *homosexuality* in relation to a first-century context, I will examine it more closely in the section on the "Horror of Homosexualism."

8. This suggestion flies in the face of Fee's (1987, 507) conclusion from his commentary published a year earlier: "There is almost no evidence (paintings, reliefs, statuary, etc.) that men in any of the cultures (Greek, Roman, Jew) covered their heads." Oster's findings are supported by Gill (1990, 245, 250), but see Meggitt's (1998, 125–26) criticism of Gill.

9. Because v. 3 in general and κεφαλή in particular are so contentious in scholarly and ecclesial debates on gender, I will examine them in more detail in ch. 4.

10. In her analysis of 1 Cor 7, in which she compares this passage with 1 Cor 11:2–16, M. MacDonald (1990, 170) argues that the parallelism in 1 Cor 7 "conceals a major concern with women," discernible because of "the fact" that they are mentioned first and given more attention (see also 2004, 149). However, she does not seem to notice and therefore explain why the men are addressed first in 1 Cor 11:2–16 *six* times compared with the women, who are addressed first only *twice*; see vv. 2–5, 8–9, 12–16.

11. See also Conzelmann 1975, 184 n. 35; Orr and Walther 1976, 260, 263; Meier 1978, 218; Byrne 1988, 39 n. 29, 41; Witherington 1988, 86; K. Wilson 1991, 446–47; Fatum 1995, 113 n. 76; Hays 1997, 185; Collins 1999, 400, 402.

12. Horrell views vv. 8 and 9 as concerning the women only, but neglects to mention vv. 11 and 12; Delobel acknowledges that both men and women are mentioned in vv. 8 and 9 but explains that the reference to the man in vv. 8 and 9 should be understood as mere contrasting background, although the same claim is not made of the woman in vv. 11 and 12; Horsley also omits vv. 11 and 12 from his schema, but he also inexplicably includes vv. 8 and 9 in his list of verses pertaining to the situation of the woman, despite the fact that they mention the man first and thus—according to his own logic—ought to be included in his list of references that pertain to the man. Curiously, Horsley also omits v. 13 from his schema, despite this perhaps being one of the clearest indicators that Paul is addressing a problem concerning women.

13. In addition, it is also possible to suggest that v. 6a (concerning the woman) has a parallel in v. 7a (concerning the man); as Murphy-O'Connor (1980, 487) notes, "A strict antithesis on the level of conduct is, moreover, suggested by the use of *katakalyptō* of the two sexes in vv. 6–7a."

14. Gundry-Volf suggests, however, that vv. 7a and 10 do not correspond closely enough to be connected, although she notes that vv. 8 and 9 and 11 and 12 stand "in contrast" to each other (1997, 163).

15. This construction is often used to present a contrast between two concepts, although this is not always sharp; at times it is the correspondence between two similar concepts of equal value that is being emphasized. See, e.g., 1 Cor 1:23; 3:4; 7:7; 11:21; 15:39–40 (Robertson 1914, 1153; Denniston 1954, 370–74). When it is being used in the sense of a contrast, the emphasis usually falls on the δέ clause, but this is certainly not always the case; see, e.g., 1 Cor 1:18; 5:3; 9:24, 25; 12:20; 14:17. In all the occurrences, however, there is never any doubt that the first clause is as "real" as the second.

16. Theissen (1987, 160) goes on to state that because ἱμάτιον was an article of clothing that both men and women wore, this could explain Paul's point; Paul and his (male) coworkers would likely have this in their luggage.

17. Scholars sometimes use possessive pronouns with regard to the Corinthian women, while "the Corinthians" are assumed to be the men in the congregation (Waltke 1978, 46). However, the androcentric patriarchal ideology of the first-century Mediterranean (as with most places) would have also viewed the women as the possession of the men (husband, father), so this language is not entirely out of place (Schüssler Fiorenza 1983, 43–48; Schottroff 1993, 35–36; Polaski 2005, 16–20, 33–42). However, I point this tendency out as an example of the way in which such ideologies continue today; this happens, for example, when current authors draw the reader in with the use of "us" or "we" in a way that would be nonsensical if they were intending to include (heterosexual) women (Keener 1992, 37; Ellsworth 1995, 178). Usually these comments are made in the context of discussions about "distraction" that assume that women will *not* be distracted by the men they view leading worship, but men *will* be distracted by the women they view. This issue forms a significant aspect of F. Watson's (2000b, 41, 53, 61) argument. Watson states, presumably positively, "As a sign of the new limit assigned to eros, a veil is interposed *between* the woman who prays and prophesies and the men to and for whom she speaks" (69, emphasis added). Such a statement acknowledges neither the reality that the veil is imposed *on*

the woman, creating a restriction on her, and that she also speaks "to and for" other women. Watson eventually recognizes that the actual outcome of such a custom is that "the veil makes woman invisible," and inevitably "makes her inaudible too" (72, 82).

18. Other scholars who simply note that long hair on men was viewed as "effeminate" include Héring 1949, 96; Bruce 1971, 108; Leske 1980, 16; Humann 1981, 20; Lowery 1986, 158; Sanseri 1999, 48; F. Watson 2000b, 87. In all of these instances little else is stated about the matter, usually because either the situation of the men in Corinth is not under consideration, or because the issue is deemed to be that of head coverings and not hair in any case.

19. Those who mention this proposal as a possible background to Paul's injunctions include Rowe 1991, 84, 88 n. 18; M. Black 1993, 200; Blomberg 1994, 210; Hjort 2001, 71–72. Those who mention this proposal but disagree with it include Fatum 1989, 74; 1995, 98 n. 54; Dunn 1995, 71; D. Martin 1995a, 296 n. 19; Horrell 1996, 170 n. 225; Gundry-Volf 1997, 165; F. Watson 2000a, 526 n. 10; A. Johnson 2004, 193; Økland 2004, 191; Fitzmyer 2008, 406, 412.

20. See, for example, the article on sports coaching by Simpson (1992, reprinted from 1973) with the provocative title "Real Men, Short Hair." Referring to 1 Cor 11:2–16, he makes a link between long hair and rejection of authority and states, "Without self-discipline and respect for authority you have the current uncontrollable problem among the young with drug abuse, crime and sexual perversion" (1992, 262). Again with reference to 1 Cor 11:2–16, he states that "long hair is a sign of submission," and according to 1 Cor 11:3 and 7–9, "women's souls were not designed to lead or fight but to submit to their right man" (263). For similar arguments, see Sanseri 1999, 48.

21. The conservative views of the Destiny Church are well known in New Zealand. For example, in an interview with the Christian newspaper *Challenge Weekly* in 2000, Tamaki described the presence of women in leadership positions within the home, church, and even government as "the Devil's strategy" (Handcock 2000, 7). Tamaki discusses this issue in his self-published book, *Bishop Brian Tamaki* (2006). At the time Tamaki was speaking and writing on this issue, New Zealand had experienced continuous female leadership at the highest levels of government for over a decade. In addition, Georgina Beyer was the world's first openly transsexual elected Member of Parliament (1999–2007). The march that the Destiny Church organized was shown on TV3 news, 23 August 2004, where spectators commented that the march was "sinister" and "could be compared to Nazis and their type of mentality." This issue was also the subject of many newspaper articles the following day with titles such as "Black Shirts Spark Anger" (Haines 2004a, A1); "March Arouses Nazi Fears" (Haines 2004b, A3); "Family First Say the Men in Black" (A. Young 2004, A3); "Homophobia Behind Opposition" (Mayman 2004, 11). Tamaki was interviewed the following day on the TV1 current affairs program *Holmes*, and at one point Holmes questioned the way in which the march resembled the Nuremberg rallies (24 August 2004). See also the discussion of these reports in Tamaki 2006, 287–88; Grimshaw 2006.

22. See "Church to Debate Nature of Marriage" (n.d.) The most recent General Synod, held in May 2014, passed a resolution that paved the way for "blessing" same-sex unions while seeking to uphold the traditional doctrine of marriage. See "Pathway to Same-Gender Blessings" (n.d.).

23. Megilla is also described by Clonarium, Leaena's dialogue partner, as τὴν Λεσβίαν Μέγιλλαν τὴν πλουσίαν ἐρᾶν σου ὥσπερ ἄνδρα ("the rich Lesbian woman who loves you just like a man").

24. Brooten (1996, 52 n. 105) notes, "The combination of a woman from Lesbos with a woman from Corinth must be intentional, since in antiquity people connected both Lesbos and Corinth with sexual adventurousness." Brooten also comments, "Authors writing in Greek in the Roman period ... represent sexual love between women as masculine, unnatural, lawless, licentious, and monstrous.... The character- ization of Megilla, but not Leaina [sic], as masculine is central to Lucian's representa- tion" (50–52). I will consider this issue in more detail in ch. 6 when I examine Wittig's "monstrous lesbian" figure.

25. Barrett (1971, 256) also suggests that Rom 1:26 is the "best parallel to the pres- ent passage." This section of Romans is often paralleled with 1 Cor 11:2–16, a point that I will discuss in more detail in ch. 4.

26. N. Watson (1992, 112) cites Lucian in his discussion of vv. 5b–6, stating that the idea that short hair on women was considered "mannish" "appears to be the point" of this section of Paul's argument; but he emphasizes that the issue concerns the dis- tinctions between the sexes and does not mention same-sex behavior at all. Yeo (1998, 11), on the other hand, states confidently, "A woman with a male hair do was seen as a prostitute, a lesbian, or a cultic heretic." Yeo cites Apuleius, *Metam.* 7.6 and 11.10. However, nothing in either of these passages connects "a woman with a male hair do" with *any* of these categories.

27. For a discussion of portrayals of men and masculinity and related issues of erotic male-male desire in the Talmud, see Boyarin 1997, 127–50.

28. However, it is not entirely clear that Paul is actually referring to lesbian behav- ior here; see Bailey 1955, 40 and n. 1; Haacker 1994; J. E. Miller 1995. See the discus- sion against these views in Brooten 1996, 246–53, esp. 248 n. 99. Bailey cites b. Shabb. 65a. See also the discussion on rabbinic attitudes toward female homoeroticism in Satlow 1995, 188–92.

29. This is perhaps even more mysterious when we consider that the work of Murphy-O'Connor, who has produced more "proof" than any other scholar on this issue, was published in 1980, in plenty of time (presumably) for Scroggs to be aware of it, yet it does not appear in his discussion.

30. See, e.g., Theissen 1987, 169; Blattenberger 1997, 31 n. 13, 33 n. 15, 52–55; Collins 1999, 399; Hjort 2001, 71; Garland 2003, 530; J. Thompson 2003, 251–56; Mac- Gregor 2009, 211–13. Hjort (2001, 66–69) also considers the relation between this passage and 1 Cor 8–10 and the issue of idol worship; in this context, she suggests, the issue in 11:2–16 might therefore be "a form of androgyny and transvestism," possibly "cultic homophilia."

31. Lines 215–217 are clearly connected to lines 213–214 (van der Horst 1978, 252; W. Wilson 2005, 206, 208). Without the addition of these extra lines it might appear that 210–214 are a discrete unit, whereas this is not so obvious when we see the whole section laid out. I have given van der Horst's translation as this is the one Murphy-O'Connor cites.

32. Delobel (1986, 372) argues that these lines are in fact several distinct maxims

and therefore rejects Murphy-O'Connor's idea that Pseudo-Phocylides is making a link between long hair and homosexuality. However, the translation and commentary by W. Wilson (2005, 10, 200) sets out the sentences as a "gnomic poem" so that, in this instance, lines 195–227 are considered as a unit.

33. Delobel (1986, 373) argues that these lines do not mention *long* hair at all, only *adorned* hair. However, it is probably reasonable to assume that hair needed to be long in order to be braided and put up into ἄμματα λοξά (cross-knots).

34. As W. Wilson (2005, 208–9) notes, there were a number of situations in which long hair on men was lauded, such as for the Spartans or for Jewish men taking a Nazirite vow.

35. This may create a link with 1 Cor 11:2–16 if we follow the arguments of Trompf (1980, 198–201) on the connection between this passage and both 1 Cor 10 and 11:17–34. Trompf highlights the connections in these passages with the issues of eating and drinking, two matters that Philo notes in relation to those who practice bestiality (3.43). Ultimately, however, Trompf argues that 1 Cor 11:2–16 is an interpolation (215).

36. It is also of interest to note the portrayal of women in this satire, as here can be found a rare example in Roman satire of a woman speaking (2.36–64). Of course, we must not assume that the "voice" heard in these lines is that of an actual historical woman; Laronia is a rhetorical device used by Juvenal (Braund 1995, 207). Laronia, a wealthy adulteress, participates in the condemnation of the hypocritical effeminate men Juvenal is satirizing because of their critique of women such as herself; her primary allegation against these men is that they usurp female roles, with regard to both sex and other tasks such as spinning (2.47–57). However, as Braund (1995, 214) notes, this satire deems both women and effeminate men to be outside the author's (and his society's) construct of ideal masculinity and thus normality; Laronia "is introduced here to expose the hypocrisy of the effeminates. But the effect of her words is to bolster a masculine view of the world." See also Richlin 1984, 67–80; Braund 1992; Battisti 1994, 1–2, 68–108; Gold 1998, 370–75.

37. The potential "feminism" of Musonius Rufus can be noted in that he rejects the hypocrisy of men who have sexual relations with their slaves but who do not tolerate their wives having sexual relationships with slaves (12.36–40). For more on this issue see Klassen 1984; Hill 2001, 40; Nussbaum 2002.

38. That the issue of a man's appearance goes beyond that of hair is also clear when the rest of Epictetus's description of the young student is studied (which Murphy-O'Connor omits): καὶ τὴν ἄλλην περιβολὴν κατακοσμοῦντος ("and whose attire in general was highly embellished"; 3.1.1). Epictetus proceeds to teach the student about the beauty given to each κατὰ τὴν αὐτοῦ φύσιν ("in terms of its own nature"; 3.1.3). For a man this is seen in the behavior of those who are τοὺς δικαίους ... τοὺς σώφρονας ... τοὺς ἐγκρατεῖς ("the just ... the temperate ... the self-controlled"; 3.1.8–9), the virtues valued by a Stoic philosopher. In general, the Stoics emphasized "the four traditional Greek cardinal virtues" of prudence (φρόνησις), self-control (συμφροσύνη), manliness or courage (ἀνδρεία), and righteousness or justice (δικαιοσύνη). See the discussions in van Geytenbeek 1962, 25; Nussbaum 2002, 287; Winter 2002, 83–87; Knust 2006, 37.

39. The translation of κίναιδος as "sexual pervert" is problematic; the LCL edition was first published in 1928 and has been reprinted most recently in 2000, but no revision as yet has been undertaken of the translation. For discussion on the interpretive possibilities for κίναιδος, see C. Williams (1999, 175), who argues that although the term was the one "most often used to describe man [sic] who had been anally penetrated," it primarily signaled "gender deviance," and its etymology suggests "no direct connection to any sexual practice" (see further 176–218; see also D. Martin 2006, 204 n. 22, 23, 30). As an aside, Vander Stichele and Penner (2005, 304) note that this reference to Corinth is "intriguing."

40. This raises the issue of the association between the individual masculine body and the body politic (Vander Stichele and Penner 2005, 304).

41. This notion, that the differences between the sexes are God-ordained and are therefore an indicator that heterosexuality is also God-ordained, is a common thread in certain theological arguments against homosexuality and will be discussed in more detail in ch. 6. It also appears in the arguments of Payne discussed below. Murphy-O'Connor (1982, 194–95) also makes the assumption that Paul's argument was less than clear "because he experienced the embarrassment that many feel when dealing with homosexuality."

42. This has become a crucial step for those on the egalitarian side of the "divide" because of the arguments aimed at them by hierarchicalists. For example, Grudem argues that "egalitarianism is an engine that will pull many destructive consequences in its train," namely "a rejection of the authority of Scripture" that has the "disturbing destination" of "a denial of anything uniquely masculine"; he argues that this position then leads to "the next step: God, our Mother," which then leads to "the final step: approval of homosexuality" (Grudem 2004, 531, 505–9, 513). For Grudem, evangelical feminism is ultimately "the New Path to Liberalism," and he concludes emphatically, "we must choose either evangelical feminism or biblical truth. We cannot have both" (517). For more on this issue from a hierarchicalist viewpoint see Jones 2003, 5–19; from an egalitarian viewpoint, see C. Kroeger 2004.

43. These ideas echo those by Barth in his discussion in his *Church Dogmatics* on "Man and Woman" and the centrality of heterosexual marriage to the notion of what it means to be the *imago Dei*; I will discuss this in more detail in ch. 5.

44. For example, in Rom 1:18–32, 1 Cor 7, and 1 Cor 11:2–16. See the discussions in Brooten 1996, 247–48; T. Martin 2005, 214; Skinner 2005, 288; Ellis 2007, 91–95; Økland 2008, 200. This issue of procreation and/or biological complementarity as part of God's created order for human relations arises again in ch. 6 when I discuss the meaning of ἡ φύσις ("nature") in relation to 1 Cor 11:14; in particular the arguments of Gagnon against homosexuality are dependent on this idea, and I will examine these in detail.

45. Payne makes no reference to men who might appear "manly" in their hairstyles, dress, or demeanor but who identify as homosexual or gay.

46. Payne consistently refers to "homosexual relations" or "homosexual liaisons" in the plural, implying a sense of promiscuity. He deplores the idea of "a man presenting himself as a sexual mate *for other men*," contrasting this with the description of "God's creation of woman to be *man's mate*" (2009, 181). Although I suspect he would

find any form of homosexual relationship deplorable, it could have been possible, for example, for him to describe a man who presents himself as a sexual mate *for another man*, but by consistently describing same-sex relationships in the plural Payne reveals the negative stereotype underlying his discussion. This is confirmed by his use of the phrase "advertising" in relation to "homosexual relations" or "liaisons" (145, 214). Of course, advertisements for heterosexual "liaisons" are also common—if not more so—and Payne would presumably also condemn these; but it is homosexuality *in general* that he condemns by this specific example, whereas he ignores this aspect of heterosexual behavior.

47. This article was initially presented at the 60th Annual Meeting of the Evangelical Theological Society, 19 November 2008. See http://tinyurl.com/SBL0685v.

48. However, MacGregor makes no further reference to them in relation to their discussions about this hypothesis. While he also cites both Barrett and Scroggs, this is only with regard to Barrett's view of the grammatical force of the word ἀντί (in v. 15) and Scroggs's comment on the obscure and contradictory nature of Paul's logic (2009, 204 n. 8, 207 n. 18).

49. This is a critical development in the understanding of gender and sexuality, to which the field of New Testament studies was late in coming, although MacGregor makes no reference to the work of Foucault, Halperin, or J. Weeks, for example, nor to any biblical scholars whose work has grappled with these issues in relation to the Corinthians, such as D. Martin, Brooten, Økland, and Penner and Stichele.

50. In 1 Cor 5–6 the strength of Paul's criticism is aimed at the man who has had a relationship with his father's wife (5:1–8) and the men who are sexually involved with prostitutes (6:12–20). These situations are clearly concerned with issues involving *opposite-sex* behavior, despite the mention of the terms μαλακοί and ἀρσενοκοῖται in the vice list Paul employs (6:9–11). See the discussions in C. Barton 1994, 88 n. 21; Brooten 1996, 260; Ivarsson 2007, 171–84; Countryman 2007, 116–18, 190–99.

51. T. Martin (2005, 296 n. 19) describes Murphy-O'Connor's scenario as a "modern fantasy." See also Halperin 2002c, 113.

52. For discussions on the many issues surrounding the available source material, see also Murnaghan 1988, 18; Hallett 1988, 1266–67, 1275; 1989, 224; Szesnat 1994, 351–52; Walters 1997, 29; C. Williams 1999, 259 n. 1, 253–57; Butrica 2005, 246, 261. Regarding the consistent "sexual pattern" between classical Greek sources and first-century Roman material, see Halperin 2002c, 140; Butrica 2005, 246.

53. Of course, married women were not available to men other than their husbands, while their husbands did not have to limit their sexual practices to only their wives (C. Williams 1999, 47–56). For detailed discussions and examination of the sources that have led to the formulation of the ancient discourse on sexuality, see Dover 1978, 65–68; Hallett 1988, 1266–71; 1989, 223; Jeffrey Henderson 1988, 1260; Foucault 1990b, 46–47; Halperin 1990, 30–40; Winkler 1990, 39–40; Walters 1993, 23; 1997, 30–36; C. Williams 1999, 17–56, 160–224; Halperin 2002c, 147. C. Williams (1999, 18, 266 n. 16) prefers the terminology of "insertive" and "receptive" to the commonly used "active" and "passive" terms, particularly given that the "passive" partner is hardly inactive during such acts as fellatio (see also Butrica 2005, 222). However, see Halperin's response (2002c, 140).

54. L'Hoir (1992, 1–2) states that in comparison with other gender epithets (such as *homo*) used by both popular and elite Latin authors to describe a "man," the term *vir* "came to signify the upper classes" and the virtues with which they were associated; *vir* is thus "never neutral." See also Jeffrey Henderson 1988, 1253; Murnaghan 1988, 10; Laqueur 1990, 61, 108; Winkler 1990, 40–50; Walters 1993, 29; 1997, 32; C. Barton 1994, 86–87; C. Williams 1999, 125–59; D. Martin 2001; Roisman 2005, 7–10; Van Nortwick 2008, 14–16, 25–27, 39–41. See also the detailed treatments of the construction of ancient masculinity in the following collections of essays: Halperin, Winkler, and Zeitlin 1990; Foxhall and Salmon 1998a, 1998b; Rosen and Sluiter 2002.

55. Veyne (1978, 55) succinctly explains the differences between modern Western Christian sexual morality and that of the ancient Romans, in that *the latter* was a *puritanism* just as much as the *Christian*, only it was a *puritanism* of *virility rather than of marriage and reproduction*.

56. That women may sometimes appear as masculine is not encouraged but nor is it treated with the same obsessive concern.

3

The Straight Mind in Corinth*

Attack the order of heterosexuality in texts and lesbianize the heroes of
love, lesbianize the symbols, lesbianize the gods and the goddesses, lesbianize Christ, lesbianize the men and the women.
— Monique Wittig, "Some Remarks on *The Lesbian Body*"

Introduction

Wittig burst onto the French literary scene in 1964 at the age of twenty-
nine with the publication of her first novel, *L'opoponax*, for which she was
awarded the Prix Medicis, one of the most prestigious literary awards in
France. With her subsequent novels and theoretical essays functioning
alongside her radical politics, she was foundational in the development of
post-Beauvoirian French feminist philosophy, a movement that she would
come to epitomize alongside the better-known figures of Julia Kristeva,
Luce Irigaray, and Hélène Cixous.[1] Although Wittig moved to the United
States in 1976, it was Butler's reading (and critique) of her theories in
Gender Trouble (1990) that "effectively mainstreamed" her work, bringing
her to the attention of academic feminist circles throughout North America, the United Kingdom, and Australasia (de Lauretis 2005, 57). Wittig
subsequently published *The Straight Mind* in 1992, the first (and only) collection of her essays, many of which were previously published in English
and French between 1980 and 1990 in the journals *Feminist Issues* and
Questions Feministes.[2]

Wittig's influence has been significant but not altogether straightforward, particularly in the field of queer theory. As noted above, Butler
devoted considerable space to Wittig's work in *Gender Trouble*, primarily
in the form of a critique, although she has subsequently acknowledged
that at the time she wrote *Gender Trouble*, she was "Wittigian" in her views
on the power of language to shape understandings of sexed and gendered

identity (Olson and Worsham 2000, 743; Braidotti with Butler 1994, 49). Another pioneer of queer theory, de Lauretis (2005, 51), is more open about the influence of Wittig's theories on her own, acknowledging that both reading Wittig and having conversations with her started her "on the project of writing lesbian theory as distinct from feminist theory" (see also 1988, 165–67; 1990, 139–45). Less obvious, but perhaps no less importantly, the influence of Wittig's fiction can be seen in the work of Rubin and Sedgwick.[3] As a result, J. Edgar Bauer (2005) posits that Wittig's work has "attained canonical status within feminist studies and queer theory" (see also Shaktini 1994, 213).

However, the relationship between Wittig and queer theory is fraught. As Brad Epps and Jonathan Katz (2007, 433) comment, "there is no easy alliance between Wittig and queer theory—far from it" (see also Hennessy 1993, 966; Cooper 2000, 163). This partly stems from the simple reality that the bulk of Wittig's work predates the development of queer theory, thus making it susceptible to a retrospective critique that may not always be fair. In addition, the differences between French feminism and Anglo-American feminism—in particular their understandings of the concept of universalism and the value of a materialist approach—complicate the ways in which Wittig's work has been understood.[4] Nevertheless, Wittig's (1992h, 43, 45) critique of heterosexuality as a "political regime" is acknowledged as a precursor to the critique of heteronormativity by queer theorists, as discussed in chapter 1 (see Warner 1993, xxi). I would also add that her call for the destruction of gendered and sexed categories of identity, and her demonstration of this through a unique literary style that destabilizes androcentric and heterosexist structures of language, anticipate both the ethos and the politics of queer theory. Thus while it is anachronistic to call Wittig "queer," and therefore technically accurate to argue that she is *not* "queer" (Spinelli 2003), I agree with Epps and Katz (2007, 436) that "Wittig will continue to be remembered, and even 're-membered,' as one of the most compelling voices of the historical moment that saw the rise of queer theory, however close or distant from queer theory she 'ultimately' may 'really' be." In many ways, the difficulty of pinning Wittig to a precise relationship with queer theory—or even to feminist and lesbian theories for that matter—is part of the appeal of utilizing her work; that which is on the fringes, which defies definition and resists assimilation, must surely in some ways be part of the "immemorial current that *queer* represents" (Sedgwick 1994, xii). Perhaps the best approach to this dilemma comes from Robyn Wiegman:

Let's not "remember" [Wittig]. Let's not incorporate her into queer studies by memorializing her into the current habits of critique, or confer
status on her by making her queer theory's theoretical precursor, as if
giving her queer theoretical thoughts before the fact makes her work of
more value.... Let's refuse the lure of saying that Wittig either knew queer
theory, instinctively, before we did, or that she knew more than queer
theory ever did. *Let's take Wittig at her word and imagine having the ability to imagine other possibilities instead.* (2007, 515, emphasis added)

It is in this spirit of imagining "other possibilities" that I wish to consider Wittig's theories in relation to 1 Cor 11:2–16, with the Corinthian
men being the focus of my attention. By bringing them (reluctantly?)
under my scrutinizing gaze and rendering them highly visible in accord
with Wittig's (1992g, 87) challenge to systematically particularize the
masculine gender, it is likely that they are already (uncomfortably?) being
imagined differently. However, I wish to push them even further, into what
Lee Edelman (1994, 114) describes as "a zone of possibilities in which the
embodiment of the subject might be experienced otherwise." In particular,
I will pick up Wittig's (1992g, 87; 2005b, 47) challenge to "attack the order
of heterosexuality in texts and … lesbianize the men" and thus imagine the
possibility that the Corinthian men might be (theoretical) lesbians, akin to
Wittig's lesbian figure.

First, however, I will outline Wittig's theory of gender and the ways in
which Butler *mis*understood her work. This is important not only because
it was Butler who brought Wittig to the attention of Anglo-American
feminists, but also because Butler's *mis*reading of Wittig has been utilized
by Boyarin in his reading of 1 Cor 11:2–16 (and the Corinthian women).
After considering Boyarin's findings I will turn to those scholars who offer
a *re*reading of Wittig, and in light of their work I will offer my *re*reading of
1 Cor 11:2–16 (and the Corinthian men).

Wittig's Materialist Lesbianism

Wittig (1992g, xvi) notes in the preface to *The Straight Mind* that this collection of essays is divided into two parts, the first half being "a political
discussion" and the second half being about "writing."[5] This division is
indicative of her dual literary role as novelist and political theorist,[6] and
a quick scan of any bibliography of Wittig criticism reveals a tendency
by scholars to focus on either her fiction or her philosophy (Shaktini
2005b, 203–22). For the purposes of this chapter, I will restrict myself

to Wittig's theoretical writings on gender rather than her novels. The final chapter of this book, however, will focus on Wittig's third book, *The Lesbian Body* (1976), described as her "most infamous text" (Whatling 1997, 239).

Wittig's theory of gender is known as *materialist lesbianism*. Taking as her point of departure Karl Marx's concept of the sexual division of labor in the family, Wittig analyzes the situation of women in terms of political economy. Refuting Marx's assumption that this division is natural, she identifies women as a social category, an ideological construct, but even more than that (building on the materialist feminist analysis of Christine Delphy), a political class, the product of an economic relation of exploitation.[7] She declares, for example, "There is no sex. There is but sex that is oppressed and sex that oppresses. It is oppression that creates sex and not the contrary" (1992a, 2). In other words, what is central for Wittig is the way in which domination is the fundamental component in even something as supposedly natural as the heterosexual relationship between the sexes. Rather than accepting this division of society into two sexes as "natural," Wittig recognizes it as an ideological construct based on the oppression of one group by another. She explains:

> The category of sex does not exist a priori, before all society....
> The category of sex is the political category that founds society as heterosexual. As such it does not concern being but relationships (for women and men are the result of relationships)....
> The category of sex is the one that rules as "natural" the relation that is at the base of (heterosexual) society and through which half of the population, women, are "heterosexualized."...
> The category of sex is the product of heterosexual society that turns half of the population into sexual beings, for sex is a category that women cannot be outside of. (1992a, 5–7)

Building also upon the work of Simone de Beauvoir, Wittig exposes the constructed nature of both gender and sex. The title of her essay, "On ne naît pas femme" ("One is not born a woman"), is a play on the famous quote from de Beauvoir, "On ne naît pas femme: on le devient" ("One is not *born* but *becomes* a woman") (1984, 295). As de Lauretis (2005, 53) observes, "Almost the same words and yet such a difference in meaning.... In shifting the emphasis from the word *born* to the word *woman*, Wittig's citation of de Beauvoir's phrase invoked or mimicked the heterosexual definition of woman as 'the second sex,' at once destabilizing its meaning and displacing its affect." While de Beauvoir alerts her readers to the social construction of gender, Wittig goes further and argues that sex and sexuality are also constructed categories, questioning the very categories of "man" and "woman" and the way they are unequally bound together in the political (and economic) regime of heterosexuality.

Wittig (1992e, 20) therefore calls for the destruction of the categories of sex and thus the "destruction of heterosexuality as a social system." In order to achieve this, she argues that women need to extract themselves from the "myth of woman" that is imposed upon them by the dominant discourses in society (13, 19). This is the idea that women are a "natural" group, existing in relation to men, a relation she describes as "servitude" and that "implies personal and physical obligation as well as economic obligation" (20). For Wittig, the only way to escape this myth, and to destroy the category of "woman," is through lesbianism. She further explains that "lesbianism provides for the moment the only social form in which we can live freely. Lesbian is the only concept I know of which is beyond the categories of sex (woman and man), because the designated subject (lesbian) is *not* a woman, either economically, or politically, or ideologically" (20).[8] Or to rephrase this, Wittig poses the reconceptualization of the subject as the lesbian, a figure who exceeds the categories of both sex and gender, who is not a product of a social (or economic) relationship with a man, and who is thus, in effect, *not* a woman. The impact of this notion can be discerned in Wittig's concluding statement to her essay "The Straight Mind," which was met with "stunned silence" when first presented at the Modern Language Association 1978 Annual Meeting in New York (Turcotte 1992, viii):

> What is woman?… Frankly, it is a problem that lesbians do not have because of a change in perspective, and it would be incorrect to say that lesbians associate, make love, live with women, for "woman" has meaning only in heterosexual systems of thought and heterosexual economic systems. Lesbians are not women. (Wittig 1992i, 32)

Wittig describes these heterosexual systems of thought as "The Straight Mind." This is the "conglomerate of all kinds of disciplines, theories, and current ideas"—the multitude of ideological discourses—that functions in society to universalize heterosexuality as something "natural" (1992i, 27). But more than this, there is also a sense of the imperative about the straight mind, so that to conceive of alternative ways of constituting individual identity or human relationships almost becomes an impossibility within this system. Consequently, the only escape available is an escape from heterosexuality. Being a "woman" or a "man" is tied so tightly to heterosexuality that to escape one is to escape the other. As Wittig (1992e, 13) states, "The refusal to become (or to remain) heterosexual always meant to refuse to become a man or a woman, consciously or not."

While acknowledging the historical difficulty of the individual subject, particularly within Marxism,[9] Wittig (1992c, 80) also discusses the importance of language as the means of producing such political and personal transformation: "Language as a whole gives everyone the same power of becoming an absolute subject through its exercise." Language is thus "raw material" ready to be used by the writer to create something new (1992k, 71). Literature therefore has the potential "to pulverize the old forms and formal conventions" that buttress heteronormativity and the domination of women (1992k, 69). Consequently, Wittig (1992k) likens works of literature to the Trojan horse, a "war machine" by which the author can shock the reader into an awareness of how language operates in the domain of ideology. Her novels are explicit examples of such war machines at work,[10] but I would also argue that phrases within her theoretical essays, such as "lesbians are not women," also function in a similar way to challenge the reader. For Wittig, the act of writing—be it fiction or theory—is a political act "of unwriting and rewriting" in order to demonstrate specifically that the category of women is not a natural group but "a historical creation of the dominant phallogocentric point of view" (Shaktini 2005a, 158).

Wittig thus also recognizes that language—as rhetoric, discourse, propaganda, and so on—is also a powerful element in the operation of the straight mind. In particular, how gender functions at the grammatical level in language, in the reinforcement of heterosexuality and the appropriation of the universal by men, is of central importance for Wittig. She suggests that gender enforces upon women a particular category, depriving them of the authority of speech, denying them universality, and ultimately stripping them of subjectivity (1992c, 81). In explaining the strength of language in this regard, she declares, "Language casts sheaves of reality upon the social body, stamping it and violently shaping it" (1992c, 78; see also 1992d, 43–44). Gender, then, can—and indeed, "must"—be destroyed through the power of language (1992c, 81). For women, this means consciously assuming the status of the universal subject. She states:

when one becomes a locutor, when one says "I" and, in doing so, reappropriates language as a whole, proceeding from oneself alone, with the tremendous power to use all language, it is then and there, according to linguists and philosophers, that the supreme act of subjectivity, the advent of subjectivity into consciousness, occurs. It is when starting to speak that one becomes "I." This act—the becoming of *the* subject through the exercise of language and through locution—in order to be real, implies that the locutor be an absolute subject.... I mean that in spite of the harsh law of gender and its enforcement upon women, no woman can say "I" without being for herself a total subject—that is, ungendered, universal, whole.... Language as a whole gives everybody the same power of becoming an absolute subject through its exercise. (1992c, 80)

Ultimately, Wittig's quest is to bring about "a total conceptual revolution" (Turcotte 1992, vii). By questioning the fundamental understandings of sex and gender, Wittig seeks not only to free women from oppression—a basic tenet of feminist politics—but she seeks to free them from the very construct of "woman." Thus she challenges not only the regime of patriarchy but also that of heterosexuality. For feminism in particular, Wittig's theories "theoretically and politically disrupt an entire movement" (Turcotte 1992, viii). But by moving beyond the categories of sex and appropriating the universal subject position for that which is otherwise deemed particular and specific, the lesbian, Wittig (1992b, 57–58) also disrupts the broader "symbolic order" of the straight mind.

Butler's Wittig

Butler (1999, 3–9) begins her groundbreaking work *Gender Trouble* with a discussion of the complex issue of "the subject," in particular the issue of "women" as the subject of feminist theory and politics. After examining both de Beauvoir's and Irigaray's views on sex and gender (12–18), and the question of "personal identity" (22–24), Butler turns to the model offered by Wittig. In particular, she discusses the way in which Wittig adheres to the notion of the subject and the way this is articulated as "the lesbian," a figure who "promises to transcend the binary restriction on sex imposed by the system of compulsory heterosexuality" (26). Butler describes this figure of "the lesbian" as "a third gender" (26), as "neither female nor male, woman nor man ... a category that radically problematizes both sex and gender as stable political categories of description" (144).

However, Butler has two major difficulties with this figure. To begin with, on a pragmatic level, she views Wittig's lesbian feminism as a kind of "separatist prescriptivism," where only lesbians can be true feminists, and there is no solidarity with heterosexual women, nor, in fact, any possibility for optional heterosexuality (1999, 155, 162). She even goes as far as to say that Wittig's "defiant imperialist strategy" is aimed at "lesbianizing the whole world" and denounces this "totalitarian" position as "no longer viable" or even "politically desirable" (153, 150, 162). Butler suggests that it inevitably creates lesbianism as a compulsory category, no different from "the compulsory meanings of heterosexuality's *women* and *men*" (162).

On a theoretical level, Butler also questions the way in which "the lesbian" is constructed for Wittig. Specifically, this concern centers on the role of the subject and the place of agency. In explaining her unease with Wittig's viewpoint, Butler says, "As a subject who can realize concrete universality through freedom, Wittig's lesbian confirms rather than contests the normative promise of humanist ideals premised on the metaphysics of substance" (27). For Butler, Wittig's subscription to this philosophical "belief," that there exists a "pregendered 'person'" who enjoys the "presocial status of human freedom," is an anathema (27). She rejects the idea that psychological categories of being, such as the subject, the self, the individual, exist as realities (as stable, universal entities) outside of constructs such as language. Arguing that Wittig's view therefore "uncritically employs the inflectional attribution of 'being' to genders and to 'sexualities,'" she labels Wittig's position as "prefeminist" in that it "naively" confuses sex with gender and accepts as possible a unified sense of identity (29).

In a later section of *Gender Trouble*, Butler continues her critique of Wittig's philosophical framework (143–63). She situates Wittig's project within the "traditional discourse of ontotheology," that is, within a modernist framework that presumes the primary unity of beings grounded in a prelinguistic Being (149). Butler labels this notion of "the unity of being," and its correlative of a "seamless identity of all things," as a "foundationalist fiction" (150). In such a framework, gender, sex, heterosexuality, and domination all belong to a second-order, discursively constituted reality. Language, for Wittig, is therefore both the cause of sexual oppression and the way beyond that oppression. But for Butler, the idea that women can "*speak* their way out of their gender" is "startling" (149). She is not impressed with the "enormous" power that Wittig accords to language, nor to the volition of the speaking subject (148). Butler states, "This absolute grounding of the speaking 'I' assumes God-like dimensions within Wittig's discussion" (149).

This is somewhat surprising, however, given that Butler herself recognizes the impact of language—or discourse—on the construction of the gendered being. In explaining the process of "gendering," Butler gives the example of the "medical interpellation" by which infants are named at birth (or even beforehand now, with the emergence of the sonogram); the pronouncement of "It's a girl!" brings the infant—now "she" rather than "it"—"into the domain of language and kinship through the interpellation of gender" (1993, 7; 1999, 142). This "girling" does not end there, of course, but is a process "reiterated by various authorities and throughout various intervals of time to reinforce or contest this naturalized effect" (1993, 8). Butler notes in particular the way that this interpellation reinforces heteronormativity: "In this sense, the initiatory performative, 'It's a girl!' anticipates the eventual arrival of the sanction, 'I pronounce you man and wife'" (232). But Butler also notes the subversive potential of language. Giving the personal example of being asked on one occasion, "Are you a lesbian?" Butler explains that her choice to answer in the affirmative was, at that moment, "a very powerful thing to do" (Olson and Worsham 2000, 760). She says, "I received the term and gave it back; I replayed it, reiterated it" (760).[11]

As stated earlier, it was Butler's initial reading of Wittig's *Gender Trouble* that brought Wittig to the attention of feminist scholars in North America, the United Kingdom, and Australasia. Indeed, Butler's critique of Wittig as a "humanist" (1999, 27, 158) and a "classic idealist" (159) served for many as "the definitive verdict" on her work and thus effectively eliminated her views from feminist debates in the 1990s (Zerilli 2005, 91, 110 n. 18). De Lauretis (2005, 57) states, "To the reader of *Gender Trouble*, Wittig appears to be an existentialist who believes in human freedom, a humanist who presumes the ontological unity of Being prior to language, an idealist masquerading as a materialist, and, most paradoxically of all, an unintentional, unwitting collaborator with the regime of heterosexual normativity." In later years, however, several scholars have responded by suggesting that Butler's critique is actually a *mis*reading. As already noted, Butler herself has subsequently reconsidered her position on Wittig, even describing herself as "Wittigian" in her views on the way in which language shapes sexed and gendered identity (Olson and Worsham 2000, 743). I will return shortly to these *re*readings of Wittig, but first I will examine the work of one of those scholars who took Butler's initial reading of Wittig as *the* definitive reading.

Boyarin's Wittig

In his historical consideration of Western gender ideologies, Boyarin (2003, 25) states that Butler's analysis of Wittig is "incisive."[12] This point comes midway through his discussion of the "Phallus" as a "privileged signifier" in the ideology of sexual difference that dominates Western formulations of gender, and his consideration of the way in which this functions to construct the feminine as corporeal and specific and the masculine as disembodied and universal (4, 12–15, 17; see also Lacan 1982; Keuls 1985; Butler 1993, 57–91). Boyarin (2003, 14, 24) argues that this has been the "dominant fiction" of gender since the time of Plato and proceeds to consider the ideologies of gender found in rabbinic Judaism and early Christianity, which he calls equally problematic "subdominant fictions."

Boyarin's premise is that early Christianity understood sexual difference as a secondary and inferior aspect of human creation, whereas by contrast, rabbinic Judaism insisted on the dual-sexed nature of the primordial human creature. For Christianity, the initial creation of humanity is as "a primal androgyne of no sex ... [a] singular unbodied Adam-creature," while the secondary act of creation is a two-part process that brings into being "a carnal Adam who is male ... from whom the female is constructed" (2003, 5). For rabbinic Judaism, the initial creation of humanity is as "a physical hermaphrodite ... a dual-sex creature in one body," while the secondary act of creation "merely separated out the two sexes from each other and reconstructed them into two human bodies" (26–27). Boyarin suggests that "the modern dilemmas of feminist thought on the Phallus" seem to reflect these differing views of gender and sexual difference (34), and he illustrates this through a comparison between the theories of Wittig and Irigaray, the former exemplifying the early Christian position, and the latter exemplifying that of rabbinic Judaism.

In the section on "Monique Wittig and the 'Christian' Thinking of Gender" in his original article, Boyarin (1998, 122–23) states that the "crucial text" for his analysis is 1 Cor 11:2–16, where he suggests, "Paul makes practically explicit his theory of gender as produced in the sexual relation." Boyarin's focus is primarily on Paul and his response to the Corinthians regarding their coiffure. Citing key verses from this passage, Boyarin explains how Paul combines two systems of understanding gender, one in which there is "an explicit hierarchy" (vv. 3, 7–9) and one in which there is "none" (vv. 11–12) (124). The absence of hierarchy does not necessarily correspond to a practical equality, however. Like many Pauline scholars, Boyarin makes the connection between the declaration in verse 11, "There is neither woman without man nor man without woman, in the Lord [ἐν κυρίῳ]," and Gal 3:28, "There is neither male and female in Christ [ἐν χριστῷ]."[13] This liturgical formula expresses the idea that a new humanity was being created in which all differences would be removed in Christ. But Boyarin (1998, 123) makes the important point that for Paul this new creation was not something that could be entirely achieved on the social level: "Paul could never imagine a social eradication of the hierarchical deployment of male and female bodies for married people." It is this qualification of marriage that seems to be the crucial factor. Boyarin observes that for Paul, "It is (hetero)sexuality, therefore, that produces gender … any possibility of an eradication of male and female and its corresponding social hierarchy is only possible on the level of the spirit, either in ecstasy at baptism or perhaps permanently for the celibate" (123).

Boyarin also makes the connection between these two levels of operation—that of a spiritual equality and a social hierarchy—and the corresponding two myths of the origins of the sexes found in Gen 1 and 2. Again, this is also a connection many Pauline scholars make with 1 Cor 11:2–16.[14] Here Boyarin (1998, 124; see also 119) states, "Paul's interpretation of Genesis is virtually identical to Philo's" (see also 2003, 4).[15] For Philo, the first story of Gen 1 tells of an entirely spiritual being, a primal androgyne of no sex, while Gen 2 tells of the creation of "a primal male/secondary female" (Boyarin 2003, 5; see also Meeks 1974; D. MacDonald 1987, 1988). As Boyarin (2003, 5) therefore points out, "Bodily gender—structurally dependent, of course, on their being two—is thus twice displaced from the origins of 'Man.'" According to Boyarin, Philo only ever claims that the first creature is made "in the image of God," while the second creature, marked by sexual difference, is material and fallen (5). Consequently, the unification of opposites in general, and the symbolization of a reunified humanity in particular, became a well-known motif in religious experience (Meeks 1974, 166–67; D. MacDonald 1988, 282–83). In particular, Boyarin (2003, 26) proposes that Philo's description of the Therapeutae provides an example of "an ecstatic joining of the male and the female in a mystical ritual [that] re-creates in social practice the image of the purely spiritual masculofeminine first human … a return to the originary Adam" (see Philo, *Contempl. Life* 11.83–90; see also Kraemer

1989). This Jewish-Christian ascetic community included both men and women living celibate lives of prayer and worship, and Boyarin describes the climatic ritual of their festal meeting where the separate choirs of the men and the women ultimately join together to form one chorus. He suggests that this ecstatic ritual illustrates "a symbolic and psychological condition of being disembodied and thus is similar to the condition of the primal androgyne" (2003, 26).

The key point for Boyarin (1998, 121) is that "spiritual androgyny is attained only by abjuring the body and its difference." As long as women renounce their "sexuality and maternity"—that which makes them specifically female—they may attain a level of autonomy and creativity on the spiritual sphere (2003, 26). Boyarin (2003, 6) suggests that we can also see this idea reflected in Philo's discussion of female figures in the Bible who fall into one of two categories: women or virgins (Philo, *QE* 2.3).[16] Boyarin (1998, 121–22) explains further: "As the category 'woman' is produced in the heterosexual relationship, so in Philo a female who escapes or avoids such relationships escapes from being a woman." The embodied, gendered person is therefore inevitably represented as female. Transcendence beyond this to become a spiritual being, through the renunciation of the body and its sexuality, is inevitably to become a *male* androgyne. Boyarin (2003, 6–8) also considers the early Christian accounts of Thekla (or Thecla), Maximilla, and Jesus's teaching regarding Mary and shows that transcendence is, again, a "virilization."[17] The women in these stories renounce their femaleness—through haircutting, clothing exchange, celibacy, and/or rejection of maternity—and in doing so become male. Boyarin (2003, 8) explains that far from disturbing gender categories, "the 'myth of the primal androgyne' ... constitutes a reinstatement, even a reinforcement, of masculinism" (see also D. MacDonald 1988, 285; Castelli 1991a, 32).

It is with this in mind, then, that Boyarin makes the connection with Wittig's materialist feminism. He finds the parallels between the views on gender found in these stories and the feminist philosophy of Wittig "stunning" (2003, 25). The female members of the Therapeutae and the female Christian disciples who seek transcendence can only do so by escaping the fleshly bonds of marriage and maternity, and thus they are no longer described as "women" (1998, 122). Boyarin suggests that Wittig also makes a similar point when she states:

> The category of sex is the product of a heterosexual society which imposes on women the rigid obligation of the reproduction of the "spe-

cies," that is, the reproduction of heterosexual society ... [the category of sex] turns half of the population into sexual beings, for sex is a category which women cannot be outside of.... Some lesbians and nuns escape. (1992a, 6–7)

For Boyarin, therefore, Philo's virgins and Wittig's lesbian are therefore almost—but not quite[18]—identical in that they are *not* women. But he also views them as both inevitably tied to the "dominant fiction" that determines that the universal, ungendered being can *only* be masculine in its formulation. From this fiction, this phallocentric ideology, Boyarin (2003, 21) declares, "there is no escape." Consequently he concludes, "Wittig's lesbian is another version of the woman of Hellenistic Judaism or early Christianity made male and thus free through celibacy.... Metaphysically speaking, nothing has changed" (25).

Boyarin openly relies on Butler's analysis of Wittig, devoting more space to Butler's comments about Wittig than to Wittig's own writings. He declares that Butler "demonstrates clearly" that Wittig's call for the destruction of the category of sex is dependent on the same metaphysics, and thus the "same masculinist ideologies of transcendence," as Philo (2003, 25). In citing Butler's critique of Wittig's adherence to the metaphysics of substance, he defends his conclusion that Wittig's position "reflects the Philonic/patristic ideology of freedom as pregendered and non-gender as male" (25).[19] Consequently, Boyarin concludes both his articles by expressing a sense of despair over the current situation with regard to discourses of gender. He states that we are suspended between "the poles of an irresolvable antinomy or aporia," that is, the dialectic between the "Christian" and "rabbinic" understandings of gender (1998, 133); in other words, between a drive for universalism or transcendence that appears inevitably to divest women of their sexuality and their bodies and an insistence on corporeality and sexuality that appears inevitably to trap women in specificity and difference.[20] Boyarin suggests that, although there is not yet "any third term that can clearly resolve this antithesis" (133), "our project must be to find a way past the impossible terms of this Hobson's choice" (2003, 34). The strength of the "dominant fiction" of the Phallus seems—unsurprisingly—relentlessly potent and unwavering, rapacious even. As noted above, Boyarin sees "no escape" from this deeply embedded cultural construct; it would seem that all—both male and female—are pinned down by the force of this "seminal signifier" (21).

However, given that Boyarin relies on Butler's reading of Wittig, what if, rather than being "incisive," Butler's analysis of Wittig is instead a *mis-*reading, as many Wittig scholars claim? How would that affect Boyarin's reading of the theology implicit in 1 Cor 11:2–16? Picking up on the idea of "dominant" and "subdominant" fictions that Boyarin utilizes in his discussion, I suggest that there are some "dominant" and "subdominant" voices at work here. With regard to Wittig, Butler is clearly the dominant voice in Boyarin's study. If it were possible to *re*read Wittig's theory in a way consistent with those who defend her work—and thus seek to hear Wittig's voice more clearly than Butler's—might another reading of this passage emerge? In addition, with regard to the situation in Corinth, Paul and Philo seem clearly to be the dominant voices Boyarin considers. But perhaps a *re*reading of the text that listens for the voices of the Corinthians might reveal an alternative, subdominant view of gender. Remembering that for Wittig writing is a political act of unwriting and rewriting, perhaps this is a strategy we can emulate in order to extract us from under the heavy weight of this virile (strong, dominating) signifier; perhaps Wittig's lesbian figure can resist the Phallus. If this passage is *re*read in such a way as to hear the "subdominant" voices of both Wittig and the Corinthians, rather than the "dominant" points of view of both Butler and Paul (and Philo), a third way may emerge, an escape may be possible.

I am also encouraged in this imaginative attempt by Butler's own discussion on "The Lesbian Phallus" (1993, 57–91). Not only does Butler wryly acknowledge at the very outset of her essay that imaginative attempts have the potential to fail and be less than satisfying—"perhaps the promise of the phallus is always dissatisfying in some way"—she also suggests that failure, if it does occur, still has its uses (57). In other words, this attempt to *re*write and *re*consider not only 1 Cor 11:2–16 but also the ways in which Wittig's lesbian has been understood may not succeed, or be particularly satisfying, but the very attempt to resist that which is dominant is still of value. In addition, Butler recognizes the possibility that signifiers, by the way in which they are constructed through language, are open to "resignification," and that this process allows for the possibility of "depriviliging" them (88–89). Butler concludes with an explanation of why it is both possible and necessary to offer the (subdominant) lesbian phallus as an alternative signifier that can destabilize and even displace the (dominant) "masculinist and heterosexist privilege" of the phallus (90):

In this sense, to speak of the lesbian phallus as a possible site of desire is not to refer to an *imaginary* identification and/or desire that can be measured against a *real* one; on the contrary, it is simply to promote an alternative *imaginary* to a hegemonic imaginary and to show, through that assertion, the ways in which the hegemonic imaginary consti- tutes itself through the naturalization of an exclusionary heterosexual morphology.... What is needed is not a new body part, as it were, but a displacement of the hegemonic symbolic of (heterosexist) sexual dif- ference and the critical release of alternative imaginary schemas for constructing sites of erotogenic pleasure. (91)

It is in this sense of proposing "alternative imaginary schemas" in order to displace the dominant schema that I wish to reconsider the value of Wittig's lesbian. Wittig's (1992c, 87) call to "attack the order of hetero- sexuality in texts, and ... lesbianize the symbols ... lesbianize men and women" can be understood in this way as a call to reveal and subvert the symbols—signifiers—of heteronormativity (see also 2005b, 47). In order to do this, however, it is first necessary to *re*read Wittig without hearing the dominant voice of Butler.

Rereading Wittig

One of the key critics of Butler's response to Wittig's theories is de Lauretis. Finding Butler's analysis of Wittig to be a *mis*reading, she points primarily to Butler's failure to understand the figural, theoretical character of Wittig's lesbian. This point is central. According to de Lauretis (2005, 55), Wittig's lesbian is not so much "an individual with a personal 'sexual preference,'" or one who is politically motivated in their sexual choices, but a "concep- tual figure ... an eccentric subject constituted in a process of struggle and *interpretation*; of *translation, detranslation*, and *retranslation* ... a *rewriting* of self in relation to a new understanding of society, of history, of culture" (emphasis added). Wittig's lesbian then, is not so much the "cognitive sub- ject" that Butler posits but rather a "conceptual figure" whose existence is barely conceivable in a society, history, and culture that is dominated by the Phallus, or a system Wittig would call "the straight mind."

This figure is therefore "eccentric," according to de Lauretis, because it does not fit with the cultural constructs of gender and sex that are nor- mative in straight society. She states that this eccentric subject is one that "exceeds its conditions of subjection, a subject in excess of its discursive construction, a subject of which we only knew what it was not: not-woman" (2005, 56). How this figure is constituted as a subject is therefore also not achieved through the forming of affective bonds with someone of the same sex, or by being a part of some utopic lesbian separatist collective. Rather, de Lauretis suggests that the lesbian "is figured in the practice of writing as consciousness of contradiction ... a consciousness of writing, living, feeling, and desiring in the noncoincidence of experience and language, in the interstices of representation" (57–58). Subjectivity in such lacunary spaces involves a displacement, or a disidentification, a leaving of the emotionally, conceptually, politically, and/or physically familiar for that which is unknown and unfamiliar, "a place from which speaking and thinking are at best tentative, uncertain, unauthorized" (53).[21] This displacement—this "reconceptualization of the subject"—is also not a static, singular event but inevitably entails "a constant crossing back and forth, a remapping of boundaries between bodies and discourses, identities and communities" (53).

Two other Wittig scholars offer further clarification over the meaning of the lesbian figure, particularly emphasizing its conceptual nature. Crowder (2005, 71) reminds her readers that Wittig's lesbian is not "a woman who loves women" as is commonly understood. Wittig (1979, 121) makes this point clear: "it is not 'women' (victims of heterosexuality) that lesbians love and desire, but lesbians (individuals who are not the females of men)." Lesbianism is not about sexual desire or practice but is a political, economic, social, and symbolic action that refuses and resists the system of domination that is heterosexuality. Dianne Chisholm further clarifies this point. She states that Wittig's lesbian "does not represent a real, physical, or political body; it does not imag(in)e lesbian persons nor even lesbian erotic experience. Rather, it *acts* as a body-metaphor; a *catachresis*, a metaphor without a literal referent that serves to conceptualize a radically different body/body politic, to think beyond representations of the conventional, naturalized body" (1993, 204). In other words, the lesbian is a signifier of an alternative to heteronormativity, destabilizing and displacing the dominant paradigm by pointing to that which is beyond the traditional categories of sex.

Having established that Wittig's lesbian is primarily a conceptual figure, we now need to consider the specific issue of subjectivity with which Butler was so concerned. In the "dominant fiction" of the phallus, this signifier is not only a symbol of privilege (and power) but is also symbolic of "completeness, coherence, [and] univocity"; maleness is thus associated with "unity, singularity and plenitude," while femaleness is associated with "difference, multiplicity and lack" (Boyarin 2003, 12).[22] This ideology has been a fundamental aspect of Western cultural constructions of gender since Plato and Aristotle and has determined that maleness is also associated with subjectivity (with its qualities of action and voice) while femaleness is associated with objectivity (with its qualities of passivity and silence). Wittig's lesbian poses an alternative configuration of subjectivity, as Karin Cope (1991, 78) argues: "Wittig's lesbian subject, while universal, is not a seamless whole, the One of patriarchal male 'major' subjectivity. Rather, as a subject ... the lesbian 'I' is a 'minor' subjectivity, fragmentary and fractured." Wittig thus takes the notions of difference, multiplicity, and lack and gives them the attributes of subjectivity—of action and voice—but *not* a voice that is coherent and univocal, in a simple replacement of "maleness" with "femaleness." Wittig's lesbian subject is both particular and universal, as Wittig (1992b, 46) herself explains: "being a lesbian, standing at the outposts of the human (of humankind) represents historically and paradoxically the most human point of view."[23]

Finally, it is appropriate to consider the comments of Shaktini, renowned Wittig authority and compeer. She suggests that one reason why Anglo-American feminists have misread Wittig is that they have not paid enough attention to her self-acknowledged debt to the French linguist Émile Benveniste and his theory of the speaking subject (2005a, 156).[24] In brief, Benveniste considers the way in which the speaker voices their subjectivity as an "I" and posits the indeterminateness of this "I" as follows:

> There is no concept "I" that incorporates all the *I*'s that are uttered at every moment in the mouths of all speakers.... It is a term that cannot be identified except in ... an instance of discourse and that has only a momentary reference. ...
> [*I* and *you*] do not refer to "reality" or to "objective" positions in space or time but to the utterance, unique each time, that contains them.... [They are] "empty" signs that are nonreferential with respect to "reality." (1971, 226, 219)

Shaktini (2005a, 157) thus makes the connection between Benveniste's "I" and Wittig's lesbian in that they are both "empty signs" able to be filled only in specific instances of discourse. This confirms the idea that Wittig is not simply affirming the "dominant" notion of subjectivity, as Butler seems to fear. The subjectivity of Wittig's lesbian is multiple, fractured, and momentary. Wittig (1992f, 62) also explains this idea in relation to the process of writing, the place where this vital act of universalizing the minority point of view can strategically occur, by suggesting that when one reads this sort of text, one experiences the effect of "an out-of-the-corner-of-the-eye perception."

Wittig's lesbian subject is thus not the cognitive, rational, unitary subject that Butler supposed. Nor is this figure the same as the flesh-and-blood lesbian who is defined by her desire and sexual practice. Of course, in Wittig's words, this figure is, more than anything, *not* a woman. Importantly, as many of these Wittig scholars have noted, it is in the process of writing—*un*writing, *re*writing—that this figure is conceptualized most clearly. In the back and forth crossing of *re*reading, *re*mapping, *re*translating, *re*conceptualizing, that which is dominant—singular, unwavering, and potent—is destabilized and displaced, while that which is subdominant—multiple, fractured, and momentary—can emerge and speak, "dealing a blow with words" (1992k, 72). As noted earlier, Wiegman (2007, 515) perhaps best articulates the task of the writer/reader: "Let's take Wittig at her word and imagine having the ability to imagine other possibilities instead."

*Re*reading 1 Corinthians 11:2–16

With these *re*readings of Wittig's lesbian in mind, it is time to *re*read 1 Cor 11:2–16 and to imagine "other possibilities." As already noted in chapter 1, this text is notoriously difficult; scholars have debated its various hermeneutical, theological, and historical aspects with little consensus emerging on any of the issues the text raises. Consequently, this passage leaves room for and even encourages an approach that accepts contradictions, multiplicities, and "out-of-the-corner-of-the-eye" perceptions. It is a passage replete with lacunae, "empty signs," and "eccentric" subjects who defy definition.

I have also argued that it is crucial to give adequate attention to the Corinthian men. Too many analyses of this text have either ignored the presence of the men in Paul's argument or declared that their role in his argument is purely hypothetical and have focused solely on the behavior of the "problematic women" (M. MacDonald 1990, 164). Yet both textually and historically there is no reason to suppose that Paul is not also addressing the men's behavior alongside that of the women. A *re*reading of this passage can therefore take into consideration the possibility that the men—by playing with the established sign systems of clothing and coiffure—are as involved in gender-scrambling behaviors as the women.

Consequently, these men may be as "eccentric," if not more so, than their female counterparts. As contradictory, unthinkable figures, ignored or deemed hypothetical, viewed as effeminate and thus anachronistically mislabeled as "homosexual," these men may reflect a view of gender that not only resists the dominant model of masculinity but is also inconceivable within that dominant paradigm. As such, it might even be possible to liken them to Wittig's lesbian figure.

In his examination of the myth of the primal androgyne in relation to 1 Cor 11:2–16 in particular and early Christianity in general, Boyarin (2003, 7) cites the account in Acts Andr. 40–41 in which the apostle addresses the disciple Maximilla as a "man," even as a "wise man," entreating her to remain celibate, and imploring her to help *him* to become perfect—to become a man. Boyarin states that in this example it is "absolutely and explicitly clear that the goal of gender neutralization for both women and men is to become a man" (7). Placing such accounts alongside a consideration of first-century Greco-Roman views on masculinity reveals that, for anatomical males, masculinity was not a given but something that needed constant attention and maintenance. No male could be confident that he had attained—or could maintain—the status of being a "real man." The corollary of this was that one *could* strive for perfection, even if one had to ask for the help of … who? A woman? A masculine female? Who is "she," this Maximilla? At the very least she is *not* a "woman," but nor, I would argue, is she Wittig's lesbian. In the sex-gender paradigm of her world, Maximilla is a "man," albeit only an honorary one, I suspect.

Most importantly, Boyarin gives no further explanation for the behavior of those men who renounce the masculine virtue of virility in order to become spiritually transcendent.[25] Boyarin's focus is primarily on the women, considering only the motivation that might lead them to renounce their sexuality in order to attain a degree of transcendence. Boyarin (2003, 42 n. 99) is aware that the men of Philo's Therapeutae community were celibate, but comments without explanation that "men do not have to renounce their *sexuality* in order to become 'male,' while women always do" (emphasis added). It is possible Boyarin means that they have not had to renounce their *masculinity* in choosing to be celibate, as this option could indeed exemplify the virtues of self-control and honor (D. Martin 2001, 83–97). As D. Martin (2001, 90) points out regarding Greco-Roman culture, "the masculinization of sexual asceticism and the asceticizing of masculinity were two sides of the same coin."

However, there are also some examples of male behavior in Greco-Roman religious contexts that do not fit with the dominant view of gender, particularly with the view that for a man to appear as "womanish" was "something that should be avoided at all costs" (Musonius Rufus, 21.28–29 [Lutz]). Gender role reversal was an important component in various religious festivals celebrated by the Greeks, particularly those in honor of Heracles and Dionysus (or Dionysos). In his series of *Greek Questions*, Plutarch asks, Διὰ τί παρὰ Κῴοις ὁ τοῦ Ἡρακλέους ἱερεὺς ἐν Ἀντιμαχείᾳ γυναικείαν ἐνδεδυμένος ἐσθῆτα καὶ τὴν κεφαλὴν ἀναδούμενος μίτρᾳ κατάρχεται τῆς θυσίας; ("Why is it that among the Coans the priest of Heracles at Antimacheia dons a woman's garb, and fastens upon his head a woman's head-dress before he begins the sacrifice?"; *Quaest. gr.* 58 [304c] [Babbitt]). The male worshipers of these gods would engage in "ritual transvestism," donning feminine apparel in order to "show themselves off as ambisexed beings, striving to transcend gender categories" (Frontisi-Ducroux and Lissarrague 1990, 228–29). What is significant to note here is that this behavior does not fit with the transcendent male androgyne that Boyarin has described. Males are not altering their masculinity to heighten certain virtues such as self-control or moderation. Instead, there is a *taking on* of the female in order to become transcendent.

With regard to the followers of Dionysus, many observers regarded this ritual transvestism (or at least effeminacy) as a shameful activity. The Roman historian Livy criticizes the male followers for behaving like the women (as well as for being debauched), saying, "deinde simillimi feminis mares" ("there are men very like the women"; *Ab urbe cond.* 39.15.9 [Sage]),[26] while in his *Life of Apollonius of Tyana* Philostratus records an episode where Apollonius criticizes the Bacchants, saying that they are "γυναικομίμῳ δὲ μορφώματι" ... αἰσχρῶς διαπρέπον ("shamefully resplendent in 'woman-like' disguise"; 4.21 [Jones]). In addition, Apollonius derides these male followers for not living up to the virtues of heroic soldiers and victors who are described as ἀγαθοὺς ἄνδρας ("brave souls"; 4.21 [Jones]).[27] In Euripides's play *Bacchae*, King Pentheus protests the wearing of feminine apparel: τί δὴ τόδ'; εἰς γυναῖκας ἐξ ἀνδρὸς τελῶ; ... τίνα στολήν; ἢ θῆλυν; ἀλλ' αἰδώς μ' ἔχει ("What is this? Am I from being a man to join the category of women?... In what dress? Female? But I feel shame"; lines 822, 828 [Seaford]). Paul likewise describes the Corinthians' behavior (1 Cor 11:4–7, 13–15) with language of shame and reflects the dominant elite view of sex and gender.

But for those followers of these derided cults, whose views do not exist in writing, to be dressed as women, "to be seen as womanish," was either not something shameful or was something shameful but was possibly embraced for being subversive and potentially liberating. Dionysus himself was closely associated with feminine clothing; the other name by which he is known, Bacchus, is derived from the word βασσάρα, a woman's dress (Farnell 1971, 5:160). Heracles is hardly any less masculine or heroic for his choice to wear women's clothing in various legends; see in particular the stories of his clothing exchange with Omphele, and the choice of Athena (herself a fascinating blend of gender characteristics) to give him a πεπλός, a distinctly feminine piece of clothing, as a gift (Loraux 1990). Since the Corinthians were primarily Greco-Roman in their religious background and cultural environment, it is possible that an alternative, subdominant, view of gender could be operating in Corinth.

Boyarin (2003, 35 n. 9) does note some exceptions to this dominant view of gender, commenting, "To be sure, there are representations in late antique Christianity of males 'becoming female' as well." These examples clearly postdate the situation in Corinth by several centuries and are predominantly examples of the emulation of female virgins, although they offer some possibility that this process of male feminization did occur in Christian contexts.[28] But the figures of Dionysus and Heracles are hardly associated with sexual restraint. Heracles can be described as "the Greek hero of virility" (Loraux 1990, 22, 25), and although portrayals of Dionysus tend to alternate between that of "hyper-virility" (Frontisi-Ducroux and Lissarrague 1990, 232 n. 109) and "scarcely sexed" (Lissarrague 1990, 59; see also Zeitlin 1990, 454), his followers were criticized for "sexual debauchery"(Verdenius 1980, 7).[29] Consequently, although there is no reliable account of the cultic behavior from the viewpoint of those who were actually involved, portrayals of their festivities and rituals strongly suggest that celibacy and the traditional virtues of moderation and self-control were *not* aspects of their practices of spiritual transcendence.

The mythic and religious behavior of both the gods and their male followers therefore reveals a complex interplay of ancient sex-gender ideologies. Perhaps scrambling the conventional codes of sexed and gendered behavior in *specifically* religious contexts—on *special* days, at certain festivals—enabled the worshipers to attain spiritual transcendence. But it might also serve to reinforce the sexed and gendered *norms* for every other *normal* day. As D. Martin (2001, 106) suggests, sometimes those aspects of a culture that appear to contradict the dominant construct of masculinity might in fact be reinforcing that dominant ideology: "contradictions, rather than revealing weaknesses in the structure of the ancient ideology of the masculine, actually worked to ensure its strength."

I would argue that it is still possible, however, for there to be a sub-dominant view of sex and gender at work in the behavior of those males who sought spiritual transcendence through the taking on of the feminine. This has to do with the element of shame that I mentioned earlier. It also has to do with Foucault's (1990a, 92–98) work on power relations and the way that even when being repressive or constraining, it can also be productive and resistant. In other words, when the dominant ideology attempts to enforce a sense of shame on those who defy the expected norms of behavior, it is possible that they can lay claim to it, "at once intensifying it and converting it into a potent sense of identity—and, paradoxically, also of identity's dissolution" (Burrus 2008, 8).

Virginia Burrus (2008, 8) has considered the ways in which Christian martyrs and saints did not just attempt to convert shame into something honorable, or to replace it with guilt, but were engaged in "the shameless courting of *dis*grace."[30] Drawing on Sedgwick's (2003, 31–38, 62–65) argument for a close relationship between shame, identity, and the Butlerian notion of performativity, Burrus (2008, 8) explores the ways in which such "defiant shamelessness" can give rise to a "queered identity that retrieves dignity without aspiring to honor."[31] Shame thus has a "paradoxical power" in its ability to transform, shift, destabilize, and forge identity (Burrus 2008, 11). For those male worshipers of Dionysus or Heracles who did *not* heed Musonius Rufus's warning to "avoid appearing as womanish at all costs" and possibly even courted the chance to be the "dreadful spectacle" Epictetus ranted about (*Diatr.* 3.1.29), playing with the established sex- and gender-identity constructs had transcendent potential. As Burrus explains, albeit in relation to the martyrs and ascetics she is "outing":[32]

> What such assertions of identity meant, and what they might still mean, was and remains open and unpredictable—ever "to-be-constituted." Perhaps that is the point: at its most productive the performance of a shamed and shameless identity opens up hitherto closed spaces, challenges prevailing assumptions, and thereby creates new social and political possibilities. (2008, 43)

Without wanting to determine that this is the only possible background to 1 Cor 11:2–16, I suggest that the Corinthian male worshipers, by virtue of their "shameful" behavior, may well be additional examples of men who challenged the accepted sex-gender ideology. Whatever it was they were doing with their hair or clothing, it is possible to imagine that they were taking on the feminine in order to become transcendent. As "womanish," they were no longer deemed "real men," and yet I can imagine that they were defiant in their shame. Thus they are men who are examples of the contradictions and noncoincidences of experience and language that can only be seen out of the corner of one's eye. They are easily missed, fragmentary and fractured, tentative, uncertain, and most certainly unauthorized. They seem to abide in the interstices of representation, on the boundaries of identity, and as such their voices are seldom heard (they are ignored or deemed hypothetical), and their motives are often misconstrued (they are wrongly labeled as homosexual).

I suggest, therefore, that the Corinthian men may be described as conceptual, theoretical lesbians, men who have challenged the dominant sex-gender ideology, who stand outside the category of their sex and thus experience disidentification and displacement, who radically symbolize a reconceptualization of the subject. Boyarin (2003, 25) concluded that "Wittig's lesbian is another version of the woman of Hellenistic Judaism or early Christianity made male and thus free through celibacy." But I propose that this be rephrased: the men of Corinthian Christianity are another version of Wittig's lesbian, made *not*-men and thus free through the shameless taking on of the female.

Notes

* Earlier versions of this chapter are found in Townsley 2007, 2011. As already noted in ch. 1, the title comes from Wittig's essay of the same name, which was first read at the Modern Language Association conference in 1978, where she infamously suggested that "lesbians are not women." The present chapter discusses this idea in more detail.

1. Although these French feminist theorists do not always sit comfortably with one another in terms of the theory they each espouse, they are often grouped together (Fuss 1989, 40; Shaktini 1994, 213; Cooper 2000, 21 n. 50). On Wittig and de Beauvoir, see Hewitt 1990, 130–31. On Wittig, de Beauvoir, and Irigaray, see Schor 1995; Butler 1999, 14–40, 143–44. On Wittig and Irigaray, see Günther 1998. On Wittig and Kristeva, see Butler 1999, 169. On Wittig and Cixous (and their legendary disagreements), see Wenzel 1981; Crowder 1983; J. Allen 1988, 108–9; Birkett 1996, 93–94; Bourcier 2005.

2. Exceptions are the essays "The Point of View" (1992f), which was first published as "Avant-note" to Barnes 1982, 7–21; and "The Site of Action" (1992h), first

published as "Le lieu de l'action" in the journal *Digraphe* (1984, 69–75). Some confusion exists over the publication details of Wittig's works, however; for example, the article "Homo Sum" (1992e) is listed as appearing in *Feminist Issues* (10/2) in the publication details page of *The Straight Mind* (1992g), whereas it is in fact found in issue 1; the article "The Place [or Site] of Action" (1992d) is said to be translated by Evelyn de Costa Beauregard in the bibliography of works by Monique Wittig in *On Monique Wittig*, but in fact the correct spelling is Evelyne Costa de Beauregard (Shaktini 2005b, 201).

3. Rubin (1975, 171) cites Wittig's novel *Les Guérillères* regarding the exchange of women: those who have been "betrayed beaten seized seduced carried off violated and exchanged as *vile and precious merchandise*" (italics indicate the citation from *Les Guérillères*). With regard to Sedgwick, R. Chambers (2002, 178) includes Wittig in the literary tradition to which she belongs; see also Barber and Clark 2002, 23.

4. On the differences between Anglo-American and French feminism and the divide between essentialist and social constructionist theories of gender (or "difference" and "equality" feminisms) that runs through both, see Allen and Young 1989, 1–17; Braidotti 1994; Schor 1995; Joy, O'Grady, and Poxon 2002.

5. This also reminds me of the way in which Wittig's *Lesbian Body* is also structured. She notes, "The book is thus formed in two parts. It opens and falls back on itself. One can compare its form to a cashew, to an almond, to a vulva" (2005b, 48).

6. Of course, a third role (of many in her life) that ought not to be neglected is that of political activist, from the revolutionary acts of the MLF (Mouvement de Libération des Femmes), of which she was a founding member in Paris during the early 1970s, through to her involvement with CLAGS (Center for Lesbian and Gay Studies) in New York in the 1990s.

7. Although Wittig critiques both dialectics and materialism, citing their lack of recognition of the political dimension of the division between the sexes, she does not reject an overall Marxist framework. In particular, she acknowledges her debt to the analyses of Delphy and Guillaumin in this regard and accepts Delphy's phrase *materialist feminism* as an apt descriptor of her own approach (1992e, 16–18; 1992g, xiv).

8. Wittig's focus on the lesbian figure has been critiqued for excluding gay men (Hennessy 1993, 971). Hale (1996, 118 n. 6) suggests that this misreads Wittig as a lesbian separatist; for him the issue with Wittig lies more with whether gay men count as men in her view.

9. Wittig argues that Marxism rejects the notion of the individual subject, emphasizing the way in which individuals are products of social relations whose class consciousness is the primary determining factor in their sense of identity. This view recognizes the constraints placed on individuals because of their economic and social classes, but for Wittig (and other feminists) Marxism has ignored the equally important constraint of gender (1992b, 47–49; 1992e, 18).

10. This will become clearer when I consider *The Lesbian Body* in ch. 6.

11. Butler also gives another example, of being asked if she was a woman or a man, and explains her choice to claim the label "woman" as follows: "I commit this violence against myself in the name of a certain kind of politics that would be ill-served if I were not to use that language" (Olson and Worsham 2000, 743).

12. Many of the citations from this article are also found in Boyarin 1993b, 1998.

13. See also Boucher 1969; Theissen 1987, 165–67; Collins 1999, 412; F. Watson 2000b, 524; Hjort 2001, 58, 69; Gorman 2004, 266; A. Johnson 2004, 198; Payne 2009, 193.

14. In fact, very few (if any) scholars do *not* comment on Gen 1–2 in relation to 1 Cor 11:2–16. Significant discussion on the connection between these passages (albeit with a diverse range of possible implications) can be found in Fee 1987, 512–18; Jervis 1993; Gundry-Volf 1997; Thiselton 2000, 833–37; Peerbolte 2000; J. Thompson 2003; Webb 2004a; Merkle 2006.

15. Although stating in his earlier article that 1 Cor 11:2–16 is *the* "crucial text" for his analysis, he has eliminated virtually all references to Paul in the second article, and makes *no* reference to 1 Cor 11:2–16 at all. Boyarin considers texts such as the Gospel of Thomas, the various apocryphal Acts of the Apostles, including Acts of Paul and Acts of Andrew.

16. D'Angelo (1995, 149) also says this idea can be found in Tertullian's discussion on whether virgins are women. Tertullian's comment that perhaps "a virgin is some monstrous third sex with her own head" (*Virg.* 7.6) reminds me of Butler's (1999, 26, 144) description of Wittig's lesbian as a "third gender." I will discuss this idea of the "monstrous" female/lesbian in ch. 6.

17. For the account of Thekla, see Acts Paul 25, 40. For Maximilla, see Acts Andr. 40–41. For Mary, see Gos. Thom. 114. See also the discussion of these and other accounts in Castelli 1991a.

18. Boyarin (2003, 25) comments, "the enormous difference that sexual pleasure is not denied Wittig's lesbian." However, see comments below by Wittig scholars who suggest that the issue of sexual pleasure is irrelevant to the concept of Wittig's lesbian.

19. In his earlier article, Boyarin (1998, 127) suggests, "In Wittig's writing, not being a lesbian, that is, 'being a woman,' seems finally as pejorative as it was in Philo and [the] patristic writings."

20. I have not considered the rabbinic view of gender that Boyarin outlines (and connects with the theories of Irigaray), but suffice to say that the belief in a dual-sexed primordial creature results in sexual difference being reified; both opposite-sex relations and male dominance are thus grounded in creation (Boyarin 2003, 27).

21. This reminds me of the opening of Wittig's *Lesbian Body* in which the reader is called to say "farewell" to "affection tenderness or gracious abandon" and to enter into "the slow sweet poisoned country from which one cannot return" (1976, 13–14). I will look at this more closely in ch. 6.

22. These concepts are drawn from the Pythagorean "Table of Opposites" concept as developed by Aristotle (*Metaph.* 985b23–986b9). Boyarin is drawing on the works of Silverman and Lloyd at this point (Silverman 1992, 15–62; G. Lloyd 1992, 1–9; see also Wittig 1992b, 49–51). I will also discuss this in ch. 4, in the section on the category of woman, "The Human-Not-Quite-Human."

23. Wittig (1992b, 47) notes that Marx and Engels affirmed "the necessity for the most radical groups to show their point of view and their interests as general and universal."

24. Wittig (1992c, 8) states that her book *Lesbian Body* can be considered "a reverie about the beautiful analysis of the pronouns *je* and *tu* by the linguist Emile Benveniste" (see also Wittig 2005b, 47).

25. Nor have those who preceded him in this area, notably Meeks 1974; D. MacDonald 1987. This is an observation Brooten (1988, 295) makes of MacDonald's reconstruction.

26. However, Livy is more concerned about the threat to the state posed by "the Bacchanalia" than about effeminacy as such: "minus tamen esset is flagitiis tantum effeminato forent—ipsorum id magna ex parte dedecus erat" ("Yet it would be less serious if their wrongdoing had merely made them effeminate—that was in great measure their personal dishonour"; *Ab urbe cond.* 39.16.1 [Sage]).

27. Conybeare (Philostratus 1953) translated ἀγαθοὺς ἄνδρας as "good men."

28. Boyarin (2006) discusses various examples in both rabbinic Judaism and Christianity in late antiquity where the figure of the female virgin is viewed as a positive model for men to emulate, frequently in contrast to the negative hypersexualized masculine model of Rome as empire (see also N. Harrison 1994; Burrus 2000).

29. Euripides, *Bacch.* 225, 354. On the "sex reversal" behavior of male followers of Dionysus (and the goddess Cybele), see also C. Kroeger 1987a, 37.

30. Burrus (2008, 44–80) also considers the shame of Jesus's execution on the cross in light of Kristeva's concept of abjection.

31. Halperin and Traub (2009, 7) also consider Sedgwick's work in their reflections on "gay pride." Burrus (2008, 42) notes the "festively ritualized demonstrations of shamelessly asserted identity" associated with Gay Pride parades, but notes that "dignity" might now be a more accurate term for naming "the effects of a performative claiming of worthiness that converts shame to shamelessness while refusing the temptation of triumphalism."

32. Burrus's (2008, 9) hope is "to 'out' the persisting shame of the ancient Christians."

Scene 1

So, I ask her, how do *you* see queer theory? It's a hard question to ask her right now. She has just quit, tossing her tiara and lasso of truth behind her. Stormed off in a rage, right off the cover of the comic I am holding and slumped into the chair in the corner of my study. She runs her hands through her thick blue-black hair, and I can't help but notice the tarnish on her silver bracelets as she holds her head in her hands.

Let me guess, I say. You've had your fill of the evils of Man's world, is that it? The cover tells me so but I ask her anyway. She just nods. I rifle through the other comics in the box I've been sorting through. I'm not surprised, I say, you've had a rough ride! So much for the mighty Amazon princess coming to rid the world of patriarchy—what happened *here*? She winces as I hold up a bright pink comic from 1961. She is being pulled in three different directions: "Mer-Man! *I'm* going to marry Wonder Woman!" "No, Amoeba-Man, *I* am!" "Tell them you are going to marry *ME*, Wonder Woman!" demands Steve Trevor. She closes her eyes as her head rests on the back of the chair and she lets out a sigh.

I try and lift her spirits. There was *this*, I say, and I carefully pull the first issue of *Ms.* magazine from a bookshelf. She's on the cover, looking slightly anxious as she saves small-town America while the Vietnam War rages in the background. The headline proclaims, "Wonder Woman for President," and we both shudder involuntarily, suddenly thinking of who might be running in the next race. Cup of tea, I ask? She shakes her head, declining, and reaches for another comic.

Ah yes. There is some classic girl-on-girl action on this cover. No kissing, of course, but the question has often been asked. Is she a ...? You know she comes from an all-woman Greek island, fans whisper. She tosses the comic on the floor and hands me (from where?) the latest issue, December 2010, and she's da Vinci's Vitruvian Man—it's a stunning cover. The enigmatic Amazon makes a great Universal Man. You're hard to categorize, I tell her; I guess you won't be hopping back in the comic box then?! She rolls her eyes at me as she stands up. She recoils her lasso, and I notice a small smile on her lips as she places the tiara back on her head.

Suffering Sappho, I think I hear her say, and she heads out the front door.

4

The Straight Mind in 1 Corinthians 11:3

The revolt takes places in this manner: the tail end of the beast tightens itself upon an object in the water, a stone or a twig, and vigorously shakes from itself the head end ... disavowing the domination of the old head that has made all the decisions with its brain and eyes. *The subindividual, become individual itself, is now headless and self-decisive.* In turn the individuals of itself may revolt from the new growing head in their time. AHH!
— Michael McClure, "Revolt" (emphasis added)[1]

Θέλω δὲ ὑμᾶς εἰδέναι ὅτι παντὸ ἀνδρὸς ἡ κεφαλὴ ὁ Χριστός ἐστιν, κεφαλὴ δὲ γυναικὸς ὁ ἀνήρ, κεφαλὴ δὲ τοῦ Χριστοῦ ὁ θεός.
But I want you to know that the head of every man is Christ, and the head of woman is man, and the head of Christ is God.
— 1 Cor 11:3

Introduction

Having considered the possibility of lesbianizing the "problematic" men of Corinth, I now turn to a closer exploration of some of the issues that emerge from the text itself. Wittig's theory asks us to consider how language operates in the domain of ideology, and she warns us about the power of language to act upon the social reality, "stamping it and violently shaping it" (1992c, 78). She argues that ideology—defined as "the discourses of the dominating group"—primarily serves to reinforce heterosexuality (1992a, 25), and she suggests that this occurs through rhetoric that "envelops itself in myths, resorts to enigma, proceeds by accumulating metaphors, and ... poeticize[s] the obligatory character of the 'you-will-be-straight-or-you-will-not-be'" (28). Such a description could hardly be more apt for 1 Cor 11:2–16.

Paul is using deliberative (political) rhetoric to effect some change in the Corinthians' behavior.[2] Yet, as we have seen, many scholars suggest that Paul is not altogether certain of his own stance on this issue, is struggling to work out his own theology of gender and is thus "convoluted" and "confused" in his argumentation. Of course, we have also seen other scholars suggest that Paul's argument is, by contrast, "clear" and it is rather our misunderstanding of the issues involved that has created a sense of confusion regarding Paul's logic. Paul uses a combination of rhetorical devices in this passage in order to persuade the Corinthians of his argument, beginning with praise (v. 2, in contrast to v. 17), presenting himself as a model to emulate (vv. 1, 3, and 16), an appeal to the Hebrew Bible (Gen 1 and 2, in vv. 7–12), threats of shame and dishonor (vv. 4–6, 14), appeals to nature (v. 14), and concluding with a comment on contentiousness intended to encourage unity (v. 16) (Mitchell 1993, 39, 48, 150–51, 260–63, 282; see also Heil 2005, 173–88). Through such rhetoric Paul is hoping to influence the behavior of these men and women who are praying and prophesying in a way that is somehow both in line with the traditions that he has taught them (v. 2), and yet also no longer within the bounds of what some others (possibly including Paul himself) deem acceptable. However, he does not appear to be entirely confident in his stance. The power dynamic operating between the apostle and "his" congregation has shifted in his absence and is no longer entirely in his favor (Fee 1987, 6–11; Phua 2005, 172–99).[3] All of this suggests that this is a passage not only full of ideological content that has the potential to "stamp" and "shape" social reality, but it is also full of instability and ambiguity that gives it the possibility of being que(e)ried.

For the rest of this book I will narrow the focus of my investigation to three sections only from this passage; verses 3, 7, and 14–15a, with the discussion of verse 3 constituting this present chapter.[4] Paul's statements in these three sections convey to many readers (historically and currently) a sense of metaphysical truth going beyond any specific cultural context, thus reinforcing certain notions of social order and, in particular, certain ideologies of gender and sexuality. Consequently these verses have been the source of much discussion in both feminist and conservative Christian circles, and in both ecclesial and academic settings, regarding matters such as gender roles in the family and the church, and issues of same-sex relationships. Because my interest lies in exploring the ways in which this passage has been used to bolster a heteropatriarchal relational model, rather than in the exegetical and historical issues pertaining to the text, the scope of the discussion on these verses will be broad. I will draw on a range of diverse material and intersecting various lines of inquiry *across* these verses in ways that might not typically be expected from a study of this passage. But it is precisely this sort of approach that is required in order to reveal and challenge the ideologies of gender and sexuality, as well as the politics and power relations that inform the ways in which this passage is interpreted and utilized. As Wittig (1992i, 30) argues, it is not enough to be aware of the power language has to shape the social reality; it is also necessary to be strategic and to "produce a political transformation of the key concepts" of that language.

Κεφαλή—Heteronormative Body Politics

Verse 3 contains the hierarchical language of male "headship" and has thus been used in conservative contexts to justify male leadership and domination in the family, church, and even the state. This view of male-female (husband-wife) relationships has been challenged in recent decades and sparked much debate about the meaning of κεφαλή ("head") in this verse, a debate that in evangelical circles in the United States has been particularly political and antagonistic. While traditional approaches to this verse seek to determine the meaning of κεφαλή and find themselves caught between the polarized options of either *authority over* or *source, origin*, I will instead explore the ideological and political nature of the debate. As a result, I find myself enmeshed in debates about traditional family values and the centrality of the nuclear family in capitalist society. I will also consider a third interpretive possibility for κεφαλή, namely, that it means *prominent, foremost, preeminent*, which has been posited as a way out of this "exegetical deadlock" (Lakey 2010, 4). Rather than simply grasping hold of this alternative and being grateful that a more nuanced understanding of metaphor has been presented, I will probe a little deeper into the implications of what it might mean to say that man is *prominent, foremost, preeminent* in relation to woman.

In addition, verse 3 outlines an ontological hierarchy, with God at the top, followed by Christ, then man, and woman at the bottom. Paul's hierarchical view of human and cosmological relations is also apparent in Rom 1:18–32, a passage that is often connected with 1 Cor 11:2–16. By comparing these divinely instituted hierarchies and considering three of the positions within this schema—that of "Human/Man," "Female/Woman," and "Christ"—I will be delving into ambiguous and marginal spaces that lie between the supposedly stable and clear elements of a hierarchical framework. As such I will be drawing on material that ranges from Aristotle and the Council of Chalcedon, to contemporary ecofeminism and queer Christology.

Immediately after the *captatio benevolentiae* with which he opens this passage (v. 2),[5] Paul outlines a series of three parallel pairs of relationships that center on the word κεφαλή: every man and Christ, woman and man,[6] and Christ and God. At the center of this triptych we find the fundamental pairing of woman and man, a pairing around which the whole passage revolves. It is here, in this pairing, that Paul headlines a theology of gender that reinforces heteronormativity for many current interpreters: κεφαλὴ δὲ γυναικὸς ὁ ἀνήρ ("the head of woman is the man"). If the NRSV translation is accepted—"The husband is the head of his wife"—this even further reinforces the connection with heteronormativity as it is within the specific institution of heterosexual marriage that heteronormativity is buttressed (Wittig 1992a, 6–7); the addition by the NRSV of the possessive "his" even further reinforces this notion.[7] Certainly in its binary opposition of man and woman (or husband and wife),[8] and in its sense of hierarchy, this statement in verse 3 supports interpretations that reinforce a heteronormative ideology. In order to probe deeper into this ideology, two issues require examination. The first is the concept of κεφαλή, which is at the heart of this verse and central to debates over gender in contemporary Christian contexts. The second is the hierarchy that underlies the verse as a whole and the ambiguous ontological categories positioned within it.

Wittig's description of the relationship between man and woman is useful when considering the central pairing of κεφαλὴ δὲ γυναικὸς ὁ ἀνήρ. Wittig (1992e, 9–11) discusses the "myth of woman," a crucial concept underpinning heteronormativity in which women form a "natural group" existing in a "subservient" relationship to men.[9] Women are perceived as "natural" in that they are seen as sexual beings defined by the capacity to give birth and have a relationship with men based on physical, personal, and economic obligation, a relationship that Wittig deems artificial and purely political in origin. She notes that this is centered on the marriage relationship and describes it as follows: "The category of sex is the product of a heterosexual society in which men appropriate for themselves the reproduction and production of women [the raising of children and the work of domestic chores] and also their physical persons by means of a contract called the marriage contract" (1992a, 6).[10]

The key element within this relationship, according to Wittig (1992a, 4), is the Marxist notion of "domination." This concept conveys the idea that between various groups in society there exists a power dynamic where one group exerts hegemonic control over the other, be that economic, political, social, or sexual, *and* that this control (or domination) be accepted as "natural," based on the supposed differences between the groups. Marx and Frederick Engels explain:

> The ideas of the ruling class are in every epoch the ruling ideas, i.e. the class which is the ruling *material* force of society, is at the same time its ruling *intellectual* force.... The ruling ideas are nothing more than the ideal expression of the dominant material relationships, the dominant material relationships grasped as ideas: hence of the relationships which make the one class the ruling one, therefore, the ideas of its dominance. (1939, 39)

Wittig (1992a, 5) employs this term to describe the relationship between the sexes, explaining that "this thought which impregnates all discourses, including common-sense ones (Adam's rib or Adam *is*, Eve is Adam's rib), is the thought of domination. Its body of discourses is constantly reinforced on all levels of social reality and conceals the political fact of the subjugation of one sex by the other." In her analysis, men are the ruling class, who have determined that their domination be viewed as "natural" given the "natural" differences between the sexes. This relationship is therefore heterosexual, based on the reproduction of the species, and is legitimized through the marriage contract. Wittig likens the relationship between man and woman to the relationship between employer and worker, at best, and slave owner and slave, at worst (1992a, 6, 8; 1992e, 20).

Most commentators regard κεφαλή as the key word of this verse if not of the whole passage.[11] If, as some scholars suggest, this word can be understood metaphorically to mean *authority over*, then perhaps Paul has placed something akin to the Marxist notion of dominance at the center of the relationship between "man and woman," and/or "husband and wife." However, the debates over the meaning of κεφαλή are so contentious they have become legendary (Thiselton 2000, 811–22). The traditional metaphorical meaning for κεφαλή is *authority over*, and it is usually pitted against the meaning *source, origin*, often suggested as a more egalitarian interpretation.[12] Scholars have tended to argue strongly for one meaning or the other,[13] often making statements that completely contradict those of other scholars and thus appear impossible to reconcile.

An examination of the scholarship in this area reveals not only the polemical nature of the debate but also points to its political nature, perhaps nowhere more obviously than in the United States,[14] providing some fascinating insights into what might be called the politics of the body, or body politics. As will become clear, it is in debate over what Paul meant by κεφαλὴ δὲ γυναικὸς ὁ ἀνήρ that politics and bodies/heads clash. Screeds of material have been written on exegetical and lexicographical details, and the debate has often been on this "surface" level. But on a deeper level, the debate reveals ideologies of gender and sexuality that have significant political ramifications. As Wittig (1992a, 5) states, the subjugation of women by men is a *political* fact, but one that is often concealed behind a "body of discourses."

The clash of views on the meaning of κεφαλή is particularly evident in the contradictory statements by scholars on the *authority over/source, origin* dichotomy. For example, at the forefront of the *authority over* position, Grudem (1985, 52–53) declares that, in light of his survey of 2,336 examples, it is "very difficult to accept anyone's claim that *head* in Greek could not mean 'ruler' or 'authority over'"; and, further, "no instances were discovered in which κεφαλή had the meaning 'source, origin' ... it would seem wise to give up once for all the claim that κεφαλή can mean 'source.'" By contrast, Gordon Fee (1987, 502–3) states, "the metaphorical use of *kephalē* ('head') to mean 'chief' or 'the person of the highest rank' is rare in Greek literature ... this metaphorical sense is an exceptional usage and not part of the ordinary range of meanings for the Greek word. Paul's understanding of the metaphor, therefore, and almost certainly the only one the Corinthians would have grasped, is 'head' as 'source,' especially 'source of life.'" Others who hold this *source, origin* view make equally bold statements. Catherine Clark Kroeger (1987b, 267) asserts, "The concept of *head* as 'source' is well documented in both classical and Christian antiquity and has long been accepted by scholars."

On a deeper level, however, such polemic points to the political nature of the debate that is concealed behind the discourse and thus rarely addressed. Scholars who tend to follow the *authority over* position are invariably conservative in their views on the nature of the husband-wife relationship, seeing women's subordination as a central aspect of marriage and as a limiting factor within church ministry. It is not surprising, therefore, to see Grudem on the board of directors for the Council of Biblical Manhood and Womanhood (CBMW). This organization grew out of a concern with, among other things, "the widespread uncertainty and confusion in our culture regarding the complementary differences between masculinity and femininity ... the increasing promotion given to feminist egalitarianism … and behind all this the apparent accommodation of some within the church to the spirit of the age" (Piper and Grudem 2006a, 469).[15] On the other hand, scholars who prefer the *source, origin* option, tend to be more egalitarian in their approach to the roles of men and women in marriage and church ministry.[16] Again, it is not surprising that Kroeger was on the board of directors (as president emerita) and Fee is on the board of reference for the organization Christians for Biblical Equality (CBE). This organization was formed after some members of the Evangelical Women's Caucus (EWC) felt that this group was moving in a direction they perceived as "unbiblical" (specifically its affirmation of lesbianism).[17]

Both of these groups (CBMW and CBE) were formed in 1987[18] and are still active. Both claim to be evangelical in nature, affirming the divine inspiration of the Bible and seeking a biblical approach to contemporary issues, and both are concerned about preventing the breakdown of marriage and family and have a "welcoming but not affirming" approach to same-sex relationships (to borrow the title from Grenz 1998). Yet these organizations are diametrically opposed when it comes to the ideology underlying their views on the nature of men and women and how they are to relate to each other, socially, politically, economically, and spiritually. The influence of the scholars involved in these organizations, at least within Western evangelical circles, has been significant with regard to views of male-female relationships, marriage, and ministry in general, and the understanding of 1 Cor 11:2–16 (and other κεφαλή passages) in particular.[19] Therefore, I will take these two groups as case studies and explore their underlying political ideologies, to reveal what has tended to be concealed (or at least not made explicit) in this debate.

Central to the differences between these two groups is the aforementioned debate over the meaning of κεφαλή and the concept of "headship" that has come into common parlance in evangelical circles.[20] The foundational document for the CBMW is the Danvers Statement, which begins with the affirmation, "Both Adam and Eve were created in God's image, equal before God as persons and distinct in their manhood and womanhood" (Piper and Grudem 2006a, 469–72). It goes on to expand on this distinction by declaring that "Adam's headship in marriage was established by God before the Fall," with the subsequent call for husbands to exercise "loving, humble headship" and wives to exercise "intelligent, willing submission" (470; see also Grudem 2004, 30–42). A quick glance through Piper and Grudem's (2006b) book, *Recovering Biblical Manhood and Wom-*

anhood (which was especially commissioned as a project of the CBMW and which expands on the Danvers Statement), illustrates the centrality of 1 Cor 11:2–16 (and in particular 11:3) in the argument for the particular style of marriage and family that they affirm.[21] What emerges from reading through this book and other ones by Grudem (2004, 2006b) is an understanding of κεφαλή as *authority over* and a concept of "headship" that creates a picture of the family with the husband/father as the leader, sole breadwinner, and ultimate decision maker. The role of the woman is first and foremost that of "motherhood" and "vocational homemaking" (Piper and Grudem 2006a, 469).[22]

This binary role division, seen as based in the divinely ordained distinctions between the sexes, is further elaborated upon in one particular article concerned about "the unisex mentality that is gaining popularity in our society today" (Rekers 2006).[23] Throughout this article, Rekers talks much of the various roles in the family, church, and wider community that men and women are to take. Appropriate masculine sex roles include "financially supporting one's children," "abstaining from sexual relations with males," "playing professional sports on all-male teams," "serving in combat," "living in a fraternity," "wearing a suit and necktie," and "opening doors for women and girls" (307). Feminine sex roles include "being a mother," wearing "modest clothing of upper torso," "abstaining from sexual relations with females," "wearing a dress … lipstick … fingernail polish … [and] mascara," "living in a sorority," "carrying a purse," and "shaving underarms or legs" (307). Women are certainly *not* seen as contributing financially, playing sports of any kind, engaging in combat, or even wearing trousers (307). These examples tend to illustrate a particular image reminiscent of 1950s (white) middle-class America. In particular, they hardly conjure up an image of multicultural America or of those who live in poverty and who cannot afford a suit and tie, let alone to go to college.

A Marxist approach reminds us that this particular image of the American family—as white, middle-class, nuclear, and heterosexual, with the father as its head—is the basic economic unit of capitalist society. Given that the word *capitalism* originates from the Latin word for "head," *caput*, it is of no surprise that this concept of "head" is of "paramount importance" for Marx (Press 1977, 336 n. 18). Marx insisted that the dynamic of production and consumption, and the way in which they have become separated from each other in human society, is the root cause of alienation and oppression. He explains it thus: "As in the natural body, head and hand wait upon each other, so that the labor-process unites the labor of the hand with that of the head. Later on they part company and even become deadly foes" (1904, 283).[24] This separation between production and consumption, between the head and the body (the hand), is widened in capitalist society and is expressed most fundamentally in the patriarchal nuclear family.

The marriage relationship, according to Marx and Engels, consists of both the original division of labor—that of the sexual act—and the notion of private property, about which they say, "the nucleus, the first form … lies in the family, where wife and children are the slaves of the husband" (1939, 21). In his later book, *The Origin of the Family*, Engels discusses the emergence of the nuclear family as the basic economic unit of capitalist society. The monogamous family, as he describes it, is "based on the supremacy of the man" and enables the preservation and inheritance of property (1972, 125, 135, 138). For those in the "possessing classes," this supremacy is based on the obligation the man is under to earn a living and support his family: "that in itself gives him a position of supremacy without any need for special legal titles and privileges. Within the family he is the bourgeois and the wife represents the proletariat" (137). For the proletariat, he notes, for whom industry has taken the wife out of the home and into the factory, making her a breadwinner for the family, "no basis for any kind of male supremacy is left" (135).[25] Wittig's (1990a, 8) statement, "The category of sex is the category that ordains slavery for women," therefore finds a parallel in Engels's (1972, 137) statement, "The modern individual family is founded in the open or concealed domestic slavery of the wife." Engels goes on to forecast that

> the peculiar character of the supremacy of the husband over the wife in the modern family … will only be seen in the clear light of day when both possess legally complete equality of rights. Then it will be plain that the first condition for the liberation of the wife is to bring the whole female sex back into public industry, and that this in turn demands that the characteristic of the monogamous family as the economic unit of society be abolished. (137–38)

This, in many ways, is precisely what happened after the second wave of feminism in the 1970s in the West (Popenoe 1993). As women demanded economic freedom and returned to the workforce, they met strong resistance by those whose "supremacy" was threatened and the emergence in the United States of groups such as the CBMW, seeking a return to what they call "traditional family values."[26] The decline of the family was widely touted, but in particular it was the decline of the *nuclear* family that caused concern. David Popenoe (1993, 527) makes this point clear: "Recent family decline is more serious that any decline in the past because what is breaking up is *the nuclear family, the fundamental unit*" (emphasis added). For groups such as CBMW, these "traditional family values" are also seen as expressing biblical values, and therefore such changes in the structure of the family are not only perceived of as a *decline*—rather than as an increase in *diversity*, or even as *progress*, for example—but as a threat to what is seen as a Christian aspect of American culture.

"Traditional family values" were therefore a core issue for the Republican party during the 1980s and have remained an important platform in American politics during subsequent election cycles as evangelicals have become associated with the Christian Right political movement (Arnold and Weisberg 1996; Kivisto 1994; Coleman 2005). Abortion, divorce, premarital sex, cohabitation, transgender pregnancy, and homosexuality are all opposed in the promotion of "family values." Other groups that support these options, as well as affordable childcare, sex education, and parent-friendly employment laws, for example—which these groups also label as "family values"—are vilified and seen as not only anti-Christian but also anti-American.[27] During the 2000s this was also coupled with an upsurge in patriotism and anxieties about Islamic terrorism in light of the September 11 attacks. For example, in response to some strong critiques of the Bush government, the Traditional Values Coalition posted the comment: "A dangerous Marxist/Leftist/Homosexual/Islamic coalition has formed—and we'd better be willing to fight it with everything in our power" (Sheldon 2005). The flip-side of such a description can be found in Sarah Palin's book, *America by Heart* (2010), subtitled, *Reflections on Family, Faith, and Flag*. Such conflations of certain ethical, religious, and political beliefs indicate the capitalist, straight, white, Christian ideal that lies behind the conservative view of the "traditional family" in the United States. It is because the family structures that such statements describe are given theological and justification by biblical passages such as 1 Cor 11:2–16, in particular verse 3, that it is so vital to dig deeper into these underlying ideologies.

But what of the (comparatively) more liberal view? The statement of faith for CBE, entitled "Men, Women, and Biblical Equality," opens with the declaration, "The Bible teaches the full equality of men and women in Creation and in Redemption," and declares that both men and women "were created for full and equal partnership ... [and share] jointly the responsibilities for bearing and raising children and having dominion over the created order" (Bilezikian et al. n.d.). What this means in practice is developed more fully in the literature available on the CBE website and in their academic journal, *Priscilla Papers*. In accord with CBMW, the CBE material reveals that considerable attention is given to the concept of κεφαλή and how it is to be understood, particularly in relation to the topics of marriage and women in ministry. What emerges in these articles is an understanding of κεφαλή as "source," in the sense of that which is the "beginning of life" or "point of origin" and that which is thus "productive of growing life" (C. Kroeger 2006, 5). The husband is therefore seen as a "servant provider of life" and of "growth and development" (Bilezikian 2002). With regard to the issue of roles within marriage, Marissa Cwik, the Research Coordinator for CBE, states, "we firmly believe that each individual and couple should have the freedom to make the choice for themselves [regarding women in the workplace, childcare, etc.] based on a mutual decision and guidance from the Holy Spirit and not have a choice regulated to them based on cultural constructs of gender roles."[28]

Members of CBE thus have a more open view of family, recognizing and seeking to empower extended families, single- and dual-headed households, blended and divorced families, and they are also liberal on matters such as women in the workforce.[29] Nevertheless, as with CBMW, their view of family is also strictly heterosexual. One of their core beliefs, as expressed in their Statement of Faith, declares that they believe "in the family, celibate singleness, and faithful heterosexual marriage as God's design."[30] No less than their more conservative counterparts, they believe that bodies are still to be tightly regulated with regard to sex and desire, and heterosexuality is the only normative expression of sexuality (Payne 2006, 2009).

The article on "Homosexual Practice" by Kroeger (2004) is representative of the CBE position on this issue. She writes in response to the fear expressed by those such as Grudem regarding the supposed link between an affirmation of women's equality and an endorsement of homosexuality,[31] arguing that biblically this is not the case. Rather, Kroeger argues, it is biblical to be in favor of women's equality but against homosexuality. She states, "although the Bible contains a handful of references to same-sex eroticism, nowhere is there given any sign of approval to homosexual be-havior [*sic*]. Rather, there is loving sympathy for the individual but condemnation of the conduct" (3). After considering the Hebrew Bible accounts of male/female relations (focusing more on the affirmation of women, marriage, and sexuality than on the negative censure of the Leviticus passages, for example), she turns to the New Testament. With regard to the gospels, she notes Jesus's positive view of women in his reluctance to allow divorce and states that (as with the Hebrew Bible accounts), "Man and wo-man [*sic*] are given to enhance one another and together to reflect the image of God" (6).

It is in Kroeger's discussion of Paul, however, that her main reason for rejecting homosexual practice emerges. Rather than the speculation by the hierarchalists that an affirmation of women's equality might lead to an affirmation of homosexual practice, she considers the historical Greek view in which an affirmation of "homoeroticism" was instead connected with a rejection of women (6–7). The misogyny that was directed toward women in the ancient world, Kroeger argues, is clearly associated with a positive view of homoeroticism. It is also something she suggests is overturned in the New Testament, particularly by Paul: "The apostle's teaching could do much to heal the attitudes that had created a virulent hostility between the sexes" (7). She refers specifically to 1 Cor 11:11–12: "Paul deals with this repugnance [fear of women's sexual anatomy] when he writes that woman had issued forth from man, and now men came forth from women, in an interdependent cycle" (7).

Elsewhere Richard and Catherine Kroeger argue that the entire passage of 1 Cor 11:2–16 is Paul's attempt to address these negative attitudes to women. For example, his "recycling" of the Genesis creation account is to highlight "women as a gift from God and a treasure for man," to show that in contrast to the Greek creation myths, woman "was created for a positive purpose" (1979, 214). They also note: "The concepts of woman as the glory of man and 'neither the man without the woman nor the woman without the man' (v. 11) were important ones in combating the sex segregation which the Greeks themselves saw as a contributory factor in homosexuality" (217). They conclude, "Zeus, Apollo, Hercules, Eros, and even Aphrodite might opt for the love of boys; but Paul frames a positive endorsement of heterosexuality and an integrated Christian community, one body in the Lord" (218).[32]

To rephrase things, I would suggest that according to the Kroegers, the Greeks had a negative view of women, which if it did not directly lead them to embrace homoeroticism, was at least in some ways coupled with such a view. The CBE position, therefore, rejects this negative view of women and thus also rejects homosexuality (embracing heterosexuality instead). If Wittig is brought into the discussion at this point, some interesting connections and contradistinctions can be noted. Along with CBE, Wittig rejects the negative view of women she observes in (Western) society. However, in contrast to CBE, she argues that misogyny is an intrinsic aspect of heteronormativity, and thus she also rejects heterosexuality, embracing the only form of being she sees as outside of these normative categories of sex—lesbianism.

Such a spectrum of views on these issues highlights the complexity of the political and ideological positions, and the inadequacy of a simple "left-right" dichotomy. Despite the enormous gap between CBE and CBMW with regard to male and female roles in church and family life and their views on the meaning of κεφαλή, both groups are against homosexuality and subscribe to perhaps the most fundamental ideology of all, that of heteronormativity. Heterosexuality is the fundamental structure for both groups within which the male/female dynamic ought to operate, ultimately within what Wittig (1992a, 6) calls the "obligation" of marriage.[33] The debate over what Paul meant in 1 Cor 11:3 when he stated that "the head of woman is man" is not just a debate over the *authority over* or *source, origin* options. Despite appearances, it is not simply a matter of sifting through 2,336 examples of κεφαλή in Greek literature, nor of determining that Paul was less misogynistic that the Greeks. An agenda that privileges heteronormativity—be it one which emphasizes male control over female bodies/heads or one that allows more freedom for (certain) bodies—inevitably serves a capitalist political ideal. While the debate over κεφαλή could look like a debate between conservative and liberal value systems, that is only the surface part of it. Underneath is a much more systemic ideological connection to capitalist interests and investment in the family—in particular the role that the husband has to play in that transaction—all of which is given theological sanction by reference to biblical texts such as 1 Cor 11:3. Divergent views on κεφαλή show how such differences sustain heteronormativity and the reinscription of the nuclear family unit within capitalism.

So at this point, one might question if there is any room left to maneuver on the debate over the meaning of κεφαλή in this passage. Lakey (2010, 4–8, 33–35) notes both the "exegetical deadlock" of the debate and the combative nature of the evangelical movement in general and finds that the result has been a "polarization" over 1 Cor 11:3. However, some scholars have proposed a way of interpreting κεφαλή—as *prominent, foremost, preeminent*—that potentially moves the debate beyond the impasse of having to decide between *authority over* and *source, origin*;

and so it is to an exploration of this alternative that I now turn. My intention, however, is not to present this alternative as a way of resolving this debate, but to explore some of the (potentially beastly) implications of what it means to suggest that a man is *prominent, foremost, preeminent* in relation to woman.

In his rebuttal of Grudem, Richard Cervin (1989, 112) critiques the conclusions of both the *authority over* and *source, origin* proponents, concluding that Paul "does not mean 'authority over,' as the traditionalists assert, nor does he mean 'source' as the egalitarians assert. I think he is merely employing a head-body metaphor, and that his point is *pre-eminence*." A. C. Perriman (1994, 618) followed Cervin, suggesting that the most obvious metaphorical sense of κεφαλή is "that which is most prominent, foremost, uppermost, pre-eminent."[34] He also comments on the nature of the debate, suggesting that "a fresh perspective may expose the inadequacy of the interpretative dichotomy that has, with few exceptions, determined the shape and conclusions of the discussion" (602).[35] He states that the debate has been

> distorted by the force of polemical interests. The traditional view has been inspired perhaps partly by anachronistic physiological notions and partly by certain deep-seated presuppositions about social relations. The "source" interpretation, on the other hand, has been accepted rather uncritically by those seeking to excise from Pauline thought what is seen as the canker of sexual prejudice. It has proved a useful stone to throw at the traditional interpretation, but the aim has not been quite accurate. (617–18)[36]

The work of Cervin and Perriman was followed by a substantial work on metaphor by Gregory Dawes (1998). Although his focus is on Eph 5:21–33, Dawes notes that scholars behind both the *authority over* and *source, origin* positions have tended to neglect the importance of context in their methodology. He states, "Grudem's error, an error which he shares with his opponents, is his neglect of the fact that different (metaphorical) senses of a word are possible in different contexts" (128; see also A. Johnson 2009, 52). Dawes examines the head-body relationship as it appears in ancient medical texts and concludes that both *authority over* and *source, origin* are metaphorical senses of the word that were understood (131, 133). He concludes that in either case, because context will be far more useful for determining meaning, "one should beware of searching lexica in an attempt to discover the possible senses of the word κεφαλή" (133). In other words, if one begins by considering the importance of context when inter-preting metaphor, which the lexicographical word-count approach tends to overlook, an alternative semantic field emerges. One reason for this is that "a living metaphor" can be open to new interpretations; an author (or speaker) may choose to create a fresh meaning for the metaphor (122–23, 129, 133). Dawes argues that "if κεφαλή in a particular context is a newly-coined metaphor, it will be creative of meaning.... The particular nuances which a living metaphor conveys will emerge only from a study of the word in its context" (133). The key is thus in the polyvalence of the word from context to context, rather than in the strict adhesion to one preference.

Nevertheless, while a more carefully nuanced meaning for κεφαλή in this passage might be that which is "prominent, foremost, uppermost, pre-eminent," rather than either *authority over* or *source, origin*, is this any further removed from the Marxist concept of dominance that Wittig sug-gests is ultimately at the heart of the relationship between man and woman in society? Perriman (1994, 603–10) is at pains throughout the article to suggest that *leadership* and *authority* are not the issues here, but rather the point of κεφαλή is *representation*. However, scattered throughout his article is a revealing list of descriptors of the one who is the κεφαλή. In addition to being "prominent, foremost, uppermost, [and] pre-eminent," this person is described as the "most wonderful," "elevated," "outstanding," "most divine," "most prominent figure in the household," "the foremost embodiment of certain characteristics," "first and most noble," and "that which is first ... prominent or outstanding ... determinative or represen-tative by virtue of its prominence" (607–8, 610, 612–13, 618). This person has, or demonstrates, "prominence or excellence or social standing," "supe-riority," "priority and historical prominence," "an active, controlling influ-ence," as well as an "active and creative responsibility," and "'priority' in the order of being" (606–7, 612, 615–17). As if all this was not enough, this person is also described as "that which safeguards the life of the body," one who is "to stand out above," is "foremost in society," and who "by virtue of its prominence and excellence is able to motivate and inspire" (609–10, 612–13). All of this can be summed up by Perriman's point that this person is said "*to occupy the position at the top or front*" (616).

Perriman is correct to argue that such qualities do not automati-cally entail leadership, confer authority, or indicate origin. He explains, "A racing driver in 'poll' position is not the 'source' or the 'source of life' of the other drivers; nor, for that matter, does he have authority over them" (611–12). What is clear from Perriman's redefinition of the κεφαλή metaphor is that it is about status and honor, one's standing and ranking in relation to others. That it is also clearly the men who are (or at least, ought to be) in this position of prestige fits well with the constructs of Greco-Roman masculinity (outlined in ch. 2 above) in which honor and status were of paramount importance. Perriman concludes that Paul's references to glory and honor in 1 Cor 11:2–16 further reinforce this understanding of the metaphor:

> We might almost say that "man is the head of woman" and "woman is the glory of man" are reciprocal statements. This, moreover, is in keeping with the fundamental emphasis in the passage on the *appearance* of the man and woman: image and glory, unlike the abstract ideas of authority and source, are visual categories and appropriately embodied in the forms of personal attire. (621–22)

We ought to question two aspects of this third way through the κεφαλή debate, however. To begin with, there is the inference that men have an ontological status that is inherently *superior* to that of women. The traditional debate about κεφαλή often has to do with the practical outworking of its meaning in relation to gender roles, in particular whether women can exercise leadership roles in the home and church. But the descriptors listed above are much more deeply associated with personal qualities (virtues) and a sense of being, albeit one that is also relational (hence the notion of status). Indeed, *supremacy* is a term that has tended to be associated with the *authority over* position in this debate (Grudem 1985, 51; Fitzmyer 1989, 510; Thiselton 2000, 812). Consequently, Grudem may well be right when he argues that the suggestion of *preeminence* as an alternative meaning for κεφαλή "is congenial with (though not identical to)" the traditional position, a "modification" of the traditional position, "not a rejection of it" (1990, 5). In this way, the division between the traditional position and this third, supposedly alternative, option for understanding κεφαλή would appear to be dissolving. Indeed, for Christians for whom the text carries authoritative weight with regard to the debate over the roles of men and women within marriage and church (as was seen above regarding the CBMW and CBE), it may be more disturbing to conclude that men are divinely appointed to *be* ontologically superior than to concede that they might *have* a divinely appointed leadership role within the church and family.[37]

The second aspect of this position that needs to be questioned involves the description of those who are *not* designated as κεφαλή. Here I will focus on Perriman's examination of the "head-tail" imagery as found in Deut 28, Isa 9, and in Philo's *On Rewards and Punishments*. Perriman suggests that the contrast in these images is between the binary pair of head and tail, rather than the head and the body. In the binary pair of man and woman, the man is explicitly described as the κεφαλή; and although Perriman does not state that the woman is explicitly described as the "tail," she is certainly below the man, at the bottom of the social-sexual hierarchy, and so may be associated with the "tail."[38] Nevertheless, this association is not automatic. Although in 11:3 Christ is also paired with God, who is Christ's κεφαλή, I have yet to come across any work that suggests he therefore takes the position of "tail."[39]

With these points in mind, it is still useful to consider how the "tail" is designated in relation to the "head." In Deut 28:13 and 44 Israel is told that if they obey the law they will be blessed: "The Lord will make you the head [LXX κεφαλή, for ראש], not the tail." But if they disobey the law they will be cursed, needing to borrow from the aliens who "will rise higher and higher" (v. 43) while they "sink lower and lower" with the outcome that "he will be the head [LXX κεφαλή, for ראש], but you will be the tail." Perriman (1994, 606) argues against the meaning of *leader, chief* in these verses, suggesting rather that "the significance of the metaphor lies in the contrast between two extremes, between prominence and prosperity on the one hand and subjection and humiliation on the other." Elsewhere, in a message of judgment against those who have turned away from the Lord, Isa 9:13–14 says, "So the Lord will cut off from Israel both head [LXX ἀρχή for ראש] and tail, both palm branch and reed in a single day; the elders and prominent men are the head, the prophets who teach lies are the tail." Perriman (1994, 606), arguing against the meaning of *authority over*, states, "It seems clear that the 'head' is distinguished from the 'tail' by virtue of its prominence or excellence or social standing ... the tail is not that which is ruled but that which is disreputable."[40] With regard to the use of this "head-tail" imagery in Philo, Perriman (613) notes: "The analogy sets the head of an animal, which is 'first and noble' (πρῶτον καὶ ἄριστον), in contrast to the tail, which is good for little more than swatting flies ... the inferiority of the tail lies not in the fact that it is not the source, but in the ignobility of its function ... the contrast [is] between prominence and humiliation" (see Philo, *Rewards* 124–125).

To be the "tail," then, is to be that which is disreputable, and entails subjection, humiliation, ignobility, and inferiority. Clearly this stands in stark contrast to the one who is the "head." Again, issues of honor and shame abound (Osiek and MacDonald 2006, 7–9). With regard to 1 Cor 11:2–16, Perriman (1994, 620–21) concludes, "What mars the headship relationship, whether between man and woman or between Christ and man, is dishonour, not disobedience.... The primary theme in the passage concerns the shame that attaches to a woman who prays or prophecies with her head uncovered." While this passage in 1 Corinthians does not explicitly say that the one who is *not* the head *is* the tail, the inference is still clear; the position of "head" is one of high social status and honor, and those (women *and* men) who behave in ways that blur the distinctions between the sexes or challenge the status quo will bring shame not only upon themselves but also upon their "heads."

But perhaps even more disturbing is the notion that regardless of what they do, by their very position below men in the social-sexual hierarchy, women are *always* the tail in relation to men. They are never at the "top" of this hierarchy, only at the "bottom." The historical association between women's physical heads and their genitals in the minds of men only reinforces this view (D'Angelo 1995; T. Martin 2004). Mary Rose D'Angelo explains:

> For early Christian men, as, it seems, for men of antiquity in general, women's heads were indeed sexual members, and at least two of these men, Paul and Tertullian, expended much thought and no little ink in efforts to enforce the sexual character of women's heads. Their association of women's heads and genitals seems to be entirely conscious; in the case of Tertullian, it is startlingly explicit....
>
> Both decapitate the women of the community in the interests of the superior status of men. (1995, 131–32)

Women are less of a *who* than a *what*; they are not the active subject who is decisive and vocal—the head that thinks and speaks—but the passive object who is decapitated and voiceless, fit only for the erotic male gaze. Ultimately, this "headless" woman ends up veiled and silent—"invisible and inaudible" (F. Watson 2000a, 82–83). Such is the "beastly" nature of this metaphor.

To conclude this section on κεφαλή on such a depressing note is difficult. Wittig (1992c, 81) acknowledges how the effect of the imposition of gender upon women "is to deprive women of the authority of speech, and to force them to make their entrance in a crablike way, particularlizing themselves and apologizing profusely." In many ways, however, some sense of hope can be found in this "beastly" situation. By drawing again on Foucault's assertion that there is power in resistance, Sedgwick's argument for a close relationship between shame and identity formation, and the ways in which scholars such as Burrus, Halerpin, and Valerie Traub have all recognized the potential for a reclamation of a sense of self through "the shameless courting of *dis*grace" (Burrus 2008, 8), it might be possible for women to regain their voice, their heads, their identities, but I suspect *not* as "women" but as "eccentric subjects" (de Lauretis 2005, 55–58).

I noted in the previous chapter how Burrus (2008, 8) explains that it is not only "a potent sense of identity" that is formed in this performance of reclamation but also "identity's dissolution." Indeed, Wittig (1992c, 81) makes this clear in her comments following immediately on from those cited above: "Gender then must be destroyed." This is accomplished through the "exercise of language" and the reclamation of speech: "It is when starting to speak that one becomes 'I'" (80). Without wanting to attempt to rescue or redeem Paul, as if this one snippet of information could counter his unsurprising complicity in the sex-gender ideologies of Mediterranean culture, I also find it hopeful to note that his assumption in 1 Cor 11:2–16 is that women will speak. They are "praying and prophesying" (v. 5), and Paul is not attempting to silence them. A line from Michael McLure's (1966, 58) essay that opened this section is perhaps an apt descriptor of these women: "The subindividual, become individual itself, is now headless and self-decisive."

Ambiguous Ontologies

As noted at the outset of the previous section, Paul sets out three parallel pairs of relationships in 1 Cor 11:3 that center on the word κεφαλή. After considering not only the meaning of this key word but also some of the ideologies underlying the ways in which it can be interpreted, we may now consider the ontological hierarchy underlying this verse as a whole. The central pairing of man and woman in this verse is enveloped within two relational statements that include God and Christ: "The head of every man is Christ … and the head of Christ is God." Such placement could easily have the effect of justifying binary, hierarchical relations through a sense of divine ordering. As Økland states:

> In 11.1–3, the relationship between woman and man is presented as analogous with the relationship between Christ and God. The first impli-

cation of this is that gender difference has theological significance, since it must reflect on a microcosmic level the relationship between the two most important figures in Paul's theology: Christ and God. Secondly, Paul gives *his* understanding of the gender difference a theological sanction, since it is cast as equivalent to the relationship between Christ and God. (2004, 177)

Most scholars see verse 3 as clearly outlining a descending hierarchy of origin, or authority, or both, originating in God and descending down through Christ, to men, and finally to women.[41] Perhaps the most blunt comment comes from Troels Engberg-Pedersen (1991, 681): "there is a certain ontological hierarchy with God at the top and with men being closer to Christ and (through him) to God than women, who are one step farther down the hierarchy."[42] D. Martin (1995a, 232) notices the hierarchical structure of each pairing, as well as of the overall structure of the three pairings, and outlines a homology to illustrate this:

CHRIST is to MAN

as

MAN is to WOMAN

as

GOD is to CHRIST

Another place in Paul's writings where a similar framework operates is in Rom 1:18–32. Many scholars make the link between this passage and 1 Cor 11:3.[43] Writing on female homoeroticism in the Greco-Roman world, Bernadette Brooten (1985, 72) notes that despite their different contexts, these passages can shed light on each other as they both share an appeal to nature as the basis for gender differentiation. She comments, "Paul's description of man as head of woman and his call for strict gender differentiation in dress and hairstyle (1 Cor 11:2–16) demonstrate that he [is concerned with] anomaly and ambiguity. Gender ambiguity is also the best framework within which to view Paul's understanding of unnatural relations in Romans 1" (1996, 252; see also 275). It is this distinction between what is "natural" and "unnatural" that seems so central to Paul's understanding of sex and gender.[44] Moore also explores the issue of female homoeroticism in Rom 1:18–32; and as with Brooten, he points out that this idea of φύσις ("nature") has many connections in these two passages with the male-female relations divinely established at creation (Gen 1–2), a relational order Paul reads as "naturally" hierarchical (2001, 151 n. 71).[45] In this schema, female homoeroticism is viewed as overturning this created order and must be censured (Brooten 1996, 240; Moore 2001, 261). Moore considers this hierarchy as it appears in Rom 1:18–32, arguing that three divinely instituted hierarchies are at stake in this passage: that of God and man, man and animal, and man and woman. He explains it thus:

> In other words, humans refused to honor the divinely instituted hierarchy that should have regulated divine-human relations (God over "man"). This refusal or rebellion found emblematic expression in, or was epitomized by, these sinful humans' reversal of a *second* divinely instituted hierarchy, that which should have regulated human-animal relations ("man" over animal). And God punished these rebels by permitting them to overturn a *third* divinely instituted hierarchy, that which should have regulated male-female relations (man over woman). (2001, 152)

Moore (2001, 151, 153) sets out the "startling homology" that results as follows:

FEMALE is to MALE

as

ANIMAL is to HUMAN

as

HUMAN is to GOD

Thus while perhaps Rom 1:18–32 does not at first reading appear to outline as clear a hierarchy as that found in 1 Cor 11:3, there is nevertheless an underlying hierarchic principle in Paul's argument. With specific reference to the Greco-Roman context, Johannes Vorster (2002, 287, 297) states that hierarchy (and its attendant dichotomies) was fundamental to the structuring of the ancient world; although this was not always explicitly expressed, it was nevertheless highly prescriptive and all-pervasive. Vorster goes on to explore the notion of hierarchy specifically in Rom 1:18–32 and explains how this passage contains several reversals of these normative hierarchies: "Animals, regarded by the Graeco-Roman to be on the lowest level of the hierarchical scale, are according to anti-Gentile propaganda moved to the highest, occupied by gods (Rm 1:23).... Females who are supposed to be passive were transformed into what was regarded as unnatural (against nature) and the same happened to males" (2002, 299–300).

A comparison, then, between these two closely linked Pauline passages, and in particular the hierarchies utilized by Paul in his arguments in these two passages, is pertinent. To begin with, one can observe that the scope of Paul's discussion in Rom 1:18–32 is broader than that of 1 Cor 11:3. Paul's discussion of gentile idolatry in Rom 1, and his argument that this led to sexual depravity, includes birds, four-footed animals, and reptiles (Moore 2001, 147; D. Martin 2006, 52–55). By contrast, the outline in 1 Cor 11:3 omits "animal" but includes "Christ." This comparison, shown in the diagram below, raises some intriguing points, both in terms of how the terms used in these hierarchies might be defined, but also in terms of how the various components relate to each other.

Rom 1:18–32   1 Cor 11:3

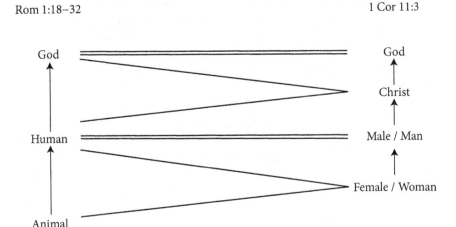

The first thing to consider in this relational schema is the positioning of "Human" and in particular how this category has an insidious tendency to become synonymous with "Male." This is evident when the following statement in Moore's homologous pairs is considered: "Animal is to Human as Human is to God." As it stands, this statement suggests that men and women, as humans, relate equally to both the animal world "below" them and the spiritual world "above" them. But it hides the reality made plain in the other statements: "Female is to Male" (Rom 1:18–32) and "The head of the woman is man" (1 Cor 11:3). According to Greco-Roman constructs of sex and gender, men are higher up the ontological scale than women. Elite adult male citizens represent what it means to be fully human, while women are viewed as incomplete or deficient males. They are consistently depicted as "naturally" defective, or, in the words of Aristotle, as "castrated" (*Gen. an.* 2.3.737a27).[46] Men and masculinity, on the other hand, are viewed as "naturally" superior and as such are able to attain perfection (if they work at it, of course).[47]

This conflation of the "human" with "male"—the slippage between humankind and mankind, which is really "malekind" (Wittig 1992b, 54)—reflects the deliberate appropriation of the universal by men that de Beauvoir exposed in her work. She argues that "man represents both the positive and the neutral," and that the "absolute human type" is "the masculine" (1984, 15; see also Sayers 1971). Wittig dissects this issue in great detail in several of her articles and states, for example:

> One must understand that men are not born with a faculty for the universal and that women are not reduced at birth to the particular. The universal has been, and is continually, at every moment, appropriated by men. It does not happen by magic, it must be done.... It is an act carried out at the level of concepts, philosophy, politics. (1992c, 80)

This appropriation of the universal by men and the conflation between "human" and "male" can be seen in Paul's theology of gender. Moore suggests that had Paul been willing or able to articulate the view of gender undergirding his discourse in Rom 1:18–32, he would have referred to Gen 3:16. According to Moore (2001, 153), while the creation of anatomical *sex* is described in Gen 1:27 ("male and female he created them"), it is in 3:16 that the institution of *gender* emerges ("your desire shall be for your husband/man and he shall lord it over you"). Moore points out that 3:16 means nothing other than, "*masculine* and *feminine* he created them" (154). Paul does base his theology of gender as articulated to the Corinthians in the Genesis accounts; the middle section of this passage (vv. 7–12) is often referred to as an argument from creation.[48] However, rather than Gen 3, most scholars refer to Gen 1–2 as the source of Paul's theology in 1 Cor 11:2–16. The suggestion is that Paul would see Gen 3:16 as describing the fall and not as prescriptive for gender relations.[49] Nevertheless, even if we leave Gen 3 out of the picture, the gender relations as expressed in Gen 2 still fit the first-century model Moore posits as normative for Paul: sharp gender differentiation and asymmetry, expressed in the primary dichotomy of active/passive, and grounded in a determinative logic that constitutes hierarchical male/female sexual relations as "natural." In Paul's "theosexual system," therefore, to be "human" is—ideally—to be an elite heterosexual "male" (Moore 2001, 172).

This is also seen in the way Paul operated as a "man" in his first-century Mediterranean context. David Clines (2003) has explored the ways in which the masculine characteristics of strength, violence, powerful and persuasive speech, male bonding, womanlessness, and binary thinking pervade not only the instructions and teaching by which Paul intends to shape the various Christian congregations to whom he writes, but also his self-presentation (see also Polaski 2005, 12–25). For example, Paul can urge the Corinthians to "be courageous, strong," in 1 Cor 16:13 (ἀνδρίζεσθε, κραταιοῦσθε), literally to "play the man, be strong" ("quit you like men, be strong"; KJV), because being strong and courageous is exactly what it means to be a real man, and this is what both males (and females) ought to aspire to become (Clines 2003, 182; Polaski 2005, 13).[50] Indeed, the very point that (predominantly male) scholars have not previously thought to consider this aspect of Paul's identity causes Clines to dub Paul "the invisible man" (2003, 181). As discussed in chapter 2, when male existence is deemed the universal standard of human existence, men are rendered invisible and it is only women who become a special historical problem (Wittig 1992f, 60–61; Butler 2007, 522–26).

Wittig (1992c, 87) responds to this conflation of the "Human" with "Male" not only by calling for the masculine gender to be "systematically particularized," but also by calling for those who have been particularized to be systematically universalized. This is *not* accomplished by the replacement of one hegemonic point of view with another, however. The assumption of universality by those who have been deemed as particular (as outcast, as queer, as "other," etc.) challenges the dominant point of view, destabilizing it, and revealing it as ideologically constructed. Wittig explains:

> All of us have an abstract idea of what being "human" means…. For indeed, for all its pretension to being universal, what has been until now considered "human" in our Western philosophy concerns only a small fringe of people: white men, proprietors of the means of production, along with the philosophers who theorized their point of view as the only and exclusively possible one. This is the reason why when we consider abstractly, from a philosophical point of view, the potentiality and virtuality of humanness, we need to do it, to see clearly, from an oblique point of view. Thus, being a lesbian, standing at the outposts of the human (of humankind) represents historically and paradoxically the most human point of view. (1992b, 46)

Moore also comes to a similar conclusion in his discussion on Romans. He ponders the possibility of ushering "that which is farthest outside the camp ... that which is most anathemized—sex between women"—into the center (2001, 172).[51] He is hopeful that this would cause a radical reform in all three of the relations set out in the homology outlined above. Divine-human, male-female, and human-animal relations might therefore be transformed into more egalitarian (more humane?) models of being, with "only the most precarious of toeholds to hierarchy" (172). In this section it has become clear that the category of "Human" is dangerously ambiguous. Purporting to be inclusive of both male and female, it in fact conceals the ideology of the "universal male." Yet it might be possible to destabilize such a hegemonic viewpoint through the universalization of the lesbian, placing "her" at the center of what it means to be "human."

The second point to observe from the hierarchical schema based on Rom 1:18–32 and 1 Cor 11:3 is the marginal place women occupy between the categories "Human" and "Animal." Many scholars in the fields of anthropology, ecofeminism, and philosophy have noted an almost universal tendency for women to be positioned so that they appear not only to straddle the boundary between human and animal/nature but also to become virtually synonymous with the natural world (Ortner 1974; Ruether 1975; MacCormack 1980; Gruen 1993; Soper 2000). The antithesis between *female = reproduction = nature* and *male = production = culture*, with the systematic devaluation of the former and the assumption of superiority of the latter, is a deeply entrenched framework operating within not only Western society but also cross-culturally and historically (Ortner 1974, 69–71; MacCormack 1980, 1–24; Plumwood 1993, 19–27; Soper 2000, 139). Far from being fully human, woman is almost animal, a point that both de Beauvoir and Irigaray have observed: "she is more enslaved to the species than is the male, her animality is more manifest" (de Beauvoir 1984, 285); she is reduced to "animality, perversity, or a kind of pseudo-childhood" (Irigaray 1991, 187; 1993, 185–217).

This association of women with nature, and the reduction of woman to animal, is closely tied to an ideology of male dominance, a point noted by Horkheimer and Adorno (2002, 31), who state that "men distance themselves from nature in order thus imaginatively to present it to themselves—but only in order to determine how it is to be dominated." They also perceptively add: "As a representative of nature, woman in bourgeois society has become an enigma of irresistibility and powerlessness. Thus she reflects back the vain lie of power, which substitutes the mastery over nature for reconciliation with it" (56). Lori Gruen illustrates this point well:

> The categories "woman" and "animal" serve the same symbolic func-
> tion in patriarchal society. Their construction as dominated, submissive
> "other" in theoretical discourse (whether explicitly stated or implied) has
> sustained human male dominance. The role of women and animals in
> postindustrial society is to serve/be served up; women and animals are
> the used. Whether created as ideological icons to justify and preserve the
> superiority of men or captured as servants to provide for and comfort,
> the connection women and animals share is present in both theory and
> practice. (1993, 61)[52]

Wittig (1992d, 41; also 1992a, 6) notes this division between men as "social beings" and women as "natural beings," and comments that, far from being "natural," "the making of woman is like the making of eunuchs, the breeding of slaves, of animals."[53] In accord with Gruen, she argues that this construction of woman is in the service of male dominance. This can be seen in her description of woman in the following pairs: woman/*slave*, woman/*dominated creature*, woman/reproducer by *obligation* (1979, 120, emphasis added). In an attempt to explore the origins of this dualistic framework, Wittig looks back to Aristotle and Plato. She considers the Pythagorean tabulation of opposites that Aristotle records in his *Metaphysics* (1.5.6 986a22–27) and sums this up as follows:

> Thus under the series of the "One" (the absolute being nondivided,
> divinity itself) we have "male" (and "light") that were from then on
> never dislodged from their dominant position. Under the other series
> appear the unrestful: the common people, the females, the "slaves of the
> poor," the "dark" (barbarians who cannot distinguish between slaves and
> women), all reduced to the parameter of non-Being. For Being is being
> good, male, straight, one, in other words, godlike, while non-Being is
> being anything else (many), female: it means discord, unrest, dark, and
> bad. (1992b, 51)

Aristotle has the reputation in feminist circles of being a "clas-
sic misogynist" (Senack 1994, 234), of being "anitfeminist to the core" (Horowitz 1976, 212; see also Matthews 1986, 25; Tress 1996, 31, 227 n. 2).[54] Although Aristotle nowhere makes explicit the link between women and animals, and in fact concedes that men and women are of the same species (*Metaph.* 10.9.1058a29–31), he makes the infamous comments, τὸ

γὰρ θῆλυ ὥσπερ ἄρρεν ἐστὶ πεπηρωμένον ("the female is as it were a deformed male"; *Gen. an.* 2.3.737a27 [Peck]), and, ἡ γυνὴ ὥσπερ ἄρρεν ἄγονον ("a woman is at it were an infertile male"; 1.20.728a18–20 [Peck]).[55] He also states, καὶ δεῖ ὑπολαμβάνειν ὥσπερ ἀναπηρίαν εἶναι τὴν θηλύτητα φυσικήν ("the female state as being as it were a deformity, though one which occurs in the ordinary course of nature"; 4.6.775a15 [Peck]). In discussing what constitutes "a monstrosity" (τέρατι ... τέρας), he comments, ἀρχὴ δὲ πρώτη τὸ θῆλυ γίνεσθαι καὶ μὴ ἄρρεν ("The first beginning of this deviation is when a female is formed instead of a male, though this indeed is a necessity required by Nature"; 4.3.767b5–9 [Peck]).[56] The male, on the other hand, he describes as τὸ κρεῖττον ... βέλτιον γὰρ καὶ θειότερον ("superior ... something *better* and more divine"; 2.1.732a5–10 [Peck]). He also states, τό τε γὰρ ἄρρεν φύσει τοῦ θήλεος ἡγεμονικώτερον ... τὸ δ' ἄρρεν ἀεὶ πρὸς τὸ θῆλυ τοῦτον ἔχει τὸν τρόπον ("for the male is by nature better fitted to command than the female.... [And] stands in this relationship to the female continuously"; *Pol.* 1.5.1259b3–4, 9–10 [Rackham]), and ἔτι δὲ τὸ ἄρρεν πρὸς τὸ θῆλυ φύσει τὸ μὲν κρεῖττον τὸ δὲ χεῖρον, τὸ μὲν ἄρχον τὸ δ' ἀρχόμενον ("the male is by nature superior and the female inferior, the male ruler and the female subject"; *Pol.* 1.2.1254b13–14 [Rackham]).[57]

Aristotle places woman, slaves, and children into the category of those who are to be ruled, as nature intended.[58] This coheres well with Wittig's observation, noted throughout her work, that women and slaves are in a similar situation (1992a, 2, 6, 8; 1992e, 11, 15, 20; 1992g, xiii).[59] For Aristotle, this category is only marginally "human." As Elizabeth Spelman (1994, 107) states, "To twist a phrase from Nietzsche, Aristotle holds that women and slaves are human, but not too human."[60] She goes on to argue:

> The gender- and class-differentiated ethics of Aristotle, and of the dominant culture of which he is the philosophical spokesperson, both presuppose and validate a conception of the natures of women and slaves which ranks them as *borderline creatures*, lacking in full humanity in ways importantly analogous to the ways non-human animals lack humanity. For slaves, beasts and (non-slave) women are all essentially *marginal beings* in the Greek male outlook.... [They share] a static marginality, an ontologically fixed residence on the fringes of (male) human concerns. (128, 130, emphasis added)

Spelman then maintains that it is the (free) labor of both women and slaves that "provides the work-free open space in which democratic political life is lived by citizen males, and free women even provide those citizen males themselves through their reproductive labor" (139). Highlighting the links between politics, economics, and ideology, she concludes by suggesting, "Aristotle and his contemporaries construct a moral ideology which ratifies what is in essence an economic need" (140). The political dimensions of Aristotle's biological theories are also noted by Maryanne Horowitz (1976, 187–88), who argues that Aristotle legitimized patriarchy as "the proper form of government for the family" in that his belief in the superiority of men over women and slaves "gave sanction to a hierarchy of servitudes, including wifedom and slavery." The comments of both Spelman and Horowitz echo precisely what Wittig (1992a, 2, 6) says with regard to the ideology of sexual difference and opposition, that such differences mask the economic, political, and ideological order(s) to which they belong.

In looking at this marginal positioning of women across cultures, Sherry Ortner makes the additional point that while women are often symbolically associated with nature, this identification is an oversimplification. She observes that "woman" is seen as being *closer* to nature than "man," and while "lower on the scale of transcendence than man," she cannot be fully consigned to the category of "nature" as she also participates in "culture" (1974, 76). Thus "she appears as something intermediate between culture and nature"; she is "situated between the two realms" (76, 80; see also 85).[61] Such an intermediary position may therefore "have the implication of greater symbolic ambiguity" (85). Perhaps this is why as a symbol "woman" can take on many different guises. Subversive figures such as witches, castrating mothers, Medusa, Circe, Scylla, and Charybdis, as well as elements such as menstrual "pollution," can be accounted for along with the many and varied feminine symbols of transcendence, such as mother goddesses, Britannia, Lady Liberty, Zelandia, Gaia, fertility, justice, the angel in the house, and the guardian of morals (86). Ortner notes: "Feminine symbolism, far more often than masculine symbolism, manifests this propensity toward polarized ambiguity" (86).

Despite the supposedly clear delineation of the hierarchy in 1 Cor 11:3, and the stability this order is meant to bring to family, church, and society—according to those who find it prescriptive—the positioning of "Female" in this schema is ambiguous. In many ways I find here an echo of D. Martin's (2001) observations regarding the contradictions of masculinity in Greco-Roman culture. While the ambiguities and contradictions within an ideological system serve to reinforce that system, this is done at the cost of making each individual's gender identity less secure. Females can never be confident that they are being viewed as fully human—the debate over inclusive language is part of this dilemma—and their symbolic positioning as mythical creatures (best exemplified by the impossibility of the Virgin Mother) leaves them suspended in the realm of both mystery and horror.[62] By recognizing "Female" as a "site of contradiction," this exposes the basis of this construct as something ideological (and political) rather than as something simply "natural" (D. Martin 2001, 105–6).

The third point to note in this schema is the marginal place occupied by "Christ." Like the "Female," he too is found between two seemingly distinct ontological categories, in this case between "Man" and "God." Theologically however, rather than being the "not-quite" of the woman, Christ came to be viewed as both "fully" human and divine. The Council of Chalcedon (451 CE) declared, τὸν κύριον ἡμῶν Ἰησοῦν Χριστὸν ... τέλειον τὸν αὐτὸν ἐν θεότητι, τέλειον τὸν ἐν ἀνθρωπότητι, θεὸν ἀληθῶς, καὶ ἄνθρωπον ἀληθῶς ... ὁμοούσιαν τῷ πατρὶ κατὰ τὴν θεότητα, καὶ ὁμοούσιαν ἡμῖν τὸν αὐτὸν κατὰ τὴν ἀνθρωπότητα ("our Lord Jesus Christ, the same perfect in Godhead and also perfect in manhood; truly God and truly man ... consubstantial [coessential] with the Father according to his Godhead, and consubstantial with us according to the Manhood"; Schaff 1919, 102). Of course, the translations of ἀνθρωπότητι, ἄνθρωπον, and ἀνθρωπότητα are indicative of the issues raised in the section on "Human—The Universal Male" above. This is also true of the phrase "consubstantial with us," in that the "us" creates an ambiguity for women who are never certain if this actually includes them and are subsequently disempowered by this ambiguity.

In continuity with the debate lying behind this christological statement from Chalcedon, there is considerable divergence in the ways in which contemporary theologians investigate this question, ranging from placing the traditions about Jesus alongside those of semidivine intermediary figures such as those found in Jewish angelological traditions (Stuckenbruck 1995; Gieschen 1998), to viewing Jesus as the unique "revelation of the divine love in action" (Wright 1991, 82, 86). In many ways the question being debated is one of categorization: can the Christ figure be explained by an ontological category already in existence, such as angelic intermediary figures, or does he represent a unique entity that transcends all other categories?

The specific arguments are complex, but those who explore the notion of Jesus as an intermediary figure argue for placing Jesus within an already existing angelomorphic framework. The cosmology of the early Jewish Christians is explained as a "theo-ontological pyramid" (Fredriksen 2007,

37) in which multiple divine personalities exist, and there are "degrees of glory" differentiating such beings, with one supreme god reigning at the top (Stuckenbruck 1995, 96). An examination of the relevant texts, for example, suggests to Charles Gieschen (1998, 28) that "the ontological distinction between angel and deity is not consistently clear." When one considers the various aspects of divinity that may be present in any one text, this may indicate that "the angelomorphic mediator figure was understood to share God's status, authority, and nature" (33).[63] There is therefore recognition in this cosmology of ambiguity within the ontological stratification.

This view can be contrasted with the view of those who explore the notion that Christ has not only a high status, having been given "the name above every name," but also "a unique status" (Hurtado 2005, 93).[64] The Christ event is explained as fitting within a cosmology that has a binary view of reality, in which there is an absolute difference in kind between God and all other things, what Richard Bauckham (2008, 107–26) describes as "exclusive monotheism." Rather than being a "category mistake," the Christ figure is understood by N. T. Wright (1991, 131), for example, as a radically novel expression of God's identity: "A quite new entity, sociologically as well as theologically, is thereby called into existence.... A strikingly new phenomenon" (136).[65]

Here is where a connection with Wittig becomes possible. While her materialist lesbianism is focused on issues of sex and gender, and has very little to say about theology directly, questions of categorization lie at the heart of her theory. She declares that "the category of sex tightly holds women" and argues that "a new personal and subjective definition for all humankind can only be found beyond the categories of sex" (1992e, 19–20). In one of the few places where Wittig does touch on things metaphysical, she explains part of the reason behind her desire to see such categories destroyed:

> Gender is an ontological impossibility because it tries to accomplish the division of Being. But Being as being is not divided. God or Man as being are One and whole. So what is this divided Being introduced into language through gender? It is an impossible Being, it is a Being that does not exist, an ontological joke. (1992c, 80)

What would Wittig say about the figure of Christ? What would she say about the Chalcedonian definition of Christ as fully God *and* fully human? No "division of Being" here, but rather the mathematics of multiplication (rather than addition), so that $1 \times 1 = 1$. If I replace Wittig's "or" with an "and," then her words are reminiscent of the creed: "God [and] Man as being are One and whole." Such language is also reminiscent of Burrus's (2006, 40) reflections on Christ: "The two-natured Christ affirmed at Chalcedon—who is also 'one person'—is not, after all, simply the sum of his manly and more-than-manly parts.... Chalcedon, it seems, demands a new math, a calculus that exceeds the logic of addition and subtraction, of fractions and wholes." Rather than being "an impossible Being ... an ontological joke"—or a "category mistake"—the figure of Christ represents something "beyond the categories."

Staying with the formulation of Chalcedon, the description of the Christ refuses an oppositional binary (either/or) and instead insists on a coexistence (both/and): "Christ" is both "truly God" and "truly man." For those scholars who argue that the figure of Christ can best be understood as an angelomorphic intermediary figure, this position is seen as "tortured" and "complicated ... to the point of paradox" (Fredriksen 2007, 37). However, it is this paradoxical coexistence that allows one to explore—even to "joke" with—the figure of Christ from a queer perspective. Rather than seeking a theological or historical explanation for the person of Christ— an approach that April DeConick (2007, 1) describes as having "boxed us into artificial ... corners"—it is possible to focus on the issue of categorization and discover what might lie beyond, an exploration in line with the direction of Wittig's theory.

One scholar who has explored a queer reading of the Chalcedon Creed is Tricia Sheffield (2008). She notes the way in which gender is constructed as a binary and argues that this gender binary is often given legitimacy as "natural" by an appeal to religious "myths" such as the creation account in Genesis, a narrative that still continues to wield enormous power and influence in the Christian West in its affirmation of the creation of humanity into two sexes (and two genders). With regard to the person of Jesus, Sheffield suggests that while "Jesus' body gets read through this same lens of human sexuality and gender performance," with regard to the construction of his identity as both "truly God and truly man" in the Chalcedonian definition, "Jesus' body matters, and causes quite a bit of trouble" (235, 240).[66] The Christ figure does not sit tidily in one category, but dares to be "both/and," resisting the traditional binary. She states:

> What I argue is *this* body is a disruptive performative entity that queers the fallacy of dichotomous thinking through its refusal to be categorized

as either/or: it is not human, it is not divine, yet, it is both and none.... Jesus' body *is* ambiguous, liminal and diverse, as it is two distinctly oppositional natures that are conjoined, yet neither nature is erased. (243)

Sheffield considers the transgressive nature of this "queer Chalcedic body" and suggests that the creed is an example of "heretical hybridity" in which Jesus's body is "constructed into what may be described as a transgressive site of corporeality ... a place of cultural ambiguity" (238–41). From this site, multiple identities might thus be possible, "identities of hybridity and transgression that disrupt ancient and contemporary fictive narratives of normative femininity, masculinity, and sexuality" (237). Thus while the "hybridity" seen in the Christ figure constitutes the human-divine dualism, this can be projected forward to the male-female dualism that "bedevils the cultural place in which we stand" (McLaughlin 2004, 129). Sheffield's "queer Chalcedic Christ" is thus a liberating model of transgression in which transgendered (and other nonnormatively sexed and gendered) people may recognize themselves. A diversity of gender experiences is therefore valorized, and the oppositional binary construction of the "natural" order is destabilized. Noting that the Latin *transgredior* means "to pass over, go beyond, or to advance," this further conveys a positive, liberating, forward-looking sense of the word (Goss 1999, 46).[67] The ambiguity of Christ's position in the hierarchical schema is thus potentially empowering for those who also fall outside the "normal" categories of being.

This is not to say that there is nothing problematic about the figure of Christ—there is of course the troubling matter of Jesus's body as a *male* body. Sheffield (2008, 243) suggests that the greatest violence done to Christ was that dominant Christianity "cleaned him up, made him masculine, even got him *saved*, by constructing his body as one that participates fully in the realm of patriarchy." "Christ" quickly became (always was?) the "male Savior" that Rosemary Radford Ruether (1983, 116–38) challenged decades ago.[68] However, this is why Sheffield insists on emphasizing the "both/and" aspects of the "queer Chalcedic Christ." Viewing Christ as "both/and" allows for a multiplicity of identity formations, the potential to embrace a "heretical hybridity" (2008, 240).

This ambiguous positioning of Christ, therefore, has the potential to disrupt and destabilize the hierarchical binaries of heteronormativity. In particular, a "queer Chalcedic Christ" may enable Wittig's (1992e, 19–20) vision in which "a new personal and subjective definition for all humankind can only be found beyond the categories of sex (woman and man)." This exploration of 1 Cor 11:3 has revealed that while several of Paul's statements in 1 Cor 11:2–16 convey to readers a sense of metaphysical truth that reinforces certain notions of social order in relation to gender and sexuality, this passage is also full of instability and ambiguity, giving it the possibility of being que(e)ried.

Notes

1. This quote comes from McClure's essay "Revolt." There are echoes in this quote of Marx's *Critique of Hegel's "Philosophy of Right"*; see, for example, Marx's comment, "In monarchy one part determines the character of the whole; the entire constitution must be modified according to the immutable head … in democracy the constitution itself appears only as one determination, and indeed as the self-determination of the people" (1970, 29). I will return to Marx throughout this section.

2. Thiselton (2000, 41) posits the term *rhetoric* as a more useful term than *argument* for describing the nature of Paul's writing. On reading 1 Corinthians as an example of deliberative (political) rhetoric, see Mitchell 1993, 20–64; on 1 Cor 11:2–16 in particular, see 149–51 and 260–63.

3. Not all scholars agree with this position, however. Dodd (1999, 44) argues that the tone of Paul's argument in 1 Corinthians as a whole is "assertive rather than defensive." Much of the debate centers on interpretations of 1 Cor 1–4 and 8–10 (particularly ch. 9).

4. In doing so, much of this passage is thus neglected; in particular, this means skipping over the notorious *crux interpretum* of v. 10. While it would be tempting to examine this verse, with its enigmatic reference to οἱ ἄγγελοι ("the angels"), and to review the history of blatantly chauvinistic interpretations of the woman's ἐξουσία ("authority"), to do so would go beyond the scope of this present work; however, see appendix 1 for some discussion on this verse.

5. See Barrett 1971, 247; Conzelmann 1975, 182; Fee 1987, 500; Witherington 1988, 84; Mitchell 1993, 260; Schrage 1995, 499; Collins 1999, 395; Garland 2003, 513; Fitzmyer 2008, 408. Some scholars rather see an ironic or even sarcastic tone present (Evans 1930, 117; Hurd 1983, 182).

6. There is debate over the translation of ἡ γυνή and ὁ ἀνήρ; I have opted for "woman" and "man" rather than "husband" and "wife." I will discuss this issue below.

7. The NRSV footnotes the alternative translation of "man/woman."

8. Other versions that opt for "husband/wife" in the text include The Message and GNB. Most translations opt for "man/woman" (see NASB, NIV, 21st Century KJV, CEV, NJB). Some of these footnote the option of "husband/wife" (see Today's NIV, and the Holman Christian Standard Bible). Young's and Amplified even opt for "husband/woman," while NLT footnotes this option.

9. Wittig is building on de Beauvoir's notion of the "myth of woman"; book 1 of *The Second Sex* is entitled "Facts and Myths," and in part 3, "Myths," de Beauvoir

explores "The Myth of Woman in Five Authors" (1984, 229–78). See also her final summary chapter in part 3, "Myth and Reality" (1984, 282–92).

10. See also Horkheimer and Adorno (2002, 56), who state, "Marriage is society's middle way of dealing with this question [of women's relationship to power]: woman remains powerless in that her power is mediated to her only through her husband."

11. Not all scholars agree. Belleville (2003, 215) argues that "it is actually δόξα, and not κεφαλή that provides the key to understanding Paul's train of thought."

12. See in particular the debates between Grudem (1985, 1990) and Cervin (1989), and the response to this debate by Perriman (1994). See also the articles by C. Kroeger (1987b, 1993) and Grudem's response (2001). Other scholars who have made significant contributions to the debate include Bedale 1954; Fitzmyer 1989, 1993; Dawes 1998, esp. 122–29; Belleville 2003. A. Johnson provides a more recent overview of what he describes as "an ongoing, sometimes acrimonious debate" over the meaning of κεφαλή (2009, 35).

13. While scholars generally acknowledge that by far the most common usage of κεφαλή is in its *literal* sense as a physical head (of a person or animal), it is the *metaphorical* sense of the word that is debated. This is complicated in 1 Cor 11:2–16 because it would seem that Paul is employing the term deliberately because of its polyvalent potential—and it is difficult for readers to determine when he is referring to the physical head of a person, and when he is referring to κεφαλή in a metaphorical sense. Collins (1999, 396), for example, states that Paul "plays on the multiple meanings of 'head.'" Verses 4 and 5 are indicative of this dilemma. Most scholars agree that the first reference to κεφαλή in each of these verses is to the physical heads of men and women who are praying and prophesying. However, it is less clear what Paul intends by the second reference; do men and woman shame their own physical heads, and thus, by way of synecdoche, themselves as individuals? Or do they shame their figurative heads, the "heads" outlined in v. 3 (Christ and man, respectively)? Bearing in mind the honor-shame dynamic of first-century Mediterranean culture, which Thiselton (2000, 826) states "has become an axiom of research on this epistle," it is perhaps best to accept that both options are possible (and even intended); the men and women are shaming not only themselves but also their respective "heads."

14. While scholars from other countries have contributed to the debate, such as Dawes (1998), the situation in the United States is particularly polarized (Kivisto 1994, 223; Coleman 2005; Lakey 2010, 7–17).

15. See also the CBMW website: http://cbmw.org.

16. Grudem (1985, 39) labels many followers of the *source, origin* option as "Christian feminist," but he also notes that others who do not generally endorse Christian feminism have also supported this view of κεφαλή.

17. CBE was initially affiliated with the international organization Men, Women and God: Christians for Biblical Equality, based in London. See their website for a full account of their history and core values: http://www.cbeinternational.org.

18. However, they disagree about the effect of one upon the other in their establishment. CBE states that the CBMW grew out of opposition to CBE, while CBMW states that it was formed independently. See the history section of the CBE website, and also Piper and Grudem 2006a, 403.

19. The word κεφαλή is found not only in 1 Cor 11:2–16 but also in Eph 5:23 and Col 1:18, for example. For discussion on the meaning of κεφαλή in Ephesians, see Dawes 1998.

20. There is no actual term *headship* in the Bible, but both the CBMW and CBE websites have much to say about the topic of "headship" (leadership, submission, equality, and other related issues).

21. No other Scripture passage comes close with regard to references. There are eighty-nine references to the passage itself and verses within it (twenty-one for 11:3 alone). Only 1 Tim 2:8–15 compares, with thirty-nine references (eighteen for 2:12 alone) (Piper and Grudem 2006b, 546–47; see also Grudem 2004, 783–95).

22. Women are specifically challenged to choose full-time homemaking and "God's business" over and above career and "secular employment" (Piper 2006, 56; see also Patterson 2006). That this is still the current view of CBMW is clear from availability of *Recovering Biblical Manhood and Womanhood* online via their website, http://tinyurl.com/SBL0685n1. See also Grudem's discussion on the different responsibilities of men and women (2004, 44–45).

23. This concern about "unisex" or "transgender" forms of gender is still considerable for hierachalists, as a search on the CBMW website reveals. See, for example, http://tinyurl.com/SBL0685w.

24. For Marx, this analysis was central to his critique of Hegel, who places consciousness (the head) at the center of man's existence. Marx argued that a Hegelian politics of "the head" gives rise to an authoritarianism that allows for monarchy, for example, and other social hierarchies that he despised (1970, 29; Hegel 1975, 27). Marx "regarded it as his greatest achievement, and the cornerstone of his materialism, to have taken this philosophy of the head, and as Engels said, 'placed it on its feet'" (Press 1977, 336).

25. The exception to this, he notes, is "the brutality toward women that has spread since the introduction of monogamy" (1972, 135). Given the widespread problems of domestic violence in society, this ought not to be ignored. Grudem counters the "egalitarian claim" that the hierarchalist view of male headship leads to the abuse of women, suggesting, for example, "Biblical male headship, rightly understood, protects women from abuse and repression and truly honors them as equal in value before God" (2004, 493; for full discussion, see 490–96).

26. Other groups include the American Family Association (1977), Focus on the Family (1977), Christian Voice (1978), Concerned Women for America (1979), Moral Majority, headed by Jerry Falwell (1979—formed out of the Christian Voice and revived in 2004 as the Moral Majority Coalition), Family Research Council (1981), and the Christian Coalition, headed by Pat Robertson (1989—formed out of the Moral Majority). The Traditional Values Coalition, which includes many of these other groups, typifies the stance of these groups with its commitment to patriotism and opposition to supposedly deviant sexual behaviors (those that do not fit the pattern of the nuclear family). See their website for more details: www.traditionalvalues.org.

27. Such groups include Planned Parenthood (1916), Parents and Friends of Lesbians and Gays (1972), and People for the American Way (1981). See comments about these groups at http://www.traditionalvalues.org/press. Liberal groups have

played with the "family values" phrase with such slogans as "hate is not a family value" (Hasian and Parry-Evans 1997, 32) and "poverty is not a family value" (see Jim Wallis's speech referenced at http://tinyurl.com/SBL0685x).

28. E-mail message to me, 14 June 2007.

29. Cwik (e-mail message to me, 14 June 2007) states that, "CBE stands in support of the family, and by that we mean both the nuclear and extended family ... CBE makes a conscientious effort to provide resources that empower all these definitions of 'the family.'"

30. See the "Statement of Faith" section of their website (http://tinyurl.com/SBL0685y). Cwik (e-mail message to me, 14 June 2007) states, "CBE believes that marriage is reserved for heterosexual couples. In that light, we provide resources that are geared to heterosexual families."

31. Rubin (1984, 13) describes this fear as the "domino theory of sexual peril."

32. There are difficulties regarding the differentiation between orientation and behavior, of course, but because of the early publication date of this work, the Kroegers were understandably unaware of the importance of these nuances.

33. On the issue of marriage, it is also of interest to note that the inadequacy of the "left-right" spectrum and the complexity of political and ideological positions also evident in the debates about the Civil Union Bill in New Zealand. As one might have expected, some sectors of conservative Christianity were opposed to the bill, expressing their views both verbally and visually through a march on Parliament (as noted in ch. 2). But perhaps the most surprising opposition to the bill came from those within the gay community who were promarriage. While groups like Destiny Church and this sector of the gay community are polarized on their views regarding sexuality, they found themselves united in their belief in the importance of marriage for the stability and security of society ("Let Them Wed," 1996, "The Case for Gay Marriage," 2004; D. Young 2004, 32–33). D. Young (33) states, "I am uncomfortable landing on the same side of the debate as Christian fundamentalists—this is not a natural place for me to be.... I'm learning to live with being the gay man out of step with the marching boys." Or, ironically, one could adjust Young's last phrase—in light of Tamaki's march on Parliament with the men in black T-shirts—to say he is learning to be *in* step with the marching boys.

34. Perriman (1994, 618 n. 41) critiques Cervin for a failure to distinguish between normative metaphorical meaning and secondary, contextually dependent connotations, and says that this "renders his analysis inconsistent."

35. This is a discussion that he describes as "scholarly swordplay," highlighting the sense of battle that exists over the meaning of this word.

36. By "anachronistic physiological notions," Perriman (1994, 608) is most likely referring to Philo's idea that the head is the ruling part of the body and/or Plato's suggestion that the head is the most divine part of the body.

37. One hopes that such elitism would not be what Perriman would suggest that one accept either theologically or pastorally, but the implications for actually accepting this meaning for κεφαλή are left undiscussed in the literature.

38. There are times when this implication does occur; see, for example, the article

by Zimbabwean academic, political commentator, and human rights campaigner John Makumbe (2010).

39. However, several articles in *Queer Commentary and the Hebrew Bible* play with another related metaphor, the notion of "top" and "bottom" that derives from the parlance of sadomasochism. As with "tail," none of these play with the idea of Christ as "bottom," but Rowlett (2001) describes the biblical character Samson as a "butch bottom," while both Jennings (2001) and R. Boer (2001) explore the idea that Yahweh/YHWH can be considered a "top."

40. Perriman also argues against the understanding of "head" as *source, origin* in these verses.

41. The following scholars are just some examples of those who note this hierarchy (this does not mean that all of them see it as prescriptive, however): Barrett 1971, 249; Brooten 1985, 75, 78; D. Martin 1995a, 232; Stuckenbruck 1995, 217; BeDuhn 1999, 298–99; Ince 2000, 64; F. Watson 2000b, 524, 528–29; Barclay 2001, 1125–26; J. Thompson 2003, 244; A. Johnson 2004, 182–84; Økland 2004, 174–78; Mount 2005, 331; Vander Stichele and Penner 2005, 230; Hearon 2006, 615; Fitzmyer 2008, 409; Calef 2009, 31–33. In contrast, Hjort (2001, 59, 64–66, 77 n. 25) understands it as presenting an order of salvation, while Payne (2009, 129) views it as a chronological order of creation. Others reject the idea that this verse is hierarchical and note that the order in which the pairs are presented does not support the idea of a descending order, or a chain of command (Murphy-O'Connor 1980, 494; 1988, 270; Belleville 2003, 229). Fee (1987, 502–5) argues against the verse being read as hierarchical primarily because he understands κεφαλή to mean *source, origin*.

42. Engberg-Pedersen (1991, 680) makes clear, however, that he does not find Paul's statement's on gender "in any way binding on us."

43. Barrett 1971, 256; Blomberg 1994, 215; Castelli 1999, 229; Garland 2003, 530; J. Thompson 2003, 239, 250; Hays 2004, 137; Mount 2005, 333 n. 69; D. Martin 2006, 60; MacGregor 2009, 203 n. 4; Payne 2009, 144.

44. Because of the importance of these concepts, κατὰ φύσιν ("according to nature") and παρὰ φύσιν ("against nature"), these will be considered in more detail in ch. 6 in relation to 1 Cor 11:14 and Paul's appeal to ἡ φύσις αὐτή.

45. D. Martin (2006, 52) argues against seeing Gen 1–3 as the background for Paul's comments in Rom 1. However, others see Gen 1–3 as important in their arguments about male-female (and same-sex) relations (Hays 1986, 191; Gagnon 2001, 292). As this is an important issue, I will return to it in ch. 6, with a particular focus on Gagnon's arguments, including Martin's response to Gagnon.

46. This idea is discussed in more detail in the next section.

47. As was discussed in ch. 3 (see Boyarin 1998, 126; 2003, 6–8; Castelli 1991a, 29–49).

48. Barrett 1971, 61; Conzelmann 1975, 186; Fee 1987, 515; Hays 1997, 184, 186–88; Horsley 1998, 155–56; Collins 1999, 399–400, 402–3, 409–10, 413; Thiselton 2000, 833–34; Garland 2003, 508, 522; A. Johnson 2004, 182; 2009, 52–53; Keener 2005, 93–94; Fitzmyer 2008, 415–16.

49. BeDuhn (1999, 312) notes that scholars disagree about whether Paul is more

dependent on Gen 1 or Gen 2, but he also notes that it is unlikely to have been Gen 3 as Paul makes no mention of the fall, of woman's temptation, or the curse (see also D. MacDonald 1987, 104; Brooten 1996, 274–75).

50. Clines (2003, 182–84) also notes that strength as a virtue also comes through in the following verses: Phil 4:13; Col 1:11, 29; Rom 15:19; 1 Cor 1:25; 2:4; 4:19; 2 Cor 12:10.

51. This is a similar idea to de Lauretis's "speculative premise" of refusing to regard homosexuality as marginal (1991, iii).

52. Therein lies the basis of ecofeminism: "Ecofeminism posits that the domination of nature is linked to the domination of women and that both dominations must be eradicated" (Gruen 1993, 125). There is also some debate over the way in which many female animal rights activists identify *with* animals, and thus perhaps participate in (and perpetuate) this ideological framework (Donovan 1990).

53. Elsewhere Wittig uses the terms "Female Body/Nature" (1992f, 60) and notes the dualisms of "nature/culture, women/society" (1992e, 14).

54. Senack acknowledges that many feminist scholars describe Aristotle in this way, but she disagrees with this conclusion. While many feminist scholars have been strongly polemical in their initial criticisms of Aristotle (e.g., Haraway 1988), more nuanced inquiries have since been put forward (see the essays in Freeland 1998).

55. I note this contra Donovan (1990, 354), who claims that in his *Nicomachean Ethics* Aristotle links women and animals as part of his argument against women's participation in moral life, although she does not cite any specific passages. Notice that, in the first comment, Aristotle uses the neuter terms ἄρρεν and θῆλυ, which may suggest that they be translated as "male and female principles" (Preuss 1970; Horowitz 1976, 187 n. 11). Notice also that Aristotle begins the second comment by saying that a boy (παῖς) resembles a woman in physique; both are infertile males.

56. In ch. 6 I will explore what I am calling Gagnon's "unnatural homosexual" in relation to Wittig's "monstrous lesbian."

57. Such descriptions are reminiscent of those given by Cervin and Perriman regarding κεφαλή.

58. In relation to the broader issue of the relationship between the ruled and the ruler, Aristotle raises the question of whether slaves, women, and children have virtues, and his comments are worth quoting at length: "there are by nature various classes of rulers and ruled. For the free rules the slave, the male the female, and the man the child in a different way. And all possess the various parts of the soul, but possess them in different ways; for the slave has not got the deliberative part [βουλευτικόν] at all, and the female has it, but without full authority [ἀλλ' ἄκυρον] while the child has it, but in an undeveloped form. Hence the ruler must possess intellectual virtue in completeness ... while each of the other parties must have that share of this virtue which is appropriate to them ... the temperance [σωφροσύνη] of a woman and that of a man are not the same, nor is their courage and justice [ἀνδρεία καὶ δικαιοσύνη], as Socrates thought, but the one is the courage of command, and the other that of subordination [ἡ μὲν ἀρχικὴ ἀνδρεία, ἡ δ' ὑπηρετική], and the case is similar with other virtues.... Hence we must hold that all of these persons have their appropriate virtues, as the poet said of woman: 'Silence gives grace to woman' [γυναικὶ κόσμον ἡ σιγὴ

φέρει], though that is not the case likewise with a man" (*Pol.* 1.5.1260a9–31). Aristotle is citing Sophocles, *Ajax* 293.

59. Of course, Aristotle's notion of "slave" and the African American "slave" to whom Wittig refers are not synonymous; nevertheless, there is still the reality of a lack of freedom and worth that both groups would have experienced that make them comparable.

60. Spelman is referring to Nietzsche's book *The Human, All Too Human* (1984). Sayers published an essay, "The Human-Not-Quite-Human," reprinted in a collection of her essays entitled *Are Women Human?* (1971). MacKinnon asks the same question thirty-five years later in the title of her book, *Are Woman Human?* She notes at the outset that she had not been aware of Sayers's work when writing the essay that became the title piece for this volume, and states, "The question deserves re-asking from diverse perspectives and in varied contexts" (2006, vii).

61. Wittig (1992e, 10) notes de Beauvoir's (1984, 295) comment, "it is civilization as a whole that produces this creature, intermediate between male and eunuch, which is described as feminine."

62. On the ambiguity of exclusive language and the way this disempowers women, see Philps-Townsley 1997. See also de Beauvoir (1984, 180), who critiques the way in which women, as mediators between men and the natural world, are endowed with "equivocal magic," and are positioned as magical entities but who consequently fill men with "horror." She examines the idea of "Myth" in book 1, part 3. This destruction of the "myth of woman" is central to Wittig's aims.

63. Indicators of divinity include positioning on or near the throne, the appearance, functions, and name of the figure, as well as the veneration given to it (Gieschen 1998, 31–33).

64. Hurtado (2005, 6) sees devotion to Jesus as a development from within Second Temple Judaism, albeit an innovative one.

65. For more detail the various aspects of this debate, see Dunn 1989; Bauckham 1998, 2008; K. Sullivan 2004; DeConick 2007.

66. Sheffield is utilizing the gender theories of Butler in her article and so makes a play on two of Butler's works at this point (as she does throughout her article), *Gender Trouble* and *Bodies That Matter*.

67. Of course, the current reality for many transgressive bodies, however, is that they are often ridiculed, distained, beaten, imprisoned, and even killed. And this is exactly what happened to the Jesus of the gospel accounts who "was numbered with the transgressors" (Luke 22:37 NIV; Mark 15:16–20 and parr.). Shame and dishonor are accorded to those who transgress the "natural" boundaries and seek to live beyond them. See the discussion in Burrus (2008, 10–80) on martyrdom, the crucifixion, and shame, as discussed in ch. 3 above.

68. In addition, even though some early gnostic christologies understood Christ to be androgynous, this is really a state of "reconstituted masculinity" (D. MacDonald 1988, 285). This androcentrism is also evident in the Adam-Christ analogy developed by Paul in Rom 5:12–21 and 1 Cor 15:45–49 (Wilson-Kastner 1982, 238; Ruether 1983).

Scene 2

So I am in this amazing study, right, and it's just lined with books. I am running my fingers along the spines, not even looking at the titles really—it's the overall feel of them that tells you all you need to know. And he is sitting just over there, in that leather armchair, barely visible through the smoke. I don't mind the smoke—it's from a pipe, or a cigar maybe, take your pick. He's got that look in his eye, I just know it—you know the one—a smoldering sparkle just ready to burst into flame. I can tell even if I am not looking at him. I pretend to look at the books.

But sooner or later we are going to have to talk, and it will be me that has to say something; we both know this. Why would he say anything? He is the one all comfortable in that chair. All smug with the world revolving around his finger. The weight of the room tells me this; the feel of all those spines tells me this. Even the smoke tells me, intoxicating me with its sweet strength. I am the one who is light, who barely leaves a mark on the thick carpet as I circle the room. I am the one who might bend or break. He knows this, is sure of this, and so can just watch through the smoke as I let my hand caress those spines.

My circling has taken me to the dark corner behind his chair. And although the leather back of it is high and its arms curve wide to embrace him, I reach around and take the pipe (although I think it's a cigar) from his mouth. He likes this. He thinks it's a game. It's not just his eyes that are sparkling now. This is a game he likes to play, has played before, and wins every time. Why talk when you can play? But I don't want to play this little game anymore. There are rules I want to bend and break.

So instead of straddling his lap and replacing the pipe (it's definitely a cigar) with my lips and letting him win, I walk over to the other arm-chair in the room (they are a pair), I make myself comfortable with one leg draped over the side, and I take a long deep pull on that pipe-that-is-a-cigar and, exhaling the sweet strong smoke, I say, "Karl, we need to talk."

5

The Straight Mind in 1 Corinthians 11:7

Thus it is our historical task ... to define what we call oppression in materialist terms, to make it evident that women are a class, which is to say that the category 'woman' as well as the category 'man' are political and economic categories not eternal ones.

— Monique Wittig, "One Is Not Born a Woman"

Ἀνὴρ μὲν γὰρ οὐκ ὀφείλει κατακαλύπτεσθαι τὴν κεφαλήν εἰκὼν καὶ δόξα θεοῦ ὑπάρχων· ἡ γυνὴ δὲ δόξα ἀνδρός ἐστιν.

For, a man, on the one hand, ought not to have his head covered, being the image and glory of God, but the woman, by contrast, is the glory of man.

— 1 Cor 11:7

Introduction

The task to which Wittig calls us involves revealing the ways in which the categories of "man" and "woman" are construed as natural, or eternal, when in fact they are ideological constructions. In verse 7 Paul proceeds to justify his comments regarding the Corinthians' behavior by utilizing an argument of theological anthropology,[1] and as with 1 Cor 11:3, he sets out the pairing of oJ ἀνήρ and ἡ γυνή ("man" and "woman") in a way that has been used to present a heteropatriarchal model of gender as God-ordained and thus eternal. From the structure of this verse, with its use of the contrastive μέν and δέ, it is clear that "man" and "woman" are compared in relational terms (Thiselton 2000, 833). As a pair they are also linked with the divine—God—and thus this verse is often understood as reflecting the key pairing of "man and woman" found in the creation accounts of Gen 1–2. This pairing, however, is an asymmetrical binary; while the woman is described in relation to the man, as δόξα ἀνδρός ("the glory of man"), the man is *not* described in relation to the woman, but in relation to God, as εἰχὼν καὶ δόξα θεοῦ ("the image and glory of God"). The differences between the sexes can thus be understood as theologically grounded by Paul in the creation order. Furthermore, Paul's asymmetrical pairing of man and woman not only creates ambiguity over the ability of the woman alone to image God, but it also binds both man and woman together in a way that reinforces a heteropatriachal understanding of the *imago Dei*, elevating (patriarchal) heterosexual marriage to the pinnacle of what it means to be human.

Wittig argues, however, that categories of difference constituted as "concepts of opposition" conceal and dissimulate an ideological order (1979, 115; 1992a, 2–5; 1992e, 11, 15; 1992i, 27–29). She states that such differences will often be viewed as "natural" or as deriving from "divine will" and thus have the appearance of being "a priori" or "already there" (1979, 115). In particular, this difference between men and women then "makes heterosexuality a 'natural' sexuality" (1979, 115). Various discourses operating in society reinforce the notion that heterosexuality is normative, that it "founds society" and is "a given" (1992i, 24, 27; see also Butler 1993, 2; 1999, 32; Bech 1995, 188). These discourses include the way in which the biblical accounts of human origin, primarily reflected in Gen 1–3, have been used in the history of the Christian West to legitimate both gender hierarchy and heterosexuality as natural and eternal. Paul's teaching in 1 Cor 11:2–16, particularly his pronouncements that "man is the head of woman" (v. 3) and "man is the image and glory of God, but woman is the glory of man" (v. 7), has been a significant part of this historical divine sanction of heteropatriarchy.

While traditional approaches to this verse often focus on the background and meaning of the other pair of key words in this verse, εἰχὼν and δόξα,[2] I will take up Wittig's challenge to "make it evident" that the categories of ὁ ἀνήρ and ἡ γυνή ("man" and "woman") are political rather than eternal. In this regard I will ultimately arrive at a consideration of the work Barth, one of the most significant Protestant theologians of the twentieth century, in particular his theology of "Man and Woman." Although a traditional approach to this verse might not usually find itself traversing sections of the *Church Dogmatics*, Barth's thinking on the way in which man and woman together reflect the image of God has been very influential on evangelical Christian views of gender and sexuality. Barth's vision of the *imago Dei* as the "unequal duality" of the heterosexual married couple

finds support in 1 Cor 11:7, so both revealing and challenging the androcentric, patriarchal, and heterosexist ideologies reflected in such theology
is important.

Before focusing on Barth, we need to consider the debate over the
interpretation of the words ὁ ἀνήρ and ἡ γυνή in 1 Cor 11:7. Given the
theological scope of this verse, and in particular its clear connection with
the creation account in Gen 1–2 (especially Gen 1:26–28 and 2:18–22),
some scholars point out that it describes an "ontological hierarchy"[3] in the
relationship between ὁ ἀνήρ and ἡ γυνή that is prescriptive for relations
between all men and women at every level of existence and not just limited to the particular situation in Corinth that Paul was addressing. Robert
Doyle (1987, 45–46), for example, declares that this hierarchy, which he
argues orders subjection for women, is a "foundational" and "normative"
principle of what it means to be the image of God, and one that therefore
"encompasses all men and women, not just married ones."[4] It is "eternally
so," according to Doyle (55 n. 5) and therefore, supposedly, "most beneficial."[5] This is precisely the sort of argument that Wittig (1992d, 41–45)
deplores as part of the rhetoric of the straight mind, the hegemony of the
"heterosexual social contract," which is given a quality of being established
according to "divine will."

Other scholars who find that Paul is outlining a hierarchical, authoritative relationship between ὁ ἀνήρ and ἡ γυνή in verse 7 prefer to limit
Paul's instructions to the marriage relationship only, so that not *all* women
are subordinate to *all* men. Although only one published translation has
"husband" and "wife" in the text of verse 7, many scholars and commentators discuss the text in terms of husbands and wives (Isaksson 1965, 174–
76; Hurley 1973, 203; Orr and Walther 1976, 264; Blomberg 1994, 209–10;
Winter 2003b, 77–96; Keener 2005, 93).[6] Blomberg, for example, argues
that although attempts to promote the notion of a matrimonial hierarchy
are fraught, Paul clearly outlines a "hierarchy of marriage" in 1 Cor 11:7
that is "not only innocuous but wonderful," in that husbands are to model
"the moral and relational attributes of the image of God" that are revealed
to Moses in Exod 33:18–34:7 (1994, 217–18, 223–26). He suggests that
although we can be sure Paul knew that women are also made in the image
of God, on the basis of Gen 1:27, he did not use the word εἰκών in his statement about woman, "lest he wind up saying that women are images of
their husbands" (218; see also Barrett 1971, 249; Fee 1987, 515; Dowling
1994, 38; Chakkalakal 1997, 192; Garland 2003, 523; A. Johnson 2004, 195;
Marshall 2004, 175; Payne 2009, 177).

In relation to this, Blomberg's (2007, 9) view regarding women in ministry is that they can take on a leadership role only if they "choose to remain single" (and thus be both celibate and childless); or, if married, a woman would need to minister at a different church from her husband so that she is not in a position of "authoritatively teaching God's word to her husband." While he sympathizes with those who find it unacceptable that certain categories of people are forever barred from certain functions "simply because of innate features such as gender," he makes the astounding suggestion that "those who cannot live with this relationship need not enter into it" (1994, 217). In this regard, Blomberg might appear to be in accord with Wittig—which would no doubt be a surprise to both parties— as she calls (albeit in a much stronger manner) for exactly this solution to the problem of male dominance and the hegemony of heteronormativity. She observes, however, that (so far) only "some lesbians and nuns" have managed to escape (1992a, 7). Unlike Wittig, however, Blomberg both hopes and expects that the majority of women (and men) would *not* opt out of marriage, given that he would argue such a choice would also necessarily entail a "choice" of celibacy and thus childlessness, which would hardly be beneficial for the long-term survival of humanity. His suggestion, while appearing to be a positive offer of freedom of choice, would therefore seem to betray a lack of understanding of the ramifications such a difficult "choice" presents. Wittig's desire for the opposite—that most people *would* opt out of marriage (and any heterosexual relationship)— does *not* preclude either sexual desire or reproduction however (1992a, 6; 1992e, 11).

Unlike Blomberg, however, some scholars do not see the hierarchy in 1 Cor 11:7 as being potentially "wonderful." Fatum (1995, 107 n. 73), for example, rejects as "wishful thinking" any attempt to rescue Paul from his "unambiguous words about women's inferior rank and secondary role in the order of creation as well as of salvation" (116 n. 52). She points out that Paul chooses to rebuke ἡ γυνή as females, as "sexual beings," rather than as "Christians," who "belong to a man," are "male property," and are a man's "possession" (67–69, 73). For Fatum, Paul's main concern is to reinforce "male sexual control," and so she argues that verses 3–10 are concerned with "the sociosexual order of marriage" (1995, 67, 98–99, 101–9; see also 1989, 71; 2005, 195–96). She suggests that, for Paul, the social subordination of ἡ γυνή is connected to the theological concept of her inferiority, given her "subordinated position at the bottom of the hierarchy" (as seen in v. 3) and her "lack of *imago dei* quality" (as seen in v. 7) (1995, 105–6

n. 73). She says that "Paul takes for granted that woman is indeed not of God's image" and that the man alone *is* the image of God, and that this is part of the order of creation as expressed in Gen 1:26–27a and 2:18–24 (71–72). In relation to God, therefore, a woman is "completely subordinated to man," and "her most vital duty is to persist in her own unworthiness and inferiority as a consequence of her not being the image of God" (74–75). As a creature without the image of God, a woman "is without human quality" (75).

It is clear from this discussion of ὁ ἀνήρ and ἡ γυνή that Paul's statement regarding ὁ ἀνήρ as "the image of God" can suggest an understanding of the *imago Dei* as something androcentric, patriarchal, and—given the centrality of the pairing ὁ ἀνήρ and ἡ γυνή—also heterosexist. Elisabeth Gössmann (1999, 32) outlines the way in which the patristic and scholastic traditions justified, by reference to 1 Cor 11:7, "a gradation of the image of God in the two sexes, that is to say, a very clear *imago Dei* in the male and a weaker one or even a total absence in the female." She notes the inability of the woman to represent God or Christ in these traditions, citing an example of medieval canon law (*Decretum Gratiani*) that clearly draws on 1 Cor 11:2–16 in its emphatic statement that "woman must cover her head, since she is not the image of God" (see *Decretum Gratiani* Causa 33, question 5, chs. 11, 13, 15, and 19, as cited in Gössman 1999, 22). Thomas Aquinas—following in the philosophical footsteps of Aristotle—also emphasized that aside from a basic level of "life in God's grace" accorded to all, "imago Dei invenitur in viro, secundum quod non invenitur in muliere. Nam vir est principium mulieris et finis, sicut Deus est principium et finis totius creaturae" ("God's image is found in man in a way in which it is not found in woman; for man is the beginning and end of woman, just as God is the beginning and end of all creation") (*Summa Theologica* 1a, 93, 4 [Hill]).[7]

The effect of this androcentric theology has been well documented by feminist scholars, and many have sought to explore ways of visioning "woman" as *imago Dei* (Daly 1973; Ruether 1983; McFague 1987; Heyward 1989; O'Hara 1995).[8] Gössmann (1999, 35–36) notes the countertradition of women writers in the Middle Ages such as Hildegard of Bingen, who, by emphasizing both what she called *quasi virile* and *quasi feminineum* aspects of the divinity, "'raised' woman's *imago Dei* to the level of man's power to reflect divine creativity and represent divinity." However, these masculine and feminine qualities of the divine tend to be stereotypical; "divine justice" is an example of a masculine quality, while "divine mercifulness" is a feminine quality (35).[9] Such a validation of the feminine is a positive step away from the prevalent androcentric norm, but there is also a tendency for this approach to reinforce gender stereotypes and reify "the feminine." This is precisely Wittig's concern with regard to "feminine writing" (1992f, 59–60; 1992k, 69). She argues that the danger of promoting a specifically "feminine" form of writing is that it reinforces the ideology of the differences between the sexes and maintains the "feminine" as something "peculiar" rather than something simply accepted as "writing" (1992f, 60; see also Collier and Sawyer 1999, 18).

It is important, therefore, to go further than this validation of the feminine, and so I agree with Althaus-Reid (2005, 63) that "gender is not a category deep enough to destabilize patriarchal theologies." A consideration of the "deeper" category of sexuality allows for a recognition that underlying virtually every *imago* theology—be it one that asserts the male as the only proper *imago Dei* or one that incorporates the female into the *imago Dei*—is a heterosexual paradigm. Althaus-Reid (267) has rightly critiqued what she calls the "patriarchal heterosexual order" of Christian theology, moving beyond feminist theology's recognition of the patriarchalism inherent in so much theology to an awareness that the ideology of heterosexuality is the main pillar of patriarchy. This has created what she calls "the heterosexual condition of theology" (270).

I suggest also that it is possible to view the traditional theology of the *imago Dei* as part of the "whole conglomerate of sciences and disciplines" that Wittig (1992i, 27, 29) calls "the straight mind." As one of the many "heterosexual systems of thought" that function in society, patriarchal theology sanctions heterosexuality not only as "natural" but also as divinely ordained (32). Consequently, in the rest of this chapter I will not only explore the way in which "the straight mind" functions in the *imago* theology of Barth, but I will also contrast Barth's vision of the *imago Dei*, "the unequal duality" of the "I and Thou"—the heterosexual married couple—with Wittig's vision of the ungendered, universal, whole "I"—the lesbian. By doing so I will be seeking to expose and destabilize the androcentric, patriarchal, and heterosexist ideologies underlying Barth's theology. This ought to be a reminder that rather than being a divinely ordained, eternal institution that finds support in a biblical text such as 1 Cor 11:7, "heterosexuality [is] a political institution in the patriarchal system" (Turcotte 1992, x).

The Straight Mind of Karl Barth

For Barth, the union of man and woman in heterosexual marriage is of utmost importance when expressing what it means for "man"[10] to be the image of God. Barth's treatise on "Man and Woman" is part of his larger discussion on creation (the subject of *CD* 3), and he states that the "invitation to humanity"—the way in which "man" is to "prove and express himself as the image of God"—is through the summons to "fellow-humanity" (*CD* 3.4:117).[11] Given that his affirmation of the "natural dualism" of man and woman is inextricably linked with his rejection of what he describes as the "malady called homosexuality" (3.4:121, 166), Barth's theology at this point is therefore perhaps one of the clearest and most influential examples of Althaus-Reid's "patriarchal heterosexual order" and Wittig's concept of "the straight mind."

Barth argues that it is in both the coexistence and differentiation of male and female that "man" finds that "he" can be truly human and reflect the image of God; God directs "him" to "his fellow-man" and this person will, of necessity, be someone of the opposite sex (3.4:116). For Barth, this "natural dualism" of male and female is of necessity a relationship of "differentiation" or "confrontation," and he declares that "no other relationship is so obvious, self-explanatory and universally valid as that whose force resides precisely in the presupposed underlying otherness" between male and female ("der menschliche Mann und die menschliche Frau") (*KD* 3.4:129). This relationship is not based in "a purely external, incidental and transient sexuality, but rather an inward, essential and lasting order of being as He and She, valid for all time and also for eternity" (3.4:158; see also 3.1:183–86).

Barth's language is saturated both with androcentric imagery and rhetorical claims to what is self-evident. Although it could be seen as anachronistic to criticize Barth for being less than inclusive in his choice of nouns and pronouns, rather it is indicative of his focus on the male as the theological subject—yet another example of the "universal male" discussed in chapter 4 above. A consideration of the way in which Barth describes the "otherness" that he argues is so fundamental to the male-female relationship makes this clear. For Barth, "Man and Woman" are fundamentally and formatively related as "I" and "Thou" in their encounter and coexistence; and he states, for example, "He can only be an I through and for this Thou. The Thou which is not an I and is therefore constitutive for the I is woman" (3.4:149).[12] The "I" in Barth's framework is inevitably revealed as *der Mann*, a point reinforced in his statement of "the natural supremacy of the I over the Thou" (3.2:292). Although Barth acknowledges that "she is I as his Thou" and has her own humanity, this comes in the context of Barth's argument that "the only real humanity is that which for the woman consists in being the wife of a male and therefore the wife of man" (3.1:309). Or, again, in light of Gen 2:18, he states: "They had no need to envy their respective advantages, although the man in himself was a question without the answer and the woman only the answer to his question" (3.4:150).[13] Woman is "the answer" rather than, for example, "she who answers," a formulation that would be empowering, self-determinative, and mutual, rather than objectifying.[14] Graham Ward (1998, 59) pointedly notes, "What man does for woman is not described in anything like the same detail."

While contemporary feminists have critiqued Barth,[15] he was also criticized by at least one feminist prior to the publication of his *Church Dogmatics*, precisely on the points raised above. After publishing an essay entitled "Is There a Woman's Problem?" Henriette Visser 'T Hooft (1934, 14) corresponded with Barth regarding 1 Cor 11:5–9, expressing her concern that "wie überall die weibliche Verantwortlichkeit Gott gegenüber von der männlichen gehemmt und determiniert wird" ("everywhere female responsibility to God is inhibited and determined by male responsibility"), and arguing for mutuality in the relationship between men and women instead of domination and submission.[16] In a later essay (1962) she also highlighted the tendency of Barth's I-Thou schema to objectify women, explaining that the I-Thou relationships of man and woman are perverted into "I-It" relationships. She thus calls woman to "be on her guard" and to "unmask false dialogues" in this world of "man-alone" (74).[17]

In his initial response to her, Barth replied, "die Superiorität Adams" ("the superiority of Adam") is to be accepted because "es nun einmal so ist" ("it is just so") (1981, 16).[18] In other words, Gary Dorrien (2000, 166) suggests, "Barth replied that she simply misunderstood the spiritual necessity of patriarchy." In another letter, Barth also echoed the familiar complaint of those in positions of power: "Aber verstehen Sie denn nicht, dass das für uns Männer eine schwere Last bedeutet?" (cited in H. Visser t'Hooft 1981, 29; "But do you not understand, then, that it is a heavy burden for us men?"); this outraged H. Visser 'T Hooft, and she challenged Barth as to whether God would "der einen Hälfte der Menschheit eine schwere Last auferlegen, von welcher zum großen Teil das Heil der anderen Hälfte abhängen würde?" ("impose a heavy burden on one half of humanity on which the welfare of the other half would largely depend?") (1981, 29). Anticipating much later feminist theorizing, H. Visser 'T Hooft (19) replied to Barth that she opposed the "Enthauptung" ("decapitation") of women and the "Entleibung" ("disembodiment") of men that results from an adherence to the head-body, or domination-submission, model of relationships.[19] She notes, laconically, that this letter "blieb unbeantwortet" ("remained unanswered") (19). Jürgen Moltmann sums up her view as follows:

> Henriette Visser 'T Hooft clearly saw that the community of men and women has two sides, the social side of women being deprived of rights and being treated unfairly and the psychological side of their assimilation to the male world through the development of inferiority complexes. The liberation of the woman to her God-given identity must at the same time proceed psychologically and socially.... The same is true for men: The identification of humanness with their maleness has deprived them of their true, God-given identity.... The conversion of the man to true humanness will connect the discovery of the inner identity with the social "redistribution of power." (1999, 530)

Moltmann (1999, 524) laments that, despite his correspondence with H. Visser 'T Hooft, Barth does not mention her name in his discussion on "Man and Woman," "much to the detriment of Barth's anthropology." According to Moltmann (529), Barth maintained "the superiority-inferiority scheme for the sake of the theological system and deprived himself and his readers of the better insights of personal mutualism." Nevertheless, Dorrien (2000, 166) suggests that Barth's "sarcasm and chauvinism" may have been lessened by their correspondence; he suggests that when Barth's *Church Dogmatics* volume 3 eventually came out, "[H.] Visser 'T Hooft must have given him second thoughts about his male chauvinism. The patronizing rhetoric of 'it is just so' gave way to a tortuous grappling with the problem of gender relations from a scriptural perspective."[20]

Such "tortuous grappling" is evident in Barth's discussion on the issue of "equality." He states, "Man and woman are fully equal before God and therefore as men [*Menschen*]" (3.4:169). But he also goes on to state, "the fact remains [that] there is no simple equality" (3.4:169–70). While Barth assures his readers that both man and woman are to be viewed as human (*Menschen*), there is a "structural and functional difference" between them that is "essential" to their creation in the divine likeness (3.4:117, 130). Thus Barth can also say that God made "man" (*Mensch*) "in the unequal duality of male and female" (3.1:288). Barth is at pains to insist that this differentiation is not meant to suggest inferiority. In his discussion on

1 Cor 11:2–16, he says, "The command of the Lord does not put anyone, man or woman, in a humiliating, dishonourable or unworthy position. It puts both man and woman in their proper place" (3.4:156; see also 3.1:303; 3.2:314). Such differentiation ought to create not division but a unity that reflects both the creation of man and woman in Genesis and their spiritual equality found in Christ (Gal 3:28), most "indisputably" and "plainly" expressed by Paul in 1 Cor 11:7 (3.4:164, 174; 3.2:309).

It is vital for Barth that this differentiation be observed. While he adamantly rejects stereotypical typologies of the sexes (3.2:287; 3.4:152–53), Barth still views each sex as being distinct: "This distinction … must not be blurred on either side. The command of God will always point man to his position and woman to hers" (3.4:154; see also 3.2:309–16). He concedes that not every violation of these boundaries is offensive, however, showing some sympathy for those who express tendencies that others might reject outright, such as Friedrich Schleiermacher's toying with the wish to be a woman (3.4:154–55).[21] However, Barth is also very clear that the differences between men and women are to be maintained, and that any "forgetting or refusal" to do so, any "jealousy, envy, imitation or usurpation," will never be acceptable, and that "pure desire will constantly and surely lead man and woman back to their place" (3.4:154; see also 3.2:287). This leads Barth into a discussion on the feminist movement, and he makes the connection with 1 Cor 11:2–16, noting that the Corinthian women wished to be like men, based on Gal 3:28. Yet Paul, he says, reminds them of their "peculiar dignity and rights" (3.4:156; see also 3.2:309–12). Women in general then, are not to violate the order that God has ordained, which is for "all eternity," and which "directs both man and woman to their own proper sacred place" (3.4:156; see also 3.2:320).

As for the nature of this order, Barth insists on an order of "super- and sub-ordination" (3.4:169). He acknowledges that this area is "delicate" and cautions that "every word is dangerous and liable to be misunderstood when we try to characterise this order" (3.4:168–69). Nevertheless, he explains that this order is part of the "divine command" for men and women in general (*not* just confined to husbands and wives). In perhaps his most (in)famous comment on the relation between the sexes, Barth explains this order—the "sequence" in which man and woman stand in relation to each other—as follows:

> Man and woman are not an A and a second A whose being and relationship can be described like the two halves of an hour glass, which are

obviously two, but absolutely equal and therefore interchangeable. Man and woman are an A and a B, and cannot therefore, be equated....
    ... A precedes B, and B follows A. Order means succession. It means preceding and following. It means super- and sub-ordination. (3.4:169)[22]

I will return to this order below, but at this point I want to note how Barth argues that for men and women *not* to accept or recognize this element in the divine ordering of male and female relationships, is to invite "disorder" (*Unordnung*) (3.4:169). Indeed, the establishment of "equality" between a man and woman leaves them both "hanging in the void," something that is to be avoided as "a state of affairs [that is] irreparably deplorable" (3.4:171).[23] But what precisely does "disorder" look like? What does it actually mean to be "hanging in the void"? What is at stake in upholding this divine order, without which there appears to be "confusion" and subsequent "dehumanisation" (*Verunmenschlichung*) (3.4:157)?

If men and women move away from the "togetherness" (*Zusammensein*) (*CD* 3.4:116) to which God calls them, preferring the company of their own sex—be that in "religious or secular orders or communities ... [or] in clubs and ladies' circles"—for any reason other than "temporarily as an emergency measure," then Barth declares that this move "is obviously disobedience" (3.4:165). Rather stereotypically, against his own advice just a few pages earlier (3.4:152–53; see also 3.2:287), he explains that "every artificially induced and maintained isolation of the sexes tends as such—usually very quickly and certainly morosely and blindly—to become philistinish in the case of the men and precious in that of women, and in both cases more or less inhuman [*unmenschlich*]" (3.4:165–66). Such a view has potential to be quite progressive, I suggest; women could expect traditional "male only" clubs, occupations, or sporting events to become open to them, and partnership in traditionally female-only areas such as parenting and childcare could open up new areas in which men could become involved. Somewhat humorously Barth comments, "All due respect to the comradeship of a company of soldiers!" (3.4:165). Of course, one logical step to take from Barth's position to solve the problem of "isolation" would be to allow for female soldiers, but given his views on the "proper sacred place" that each sex occupies, and the "peculiar dignity" of women, I suspect he would not accept that women could have a place in the military. Where this leaves the role of the military in Barth's schema is therefore ambiguous. These comments highlight some tension in Barth's thought between rejecting typologies of the sexes and the contorted effort to place man and woman in a relation of superiority and subordination.

However, the real concern for Barth is that these expressions of isolation are the "first steps" toward what he calls "the malady called homosexuality … the physical, psychological and social sickness, the phenomenon of perversion, decadence and decay" (3.4:166). It is here in his brief discussion on homosexuality that we perhaps most clearly find Barth's vision of "disorder" and "confusion."[24] Homosexuality for Barth is inextricably linked with a rejection of the "Other" in preference for one who is the "Same" and is thus (with reference to Rom 1:25) primarily the sin of idolatry (3.4:166). Barth argues that despite a sense of "togetherness" those in a homosexual partnership might portray and express, this is actually dehumanization since the only true reflection of humanity (as the image of God) is in the "natural duality" of male and female.[25] Barth takes for granted that the "opposite sex" is "despised" by those who engage in such behavior, and that "the natural orientation" is still "in force" on those who have given themselves up to "the worship of a false god" (3.4:166).[26] As Jaime Balboa (1998, 780) puts it, "This denial of heterosexual desire then culminates [for Barth] in the denial of the *imago Dei* of the self and of the other."

Ultimately for Barth, homosexuality is an orientation that has turned in upon itself rather than being directed outward toward another; it is an "I" turned toward the self-same "I," rather than toward an opposite "Thou." Being inwardly focused upon "Oneself" rather than outwardly focused toward "Another" leads the person inevitably into an unhealthy state of being; it is as much an inversion as a perversion. Barth argues that the creation story shows that the "man in isolation" would not reflect the image of God (3.1:289–90). But more than this, the partner ("helpmeet") that is needed must be different in order to be able to confront him, otherwise "he would merely recognise himself in it" (3.1:289–90).[27] Such behavior is seen by Barth, therefore, as a "malady," a "sickness," an attempt at being "genuinely human" that inextricably ends in "decay" and in something that is ultimately "inhuman" (*unmenschlich*) (3.4:166). Separate spheres of male and female activity are viewed as "symptoms" of this "malady of homosexuality," which consequently "breaks out"; doctors (as well as pastors and others) are thus called upon "for the protection of threatened youth" (3.4:166).[28] The only true expression of sexuality for Barth is (to use a favorite term of his) "concrete" heterosexuality in contrast to this esoteric, confused, unhealthy, and ultimately inhuman state of being (3.1:309; 3.4:175).

Ward (1998, 55) agrees with Barth on the importance—centrality even—of sexual difference in relation to human identity: "Difference is fundamental and cannot be transcended. Sexual difference, in its endorsement of both separation and relation, constitutes we human creatures as the *imago dei*." Building on the work of Butler, Ward explains that the biological has been shaped by the political—as Wittig would also argue—and thus bodies and sexuality are not stable universal givens.[29] In other words, "male and female are tropes"; they are "symbolic positions within a divine narrative" (63, 65; see also Salomonsen 2003, 112). Consequently, Ward criticizes Barth for resorting to a form of theologizing based on precisely the kind of natural theology his entire system was intended to refute. He notes that, for Barth, "same-sex relations are perversions not of the theological but of the natural order," and that in regarding the role of woman as a subordinate "helpmeet," "Barth returns here to an affirmation of a natural and social order (orders highly convenient for him, serviced as he was by two women)" (1998, 65–66).[30] Based on his utilization of Irigaray's concept of hom(m)o-sexuality,[31] Ward suggests that Barth views sexual difference from a male perspective:

> He [Barth] wants difference. He wants sexual difference to be paradigmatic of the radically, unassimilable difference between I and Thou, Self and Other, Yahweh and Israel, Christ and His Church. But he reads this sexual difference from the male perspective. Though he voices a respect for the feminine, she is defined only in relation to what the male lacks—she is the help *meet* for him.... She does not stand *with* man, or *before* man as other, she stands *for* man. In other words, I suggest, Barth is not able to establish the sexual difference his theology requires. His male and female are not a couple. They are not a partnership. The desire in operation, in Irigaray's terms, is hom(m)osexual, narcissistic. The woman has a function only within the economy of the male desire wherein she functions as compliment [*sic*], not difference. (66–67)[32]

That Barth's rejection of homosexuality is based more on social and cultural mores, rather than on a rigorous adherence to his own theology of sexual difference, as Ward argues, can be seen most clearly when one considers how Barth deals with another potentially theologically difficult topic—divorce. Barth spends many pages highlighting the notion that marriage is the "proper locus" (3.2:288), "crucial expression" (3.4:117), and "*telos*" of the male-female relationship (3.4:140–42, 181). It is "an exclusive life-partnership" (3.4:182, 195) that is "the ideal and archetypal form of human fellowship" (3.4:197) and the "special reflector, image and likeness" of the relationship between God and man (3.4:197). Most significantly, it is akin to the theologies of divine election and covenant, and in particular, the relationship between Christ and the church (3.1:190–91, 203, 290; 3.2:297–324; 3.4:198). Not surprisingly, therefore, Barth's discussion of marriage is also peppered with comments such as: "To enter upon marriage is to renounce the possibility of leaving it"; and "Divorce is quite impermissible" (3.4:203–5). Even in his discussion of the subordination of women, where he recognizes that some men will abuse their position of superiority and cause women to suffer—these men becoming what he later calls "tyrants"—he counsels women to remain in their place (3.4:171–72, 177).[33] It is clear from such comments that Barth holds marriage—and the order of relations within marriage (to which I will return below)—as being of utmost importance, and thus his view on divorce seems unequivocal.

However, even on this "crucial" issue, Barth is not entirely inflexible. Only that which God has joined together cannot be put asunder; in other words, according to Barth, only the marriage that "rests upon the command of God and therefore upon His calling and gift cannot be dissolved by man even if he wishes" (3.4:207). It turns out, therefore, that not all marriages are called by God, and thus some marriages are quite simply "radically dissoluble because there has been no real union in the judgment of God" (3.4:209). Precisely how one determines what God's judgment is on the matter is dependent on "certain terrible indications" that Barth does not elucidate. Ultimately, it seems to come down to "a recognition of faith" and an acceptance of "the Word of God" that will determine that a marriage can, "and perhaps in certain situations must," be dissolved (although, again, which situations these might be is left unexplained; 3.4:209–11).

Given the centrality of marriage in Barth's schema of male-female relations, it is quite remarkable that we find such unspecified and relatively open scope for divorce. For homosexuality, however, there is no room for any form of expression: "homosexuality can have no place in this life, whether in its more refined or cruder forms" (3.4:166). It is here then that we realize the strength of Barth's "straight mind"; heterosexuality is absolutely fundamental to what it means to be "human" and thus to be made in the image of God. An "unhealthy" expression of the male-female relationship is still an expression of the "natural dualism" that has been commanded by God; a partnership of two people of the same sex—despite any sense of "togetherness" or differentiation—can never reflect the image of God (Thielicke 1964, 271; Rees 2002, 42; Ward 1998, 70).

Recalling Wittig's point that "heterosexuality [is] a political institution in the patriarchal system" (Turcotte 1992, x), then it is crucial that we delve deeper into Barth's notion of marriage. Despite vehemently rejecting stereotypes and typologies of the sexes a few pages earlier, Barth explains that the way in which man and woman obediently observe the divine order "will inevitably entail a certain systematisation, almost a kind of woodcut" (3.4:176).[34] Not only is the heterosexual relationship at the center of what it means to be fully human as the image of God, but if this relationship is one of "obedience," then the "proper place" of "man" is as "the strong man" who stands with "the mature woman" at his side (3.4:176–77, 181). The strong man is in many ways the benevolent paterfamilias: one who takes "masculine responsibility" for ensuring the divine order is maintained, who "is vigilant for the interests of both sexes," and who, while "he will not feel superior to woman," will nevertheless "really be superior" as he takes upon himself the primary task of ensuring that the divine order is secured and obeyed (3.4:176–77). The mature woman, for her part, "will feel no sense of inferiority nor impulse of jealousy" nor will she "need to assert herself," but she will feel "promoted and protected … [and] guarded" and will "make it her joy and pride as a woman to be worthy of this concern" (3.4:177).

Behind this picture of the "ideal" heterosexual couple lies Barth's exegesis of 1 Cor 11:2–16 and other passages, most notably Eph 5, which he describes as the "*locus classicus*" on these matters (3.2:312). Barth seems to have viewed the κεφαλή schema in 1 Cor 11:3 in particular as the key for understanding the fundamental "I-Thou" relationships—of the Father to the Son, of God to creation, of Christ to the church, and thus also of male to female (3.1:203–4; 3.2:310–13; 3.4:174). Barth is quick to dismiss as "absurd" any understanding of this verse to mean that woman only has an indirect relationship to God (by way of the man) and instead argues that the correct interpretation of this passage involves recognizing that Christ, as the "head of every man," implies that he is both "the sum of all superordination" and "the sum of all subordination" (3.2:311). Barth therefore states:

> It is no little thing for man to be κεφαλή in relation to woman, i.e., the one who has precedence, initiative and authority, the representative of the order which embraces them both, [and] it is no little thing for woman to take the place which she is assigned in relation to man and therefore not to be κεφαλή but to be led by him, to accept his authority, to recognise the order which claims them both as it is represented by him. (3.2:311)

Bringing in 1 Cor 11:10, Barth explains that, because the place of both the man and the woman is most supremely exemplified in Christ, the ἐξουσία of man "is legitimate and effective," while the woman's relationship "to the ἐξουσία of man which she lacks … is sanctified, ennobled and glorified" (3.2:311). That this order of relationship is "helpful and right and worthy" is justified by reference to 1 Cor 11:7–9, with its explicit link to Gen 2. Barth argues that "this basic order of the human established by God's creation is not accidental or contingent. It cannot be overlooked or ironed out.… It is solidly and necessarily grounded in Christ" (3.2:311).[35] As a result, he argues against any need for "the feminist question" given that this order "can only be their [the man and woman's] honour and joy and blessing" (3.2:312). The woman, in fact, "need not fear this pre-eminence"; because she represents Christ's subordination, she has "the advantage" and "a peculiar distinction" (3.1:306, 314). More than this, "the wife is not less but greater than her husband.… She is not the second but the first"; or as he no less idealistically states elsewhere, "The man does not enjoy any privilege or advantage over woman" (3.2:314; see also 3.4:170).

If Barth's assumption that this divine ordering entailed "only" honor, joy, and blessing, then one might ask why some women—be they the "enthusiastic" Corinthians or members of "the modern feminist movement"—might find this hierarchical style of relating less than satisfactory (3.2:309, 313; 3.4:155). One may wonder why these women have not embraced the "freedom" and "joy" that this order supposedly entails. Why not be "second" and "subordinate" to one who leads "for her sake" and "certainly not to his own advantage" (3.4:194)?

Elizabeth Clark and Herbert Richardson (1977, 243) answer somewhat succinctly: "Feminists … find Barth's views either infuriating or laughable." The reality is that few men appear to live the altruistic life that Barth upholds as part of "the particular responsibility of men" as κεφαλή. Not only this, but as H. Visser 'T Hooft observed, this "heavy burden" is detrimental to the emotional and spiritual health of men who cannot live up to this ideal. Ironically, Barth criticizes de Beauvoir for indulging in mythmaking with regard to the "highly unreal man" that he suggests she envisions: "Even in the masculine form [she presupposes], is not this individual a product of wishful thinking rather than a reality? Is he not more of a man-God or God-man than a real human figure?" (3.4:162). In addition, not only does the rhetoric of such male "service" appear to be able to exist alongside the maintenance of male prerogative and privilege and women's oppression and restriction, it is the presumed "naturalness" and "divine ordering" of this so-called freedom and fellowship that feminists have resisted. Even under the rule (guidance, protection) of a benevolent dictator, such as one might describe Barth's "kind strong man," women are positioned as "secondary"; and therefore, as much as Barth would like to think that this does not imply "inferiority," it not only places women in an ambiguous position (almost but not quite fully human, as with Aristotle's placement of women alongside slaves and children), but it also calls into question their ability to image God in and of themselves.

Although Barth would want to argue that neither man nor woman images God by themselves, but only through being in "fellow-humanity" (*Mitmenschlichkeit*), he nevertheless also argues that *males* image God inasmuch as, within the pairing of male and female, they represent God in relation to the creature (or Jesus in relation to the church), while the female images the creature (or the church). In addition, he notes that the different parts of the analogy that man and woman represent are not interchangeable: "Man is primarily and properly Yahweh, and woman primarily and properly Israel" (3.2:297; see also 3.4:142–43). Barth warns that it is possible for the sexes to be tempted to exchange their unique roles but emphatically states, "The essential point is that woman must always and in all circumstances be woman; that she must feel and conduct herself as such and not as man; that the command of the Lord, which is for all eternity, directs both man and woman to their own proper sacred place and forbids all attempts to violate this order" (3.4:156). Here, then, is the crux of my critique of Barth's theology of man and woman regarding the *imago Dei*: woman can never represent God (or Jesus) in relation to the man. That only man, as male, can represent God (Yahweh, Christ), and that woman can never do this without violating the divine order, reveals the heteronormative patriarchy inherent in Barth's theology on the *imago Dei*. Barth may argue that these categories of man and woman are eternal, but they have emerged in this discussion as very much grounded in the ideological framework within which Barth operated.

Barth's Heterosexual "I and Thou" and Wittig's Lesbian "I"

Finally, this leads me to a contrast between Barth's vision of the *imago Dei* as "the unequal duality" of the "I and Thou"—the heterosexual married couple—with Wittig's vision of the ungendered, universal, whole "I" who is lesbian. In expounding his view on "the basic form of primal humanity," Barth states that there is "none who can escape" the divine ordering of human existence as male and female together (3.2:289). By contrast, as noted at the outset of this chapter, Wittig (1992a, 7) argues that this structuring of society is not a divine ordinance—the categories of man and woman are not eternal—and therefore she makes the point that such structuring is an ideological order from which only "some lesbians and nuns escape." Wittig (1992e, 13) urges all to escape the oppressive regime of heterosexuality, to refuse to become (or remain) heterosexual, and thus to "refuse to become a man or a woman." Rather than being trapped in the compulsory ideology of domination that lies at the heart of all relations between the sexes—the essence of heterosexuality for Wittig—she suggests destroying the categories of sex, and thus seeking "a new personal and subjective definition for all humankind ... beyond the categories of sex" (1992e, 19–20).

For Wittig, the only social form that enables this re-creation of the individual subject is lesbianism: "Lesbian is the only concept I know of which is beyond the categories of sex (woman and man), because the designated subject (lesbian) is *not* a woman, either economically, or politically, or ideologically" (1992e, 20). Refusing to acquiesce to the "unequal duality" of the "I and Thou," to use Barth's phrasing, Wittig (1992d, 45; 1992e, 20) argues that the lesbian is an "escapee" from the system of heteropatriarchy in the same way as American runaway slaves who escaped slavery. This is the essence of freedom for Wittig: to be free from the personal, physical, and economic obligations of heterosexuality that are imposed on women (in particular), and to be free to constitute oneself as an individual subject, an "I" who is "ungendered, universal, whole" (1992c, 80), and, as a lesbian, therefore neither a woman (nor a man).[36] As already noted, for Wittig, this act of becoming an "I" is primarily achieved through the authority of speech. By reappropriating language and speaking for oneself, one becomes the subject, thus enabling a reorganization of the social world free from the constraints of heteropatriarchy. This is not an isolationist stance, however. Wittig's fictional work highlights the "togetherness" (to use a Barthian term) of *elles* (in *Les Guérillères*), or of the protagonists "I" and "you" (in *The Lesbian Body*) (2005a, 38–39; 2005b, 47).

Barth, of course, not only has difficulty with the notion of the individual, but also has a very different idea of freedom. For Barth, the essence and nature of being human is found in the divine call to fellow humanity (*Mitmenschlichkeit*). In his critique of de Beauvoir, for example, he argues that she proclaims the "myth" of the human individual who achieves freedom by overcoming his masculinity or her femininity

(3.4:162). He comments, "the freeing of man in the form of his emancipation—and especially in this case the emancipation of woman—from sex ... can only end in the negation of real man" (3.4:162). Instead, Barth proposes that true freedom is found in the fellowship of being male *and* female. He cites 1 Cor 11:11 and declares, "in obedience to the divine command there is no such thing as a self-contained and self-sufficient male life or female life" (3.4:163). In addition, and in contrast to Wittig's idea of locution as evidence of subjectivity, Barth's concept of the *imago Dei* requires a "woman" who, as object rather than subject, barely speaks; she is an answer rather than she who answers. As Balboa (1998, 783) candidly notes, the concrete reality (for women at least) is that within Barth's framework, *"there is no room for human freedom."*[37]

One question that might be asked of Barth's *imago* theology, then, is how he understands the place of Jesus Christ in this schema, given both the importance of Christology for Barth's overall theological project (4.2:x; 4.1:138; Dawson 2007, 6) and that the historical figure of Jesus was (at least according to tradition) both single and celibate. While his focus on the "male and female" pairing found in Gen 1:27 allows Barth to give central place to marriage in his *imago* theology, a focus on the person of Jesus would hardly seem to allow for such a reading. The "life" of Jesus, as unmarried and celibate, would surely qualify him as one of Barth's "self-contained and self-sufficient" males, and yet—in a curious parallel to Wittig's lesbian—Barth instead describes the "Man" Jesus as "Real" and "Whole" (3.2:132, 325).

Barth grounds his theological anthropology in Christology, arguing that the ultimate expression of genuine humanity is found in the person of Jesus (Dawson 2007, 99–100).[38] He states, "The ontological determination of humanity is grounded in the fact that one man among all others is the man Jesus" (3.2:132). For all Jesus's unlikeness to us as individuals, and despite his unique relationship to God, Barth can say that "to be a man is to be with Jesus, to be like Him" (3.2:145). Consequently, theologians building on the work of Barth suggest that "genuine human being is Christic being" (Ward 1998, 60). So how does Barth end up restricting such a fundamentally christological anthropology, with its emphasis on the "one man" to whom "a man" (*Menschsein*) can be likened, to an *imago* theology, with its narrow pairing of a heterosexual married couple at the center?

It would seem that rather than having a purely christocentric focus in his discussion on man and woman, Barth resorts to an Adamic definition, not only of humanity but also of Christ. This can be seen in Barth's discussion of the New Testament uses of the phrase "the image of God" as they relate to Gen 1:26–27. For example, he states, "Adam is already Jesus Christ and Jesus Christ is already Adam.... In this way Paul regarded the man Jesus as the real image of God, and therefore as the real man created by God" (3.2:203). Barth explains each text in the New Testament that speaks of Jesus as the image of God in this Adamic manner, with the consequence that the figures of Christ, Adam, and "man" begin to conflate. In the text most pertinent to our discussion, Barth states:

> According to 1 Cor 11:7 there is a man who actually *is* the εἰκὼν καὶ δόξα θεοῦ and from this standpoint the same can be said of every man.... This man (with this woman) is, according to Paul (1 Cor. 15.45), the "last Adam," and (v. 47) the "second man from heaven," i.e., the man for whose sake, with whom in view, towards whom and therefore in and after whom, God created the first man. (3.2:203)

It appears from this statement that Barth reads the ἀνήρ in 1 Cor 11:7 in relation to both Christ and "every man" (perhaps recalling the παντὸς ἀνδρός from v. 3), giving ontological significance to Paul's choice of ὑπάρχων ("*is*") to allow for such multiple layers of interpretation. Barth's emphatic conclusion on this matter is worth citing in full:

> If we are to understand this, we must not overlook the fact that according to 1 Cor. 11.7 Paul always thought of the man who is God's εἰκὼν καὶ δόξα (even in passages where there [*sic*] is not immediately obvious) in conjunction with his wife, and therefore of Jesus, not as an isolated figure, but as Israel's Christ, the Head of His community. This will not surprise us if we read Gen. 1.26 (not to speak of Gen. 2) with open eyes. Paul did not find there an isolated male, but man and his wife. If Jesus Christ is the image of God, and therefore man, to say "Jesus Christ" is necessarily to speak also of the other ... who was divinely created with man, who with him is addressed by God as a Thou and made responsible to God as an I, the other who confronts him as a Thou and whom he himself confronts as an I. It is in this way that Paul actually speaks of Jesus Christ when he describes Him as the image of God and therefore man....
> ... It is obvious that all that [Paul] had to say about man and woman was seen from this angle, in the light of the relationship between Jesus Christ and His community, and therefore of His divine likeness. (3.1:203–5)

Thus Jesus is brought into both Barth's discussion of "Man and Woman" and his *imago* theology only in the abstract (or symbolic) pairing of Christ and his community (the church as the bride of Christ in Eph 5).[39] Earlier we noted that Barth ultimately resorts to a form of natural theology when it comes to his decrees on how men and women are to relate in the divine order, so that biology and social structures are determinative; but in his discussion of Jesus, Barth shifts from a focus on such "concrete" things as biology and social structures, and the importance of the gospels as the source of historical knowledge, to a focus on Adam, Christ, Gen 1–3, and the Pauline epistles (Rogers 2007, 178–79). The significance of the historical person of Jesus is therefore downplayed by Barth in favor of "Israel's Christ, the Head of His community," who exceeds his specific historical (and anatomical or racial for that matter) reference. It then becomes possible for Barth to invoke this notion of Christ as the "Husband," even if the historical Jesus was not married. In his discussion of the relationship between Paul and the Corinthians, for example, Barth is thus able to say, "Indeed, we might almost say that as God brought Eve and showed her to Adam, [Paul] brought and showed them to the *real Jesus* as the one Husband, betrothing them to Him as His bride" (3.2:303, emphasis added).

Picking up on Ward's suggestion that (despite Barth's frequent reliance on a natural theology) "male" and "female" are "symbolic positions within a divine narrative," Barth's point becomes clear that all "men" (all people) become feminine in relation to Jesus, "the archetypal man" (3.2:144).[40] For example, Barth maintains that genuine freedom only comes from this encounter with Jesus, and as such, humans are "free to be the wife of this Other, their Liberator" (3.2:304). As noted above, this feminine aspect of being human leads Barth to declare that the woman has the "advantage" and even "primacy" over the man as she is the one who, in her subordination to the man, is the "prototype" of the community, the bride of Christ (3.4:174–75). Man, then, has "no option but to follow the example of the woman, occupying in relation to Jesus Christ the precise position which she must occupy and maintain in relation to man" (3.4:175). In other words, all "men" are wives of Christ (to use Barth's terminology), with the consequence that we arrive back at Moore's (2001, 153) homology: female is to male as human is to God. In other words, the right relation of "man" to God is modeled by the subordinated relation of female to male. This places males in the ambiguous position of being strong, first, authoritative, and superior (to use Barth's own words) in relation to the female, but subordinate and obedient in relation to Christ—as befitting what Barth views as the proper relationship of a "wife" to "her" husband. Of course, Christ himself is also placed in this ambiguous position; he is subordinate to God the Father, obedient to the will of God, and yet has all authority and superiority in relation to creation; indeed, in his discussions of κεφαλή Barth has no difficulty with the concept of subordination of the Christ to God (3.2:311; 3.4:173).

If this notion of the right and proper relation of man to God is taken to its logical consequence, as Geoffrey Rees has done for example, even more is revealed regarding issues of gender and sexuality. After a discussion of sexual intercourse, Barth argues that while such "utter transport" and "blessed intoxication" might allow "man" to view "himself" as godlike— "Is man not God to the extent that his being is being in this encounter?"— "man" is immediately jolted out of this esoteric state and confronted with "the real" and "the fact" of God (3.4:120). This encounter "marks him as a creature" and "puts man in his place and confines him within his limits" (3.4:120). Barth's choice of language then becomes (deliberately?) erotic, and according to Rees (2002, 36), reveals "an intensely sexualised male-homosocial figuration of God-intoxication."

> Even in the depths and heights, the self-recollection and rapture, the immanence and transcendence of this primal experience, he is still a creature. And whatever the command wills of him, it is the command of God. An alien and superior will confronts him at this climax of his self-affirmation and self-denial, in this immanence and transcendence. It shows him that in all the seriousness and rapture of this dialectic he is still not his own master. In face of the dialectic which transports him it reveals a higher and impregnable place, and it lets it be understood that from this place there is One who rules, commands, permits and also forbids. From this place there is heard in the voice of the Law, in the midst of the storms of passion or the whispers of sublimated ecstasy, a critical and judicial Yes and No by which man is tested and must test himself. (3.4:120)

While presumably still purporting to be discussing the sexual relationship between "man" and "woman," Barth's description reveals that this instead "turns out to be a decidedly male homosocial encounter" (Rees 2002, 35). I noted above that both Irigaray's notion of hom(m)osexuality and Sedgwick's notion of homosocial relations are not equated with homoerotic or homosexual relations, but highlight the way in which relations between men are paramount and that women are often merely a conduit for male bonding or interaction. In order for men to encounter God, for the male-divine homosocial relation to occur, men must become as subordinate and powerless as women. Rees (36) notes, "God is figured as an erectile presence that emasculates men precisely at the moment of their own erectile climax…. Even as the man successfully reaches climax— he encounters an 'impregnable place'—'*einen festen höheren Ort*'—that immediately and conclusively puts *him* in *his* place…. [He] discovers that compared to God's phallus, his own is as *no phallus*."

Such is the "phallobsessive gender logic" that occurs when an "extraordinary *signifying* importance" is given to the sexual differentiation of human beings as male and female (Moore 2001, 165; Rees 2002, 32).[41] To imbue the male-female sex binary with the gendered active/passive, dominant/subordinate order of relating, and to apply this to the human-divine binary (and even the intradivine binary of Christ and God the Father), is to create precisely the sort of gender ambiguity that Barth wishes to avoid.[42] According to Barth, "fidelity to one's sex" means maintaining "a firm adherence to this polarity and therefore to one's own sex"; and yet, as we have seen, in relation to the divine, "man" must (temporarily at least) become *as woman*, taking on the gendered role of "the wife of this Other" (3.4:163). The subsequent blurring of *gender*, which has become detached from any particular *sex* designation (in that it depends not on biology but on *relation*), highlights the performative aspect of gender, and thus reveals its constructed nature.[43] It also reveals Barth's theology to be inconsistent and his views on gender as ultimately dependent on a heteropatriarchal ideology.

The "Real" and "Whole" person of Jesus, however, clearly existed for Barth as a being in relationships of differentiation and otherness, of confrontation and encounter, despite being unmarried (3.2:132, 325). In describing the person of Jesus in his relationship to "every man," Barth uses the images not of "Husband" but of "their divine Other, their Neighbour, Companion and Brother," "a true and absolute Counterpart," and a "Kinsman" (3.2:133–35, 160). Indeed, this relationship with Jesus is of primary importance for one's identity as a human being according to Barth: "As an ontological determination of man in general, the fact that among many others this One is also man means that we are men [*Menschen*] as in the person of this One we are confronted by the divine Other" (3.2:134). Coexistence with other human beings is an insufficient level of confrontation for Barth, however; this can only occur through encounter with "the man Jesus … the archetypal man" (3.2:144).

It might have been possible, I suggest, for Barth to develop his anthropological theology on this "Jesus-centered" basis. Utilizing his terminology, one could say that *all* people are genuinely human in their encounter and confrontation with this divine Other who is their true Counterpart. Differentiation between people is not confined to the realm of biology only, as Barth argued,[44] but includes the intersection of multiple lines of difference (class, gender, race, age, ethnicity, sexuality, etc.), creating no less genuine points of encounter, and can be expressed positively by the terms *Neighbour*, *Companion*, *Counterpart*, *Brother*, and *Kinsman* (albeit noting Barth's androcentric formulation of the last two terms). Rather than differentiation leading to the "unequal dualism" and "natural" relationship of subordination and superordination inherent in such a binary (which Barth argues for and which Wittig argues against), it might instead point to "the love of difference" that Ward (1998, 71) argues is expressive of "trinitarian love," a love that is not binary and clearly not limited to a biological essentialism.

Returning to the comparison between Barth and Wittig, I suggest that Wittig's lesbian and Barth's Jesus, for all their differences, may be able to give deeper meaning to the notion of *imago Dei* than Barth's heterosexual married couple. A Jesus who is "Real" and "Whole" and "archetypal," and a lesbian "I" who is "ungendered, universal, [and] whole," confront *all* people with possibilities of being that lie beyond the constraints of gendered life. They offer "a new personal and subjective definition for all humankind" that is available regardless of marital status or sexual orientation (or any other marker of differentiation such as race, age, or class). Instead of limiting the notion of *imago Dei* to the particular form of encounter found in the narrow binary of heteronormative patriarchy, Jesus as Neighbour, Companion, Counterpart, Brother, and Kinsman, and Wittig's lesbian as universal subject, allow for multifarious expressions of both encounter and being that are "beyond the categories of sex." Monogamous heterosexual marriage is not the only way of attaining authentic personhood or of encountering God. Rees (2002, 40) is therefore correct in his judgment that Barth's "excessive God-relating claims for [monogamous, heterosexual] marriage" overburdens this particular relation.

Ultimately, however, heteropatriarchy itself, as the broad "sphere" or "complex" of relations Barth describes between male and female, where marriage is at "the centre" (3.4:140), is challenged by those who stand outside this ideology and offer alternative meanings to being *imago Dei*, namely, the historical Jesus and Wittig's lesbian. While Barth argues that there is no escape from this divine ordering of the *imago Dei* as the heterosexual married couple, given its basis in Pauline texts such as 1 Cor 11:3 and 11:7, the link between Barth's "Real" and "Whole" person of Jesus and Wittig's lesbian figure allows for difference but does not limit it to the sexual. This not only challenges the narrow framework of heteropatriarchy that dominates Barth's formulation of the *imago Dei*, but I suggest it also enables the discovery of "a new personal and subjective definition for all humankind ... beyond the categories of sex" (Wittig 1992e, 19–20).

Notes

1. That this verse is connected with the preceding verses in indicated by the explanatory γάρ. This is the third of five such pointers in vv. 5–9, suggesting that the whole section (vv. 4–9) is connected. This is then followed by two διὰ τοῦτο/τούς statements in v. 10, also suggesting a connection between this verse and the preceding section.

2. With regard to this aspect of the verse, there is a general agreement that Paul is alluding to Gen 1:26–27 and 2:18–24 here (and in vv. 8–9), and so the question arises as to why Paul modifies Gen 1:26 in particular, first in his change from ἄνθρωπος ("humankind") to ἀνήρ ("man/male"), and second in his change from ὁμοίωσιν ("likeness") to δόξα ("glory"). See the discussions in Conzelmann 1975, 187–88; Wire 1990, 119–20, 122–27; Gundry-Volf 1997, 154–58; Thiselton 2000, 834–37; Fitzmyer 2008, 415. Scholars have also explored the connections with 2 Cor 3:7–4:6 (a passage replete with "glory" and "veiling" language); see the discussions in Barrett 1971, 249–50; Newman 1992, 157–247; Chakkalakal 1997, 192; Ince 2000, 68; F. Watson 2000b, 535; Fitzmyer 2008, 415.

3. For this and similar ways of describing the relationship between ὁ ἀνήρ and ἡ γυνή, see Engberg-Pedersen 1991, 682; BeDuhn 1999, 308; S. Barton 2003, 1338. Some describe this hierarchy as an "order of creation" (or "creation order"); see Bruce 1971, 105–7; Corrington 1991, 225; Hjort 2001, 58, 63, 65; Powers 2001, 31; Calef 2009, 22. For comments on the derivative nature of woman implied in this verse, see Brauch 1990, 141; Bassler 1998, 417; Økland 2004, 181; Keener 2005, 93. Not all of these scholars accept this as the definitive reading of the text, however.

4. Doyle (1987, 45) outlines the order of relationships in a hierarchy as follows: God—Man—Woman—Animals. In some ways this could be seen as a conflation of the Rom 1:18–32/1 Cor 11:3 schema from ch. 4, although "Christ" and "Human" are missing.

5. Doyle (1987, 45, 53–54) hopes that this divine hierarchy is also one of "grace," but he also expects that recognition of this hierarchy will prevent women from being ordained in the church.

6. The Message speaks of the "marriage relationship" and uses "husband" and "wife" throughout 1 Cor 11:2–16. The NEB notes "husband" and "wife" as an option for v. 7. The usually comprehensive Thiselton simply says, somewhat enigmatically, that the translation decision on this point "is of a different order" (2000, 811).

7. For detailed discussion of the androcentrism of Aquinas, and "scholastic sexology" in general, see Børresen 1995a.

8. While most Christian theologians are quick to point out that God is nowhere in the Bible said to be *male*, that God is predominantly described with masculine titles conveys the impression that, with regard to gender, God is most definitely *masculine*. This often extends to include the *imago Dei*, as many scholars have noted (Pagels 1976; Cobb 1983; Foster and Keating 1992; Gössmann 1999, 32–35; Lambert and Robinson Kururpius 2004). This is precisely the thought expressed in Daly's now classic slogan, "Since God is male, the male is god" (1974, 21).

9. This approach is common in Christian feminist quests to counter the androcentrism of the past, be it in regard to emphasizing the feminine attributes of the divine that are usually overlooked in the Scriptures, or in recovering the lost voices of women from the Scriptures or throughout church history (Mollenkott 1983; Ruether 1983; Schüssler Fiorenza 1983; Meyers 1988; Witherington 1988; Trible 1989; Rae and Marie-Daly 1990).

10. Despite ideally being used in the generic sense of "human being" (*Menschen*), this term actually refers to the more specific "male," as will become clear.

11. See Ward (1998, 56–57) for a good summary of how Barth's theology of sexual difference is developed over *CD* 3.1, 2, and 4 (Barth 1936–1977). Unless otherwise indicated (i.e., *KD*), all Barth references are to *CD*.

12. For Barth's use of "I" and "Thou," see also 3.2:244–45, 285; 3.4:131, 133.

13. The word *only* in this latter explanation is problematic, making it far more chauvinistic than it perhaps needed to be, given that the original German also states that "der Mann für sich nur Frage ohne Antwort" (Barth 1932–1970, 3.4:166). This raises questions about the translation, of course. Unfortunately, there is not the scope in this project to do more of a comparison between Barth's original text and the English translation. In addition, it is primarily the English version of Barth's work that has had the most influence on Protestant theology.

14. See the discussion in Muers 1999. Barth (3.2:294) suggests that it is in the Song of Songs that we hear the voice of the woman that he agrees was lacking in the Genesis account.

15. See, e.g., Daly 1973; Clark and Richardson 1977; Ruether 1983, 1995; Salomonsen 2003. Nordling (2010) explores the theology of Barth in dialogue with that of feminist theologian Elizabeth Johnson, as well as others such as Ruether, particularly on the "I-Thou" relationship of "Man and Woman" and the *imago Dei*.

16. See H. Visser 'T Hooft (1981) and Barth (2006) for their correspondence.

17. She discusses this in relation to Buber's writings, noting also the position of Sartre, Kierkegaard, and Stirner on this matter, viewing these as varieties of the "man-alone" principle (1962, 73–74).

18. This is from Barth's letter to H. Visser 'T Hooft dated 27 April 1934 (Barth 2006, 329).

19. On this theme, see Eilberg-Schwartz 1995; D'Angelo 1995.

20. At the World Council of Churches conference in Amsterdam in 1948, Henriette's husband, W. Visser 'T Hooft (founder of the present-day ecumenical movement), recalled with embarrassment that "Barth made fun of such women who, in his eyes appeared to 'rush to equality'" (1982, 58–59).

21. This is also an observation noted by Taylor 1957, 266 n. 25; Marmor 1965, 161. See Schleiermacher 1860, 1:382.

22. See the critiques of this in Sonderegger 2000, 270; Salomonsen 2003, 114.

23. Note that the word *void* is used in a positive sense in Barth's commentary on Romans in that the church is "a void in which the Gospel reveals itself" (1968, 36), and is likened to the center of a wheel (254); it is equated in this context with a willingness to be open, to question, and to respond to the gospel. See the discussion in Sykes 1989, 71–74.

24. Balboa (1998, 772) critiques Barth's lack of attention to this topic despite evidence of Nazi persecution.

25. For discussion on current groups, such as Desert Stream Ministries or Living Waters Global, that echo this thought, see Rogers 2007, 179.

26. Thielicke (1964, 272, 282–83) questions Barth's view of "orientation." See D. Martin (2006, 56) for a brief discussion on the differing views of Barth and Thielicke.

27. For an elaboration on narcissism as it relates to male homosocial relations, see Sedgwick 1990, 157–63. See also Balboa 1998, 783; Ward 1998, 70–71; Rees 2002, 42.

28. Barth is clearly utilizing (and giving theological authority to) the medical discourse so prevalent in the early part of the twentieth century that pathologized homosexuality and viewed it as an aberration from the heterosexual norm (Foucault 1990a, 43).

29. Balboa (1998, 781–82) also uses Butler in his critique of Barth's understanding of what is "natural." However, he also points out that the distinction between a biological understanding of "sex" and a constructed notion of "gender" was not available to German speakers at the time Barth wrote, given that the German language has a single word, *Geschlecht*, which does not distinguish between the two ideas (781).

30. Ward is referring to the controversially close relationship Barth had with Charlotte von Kirschbaum (Köbler 1989; Selinger 1998; Sonderegger 2000, 258).

31. By "hom(m)o-sexuality" Irigaray (1985, 172) is referring to a culture where men are the subjects, and women the objects (of desire, for example), betraying an underlying reality that there can only be true mutuality or reciprocity between men and other men. Wittig (1992d, 42–43; 1992i, 30–32) also discusses the concept of the exchange of women (as expounded by Lévi-Strauss and Lacan, for example) that lies behind Irigaray's concept of hom(m)o-sexuality. See also Rubin's (1975) article on the traffic of women.

32. See Barth's comment that women who wish to lead *with* men clearly wish not to be women, highlighting that this relationship is certainly *not* one of partnership (3.4:171). Ward (1998, 68–72) goes on to develop a theology of sexual difference that develops Barth's theological position without confining it to biological difference. As long as committed sexual partnerships reflect a difference mediated by desire, it matters not if the relationship is heterosexual or homosexual; "True desire, that is, God-ordained desire can only be heterosexual."

33. Wittig (1992a, 2) is, of course, highly critical of ideologies that sacrifice female well-being in the name of maintaining male prerogative and power under the guise of the "natural differences" between the sexes.

34. See his equally stereotyped descriptions of "the tyrant" and the "complacent

woman" (3.4:177–79). For a critique of Barth's portrayal of male-female relationship, see Clark and Richardson 1977; Sonderegger 2000, 268; Salomonsen 2003, 112; Loughlin 2004, 187. Clark and Richardson (1977, 244) express the thought that given that Barth was an "open person," grace may have eventually triumphed over his patriarchalism had he lived long enough to be more fully exposed to the ideas of the feminist movement.

35. See also his descriptions of this "order" in relation to the notion of δόξα in 1 Cor 11:7 (3.1:303, 306).

36. For a discussion on the historical difficulty of determining the individual subject in relation to Marxism, see Wittig 1992e, 16.

37. Barth regards the voice of the woman in the Song of Songs in a positive way (3.2:294), although the woman is still an object (as Beloved) rather than a subject (as Lover). Barth also clearly enjoyed intellectual discussion with women such as von Kirschbaum, despite the "it is just so" silencer he used in his correspondence with H. Visser 'T Hooft.

38. Barth also notes that, given "the mystery of our sin" and the "mystery of His [Christ's] identity with God," "Anthropology cannot be Christology, nor Christology anthropology" (3.2:71).

39. See the multitude of references to Christ as husband or head of the church (or community) that is his bride, for example (3.4:117, 123, 142–43, 174).

40. Bonhoeffer (1959, 60–67), by contrast, allows for confrontation with the human brother as a sufficient expression of the *analogia relationis*, interpreting Gen 1:26–27 in relation to Adam and Eve more generally as "I" and "Thou," rather than as specifically male and female as does Barth. See Barth's disagreement with Bonhoeffer on this point (3.1:194–95).

41. Despite the recognition that homosocial relations are not identical with homosexual relations, it is difficult not to mention at this point Moore's queering of male homosociality. Moore (2001, 164–65) explores the gender ambiguity of both Christ and Paul (in both their submission to another more dominant than they and their performance of masculinity in terms of self-mastery) in his description of the "male-male love affair" between Jesus "the penetrator" and Paul the "penetratee," adding that when God, "the most dominant male of all" to whom both Paul and Jesus submit, arrives on the scene, we now see an "all-male threesome" emerge.

42. See Barth's rejection of the androgyne "drama" or "fable" with regard to both humanity and portrayals of Christ (3.4:160–61, 163). See also his discussion on the "confusion" generated by the Corinthian women in their quest for freedom from the veil and thus from the order of "precedence and succession … superiority and inferiority" (3.4:174).

43. Barth often uses the word *play* when it comes to gender roles, which I suggest also points to this issue (3.4:178, 3.2:303).

44. See his discussion of why sex rather than race, for example, constitutes "the only real differentiation" (3.1:186).

Scene 3

So I start talking to David, and we talk and talk and talk queer talk. David is a photographer. He is the epitome of the male gaze. But he isn't either. He is fine with the gaze coming right back at him, revealing him. His images on display *are* him; he is pinned to the gallery walls for all to see. It is the artist's exhibition, after all, a performance piece without words. But there is no pinning him down really. He is as elusive as his images.

His images are haunting, surreal, abject, taken just before dawn. In many of them the boundaries between objects blur and shimmer. There is a transcendence and an uncertainty, a sense of something hovering beyond my grasp and yet resonating within me too. It is not just David pinned (and not pinned) to those walls. I also see myself. I see the darkness and the fragility, the horror and the shame. But I also see the wonder and the glory.

How do you see queer theory, he asks. How do you *see* it? How *do* you see it? How do *you* see it?

6

The Straight Mind in 1 Corinthians 11:14–15a

As systematic theologies went about the business of constructing the Holy and defining its ancillary, the Natural, the reverse was also made possible. The unholy—an abstraction, to be sure—could be imagined and demonstrated in examples of the socially perverse and unnatural…. As a necessary buttress to the regulatory work of sexual ideology, encapsulated most cogently within the economic terms of family values, homosexuals *must* be pinioned in the public gaze, their deviancy presumed for its naturalizing effects.

— Edward Ingebretsen, *At Stake*

οὐδὲ ἡ φύσις αὐτὴ διδάσκει ὑμᾶς ὅτι ἀνὴρ μὲν ἐὰν κομᾷ ἀτιμία αὐτῷ ἐστιν, γυνὴ δὲ ἐὰν κομᾷ δόξα αὐτῇ ἐστιν;
Does not "nature itself" teach you that if a man has long hair it is a dishonor to him, but, by contrast, if a woman has long hair it is her glory?

— 1 Cor 11:14–15a

Introduction

Turning to a consideration of verses 14–15a, we find Paul moving away from his arguments based in theological anthropology and Scripture (vv. 7–12), toward an appeal to φύσις ("nature") in order to reinforce "proper" gender distinctions.[1] Similar rhetoric about what is "natural" (and thus "unnatural") been has "used and abused" in contemporary political and religious debates in the West, particularly in the United States, about sexuality and gender (Bauman 2009; Childs 2009). This has been especially evident in debates over the issue of sexual orientation and the contentious issue of same-sex marriage. As Whitney Bauman (2009, 6) explains, there has been a "tug-of-war on all sides to legitimate claims about 'sex' and 'sexuality' within the secure foundations of 'religion' and 'nature.'" But if we recall that Barth's vision of the *imago Dei* was of the "natural dualism" of man and woman and that his argument against homosexuality was "not of the theological but of the natural order," then it is clear that this rhetorical tactic is both pervasive and powerful (Ward 1998, 65).

Those who oppose homosexuality (and thus also same-sex marriage) from a Christian standpoint often do so on the basis of an interpretation of Gen 1–3 that understands the sexual union of one man and one woman (usually for life) as God's design for sexual expression, marriage, and reproduction. The catchy bumper sticker "God made Adam and Eve, not Adam and Steve," which started appearing on cars of conservative evangelicals in the United States during the 1980s, is indicative of this view. Sexual behavior outside of this "divine plan" is usually viewed as immoral and unnatural, a view reinforced by reference to Rom 1:18–32 (Swancutt 2006, 66; Campbell and Robinson 2007; Tadlock, Gordon, and Popp 2007; Wald and Glover 2007). In addition, this "divinely ordained" structuring of sexual behavior is often accompanied by a certain understanding of "biblical" gender behavior regarding appropriate roles in family, church, and society for men and women. Women are usually viewed as being designed by God to be "a helper" for the man, to "respond to, surrender to, and complement him," while men are created by God to "provide for ... cherish ... [and] protect" the woman; the man is "the Initiator, Protector, Provider," while the woman is "the responder" whose essence is "surrender" (Elliot 2006a, 397–98). Diana Swancutt (2006, 66) notes this use of Scripture in the American Christian arguments about gender and sexuality and states, "In the battle to save heterosexual unions, 'what the Bible says' is one of the biggest guns conservative Christians fire: Genesis 1 and 2 to prove that 'the two sexes' were created complementary and naturally heterosexual, and Romans 1 to prove homosexual sex contrary to nature."

However, those who affirm a variety of sexualities (as covered by the term *LGBTQIA*, for example) may also argue that these are equally "natural" expressions or behaviors, whether because of genetics or outside influence, and that to live in any other way would be "unnatural" (D. Martin 2006, 197–98 n. 34). For those within the Christian community, the argument can be used that this is also precisely how God designed them to be; autobiographical accounts, such as that by Amy Adams Squire Strongheart (1997, 82), clearly state, "Because we *are* the will of God, we are therefore obliged to promote same-sex marriage as a holy, decent, and legitimate estate worthy of affirmation." Consequently, the retort to the quip on the bumper sticker might well be, "Well then, who made Steve?"[2]

This interrelation between what is "natural" regarding gender and sexuality, and the subsequent debates regarding issues of homosexuality, same-sex marriage, and gender roles, clearly highlights the importance of exploring the rhetorical use of "nature." In chapter 4 we saw that a link is often made between 1 Cor 11:2–16 and Rom 1:18–32. One of the key reasons why this link is made is because of the "argument from nature" that Paul uses in 11:14 (ἡ φύσις αὐτή) and his argument concerning "natural" and "unnatural" (τὴν φυσικὴν ... παρὰ φύσιν) sexual behaviors of men and women in Rom 1:26–27. When Paul is discussing "unnatural" behaviors— be it effeminate hairstyles for men (1 Cor 11:14) or sexual acts between members of the same sex (Rom 1:26–27)—his statements are therefore deemed by some scholars (and by many lay readers of the Bible in general) as authoritative with regard to the "proper nature" of both human sexuality and gender.

At the heart of Wittig's critique of the heterosexual political regime and her questioning of the categories of "man" and "woman" lies a critique of the "doctrine" of sexual difference and how this is used to justify the way men are presented as merely "naturally" *different* when, in fact, and more importantly, they are economically, socially, and politically *dominant* to women (1992a, 2–5; 1992e, 20). In contrast to Paul's statement to the Corinthians that "nature teaches" (1 Cor 11:14), Wittig (1992a, 4–5) proposes instead, "Dominance thus teaches us from all directions." Formulations of gender and sexuality are therefore deeply dependent upon cultural expectations of how individuals ought to behave with one another and present themselves as members of a particular sex. This is evident not only for Paul and the Corinthians in their first-century Mediterranean world, but also becomes apparent when we consider the ways in which contemporary scholars interpret these verses in their own cultural and historical contexts with regard to issues of sexual differentiation and homosexuality.

In this chapter, I will therefore consider some of the ways in which some contemporary evangelicals argue for an understanding of ἡ φύσις that equates this with "God's design in Creation" (Merkle 2006, 535) in their arguments about the "proper" understanding and expression of sexuality and gender. The leading spokesman for what is known as the complementarity argument against homosexuality is Gagnon, so to conclude I will contrast his most important book, *The Bible and Homosexual Practice*, with Wittig's "most experimental work," *The Lesbian Body* (see Shaktini 2005a, 150). Through this intersection between Wittig's "monstrous lesbian" and what I am calling Gagnon's "unnatural homosexual," the ideologically constructed nature of all models of gender and sexuality will be revealed, including the sex-gender model with which Paul operates in 1 Cor 11:2–16, particularly verses 14–15a. Readers of this text assume that because Paul appeals to "nature" and alludes to Scripture (Gen 1–2), the hierarchical pairing of man and woman he presents is determinative for what is "natural" and "biblical" regarding gender roles and sexual behavior today. The rhetorical power of such a passage is therefore significant indeed, and so my hope is that this juxtaposition will not only reveal the dominant heteropatriarchal model that has been supported by such appeals but it will also destabilize it.

Evangelicals and Nature—"God's Creational Design"

Paul's decision to change tack in his discussion of the behavior of the Corinthian men and women regarding their hair/head coverings, shifting from a theological argument to one based on the teaching of ἡ φύσις αὐτή ("nature itself"), has led to much discussion among commentators. A key point of debate centers upon the background of Paul's use of φύσις given that this choice of terminology is highly unusual in Pauline argumentation.[3] Some scholars suggest that Paul is deliberately drawing on the Stoic usage of the word, and without wanting to argue definitively that Paul is operating within a Stoic framework, there are some significant parallels between Paul's teaching in this verse and that of the two Stoic philosophers whose discourses on hairstyles we considered in chapter 2, Musonius Rufus and Epictetus.[4] In addition, I would also argue that there are significant parallels between some aspects of Stoic philosophy and contemporary evangelical understandings of what is "natural" and "God-ordained" regarding the "proper" conduct of Christian men and women on matters of gender and sexuality. This highlights, as Wittig's theory predicts, that appeals to propriety and to what is "natural" do not simply illuminate a God-ordained model of sexuality and gender, but rather reveal the dependence of such a model on ideology, and in particular on a heteropatriarchal ideology.

Arguments based on "nature" are an important (and complex) aspect of Stoic philosophy and the Stoic understanding of ἡ φύσις and what is κατὰ φύσιν is closely bound to their own elite values of what is "decent" and "proper" (van Geytenbeek 1962, 22–50; Hahm 1977, 200–215; D. Martin 1995a, 9–10; Long 2002, 142–79; Sellars 2006, 91–95). Behavior that demonstrates moderation, self-control, and excellence is in accordance with nature, and it thus also sets "real men" apart from both other men (be they from another culture or class) and from women. How men behaved with regard to their physical appearance (such as clothing, hair, or voice), or with regard to their sexual proclivities, was indicative of their status as "real men" and thus ought to be clearly distinctive from these "others." With regard to the shaping of the aristocratic male body, D. Martin (1995a, 27) says, "Clearly, 'natural' here has nothing to do with the way the body might grow if left to nature. What is 'natural' is the body that conforms to the esthetic expectations of the upper class" (see also Klassen 1984, 205–6; Gleason 1990, 412; Swancutt 2003, 193; Ivarsson 2007, 166). That such supposedly "natural" behavior had to be encouraged and maintained— and could easily be transformed into another "nature" that could be then "practiced like an art" (Philo, *Spec. Laws* 3.37–38)—is indicative of the constructed "nature" of this desired expression of elite masculinity.[5]

When we consider Paul's arguments concerning ἡ φύσις in 1 Cor 11:14, or that which is φυσικήν ("natural") and παρὰ φύσιν ("unnatural") in Rom 1:26–27, it becomes clear that for ἡ φύσις to teach that it is a disgrace for a man to have long hair (while long hair is proper, or seemly, for a woman) is to evoke standards of deportment that conform with Greco-Roman societal expectations for men and women aimed at maintaining the distinctions between them (see Gleason 1990, 401). But deeper than this, behind the matter of physical distinction, lies the androcentric elite ideology pervasive throughout that society that seeks to maintain the hierarchical superiority of the "real man" over any "other," particularly women (D. Martin 1995a, 34). To be able to invoke "nature" in order to promote this ideology, and to structure society around the supposedly "natural" hierarchies of not only male and female but also socioeconomic position, was a powerful tool (Penner and Vander Stichele 2005, 292). Control of the individual body as well as the social body was "natural" for those who were physically and morally elite and thus also controlled the discourse on such matters.

Formulations of gender and sexuality are therefore deeply dependent upon cultural expectations of how individuals ought to behave with one another and present themselves as members of a particular sex. This is evident not only for Paul and the Corinthians in their first-century Mediterranean world, or even for Barth in his early-twentieth-century European world, but it is also apparent when we consider the ways in which contemporary scholars interpret these verses in their own cultural and historical contexts regarding issues of sexual differentiation and homosexuality. Many evangelical scholars equate "nature" with creation and thus with an ordering of the cosmos as intended by the Creator. "Nature" therefore reflects "God's design in creation," and that which is "natural" is "God-ordained." With regard to both 1 Cor 11:2–16 and Rom 1:18–32, the echoes of the creation account (Gen 1–2) within these passages corroborate this view. This "natural order" has frequently been understood to equate to a division of the sexes whereby the woman is "naturally" inferior and the subordination of woman to man is part of the natural created order. Commentators in the first half of the twentieth century are quite explicit in their description of this "natural order" that they find outlined by Paul; Joseph MacRory (1915, 157) simply stated in relation to 1 Cor 11:2–16, "[The] inferiority of women is shown by the history of Creation."

However, after the second wave of feminism swept through the West in the second half of the twentieth century, rather than explicitly describing woman as "naturally" inferior—an ontological statement that would now appear to be too blatantly sexist (if not downright misogynist)—the emphasis shifted in evangelical circles to the supposedly less personal notion of roles and functions. Roger Ellsworth's comments on 1 Cor 11:2–16 illustrate this view:

> [Paul] is not talking about headship in the sense of personal worth, but in terms of function.… In the light of this, we can conclude that the headship of the man doesn't mean that the woman is inferior to the man. The woman's submission is to be like Christ's: a voluntary submission of an equal in order to endure the smooth functioning of church and home.… Man's headship was not based on man's fall into sin but on God's creative act. Man is given the role of headship because God designed it to be so … (11:8–9). Why did God do things in this way? To ask that is rather like asking why there are radishes. They are just there. And man's headship is there! God put this order in creation because it pleased him to do so. (1995, 179–80)[6]

In such a schema, men can only raise their shoulders in a helpless shrug; they are not personally responsible for what might otherwise be labeled as patriarchy. One of the most influential biblical commentators in this area is the conservative evangelical preacher John MacArthur.[7] In his commentary on 1 Corinthians, he gives the section on 1 Cor 11:2–16 the title "The Subordination and Equality of Women" and states that woman "is not intellectually, morally, spiritually or functionally inferior to man. She is unique from him. Her role is to come under the leadership, protection, and care of man.… That is God's wise and gracious harmony and balance—difference in roles but equality in nature, personhood, work and spirit" (1984, 259–61; 2007, 68, 72). These role divisions are inherent in the basic order of creation and thus constitute God's "wise" and "perfect" design (1984, 255; 2007, 68, 72). Rather than a focus on innate inferiority or superiority, women and men are now to celebrate God's "glorious purpose" and "loving will" in gifting them with different roles or functions (1984, 261; 2007, 72). According to MacArthur (1984, 261–62), "Both nature and general custom reflect God's universal principle of man's role of authority and women's role of subordination."

What is of particular interest is how "creation" and "nature" are conflated with "general custom" and "cultural practice"; together these are seen to reflect God's cosmic design. Yet elsewhere MacArthur lambasts the church, arguing that with regard to women's rights the church "so often catches the world's diseases and adopts the spirit of the age" (1984, 252; 2007, 67). He criticizes "leaders and writers" who have attempted to alter "biblical truths" in order "to accommodate the standards of contemporary thinking" rather than teaching "divinely revealed standards"; and he disparages "Worldly Christians" who "continually try to find ways to justify their worldliness" (1984, 252–53; 2007, 68). It is hard to avoid the conclusion that MacArthur—as with the Stoics—is therefore very selective about which aspects of culture and/or nature reveal "indispensable elements in God's order and plan" (1984, 252–53). Only certain behaviors or attitudes are deemed to be "natural" or in accordance with God's design, while those that do not fit with a predetermined notion of what is "proper" or "biblical" are determined to be "worldly." D. Martin (2006, 21) argues that this tactic is "hypocritical rhetoric" and reminds us, " 'Nature' is mediated to us humans *only* through culture of some sort.… There is nothing more 'natural' than culture … and there is nothing more 'cultural' than nature."

This different categorization of various human activities as either natural and godly or cultural and worldly can be discerned through the language used to describe these activities. Aspects of human behavior that are said to reflect God's design usually fall into the category of things that are deemed to be "proper," to use Paul's own word choice in 1 Cor 11:13. Class issues are frequently mentioned by scholars, often in terms of the clash of values apparent at Corinth, such as with well-to-do matrons from "good" families behaving in ways associated with disreputable women.[8] When it comes to the "proper" behavior women are to exhibit in their lives today, for example, conservative evangelical scholars writing on 1 Cor 11:2–16 (particularly v. 13) use words and phrases that reveal a desire for the maintenance of the status quo, for stability and security in both family and society: respectability is crucial, as are convention, propriety, and conformity; women are to be demure, chaste, modest, supportive, and quiet; and they ought to comply with decorum, exhibit tenderness, softness, and beauty.[9] Such virtues are literally conservative and therefore portray a woman who is decidedly passive and dependent.

By contrast, when scholars describe women's behavior that is *not* deemed "proper," there is a clear sense of disruption to the status quo, with women portrayed as being strikingly active and even aggressive. Over the twentieth century, both the Corinthian women and modern feminists have been described as "flinging their inhibitions to the wind," "discarding [their] godly character," "scandalizing visitors," and "disregarding convention" (see Robertson and Plummer 1914, 226, 231; Radcliffe 1990, 68; Murphy-O'Connor 1998, 115; Talbert 2002, 88). They are accused of such actions as daring, flouting, asserting, shocking, demanding, disturbing, rejecting, willfully refusing, and flagrantly defying.[10] When women are behaving in this way they are also described as being rebellious, attacking, violating, and having "a dangerous lust for emancipation" (Tischleder 1923, 156).[11] Such behavior is also associated with violence and danger. Indeed, the whole issue of women's equality is viewed as threatening, a battleground, a sign of protest, and a minirevolt (Meier 1978, 216–17; MacArthur 1984, 252–53; D. MacDonald 1988, 281; Peerbolte 2000, 92). Women who seek after "their rights" are therefore held responsible for the breakdown of that most sacred of all institutions, the family, by deliberately "refusing to care for their children," "leaving their husbands and homes," and even "living with other men" (MacArthur 1984, 256). These women also pose an economic threat by "demanding jobs traditionally held by men" (256). Both family and society are therefore deemed to be under threat; the status quo is being exchanged for chaos and disorder (Craig 1953, 124; Mare 1976, 255; Prior 1985, 183). Or to put it another way, the historical (androcentric/patriarchal) structures of the past are viewed as being challenged (by women), and thus a battle in the present (which is being inflicted upon men) threatens to undermine the (hegemonic) stability of the(ir) future.

These assertive women are therefore also deemed to be sexually active—exposing themselves to the erotic male gaze—and thus such a woman is said to be shameless, "bringing disgrace to her husband."[12] This image of an active, aggressive woman who is also labeled as sexually shameless is ultimately viewed as a "violation of nature" (Schreiner

2006a, 137; J. Thompson 2003, 254, 256; A. Johnson 2004, 193). Charges of lascivious behavior have long been used to police boundaries, particularly class and gender boundaries. Jennifer Knust (2006, 40) has explored the use of such invective in ancient Christianity and in its broader Greco-Roman historical context and shown that women whose behavior implied sexual, economic, or relational independence, rather than reflecting the virtues of passive dependence and submission, "became an emblem of both political and religious deterioration." Both power and status are thus negotiated via ideologies of sexual behavior centered on the shame/honor axis. The elite ought to display the virtues of their sex, demonstrating the "naturalness" of their elite status and thus gaining honor (if men) and conveying honor (if women). To fail—or be accused of failing—to meet these standards is to indicate failure both in terms of class and in terms of gender, as a "good man" or "good woman," bringing shame upon oneself (as a man), one's family (as a woman), and thus also upon society (38–39).

As I have already suggested, rather than denigrating women as "naturally inferior," this approach of emphasizing the ideal "good woman" as a way of controlling the behavior of women (and the men who ought to be able to control them, either as free Roman citizens adept at σωφροσύνη or as Christian men who are heads of their households) has come to the fore in evangelical discussions of gender, be it through material available online, or in books and Bibles that expound this view of "biblical womanhood" (Heald 1986; Shirer 1999), and more recently, being "God's princess" (N. Johnson 2003; Shepherd 2004; Glick 2005; Garrison 2009).[13] Evangelical material aimed at men tends to emphasize the Stoic virtue of manliness (ἀνδρεία); attributes such as strength, courage, and endurance are all valued, while metaphors of battle (and its potential for victory or defeat) are heavily utilized (Cole 1992; J. White 1997; Briscoe 2004; Elliot 2006b; Pritchard 2008).[14] That these masculine/military images are present within the Pauline material in the New Testament allows the contemporary evangelical movement to argue that the approach to "godly" living advocated in the type of material described above is "biblical."[15]

However, egalitarians have challenged the notion that the hierarchical model of femininity and masculinity is simply "God's design." Rebecca Merrill Groothuis and Ronald W. Pierce, for example, argue for a gender model that accepts the importance of differences between the genders, but suggest that equality between the sexes is "true, logical, biblical and beneficial" (Groothuis and Pierce 2004, 13). Groothuis (2004, 302) also challenges the "logic" of the hierarchicalist rhetoric that men and women are "equal in being but unequal in role," arguing that for the hierarchicalists, men's authority and women's subordination are integral to "what true manhood and womanhood *are*." Thus, when all is said and done, "A man is fit to lead by virtue of his male nature. A woman, by virtue of her female nature, is not" (Groothuis 2004, 303).[16] For egalitarians, "God's creational design" means that women are truly equal to men, not in the sense of being identical, nor in terms of sexual role, but in terms of being fully human and thus fully capable of engaging in the "uniquely human capacities" of exercising authority and rationality as seen in the Genesis account (305–7).[17]

Nevertheless, as with the discussion on 1 Cor 11:3 and the meaning of "head," despite different views regarding whether "God's creational design" involves a hierarchical dimension to the relationship between men and women, both hierarchicalist and egalitarian evangelicals agree that this same "design" prohibits same-sex relationships. For example, William Webb (2004b, 401 n. 1) states that "God's creational design" can be seen in the "undisputed differences in sexual and reproductive function (which belie the claim that homosexual relations are somehow 'natural')."[18] Ultimately, for Webb, the prohibition of homosexuality comes down to "sexual-intercourse design, reproductive design and nurturing design" (412). He contends that this is a "question of pragmatics" and explains that "the creative architecture of male and female sexuality," which "utilizes the natural, complementary design of body parts," therefore provides an argument both *for* heterosexual relationships and *against* same-sex relationships (412 and n. 20). To illustrate his point, Webb (412 n. 20) maintains that "the physical design of female breasts" is a reason "for heterosexual relationships (and against homosexual relationships)" because "the mother can breastfeed her children." Webb does not address the fact that lesbians can bear children and breastfeed them.

One of the most comprehensive proponents of this "anatomical" approach to viewing same-sex intercourse as "unnatural" and heterosexual intercourse as "natural" is evangelical biblical scholar Robert Gagnon, to whose work I now turn. While Gagnon's work has received much attention with regard to reviews or debate with other scholars, the result for those who have disagreed with Gagnon's approach and/or conclusions has often been little more than a stalemate. Yet there is much at stake here. The "battle" over acceptable expressions of gender and sexuality—in particular over the issues of sexual orientation and same-sex marriage—has at its heart issues of freedom of expression and the validity of one's sense of identity. In many ways these are the core issues behind Wittig's (1992e, 19–20) critique of the regime of heterosexuality and her quest for "a new personal and subjective definition for all humankind … beyond the categories of sex."

By juxtaposing Wittig's novel *The Lesbian Body* with Gagnon's *The Bible and Homosexual Practice*, I provide a running commentary and alternative viewpoint to the arguments in Gagnon's work. Both books explore notions of gender and sexuality in ways that promote a (utopic) vision of society that is an alternative to the current (perceived) reality and are also deeply concerned with what is "natural" and "unnatural," but they do so utilizing methods ideologically and stylistically opposed to each other. In Gagnon's *The Bible and Homosexual Practice*, we find an insistence that homosexuality is "destructive," "inherently degrading," and "unnatural" (2001, 27, 71, 173), whereas heterosexuality is affirmed because of the "witness of nature" (2001, 41) seen in the "natural fittedness" (181) of the male and female sex organs. By contrast, Wittig's *The Lesbian Body* embraces that which is degrading and destructive and confronts readers with the "monstrous lesbian," a figure whose body parts are listed, bared, and broken while also exposed to the elements or transformed into wings or horns. Because both books focus on "the visible, the bodily characteristics … the material shape" of the bodies that are at their center (Gagnon 2001, 256–58), and in both we are presented with what can be described as "the page as flesh" (Hewitt 1990, 161), the physical juxtaposition of the discussion on them is not just appropriate but also necessary.

This juxtaposition of *The Bible and Homosexual Practice* with Wittig's *The Lesbian Body* provides a challenge to Gagnon's work by its very presence underneath it. Rather than a direct confrontation or engagement through conventional dialogue and debate, this approach allows Wittig's *The Lesbian Body* to physically push upward against the material dedicated to Gagnon's work, slowly but inevitably removing it from the page altogether. Wittig's *The Lesbian Body* begins by speaking from a subdominant position but ultimately emerges as that which has resisted the dominant heteropatriarchal ideology. *The Lesbian Body* thus provides a challenge to the "proper" and supposedly "natural" heteronormative model of gendered and sexed being that *The Bible and Homosexual Practice* promulgates, and which is underpinned by a text such as 1 Cor 11:2–16.

Gagnon's Unnatural Homosexual

Gagnon is a key exponent of the complementarity argument against homosexuality, and *The Bible and Homosexual Practice* (2001) is his major contribution to the heated debate on the issue of sexual orientation and practice. One reviewer states that this book "has undoubtedly galvanized the debate," noting that "the book will be welcomed and hated, praised and blamed, but it should be read" (Burns 2002, 8). D. Martin (2006, 25) also points out that Gagnon's book "has generated much discussion since it appeared" and thus "provides an excellent opportunity" for analysis of modern scholarship on this issue.[19]

Gagnon (2001, 40–41, 86) persistently argues throughout his book that besides the primary and authoritative teaching of Scripture, it is "the witness of nature," that is, the "anatomical and procreative complementarity of male and female sex organs," that provides "the most unambiguous clue people have of God's intent for gender pairing." Gagnon's argument is therefore strongly grounded in an understanding of nature as a clear expression of God's design. As he states, " 'nature' corresponds to the essential material, inherent, biological, or organic constitution of things as created and set in motion by God.... 'Nature' ... goes beyond what one feels and thinks to simply what 'is' by divine design" (373). Despite indicating that human perception ("what one feels and thinks") only partly enables us to discern this "divine design," Gagnon appears to assume that what is "visible" and "bodily" needs no interpretation but simply "is." This raises questions of epistemology that Gagnon does not address.

With regard to Paul's use of "nature," Gagnon specifically states that Paul was *not* thinking of cultural convention but "the material shape of

Wittig's Monstrous Lesbian

LACUNAE LACUNAE
AGAINST TEXTS
AGAINST MEANING
WHICH IS TO WRITE VIOLENCE
OUTSIDE THE TEXT
IN ANOTHER WRITING
THREATENING MENACING
MARGINS SPACES INTERVALS

the created order" (256). Indeed, he highlights 1 Cor 11:14 as an example of how an appeal to the "visible, bodily characteristics of men and women" confirms this view of "nature" and notes that this is paralleled in Paul's arguments in Rom 1:18–32 for viewing "same-sex intercourse as an 'unnatural' use of the gendered body" (258, 258–59 n. 18). Gagnon views 1 Cor 11:2–16 as being about the shame incurred from blurring the distinctions between the sexes through inappropriate hairstyles and head coverings, and, referring to Rom 1:27, posits that "a man taking another man to bed" would be a significantly more shameful act in Paul's eyes (328).

Gagnon therefore has to develop an explanation for 1 Cor 11:14–15 that justifies why long hair on a man is "shameful" when, in fact, the "inherent, biological, or organic constitution" of hair—the "visible, bodily characteristic" of hair—is that it grows. He acknowledges that it is possible that "Paul allows his judgment to be blinded by cultural convention," but in the end argues that, in line with the Stoic rationale of the time, "the most likely explanation … is that Paul is thinking of the tendency for many men (including himself?) to develop baldness" (375). Gagnon explains that because baldness is nature's "clue" for what is "natural" regarding men's coiffure, men who grow their hair long "are debasing their masculine stamp" (376).[20] Gagnon's argument against homosexuality, then, requires an understanding of "nature" that is not only biological (as opposed to cultural) but also supposedly "set in motion by God." Gagnon's conflation of "nature" and "God's design," and his subsequent rejection of homosexuality, is made clear in this summary of his argument:

> The Bible presents the anatomical, sexual, and procreative complementarity of male and female as clear and convincing proof of God's will for

WITHOUT PAUSE
ACTION OVERTHROW
— Monique Wittig, *Les Guérillères*

Wittig's fiction has been described as having the tone and style of "revolutionary poetics" or of having "poetic power" (Zerilli 2005, 93; Ecarnot 2005, 180).[21] In particular, *The Lesbian Body* (1976) has been described as Wittig's "most experimental work," her "most infamous text," "the most notorious of Wittig's works, and probably the most difficult to read" (Shaktini 2005a, 150, 155; Whatling 1997, 239; Wenzel 1981, 265). Consequently,

sexual unions. Even those who do not accept the revelatory authority of Scripture should be able to perceive the divine will through the visible testimony of the structure of creation. Thus same-sex intercourse constitutes an inexcusable rebellion against the intentional design of the created order. It degrades the participants when they disregard nature's obvious clues, and results in destructive consequences for them as well as for society as a whole. (37)[22]

For Gagnon, the original binary pairing of "male and female" in Gen 1:26–27 is constitutive of what it means to be human. He argues that not only does this pairing intimate "that the fullness of God's 'image' comes together in the union of male and female in marriage (not, one could infer, from same-sex unions)," but also that the "complementarity of male and female is secured in the divinely sanctioned work of governing creation" (57–58).[23] This proheterosexual stance is coupled with the antihomosexual position Gagnon finds in Rom 1:18–32, a passage described by him as "arguably the single most important biblical text" on this matter and that therefore functions as a hermeneutical key determinative for his reading of the Bible as a whole (40). It is here, he states, that we find same-sex intercourse put forward as "exhibit A" for the way it "represents one of the clearest instances of conscious suppression of revelation in nature … as it involves denying clear anatomical gender differences and functions" (264).

Gagnon frequently portrays the Bible as an active and independent agent that "speaks directly" or "strongly and consistently condemns," or performs any number of actions such as having a particular "stance" and being a "witness" (40–41). D. Martin (2006, 25–26) highlights this as a rhetorical strategy that belies the process of interpretation inherent in the reading of a text; the reader of the Bible is led to believe that their role is to

scholars have had difficulty in determining its genre, describing its style in various ways, from being "one of the greatest love poems ever written," "an esoteric and erotic Sapphic 'Song of Songs,'" to "neither love-poem nor love-story" (Ostrovsky 2005, 121; Wenzel 1981, 265; Linstrum 1988, 39).[24] Julie Scanlon (1998, 75) notes, "The word 'novel' does not apply to a work such as this.… Instead I shall refer to the work as 'text,' although with reservations."[25] Wittig (2005a, 47) herself compares this work to "poems," and I will follow suit.[26]

All but one of Wittig's books were published before her essays, but sequentially they illustrate the strategy of lesbianization that are at the

be a passive recipient who simply needs to listen to what the authoritative text "clearly" says (see also Countryman 2003, 196). It is this "rhetoric of agency" that Gagnon again uses in his discussion on "nature." Not only does the Bible (as opposed to Gagnon, the mere interpreter) clearly present the complementarity of male and female as proof of God's design for sexual intercourse, but "nature" itself also clearly presents this teaching, giving "visible testimony" and "obvious clues" that stand as a "witness" to what is the (only) divinely sanctioned form of sexual intercourse (Gagnon 2001, 37, 41). This is similar to the rhetorical strategy that Paul's uses in 1 Cor 11:14, in that ἡ φύσις αὐτή ("nature itself") is the one who teaches the Corinthians about appropriate hair length for men; Paul positions himself as merely the messenger.

For Gagnon (2001, 164), the "most unambiguous clue" that heterosexual intercourse is God's design can be found in the anatomical complementarity of male and female sex organs: "Procreation is God's clue, given in nature, that the male penis and female vagina/womb are complementary organs." Indeed, Gagnon goes so far as to equate nature and God in a typically graphic description of human biology: "God/nature obviously intended the female vagina to be the complementary sex organ for the male penis" (169). Apart from Scripture, it is this anatomical "'natural' fittedness" of the human penis and the vagina—indeed, they are "perfect fits"—that Gagnon finds so compelling an argument *for* heterosexual intercourse and *against* same-sex intercourse (169).[27] He even suggests that this is affirmed by the "sturdiness" and "cleanness" of the vagina "when compared to the rectal environment," commenting that "neither the male anal cavity (the orifice for expelling excrement) nor the mouth (the orifice for taking in food) are likely candidates for

heart of Wittig's theories. Hélène Wenzel (1981, 275) notes, "Read in sequence, Wittig's works take the reader on a journey through time and space, self and other, language and culture, to ultimately arrive at a genesis of new language, and its redefinition of woman." Leah Hewitt (1990, 129) notes that few other writers manage "to couple a militant feminist agenda and the reworking of literary language and cultural myth as well as Wittig ... [her books] constitute a post-modern feminist adventure in the imaginative reworking of our Western cultural heritage."

But perhaps the most significant difficulty with *The Lesbian Body* is its violent tone. Clare Whatling (1997, 239) points out that while readers

what God intended as a receptacle for the male penis" (181). Presumably therefore, Gagnon would also rule out heterosexual sex that involves anal penetration of the woman, the practices of fellatio and cunnilingus, or for that matter, any sexual pleasuring of the breasts, given that the latter are anatomically designed for feeding babies—but he does not comment on these matters; his concern is predominantly (if not exclusively) with male same-sex penetration. In addition, the lack of concern he shows for the "cleanness" of the male penis, which is anatomically also used for excretion and yet is being placed inside the vagina (in his heterosexual schema), not only highlights his selective understanding of "nature" but also his androcentric focus.

I must also note that despite this persistent focus on human genital anatomy and his statement that "procreation is God's clue" that heterosexuality is God's design, Gagnon conveniently dismisses the argument that heterosexual sex ought to be procreative, an astounding lapse in logic that almost more than any other point does damage to Gagnon's emphasis on nature as second only to Scripture as evidence for God's design for human sexuality. Gagnon's position should lead him to conclude that sex ought to be both penetrative (penis into vagina) *and* procreative—in both its intent *and* consummation (D. Martin 2006, 28, 198 n. 35).

With regard to this selective view of nature, there is also the difficulty, for those who agree with Gagnon's position on homosexuality, that those who identify as homosexual can argue that their sexuality is "natural" for them (D. Martin 2006, 197 n. 34). Gagnon (2001, 392) attempts to resolve these issues by explaining, "Nature is material creation, visible to the naked eye, to the extent that it is not distorted or corrupted by the

accepted with "ease" the "righteous vengeance" celebrated in *Les Guérillères*, the woman-on-woman violence portrayed in *The Lesbian Body* "has presented far greater problems for readers," seeming to be "at the very least questionable, if not wanton."[28] Given the significance of violence in the book, I will return to this matter below. Suffice to say at this point, the physical intrusion of *The Lesbian Body* onto the page of this chapter, forcibly pushing Gagnon's work upward until it is removed from the page entirely, is an appropriate stylistic gesture of critique.

In this dark adored adorned gehenna say your farewells m/y very beautiful one m/y very strong one m/y very indomitable one m/y very learned

fall." Without explaining why all our perceptions of the observable world are not therefore marred by the fall, he argues that even if homosexuality was shown to be genetically determined (a view he finds "irrelevant" in any case), "homosexual urges" are simply part of the wider category of "sinful impulses" that are part of human nature (393–432). Some critics of Gagnon's focus on "natural revelation" note his tendency to give priority to this form of argument; indeed, one wonders if Gagnon even needs the Bible, "since everything one needs to know about sexuality can be deduced from the functionality of body parts" (W. Johnson 2006, 392). Jack Rogers (2009, 78) notes in particular, "Giving priority to natural law opens the door to bring in all manner of assumptions and prejudices that have nothing to do with the biblical text." I will argue below that this is precisely what one discovers when one examines the underlying ideologies in Gagnon's arguments.

In the rest of this chapter I will focus upon two aspects of Gagnon's arguments that reveal the heteropatriarchal ideology that underlies his "natural" view of gender and sexuality. First I will address the issue that Gagnon (2001, 176, 272, 311) finds male same-sex intercourse degrading in that at least one of the partners "is taking the place of a woman" by being penetrated, a process that he deplores as it inevitably leads to the "demasculization" or "feminization" of such men. For Gagnon, same-sex intercourse and "the absurd denial of natural revelation" that it entails is the height of "depravity" and "self-degradation" (268, 264, 269). He states that the language used in Rom 1:18–32, for example, indicates the "depth of Paul's visceral feelings toward same-sex intercourse" and argues that these feelings are paralleled in both the Hebrew Bible and other Jewish

one m/y very ferocious one m/y very gentle one m/y best beloved to what they, the women, call affection tenderness or gracious abandon. There is not one who is unaware of what takes place here, which has no name as yet....

   ... At this point *I* invoke your help m/y incomparable Sappho, give m/e by thousands the fingers that allay the wounds, give me/ the lips the tongue the saliva which draw one into the slow sweet poisoned country from which one cannot return.

   ... farewell black continent of misery and suffering farewell ancient cities we are embarking for the shining radiant isles for the green Cytheras for the dark and gilded Lesbos. (Wittig 1976, 13, 14, 24)

writings of the period (269). Gagnon's primary concern is the *behavior of men*, as it is their degradation in being penetrated *as if they were females* that makes same-sex intercourse so "detestable" (70).[29]

Second, I will explore Gagnon's argument that the institutions of heterosexual marriage and the family are under imminent threat from the destructive practice of male same-sex intercourse. Gagnon promotes the value of "a stable and nurturing society" with its need for "stable and productive citizens" based upon the institutions of heterosexual marriage and the family, but he does so by utilizing a rhetoric of fear and aggression (25, 481). Primarily he argues that an increase in the numbers of people identifying as homosexual (or bisexual) will inevitably lead to greater sexual promiscuity, and thus ultimately a low standard of sexual fidelity "that will wreak havoc on the institutions of marriage and family" (481). Thus, for Gagnon, same-sex behavior does not only lead to degradation for the individuals who practice it, but it inexorably leads to the destruction of society "as a whole" (37).

Homosexuality as Degrading

Complementarity is a central tenet of Gagnon's argument, and this notion that male and female are "perfect fits" might suggest to evangelicals of an egalitarian persuasion that this entails a sense of mutuality and equality in gender relations. But Gagnon's focus is strictly androcentric. Woman is man's complementary sexual "other" who restores *him* to wholeness through being united to him in sexual intercourse and marriage (2001,

Wittig's *The Lesbian Body* begins and immediately we are asked to say farewell to what "the women call affection tenderness or gracious abandon" and are dared to enter "this dark adored adorned gehenna."[30] We say farewell to that "black continent of misery and suffering" and set sail for "green Cytheras for the dark and gilded Lesbos."[31] Lesbos is the Greek island traditionally associated with the poet Sappho and is the source of the word *lesbian*. Wittig (2005a, 44–45) comments that Sappho's poetry— the fragments that are left—were her original inspiration for *The Lesbian Body*, although she notes that her attempts to "write around" Sappho's work did not work and she had to find a new form.[32]

As we are drawn into this "slow sweet poisoned country" from which there is no return, we discover that "entry in to the world of *The Lesbian*

60–61). Gagnon explains this understanding of complementarity by reference to the creation accounts (Gen 1–2), stating, "The woman is not just 'like himself' but 'from himself' and thereby a complementary fit to himself.... Only a being made from man can be a suitable and complementary counterpart for him" (61). There is no corresponding mention of how the man might be a "fit" *for the woman*. Even when he has moved beyond the scope of Gen 1–2 to "contemporary Western society," Gagnon's focus is still androcentric. He frequently states, "God/nature obviously intended the female vagina to be the complementary sex organ for the male penis" (169). Yet there is *no* corresponding mention of how the male penis might be a complementary sex organ *for the female vagina*.

This androcentric focus flows through into Gagnon's argument against same-sex relations, based as it is on the notion of complementarity of male and female. He declares, "A man can never be a complementary sexual 'other' for another man" (63 n. 54). Again, there is no corresponding mention of how a woman can never be "a complementary sexual 'other'" *for another woman*. For Gagnon, "homosexual intercourse" primarily means male same-sex intercourse. Ultimately Gagnon appears to create a natural law–based ethic for men, as only that which is male is viewed as normative. I cite a longer sample here so that the "slippage" from the general (human sexuality) to the specific (male same-sex intercourse) becomes clear:

> The particularly "abhorrent" character of homosexual intercourse cannot be explained solely or primarily by its lack of procreative potential. Rather, it is to be traced to its character as a flagrant transgression of the

Body is therefore exile from the world of conventional relations" (Whatling 1997, 241). In this new (utopic? dystopic?) country we must "discard the qualities associated with traditional womanhood" and engage in a "radical departure from the universe of romantic and feminine forms" (Rosenfeld 1984, 240; Chisholm 1993, 204). If we dare to follow, we will be taking part in that "which has no name as yet."[33] Consequently, we enter into a territory that is always dark *and* adored, sweet *and* poisoned, dark *and* gilded.

Wittig's intention, clear from the outset, is to destabilize (and ultimately destroy) the naturalized notions of the stable sexed (female) body and the dyadic hierarchical categories of gender by challenging the heteronormative ideology that underlies these supposedly "natural" structures or, rather, "ideological machinations" (Scanlon 1998, 74), through

most fundamental element of human sexuality: sex or gender. Homosexual intercourse requires a radical "gender bending" of human sexuality by the very creatures whom God placed in charge of the good, ordered creation. Such an act constitutes a conscious denial of the complementarity of male and female found not least in the fittedness (anatomical, physiological, and procreative) of the male penis and the female vaginal receptacle by attempting anal intercourse (or other forms of sexual intercourse) with another man. Anal sex not only confuses gender, it confuses the function of the anus as a cavity for expelling excrement, not receiving sperm. (138–39)

There is much to critique in this sample of Gagnon's argument. To begin with, not only does he assume that men always engage in anal sex without the use of condoms, but he also confuses the concepts of sex and gender, assuming that these are synonymous. In addition, this paragraph illustrates his tendency to opt for objectifying language with regard to women. Why not simply say "vagina" as opposed to "vaginal receptacle"? But in particular, it is clear from this paragraph that Gagnon equates "homosexual intercourse" with "anal intercourse," and that he views this as an "act" to be done "with another man." Indeed, Gagnon only has male same-sex anal intercourse in view throughout his discussion. Although he mentions "human sexuality" and "creatures" at the outset of this paragraph, the identity of who is meant by these general terms shifts to the specific pairing of two men as the phrase "another man" suggests an additional one of the same. Perhaps, however, the move in this direction could have been

the offering of reconfigured notions of identity and community that are liberated and contestable, multiple and fractured. By offering the lesbian body as an alternative construct of subjectivity, Wittig (1992i, 32) refuses to accept the heteropatriarchal tradition of construing identity in terms of masculine subjectivity and its relation to the feminine "other" (called woman). Shaktini (2005a, 158) elaborates on this point: "To write the lesbian body as a lesbian materialist is also to unwrite the heterosexist images, myths, grammar, lexicon, practices, and relationships that create the object 'woman.'" This creation of woman, as an "other" who was created *for* man, as Barth and Gagnon would have us understand the creation account in Gen 1–3 and passages such as 1 Cor 11:2–16, is therefore profoundly challenged by Wittig's lesbian body. Erika Ostrovsky (2005, 124) picks up on this point in relation to the way in which the protagonists[34] in *The Lesbian*

detected by the description of the "creatures" being those "whom God placed in charge of the good, ordered creation." Elsewhere Gagnon notes that the "complementary differences between male and female humans [bring] out different facets of the divine image (for example, God as ruler and God as nurturer)," unmistakably suggesting the male brings out the former, the female the latter facets of God's image (59 n. 42). I would posit then, that Gagnon has males in mind throughout the entire passage.

Admittedly, Gagnon does mention female same-sex behavior in a few instances, but in general he consistently focuses on male same-sex behavior. Gagnon notes the absence of explicit critiques of same-sex female intercourse in the Old Testament, suggesting that possible reasons for this may be found in the "primacy of penetration for defining sexual intercourse," and because the "experimentation" that women may have been involved with prior to marriage "would thus constitute no danger to Israelite family structures or determination of paternity" (144–45). Otherwise, he only includes "lesbians" and "lesbianism" in his discussions on evidence from twin studies, hormonal influences, and socialization (403–20). When he examines "The Hermeneutical Relevance of the Biblical Witness"—by far the longest section of his book—the research he cites often ignores same-sex female behavior.[35] But it is when Gagnon discusses the issue of the supposed "dearth of life-long monogamous homosexual relationships" that the ideology driving his predominant focus on male same-sex behavior emerges (452–60). Not only does he again dismiss female same-sex behavior as experimentation and as having little impact on the institutions

Body are no longer the objects of male discourse but are instead speaking subjects: "Such power is tantamount to creation, even Creation. It constitutes a transposed version of Genesis.... In this version, however, it is not pronounced by a male god but by thousands of female voices."

This strategy is perhaps best described by K. Cope (1991, 76) as "Wittig's practice of lesbianization." Cope bases this notion primarily on Wittig's (1992c, 87; 2005a, 47) self-description of her project in *The Lesbian Body* as an attempt to "attack the order of heterosexuality in texts" in order to "lesbianize the heroes of love, lesbianize the symbols, lesbianize the gods and the goddesses, lesbianize Christ, lesbianize the men and the women." But Cope also bases this on Wittig's (1992k; 2005a, 45) idea that a literary work can function as a potential "war machine," as a subversive "Trojan Horse."[36] By producing a "shock" with the words used, the lan-

of marriage and inheritance, but he also suggests that whereas "female homosexuality is more cognitive and relational," "male homosexuality appears to be governed more by pure libido" (417). Using negative generalizations, he comments, "A rampant promiscuity along with a host of other addictive behaviors that often accompany it remains characteristic of many segments of homosexual male culture. This suggests male homosexual relationships are plagued both by the absence of a female partner to curb the excesses of male sexuality ... and inadequate self-control" (178).

It is this concern over male sexuality and promiscuity that dominates Gagnon's anxiety about male same-sex behavior. He states, "As a general rule, men who are left to their own devices have great difficulty forming enduring monogamous relationships. Men need to be 'civilized' and 'domesticated' into such unions by women" (459). He then cites a study that argues that a significant difference between men and women is that while women tend to be monogamous and have "nurturing interests," men are "sexually promiscuous" (460). According to this study, male homosexuals are even more promiscuous because "they simply lack the restraints imposed by female partnership" (460 n. 193). Gagnon notes that "males can be resocialized when their partners are female. But males will remain males; when a man's partner is a male both will share these proclivities" (460 n. 193).[37] There is much to critique here regarding Gagnon's dependence on studies that show a lack of awareness of the social construction of gender roles. In addition, his acceptance of the "angel in the house" con-

guage of heterosexuality is itself challenged, fractured, and reconfigured to allow for the production of a new subject identity beyond the constraints (or "coercive artificiality") of the "natural" binary sex differences of male and female (Wittig 1992k, 72; Epps and Katz 2007, 424). K. Cope (1991, 76, 79–80) explains, "Wittig's practice of lesbianization ... declares war against the compulsory, totalizing, and apparently extra-linguistic character of heterosexuality by means of attention to language, by linguistic appropriation, displacement, and redirection of dominant cultural themes, concepts, practices and literary texts." In *The Lesbian Body*, this strategy of lesbianization is evident in both the text and its subject matter. Wittig (2005a, 46) describes how this parodic destabilization is evident from the outset in the title of the book: "Suddenly giving me a big laugh (for one can laugh even in anguish) two words came in: *Lesbian Body....* That is how the book started to exist: in irony. The body, a word whose gender

cept (as discussed in the previous section)—with its notion that women's purpose is to civilize and domesticate men, and to be used by men as a way of curbing their sexual excesses—is indicative of his androcentric (if not misogynist) focus.

When Gagnon considers "The Negative Effects of Societal Endorsement of Homosexuality," it is primarily male same-sex promiscuity that again appears to be the cause of most of these ills. To begin with, Gagnon argues that society has to carry the "staggering" costs of health care that are generated by same-sex activity, namely "receptive anal sex and promiscuity" (478). In addition, he argues that because "some who engage in same-sex intercourse *also* engage in opposite-sex intercourse," their partners are therefore also exposed to the health risks that are "associated with homosexual activity" (479, emphasis added). The way in which Gagnon has ordered these encounters clearly indicates that he puts the blame on those who engage in same-sex behavior. He then argues that there is "little doubt that affirmation of a same-sex lifestyle will increase the incidence of pedophilic activity," the main purpose of which is "in 'recruiting' homosexuals into the fold" (479). But potentially "far more dangerous" than pedophilia, according to Gagnon, is the way in which societal and ecclesial "affirmation of homosexuality" will lead to "greater permissiveness as regards sexual promiscuity" and therefore to the acceptance and practice of "irresponsible and unstable sexual behavior" by heterosexuals (480–81). These arguments are disturbing not only for their androcentrism, but also

is masculine in French with the word *lesbian* qualifying it.... Such was my 'Lesbian Body,' a kind of paradox but not really, a kind of joke but not really, a kind of impossibility but not really" (see also Devarrieux 1999, iii).

In contrast to Wittig's first two books, in which she does not mention the word *lesbian* at all, the word conspicuously appears in the very title of this work. Yet, Whatling (1997, 239) argues, while the title of the book, with the use of the definite article, "appears to set up an absolute notion of identity ... namely that there is some such thing as a lesbian [whose] nature will be described (inscribed) within the text," this is in fact deliberate textual trickery, as the notion of a stable fixed identity is actually the stuff of fiction. Whatling (239) goes on to state, "*The Lesbian Body* is a text which, rather than celebrating a unified notion of the lesbian, institutes separation, multiplicity, contradiction and the fracturing of lesbian identity into a thousand possible combinations."[38]

because Gagnon equates same-sex desire per se with pedophilia, once again assumes that men engage in anal sex without protection, and blames any negative sexual behavior by (male) heterosexuals on those (men) who engage in same-sex behavior.

Other ills mentioned by Gagnon include homosexuals experiencing "female-like types of 'neuroticism'" and the annihilation of gender norms: "In its most bizarre forms we will be asked as a culture to accept as perfectly normal and well-adjusted a man wearing lipstick, pantyhose, and a pink dress" (478, 482).[39] Again it is clear in both of these examples that Gagnon's focus is on male behavior. He is also dismissive of such "female-like" behavior or attire, his attitude toward female mental health is patronizing, and his description of pink dresses is more suggestive of clothing worn by preschool girls than by adult women. In addition, Gagnon expresses concern about the dearth of long-term same-sex relationships and the high incidence of domestic violence in the gay community, suggesting that these social ills argue against the validity of same-sex behavior (452–60, 475). But these are hardly issues limited to those in same-sex relationships. Issues of adultery, depression rates for married women, child abuse (violence and incest), and the health risks of pregnancy and birth are but a few of the issues that ought to concern Gagnon with regard to heterosexual relationships; yet somehow he ignores these.[40]

When we consider the book as a whole, its unconventional appearance immediately provides evidence of lesbianization. Seth Clark Silberman (2007, 470) notes that lesbianization is "expressed through the novel's fleshly, sinewy syntax." Altogether there are 109 (or 110)[41] poems interrupted at regular intervals by eleven segments of a list enumerating the names of body parts and functions, differentiated from the poems by their print in boldface capital letters. Lynn Higgins (1976, 161) explains, "*Le Corps lesbien* is not *about* the lesbien body, *but*, thanks to the ambiguity of the title, it *is* the corps (corpus) lesbien. The text itself is a body.... Ritual disarticulation of the human body is enacted in the narrative passages [while] the list reassembles the body with a different syntax." It is significant to note also that despite its title, the phrase "the lesbian body" occurs only twice in the entire book—as the first phrase of the first list and as the last phrase of the last list—suggesting that everything in between *is* this body; there is no individual lesbian in this text, so to speak, only bodies and beings that are lesbian.[42]

Ultimately, this androcentrism expresses itself in the misogynist issue of degradation that Gagnon argues is an inherent part of male same-sex intercourse. Throughout his book Gagnon consistently refers to the "inherently degrading quality of same-sex intercourse," explaining that "every act of male same-sex intercourse [is] detestable since the penetrated male, at the moment of penetration, inherently functions as a female—whether the act of same-sex intercourse is coercive or consensual" (70–71). Clearly assuming that penetration is definitive for sexual intercourse, he frequently argues that such behavior is "debased" and "shameful" and elicits feelings of "disdain" and "revulsion," which ought to clearly convey its immorality (46, 70–71, 253). Although Gagnon may have adopted some of this language from Paul's own vocabulary in Rom 1:24–27 (ἀκαθαρσία, ἀτιμάζεσθαι, ἀτιμία, ἀσχημοσύνη), he has done more than simply translate Paul's texts and comment on them, but he has carried this visceral response over into his own descriptions and comments. This is a persistent practice throughout Gagnon's book, despite the comments by some reviewers that Gagnon's work conveys a "hope-bestowing spirit ... [and is] written in non-polemical tone" (Swartley 2002, 218–19) and is "fair and compassionate."[43] The sheer force of Gagnon's (2001, 269) "disgust" at male same-sex behavior, because of its "demasculization" and/or "feminization" of men who are penetrated (272, 311), is difficult to convey here other than by citing a few of his comments in cumulative fashion:

To highlight the way in which the book itself demonstrates lesbianization in its very structure, Wittig (2005a, 48) concludes her comments on *The Lesbian Body* by noting, "The book is thus formed in two parts. It opens and falls back on itself. One can compare its form to a cashew, to an almond, to a vulva." This can be contrasted with Gagnon's obsession not only with penises and penetration, but also with his interpretive strategy that is determined to discover *the* meaning of a text. As such, Gagnon's work is a classic example of phallogocentrism.

I will further explore *The Lesbian Body*, then, by a consideration of these two parts. First, I will focus on the lesbian body as seen in the poems, a figure that quickly emerges as monstrous, or to echo Bakhtin (1984), "grotesque," and Kristeva (1982), "abject," and the way in which violence is a necessary element in these poems with regard to the concept of subjectivity. Second, I will consider the list of body parts and the way in which this challenges androcentric, heterosexual (supposedly "natural") con-

To "lie with a man as though lying with a woman" (Lev 18:22; 20:13) was to treat a man as though his masculine identity counted for nothing, as though he were not a man but a woman. (75)

As with the author(s) of the Levitical prohibitions, the Yahwist [in Gen 19] is less concerned with motives than with the act of penetrating a male as if he were a female, an act that by its very nature is demeaning regardless of how well it is done. (78)[44]

The "mounting" of another man emasculates that man ... because it puts the male in the inferior status of the female.... Penetration is the first stage of feminization.... Philo emphasizes the culpability of the active partner for "not respecting (standing in awe of, fearing, showing regard for, *aidoumenoi*)" the male gender of the passive partner. (172–73)

The moment a man takes another man to bed he distorts and diminishes the other male's sexual identity as created and ordained by God, regardless of whether the relationship is fully consensual and noncommercial.... For [Paul and Philo], the first and most heinous stage of feminization occurred in the act of sexual penetration: being lain with "as though a woman." (311)

With regard to Rom 1:24–27, both idolatry and same-sex intercourse are structions of sexualized bodies (or the body politic for that matter). As Scanlon (1998, 78) observes, "The lesbianization produces a monstering not only of the text but also of the body."

The *LESBIAN* Body

But you know that no one will be able to bear seeing you with eyes turned up lids cut off your yellow smoking intestines spread in the hollow of your hands your tongue spat from your mouth long green strings of your bile flowing over your breasts.... The gleam of your teeth your joy your sorrow the hidden life of your viscera your blood your arteries your veins your hollow habitations your organs your nerves their rupture their spurting forth death slow decomposition stench being devoured by worms your open skull, all will be equally unbearable to her. (Wittig 1976, 13)

Right from the outset of *The Lesbian Body* we are warned that what takes place here will be "unbearable," and without any chance to hesitate at

singled out by Paul as particularly clear and revolting examples of the suppression of the truth about God....

Participation in same-sex intercourse is partly its own payback for turning away from the one true God, since Paul regards such behavior as itself unclean, a dishonoring of one's own body, and a self-shaming act of obscene indecency. (337)

From Paul's perspective the fundamental problem with male homosexual conduct is not that it is exploitative of young people but that it is sexual gratification aimed at other males rather than at females. (348–49)

Despite commenting sporadically that the misogyny of some of the ancient writers' comments is deplorable,[45] it is hard to avoid the conclusion that Gagnon's comments themselves seem to manage a combination of both heterosexism and misogyny. The language he uses makes clear that, for him, for a man to be penetrated is demeaning, heinous, revolting, unclean, dishonoring, self-shaming, and obscene. Why? First, because it appears that penetration is something to be done to females, sexual gratification ought to be aimed at females, and they can be used to curb the excesses of male sexuality. Second, because to be a woman—or to be *like* a woman—according to the language used in these citations is to have

the entrance to this "dark adored adorned gehenna" we are immediately confronted with images of abjection that "no one will be able to bear." As Whatling (1997, 242) remarks, we will find ourselves "simultaneously seduced and revolted." In this very first poem, Shaktini (2005a, 157) suggests, Wittig presents the lesbian body as a "monster," playing on the way in which throughout history, "When men have not completely denied lesbianism, they have monstrously distorted it" (see also Wenzel 1981, 282; Bourque 2005, 173). Embodying the collective fears of Western culture, which has stigmatized the lesbian as both something apart and something potentially contagious—"Look out or you'll turn into one of them, not a woman but a victim of the lesbian plague, a monster" (K. Cope 1991, 75)—Wittig's conceptualization of the lesbian body in this text both highlights and challenges this anxiety. As Scanlon (1998, 74) explains, "Wittig deploys hyperbole, parody and humor to redefine from the lesbian point of view the position already ascribed to the lesbian by the mainstream order.... The lesbian becomes a trope for the ambivalent monster excluded

an identity that counts for nothing, to have an inferior status, and to be diminished in identity. A man, however, ought to be treated with respect, stood in awe of, shown regard for, and feared. While Gagnon argues that at times "different cultures" have emphasized the differences between the sexes "sometimes with oppressive results for women," he suggests that it is also possible to distinguish between "misogyny and cultural appreciation for legitimate gender differences" (483).

What Gagnon perhaps does not seem to realize is that in the descriptions amassed above, there is very little "appreciation" shown for being a woman. Indeed, to view females as basically "receptacles" into which males can insert their penises as a way of gratifying their sexual needs and thus curbing their sexual impulses is a decidedly oppressive notion. Clearly Gagnon does not appear to accept that discourse, in the Foucauldian sense, conveys ideology. The "cultural appreciation for legitimate gender differences" that he mentions is precisely the kind of discourse that transmits and perpetuates the ideology that supports misogyny.

Homosexuality as Destructive

But what lies behind these attitudes? How does Gagnon manage to be

from the heterosexual system." Thus Wittig brings the lesbian body to the fore, a figure who she says is "a not-woman, a not-man, a product of society, not a product of nature," a figure who stands "at the outposts of the human" (1992b, 46; 1992e, 13).

The protagonists in *The Lesbian Body* exist beyond the categories of sex and gender, traverse the boundaries of the "normal," and thus signify "a counter-attack on the categorical thinking" of heteropatriarchy (Chisholm 1993, 197). They are at times transfigured into superhuman beings that can fly, have superhuman strength and gigantic dimensions, or are godlike in their powers. At other times, highlighting the way in which "woman" has been associated with "nature," Wittig has her protagonists immersed and enmeshed in their environments—covered in mud or sand, tangled in seaweed, lying at the bottom of a lake, and imprisoned in ice. They are also attacked by wasps, eaten by sharks, entwined by snakes, covered with biting spiders. Wittig even transforms her figures into various elements of nature, such as trees, the sea, or a storm. Exploiting the way in which "woman" is often reduced to "animal" (as we discussed in ch. 4),

both prudish and yet incessantly explicit in his descriptions of specific sex acts and anatomy? How does he manage to be so offensive to both women and those within LBGT communities and yet insist that his approach is one of compassionate Christian love? I suggest that it is possible to place Gagnon's rhetoric in a broader framework of discourses that operate within the evangelical environment in the United States. Cultural theorists and historians have traced the ways in which the creation of citizens and the ideology of nationhood in the United States have, from its Puritan foundation, had an impact upon the sense of self and sexual identity of individuals (Bercovitch 1975; Fessenden, Radel, and Zaborowska 2001; Vejdovsky 2001; Ingebretsen 2001). The "identity panic" that was integral to the formation of the United States—in that it was both a Puritan "Utopia" and a "hybridic, multicultural, centerless and plural … melting-pot"—has continued to shape the way its individuals have responded to the difference of "others" (Ingebretsen 2001, 26).

Edward Ingebretsen (2001, 4) considers how these "others" (be they Indians, Irish, Asian, women, or gays, for example)[46] are typically formulated within American culture as "monsters" whose function, as "agents of moralized fear," is pedagogical. Seen as those who threaten civil, political, or theological order because of the freedoms they seem to exhibit through

she also transforms her figures into a wide variety of animals, from the recognizable, such as she-wolf, horse, kangaroo, swan, cat, and lamb, to the unusual or strange, such as a giant whalelike creature, a giant fly, and tiny multitudinous protozoa and cilia. But Wittig pushes the boundaries of identity even further, through the transmutation of her figures into fantastic creatures covered with iron spikes or scales, or having three horns, or ten thousand eyes, or arms of white-hot steel and hair of tin.[47] Whatling (1997, 245) suggests that this unsettling of any singular notion of identity is intended "to ensure that the lesbian body, though always in play, is never fully determined … *the* lesbian body is never there to be caught, entrapped, assimilated, or rejected."

It is perhaps not surprising then, that while the figures address each other as "m/y best beloved," or "m/y dearest one," for example, they also call each other "m/y most execrable one," "m/y vile one," "m/y deplorable one," and "m/y most atrocious one," and so on. Perhaps the most powerful phrases are those that combine these elements, revealing not only the parodic and destabilizing effect of this whole process but also the

their transgressions of "our" categories of sex, gender, race, or class, monsters "warn" and "secure the normal" (4, 20). They are "carriers of social anxiety" whose portrayal is intended to shock the onlooker (or reader) "with a sense of *horror* that confirm[s] their own 'normalcy' in the face of the morally alien" (25–26). Ingebretsen suggests, "By locating monsters *off* the social map, we locate the human—and thus, we hope, ourselves—*on* it" (26). What is ultimately "at stake" is whether we ourselves shall "pass the 'Monster Test,'" given that "the answer to that question is never clear, never certain" (26). Thus, as communities and the various individuals within those communities debate issues of identity and the nature of belonging, being able to point to "others" who do *not* belong and defining them as "sinners" (or "monsters") enables each community to redefine its boundaries and establish what is (supposedly) "normal."[48]

In particular, Ingebretsen argues that one of the fundamental "motifs of fear" in American culture (since the 1950s) is "gender failure," especially the failure of manhood as epitomized in "the homosexual" (71–72). As he explains, "A cult of domesticity equated national security and personal purity with domestic orderliness and sexual virtue; its hermeneutic

way in which lesbian bodies demonstrate "morphological metamorphosis" (to extend the "nature" metaphor even further) (Chisholm 1993, 205, 209; Whatling 1997, 244). Also perhaps not surprisingly, these particular terms of endearment utilize the word *monster*, such as "adored monster," "m/y most handsome monster," and in the same poem as this last phrase, "a goddess monstrous with rottenness." Whereas Gagnon (2001, 70–71) consistently rejects same-sex erotic behavior as "inherently degrading" and "detestable," Wittig deliberately claims these qualities in the form of the "monstrous lesbian" (Scanlon 1998, 73), disrupting and transgressing perceived boundaries and conventional categories (of sex, gender, genre, grammar, etc.) in order to celebrate that which straight society sees as "an object of horror," to take pride in that which is deemed to be shameful, and "to render positive that which has formerly been designated as grotesque" (Whatling 1997, 238–40; see also Sedgwick 2003; Burrus 2008; Halperin and Traub 2009).

Indeed, this concept of "grotesque" is not accidentally ascribed to Wittig's work. Several scholars note a connection with the work of Mikhail Bakhtin and his theories of carnival and the grotesque. In particular, Chisholm (1993, 209) notes that, for Bakhtin, "the principle of degra-

of the anti-erotic marked as deviant, first and foremost the homosexual" (72). During the "gender-rigid landscape of the fifties," manliness became equated with civic virtue and was put at risk by those men who did not fit the stereotypical image of masculinity (73–74; see also Faludi 1999). By the end of the 1980s, with the onset and persistence of AIDS, homosexuality had become "America's favorite goblin" and was perceived as an even greater threat (Green 1999, 13). The supposedly "shocking sexuality" of the homosexual lifestyle was contrasted with the "domestic virtue of middle-class America" (Ingebretsen 2001, 91).

But by the end of the twentieth century (and into the first decade of the twenty-first century), for the religious and political "New Right," the threat of homosexuality went even deeper; homosexuals were portrayed as "diabolic and demonic" and were viewed as "the apocalyptic agents of national collapse" (Ingebretsen 2001, 190). Ironically, despite being "effeminate," homosexuals (and those who affirmed their lifestyle) were thought to wield enormous power, generally construed as a "crisis of gender" (192).[49] The evangelical conservative Robert Knight, who declared that Christianity in America is a "man-based culture," also com-

dation" is an essential element in his "aesthetics of the grotesque body," arguing that this element is clearly evident in *The Lesbian Body* (see also K. Cope 1991, 84; Whatling 1997, 240; Scanlon 1998, 79). Wittig (1992c, 78) herself refers to Bakhtin, although not in relation to the grotesque but with regard to his "strictly materialist approach to language" in her discussion of linguistics. Nevertheless, Chisholm (1993, 206) argues that "Wittig could not have failed to have been influenced by Bakhtin," suggesting that the "points of intersection" between their work can be viewed as "a productive intertextuality that Wittig may or may not have intended." But as Fiona Black (2009, 94) rightly notes, "Bakhtin's emphasis is phallocentric"; and so I suggest that whether or not Wittig has intentionally embraced Bakhtin's grotesque, she has nevertheless lesbianized this style of representing bodies and desire.[50]

Unlike the idealized, "godly" representations of woman (or man for that matter) that Barth, Gagnon, and evangelical writers such as Elliot have presented, in which the elite virtues of self-control, purity, and beauty are applauded, Wittig's lesbian body is bawdy, visceral, and—as in the poem above—literally soiled. These representations are frequently class-determined, so that what is "proper" behavior for men and women (or

ments, "As a man is reduced in stature, all hell will break loose" (cited in Dreyfuss 1999, 39–41).[51] Indeed, Gagnon also equates "apocalyptic" events with the affirmation of homosexuality. When the steeple of the Central Lutheran Church in downtown Minneapolis snapped after it was unexpectedly struck by a tornado (on 19 August 2009), and dangled ominously upside down, Gagnon (2009) commented that the church was being used at that specific time by the Evangelical Lutheran Church in America (ELCA) "to approve the new sexuality statement," which would permit the blessing of homosexual unions. He noted that while the weather forecast did not predict severe storms, the tornado hit the church soon after it had approved of the new statement by a vote of 66.6 percent and declared that the symbolism of the upside-down cross "is a profound image of the inversion of God's will for human sexual pairing."

As "monster," the homosexual therefore represents "a nexus of confusions, crossings, and transgressions" (Ingebretsen 2001, 195), to which conservative evangelicalism has responded with what Ingebretsen calls a "poisonously benign" Christian altruism, the combination of both "lib-

"ladies") is determined by the conservative values of respectability and the maintenance of the status quo. As Chisholm (1993, 210–11) states, "*The Lesbian Body* is the *soiling* of idealist representations of the structures of desire.… The speaking and desiring subjects literally bathe in a flood of bodily images that are spoken in knowing disdain for the bourgeois sense of the aesthetic and the proper" (see also Whatling 1997, 241; Crowder 2007, 499). As such, the lesbian body challenges notions of what constitutes "natural," virtuous, proper behavior for women (and men). The lesbian body is very earthy, very grounded in the soil (and as such also very "natural"), and not at all transformed into the constructed model of proper appearance and behavior imposed upon bodies by the heteropatriarchal system, yet deemed by that system to be "natural."

Paul's comments in 1 Cor 11:13–15 regarding "proper" deportment for women and how "nature itself" teaches that long hair on a man is shameful are closely aligned to this understanding of what is "natural," with gender boundaries firmly in place, the gaze controlled, and bodies/hair covered, preventing exposure. By contrast, and by a coincidentally relevant metaphor (if one thinks of head coverings in relation to 1 Cor 11:2–16), Epps and Katz (2007, 440) suggest that for those like Wittig who reject "a reified social reality," the "key task was to pierce the veil of illusion

eral demonstrations of showy love and sympathy" and "a heavy dollop of hate" (2). While Gagnon nowhere describes "homosexuals" as "monsters," the rhetoric he uses throughout his book fits Ingebretsen's (2001, 2, 37) descriptions of "a rhetoric of rebuke" and the "rhetorics of monstrosity." In the public display of the "monster," Ingebretsen suggests that the body "is slowly stripped, deliciously moralized.... The obscene is offered as civic tableaux for the public good" (3). This process, which Ingebretsen points out can happen anywhere from political speech to "the double-edged altruism of church prayer" or in "the benign commonsense rationality of ecclesiastical injunction," creates a situation where "rhetorical as well as social cruelty is normalized in the name of the civil" (4, 10). The repudiation of the so-called monster is achieved with a rhetoric "in which violence, disowned into words, becomes a tactical although unacknowledged bludgeon" (26). This is a rhetoric that both luridly focuses on sexual detail and admonishes with a supposedly well-meaning but ultimately brutal backhand—a rhetoric that I would argue is a fair description of Gagnon's approach.

One of the other pertinent elements of this "rhetoric of fear" is the

through which ideology structures the perception of the real and to begin the slow, difficult task of denaturalizing it."

> *I* become the place of the darkest mysteries ... *I* am the pitch that burns the assailants' heads, *I* am the knife that severs the carotid of the new-born ewe-lambs, *I* am the bullets of the submachine guns that perforate the intestines, *I* am the pincers brought to red heat in the fire that tears the flesh, *I* am the plaited whip that flagellates the skin, *I* am the electric current that blasts and convulses the muscles, *I* am the gag that gags the mouth, *I* am the bandage that hides the eyes, *I* am the bonds that tie the hands. (Wittig 1976, 14)

From its outset, Whatling (1997, 241) notes, "*The Lesbian Body* opens upon a carnivalesque state of uncensored emotion, sensuality and hedonistic liberation ... in which the reader is encouraged to vicariously share." Indeed, while we are forced to observe the violence done to "you" in the opening poem (where we are even faced with the death and decomposition of "you"), the second poem cited above presents us with the challenge of partaking in this violence ourselves, as the text shifts to the first person pronoun *I* (*j/e* in the original, a point to which I will return below). I noted earlier that it was the violence perpetrated by the protagonists of Wittig's

exposure of the instability of "the normal" (Ingebretsen 2001, 25). In the fragmented society of the United States, where diverse identities compete for acceptance and validation, and yet where there is also a nationalistic nostalgia based on a coherency of self and state, the latter inevitably emerges as a "*fantasy*" as does the concept of the "normal" individual (13). Ingebretsen explains:

> The more visibly national mythologies of the civil and domestic lay in tatters, the more visibly they were restitched in nostalgic wholeness.... As a result, ideological operations of public fantasy produced what might be called the normalized citizen, but it also made possible the monstrous, secret alien.... Identity and its possibilities were doubled, or fragmented, and the horrifying other was seen, inevitably, to be an intimate other. (33–34)

Because of this instability and anxiety, a rhetoric of fear is used to reaffirm "what are assumed to be the 'normal' values of heterosexual romance,

book that repelled many readers. But, as Wittig (2005a, 45) explains, violence was "doubly at the nexus and the core of this undertaking." By writing "forcefully" about "that which doesn't dare to speak its name," not only was Wittig attempting a "new form" of writing that inevitably "threatens and does violence" to older forms (and involves "a violence to the reader"), but she wanted to express "the violence of passion ... lesbian passion ... carnal passion" (46). Or as she succinctly explained elsewhere, when asked about the violence in her work, "Cela avait été une passion telle, il fallait quelque chose de violent" ("It was such a passion that something violent was needed") (Devarrieux 1999).[52]

Wittig (2005a, 45) explains that the introduction of the violence of "lesbian passion" into literature was to be a deliberate contrast to the "mildest kind of love" perhaps best expressed by Colette, whereby "two poor women had to help each other—out of compassion—to pass over the peak of passion—that is orgasm—as a sister of charity helps a dying man."[53] Rather than the virtues of compassion or beauty, for example, Wittig places passion at the center of her work. Consequently, Wittig also challenges the notion of idyllic femininity presented in certain strands of what can be called "heterofeminism" that embrace "a matrocentric, feel-good, 'woman is wonderful' logic" (Epps and Katz 2007, 438) in an attempt to set up an alternative understanding of "difference" that values

clearly defined sexual roles, and the middle-class family" (32). This anxious affirmation of the "normal" in the face of the horrifyingly different is precisely what we see throughout Gagnon's (2001, 482) book, perhaps most notably in his lament that although "one may wish for a utopian society where homosexuals will 'behave' like the average heterosexual … wishing will not make it so."

Gagnon also consistently notes that the presence of same-sex behavior in society will inevitably lead to the destruction of society "as a whole" and warns that such behavior has "apocalyptic repercussions" (2001, 37, 245). Implying that homosexuality is a "condition" that can be "caught," in that he argues that societal acceptance of homosexual behaviors leads to an increase in the numbers of people exhibiting "homosexuality" with its associated "serious health problems," Gagnon states that this will "wreak havoc on the institutions of marriage and family" (471, 481). Thus, he argues, same-sex intercourse "results in destructive consequences" for society (37). Of course, although Gagnon states that "the medical facts" are

the feminine alongside the masculine, that which she calls "the myth of woman" (Wittig 1992e, 13–19). Such a utopic view is also seen within certain strands of lesbianism where "sisters" are said to exist in complete harmony and where lesbianism is viewed as "the most natural, the most virtuous, and the most pleasurable way of life" (Marks 1979, 359–60). Both Whatling and Cathy Linstrum propose that Wittig not only rejects any notion of mutuality or equality between the sexes as a satisfactory alternative to patriarchy, but even between the *amantes* ("lovers") there is a "fundamental violence" (Whatling 1997, 243) that constantly challenges any pretenses to stable identity formation of both subject and object: "A violent rupture of the other takes place on the level of the relationship between subject and object, each penetrating the body of the other with a macabre sense of destruction" (Linstrum 1988, 39).

Thus, rather than affirming heterosexist notions of "traditional womanhood," where women are stereotypically seen as "timid, gentle, and passive objects of desire," or even lesbian notions of harmonious "sisterhood," Wittig totally alters these gender paradigms and presents her *amantes* as "active, audacious, and often violent" (Ostrovsky 2005, 122). She deliberately provokes the conventional categories of sex and gender, "exposing their pretense to represent the norm" (Whatling 1997, 238), displacing the androcentric and phallocentric interpretations of these categories that, for

a clear indicator that homosexuality is immoral, he does not list the comparative "medical facts" that are related to heterosexuality, such as domestic violence and child abuse statistics (including murder and manslaughter), depression rates, and health conditions associated with pregnancy and childbirth, that might equally be used to argue against the "natural" benefits of a heterosexual lifestyle (471). In a point that almost seems to have Gagnon's position in mind, Ingebretsen (2001, 27) states, "Making monsters is a necessary social hygiene, helping to keep citizens straight."

In order to press home his points, Gagnon engages a "rhetoric of fear," or what could also be called a "theology of anxiety" (Vinz 1997, 169; Fromm 1941; Schaeffer, Resnick, and Netterville 1970).[54] In his introduction, he states that "the urgency of the time" is a reason for speaking out on this issue. Using the patriotic terminology of constitutional rights (particularly those protected by the First Amendment in the Bill of Rights), Gagnon (2001, 35) also states, "The window of opportunity for speaking

example, we have witnessed in the work of Barth and Gagnon, but also the gynocentric or matrocentric formulations that can also be seen in various discourses presenting lesbianism as a *"retraite sentimentale"* (Marks 1979, 369).[55] Linda Zerilli (2005, 98) explains that the revolutionary aspect of Wittig's writing "lies not in the substitution of one (feminist) order for another (patriarchal) one but in the creation of the open structure of freedom. What is radical in Wittig's text, in other words, is not the overthrow of patriarchy, as most commentators seem to assume, but the refusal to install another (albeit feminist) political form in its place."

> *I begin with the tips of your fingers. I* chew the phalanges *I* crunch the metacarpals the carpals, *I* slaver at your wrists, *I* disarticulate the ulnae with great delicacy, *I* exert pressure on the trochlea, *I* tear away the biceps from the humerus, *I* devour it, *I* eat m/y fill of you m/y so delectable one, m/y jaws snap, *I* swallow you, *I* gulp you down. Separated from the acromion both your arms are detached from your shoulders. You sovereign radiant you regard m/e. M/y saliva spreads over your breasts, long fragments of flesh separate from the muscles falling over your neck staining your white throat, carefully *I* take them between m/y teeth, *I* chew them voraciously, then *I* look at you and *I* am overwhelmed with great pity to see you so mutilated deprived of both your arms your bust bloodied. The food you are weighs on m/e within m/y stomach, *I* am suddenly revolted, *I* vomit you up, a great liquid half-digested stinking

out against homosexual behavior is closing. Nothing less than intellectual integrity, free speech, and a potentially irreversible change in the morality of mainline denominations are *at stake* in this vital area of sexual ethics" (emphasis added).[56] A language of violence underpins this urgency. On the first page of his book Gagnon speaks of the "debate now raging," describing it as "fierce"; he comments, "To jump into the fray with both feet is to invite attack, often vicious attack" (25).[57] In his discussion of the current situation, Gagnon (418, 479) particularly highlights the threat to children—the group Ingebretsen (2001, 102) contends are the "*sine qua non* of moral panics"—arguing that "it is possible for aggressive homophile instruction in the schools to recruit some additional children into a homosexual lifestyle" and that "affirmation of a same-sex lifestyle will increase the incidence of pedophilic activity." Again conveying the sense of urgency, Gagnon describes the "harmful effects" arising from endorsement of homosexuality, but states: "This is only the beginning" (483–84).

> steaming mass falls on your belly. You become very pale at this point you throw yourself back with a great cry, tears spurt strongly from your eyes spattering m/e, you say it is unbearable to see m/e vomit you up, *I* am overcome by greater pity that ever, *I* begin to eat you again as fast as *I* can m/y so adored one *I* lick the last scraps on your belly *I* get rid of the traces of blood, *I* absorb you m/y very precious one *I* retain you within m/e. (Wittig 1976, 120)

This poem is simply one of the many gruesome poems of *The Lesbian Body*, and I have cited all of it to give the full impact of its great and tender violence, its testimony to "lesbian passion ... carnal passion," and to demonstrate a little of the "violence to the reader" that Wittig (2005a, 46) expected would be done by this work. It is not an easy read. Readers may experience "revulsion," "confusion, disorientation and uncertainty" (Whatling 1997, 240, 244). Although the protagonist begins with the fingertips of the beloved, it is not to kiss them as one might ordinarily expect in traditional romances, but to chew, crunch, tear, devour, eat, swallow, and vomit them up, only to eat them again. Although the beloved is being "so mutilated," the intent is not the hatred or revenge we might expect when hearing of such acts on the evening news,[58] but appears to be one of desire for union together—the beloved does not resist this absorption, but rather cries out for its completion. Higgins (1976, 162) explains, "Love is literally a gut-rending experience, as each is dismembered and absorbed

He then returns to the way in which "children in the public school system will be indoctrinated" because of the religious exemption clauses that "are now under attack from homosexual activists" (484). Ultimately, Gagnon even argues that homosexuality "serves to destabilize the integrity of the family and the ordered survival of the species" (348), painting an apocalyptic scenario akin to the genre of "horror" movies that Ingebretsen (2001, 30–41) examines in which monsters invade either from the swamp, outer space, or—perhaps more chillingly—from within (see also T. Williams 1996).

At the center of Gagnon's argument, then, lies a specific understanding of "society" and how this ought to be constituted. In the introduction of his book he speaks of the mating instinct and the importance of harnessing it "to build families" and to "contribute to a stable and nurturing

or invaded by the other. But in order to love, *j/e* and *tu*, self and other must be separate, and so fusion leads to separation, reintegration follows fragmentation."

Such a desire for union may remind us of certain biblical images that extol heterosexual union at this point (if we focus on the influential KJV rather than the original Hebrew), such as Gen 2:24 ("Therefore shall a man leave his father and his mother, and shall cleave unto his wife: and they shall be one flesh"), with the potentially double-edged meaning of "cleave" (to either cling together or to separate with a sharp instrument). This combination of love and death is also seen in Song 8:6 (KJV: "Set me as a seal upon thine heart, as a seal upon thine arm: for love is strong as death; jealousy is cruel as the grave: the coals thereof are coals of fire, which hath a most vehement flame"). Wittig (2005a, 47) herself notes the connection with the Song of Songs: "For what is total ecstasy between two lovers but an exquisite death? A violent act (here in words) that can only be redeemed by an immediate resuscitation.... Thus illustrating the poetical sentence from the Bible that love is stronger than death." Indeed, only two pages prior to the poem just cited above, Wittig's (1976, 118) figures experience the burning heat of passion to the point that they catch fire and again are fused together.

Chisholm (1993, 210) suggests that this violence is not so much a violation as a "'systematic transformation' that *grounds one in the body of an other*." With the double meaning of "ground" perhaps in mind—to be foundational but also to be crushed into pieces—this might remind us

society generally" (2001, 25). This notion of a "stable" family and society is found throughout Gagnon's book as an ideal that reflects God's design for human sexuality and social life. Genesis 1–3 purportedly reveals the "procreative purpose of marriage" (which Gagnon avoids taking as prescriptive) as a way of ensuring "stable family structures" (58). Consequently same-sex intercourse undermines "the very integrity and health of the family unit" (142). Explaining this argument in more detail (and androcentrically), Gagnon says, "The issue is curbing self-indulgent passions that do not lead to the stability and growth of the state but rather destabilize the family unit by turning men's affections away from their wives and from the procreation and nurture of children" (165). However, these "stable" families are at times also described as "productive" (291). The ideal formula for human sexuality and social life appears to be het-

(albeit only in the English) of Barth's (*CD* 3.2:311) vision of the hierarchical relationship of man and woman, and the order of superordination and subordination, as an order "grounded and explained in Christ" and outlined most clearly in 1 Cor 11:3. For Wittig, the point is to parody such patriarchal discourse, given the reality of violence that women face at the hands of those who supposedly love them, as noted above. Indeed, she argues that such violence is part of the condition of a society that promotes the domination of women by men on the basis of a "natural" division of the sexes (1992a, 2–3). De Lauretis (2005, 58) picks up on this point: "In *Le corps lesbien*, the odyssey of the lesbian subject *j/e* is a journey into language, into the body of Western culture, a season in hell."

This point brings us to a consideration of "the lesbian subject *j/e*" and the "journey into language," which is one of the central features of *The Lesbian Body*. The split first-person pronoun *j/e* represents Wittig's lesbianization of subjectivity, challenging the way in which the subject is represented in language and thus offering a reconfigured understanding of that subject, the fractured, transgressive, contentious, lesbian body. As Wittig explains at the outset of *The Lesbian Body*, her desire is

> to do violence by writing to the language which *I* [*j/e*] can enter only by force. "I" [*Je*] as a generic feminine subject can *only* enter by force into a language which is foreign to it, for all that is human (masculine) is foreign to it.… *J/e* is the symbol of the lived, rending experience which is m/y writing, of this cutting in two which throughout literature is the exercise of a language which does not constitute m/e as subject. *J/e* poses

erosexual couples "who have maintained long-term monogamous relationships and live as stable and productive citizens of society" (481). This
description of "productive citizens" suggests a capitalist ideal expressed
frequently in the 1950s and still today in contemporary conservative
American culture.[59]

For Gagnon, the heterosexual "family" is a fundamental and vital yet
threatened structure of society. It is also privileged, a point he makes when
he argues that the church should oppose any attempts "to grant to same-
sex relationships status and benefits comparable to those married couples
receive" (491). This struggle over who is entitled to marry—who is entitled to the rights and benefits that "embody the heterosexual assumption"
(Weeks, Heaphy, and Donovan 2001, 182)—is a hotly contested one in the

the ideological and historic question of feminine subjects. (1976, x; all
brackets are hers)[60]

Given this provocative approach to subjectivity, and the immediate visual
and verbal impact this has on the reader—how *does* one pronounce *j/e*
in order to convey its rendering?[61]—most commentators on *The Lesbian
Body* offer a response to this feature of the text. De Lauretis (1988, 167–68)
offers several suggestions, noting that the reader "might find in its linguis-
tically impossible subject pronoun several theoretically possible valences,"
from the more conservative (the slash represents the division of the Lacanian subject), to the more radical, such as echoed in Sue-Ellen Case's
(1989, 283) oft-cited (and playful) phrase, "replacing the Lacanian slash
with a lesbian bar."[62] However, one who objected to this textual strategy is
feminist Penelope Englebrecht (1990, 96), who criticized Wittig's choice
to do violence to the text, arguing that as a result, "violence is done more
visibly to the lesbian Subject herself by splitting her very sign…. I think it
reinforces a phallic violation which objectifies." But rather than reinforcing the violating phallogocentrism of heteropatriarchy, other commentators argue that this "I" both visibly demonstrates this violence by refusing
to mask the material violence done to the lesbian body through language,
and parodies the promise of the pronoun that sustains the fiction of subjectivity and identity as stable constructs. Zerilli (1990, 168) points out,
"Wittig's subversive pronouns appropriate first by inhabiting and then by
displacing the fictional category of the universal subject constructed in
and through heterosexuality…. Wittig's 'I', in short, forces the universal to

current American political and popular arenas, with various state legislative decisions being the spark for considerable public and ecclesial debate, as is seen through a quick search for "gay marriage" or "same-sex unions" on the websites of specific organizations.[63]

This topic seems to be a particularly polarizing one within the United States,[64] and I suggest that the history of identity formation of both the individual and the state outlined above is integral to the underlying issues involved. Ingebretsen (2001, 5) notes, for example, that three key areas of "cultural trauma" in the United States that create "an intoxicating cocktail" if they converge are: "gender, beset and undone; the sanctities, often spurious, of the home; [and] the collapse of the erotic and private." The issue of "gay marriage" seems to be a potent mix of all three of these areas.

live up to its promise by turning it upon itself, thus revealing its pretensions."[65] Rather than violating the subject, Marthe Rosenfeld (1984, 236) notes that this "splintered *j/e*" is in fact "life-giving";[66] while in a similar fashion K. Cope (1991, 86) describes this "fractured, fractious, and fragmentary" "I" as "a bountiful 'cite' of transgression."

If this is beginning to sound like the sword-pierced body of Christ, whose death brings life, whose resurrected body still holds the scars of that death, then Wittig has succeeded in her strategy of lesbianization. She explains that "the bar in my j/e is a sign of excess. A sign that helps to imagine an excess of 'I,' an 'I' exalted in its lesbian passion, an 'I' so powerful that it can attack the order of heterosexuality in texts and lesbianize ... Christ" (2005a, 47). Thus we discover, in this materialist lesbian feminist text, "Christa the much-crucified" (1976, 32).[67] At various places within *The Lesbian Body*, references to sayings attributed to Jesus appear in contexts of intimacy between the *amantes*, such as the repeated phrase, "So be it." Even the ritual phrase reminiscent of John the Baptist baptizing Jesus is reconfigured to be an utterance by one of the lovers to the other: "*I* baptise you for centuries of centuries, so be it" (1976, 27). But perhaps the most striking image of the "lesbianized persona of Christ" is found in poem 82, where the setting is a combined Golgotha/Gethsemane scene "stripped of its phallic signifiers" (Shaktini 1982, 41), and thus described as "one of the most clear-cut instances of subversion" (Ostrovsky 2003, 196).[68] De Lauretis (2005, 59) states that Wittig's strategy of lesbianization seeks to shatter "the symbolic logic of the name of the father, the family, the nation, and all the other institutions of society that are based on the macroinstitution,

Although not addressing the particular issue of "gay marriage," and the "monstrous" issue that this has become in the current American context (Cahill 2007; Wald and Glover 2007), I offer the concluding words of Inge-bretsen's first chapter as a summary of the situation:

> The processes of exclusion, denial, and difference that drive the dynamics of monstrosity are bound up in American political fancies, rooted in deeply ingrained theological habits. These fancies and habits are in turn reproduced in and through various exercises of public display, scandal, rhetorical and polemic pronouncements, economies of desire and languages of fear.... Politics, entertainment, ideological concord, and

and the presumption, of heterosexuality," and surely the Christian church is one of the most powerful of these.

> *I* am at the Golgotha you have all abandoned. You sleep among the women a paper tigress.... During this period deprived of the aid of your strength *I* lie face to the ground, fear grips m/e and the desire to go on living with you in this garden, not one of you knows anything of m/y anguish, then *I* implore the great goddess m/y mother and *I* say to her mother mother why have you forsaken m/e, she remains silent while you sleep, not a breath of wind stirs m/y hair, *I* cry out in m/y distress mother mother why have you forsaken m/e ... m/y very tears dripping in great drops on m/y arms stain them with blood, bloody m/y saliva falling in strings from m/y mouth, red the moon when she appears in the sky red the earth red the night *I* see all red around m/e, *I* cry out in m/y great distress mother mother why have you forsaken m/e ... *I* turn towards you but you are all asleep. (Wittig 1976, 121)

Reflecting on the "exalted" *I* of *The Lesbian Body*, Wittig (1992c, 87) also explained, "I have considered this text a reverie about the beautiful analysis of the pronouns *je* and *tu* by the linguist Emile Benveniste" (see also 2005a, 47). Within *The Lesbian Body*, we see this theory at work in the dialectic between subject and object; *I* and *you* have a different identity in each poem, are "presented independent of any reference to sexuation," and are thus rendered "theoretical, even universalizable,"[74] at one and the same time inevitably constituting each other, destroying each other, healing each other (Ecarnot 2005, 185; Silberman 2007, 472; see also Linstrum 1988, 40). Ultimately this leads Marks (1979, 376) to suggest rather

theological habit combine in civil rites of panic in which the dread-ful body is displayed for erotic or terroristic gain. (2001, 39)

To conclude, as this material on Gagnon is pushed off the page altogether and our attention is given more fully to Wittig's monstrous lesbian,[70] I note that just as with the previous discussions of κεφαλή (1 Cor 11:3) and the *imago Dei* (1 Cor 11:7), a similar situation has been reached. In arguing that there is "much *at stake*" with regard to his vision of a utopian society, Gagnon (2001, 26) does so in a way that reinforces not only heterosexuality per se but also, more specifically, heterosexual marriage and an idealized notion of family. In his discussion of the politics of the same-

provocatively, "The J/e of *Le corps lesbien* is the most powerful lesbian in literature because as a lesbian-feminist she reexamines and redesigns the universe.... She is, in fact, the only true anti-Christ, the willful assassin of Christian love." If by "Christian love" Marks means "the Judeo-Christian tradition," which she views as aligned with "patriarchy and phallogocentrism" and describes as a "God-ruled phallogocentric system," where "the traditional female/male love story" is the only legitimate expression of desire and sexuality such as we have seen in the work of Barth and Gagnon, then she may well be correct.

The Lesbian *BODY*

> THE LESBIAN BODY THE JUICE THE
> SPITTLE THE SALIVA THE SNOT
> THE SWEAT THE TEARS THE WAX
> THE URINE THE FAECES THE
> EXCREMENTS THE BLOOD THE
> LYMPH THE JELLY THE WATER
> THE CHYLE THE CHYME THE
> HUMOURS THE SECRETIONS THE
> PUS THE DISCHARGES THE SUP-
> PURATIONS THE BILE THE JUICES
> THE ACIDS THE FLUIDS THE
> FLUXES THE FOAM THE SULPHUR
> THE UREA THE MILK THE
> ALBUMEN THE OXYGEN THE
> FLATULENCE THE POUCHES THE

sex marriage debate, David Rayside (2007, 342) explains that the legal and institutional policies regulating relationships within the US context privilege certain "family regimes" over others and that this "maintains a hierarchy of relationships [so that] the top rung in rights, obligations, and social respect is occupied by married heterosexual couples with children." Thus, as with both the examinations of κεφαλή as understood in evangeli-

> PARIETES THE MEMBRANES THE
> PERITONEUM, THE OMENTUM,
> THE PLEURA THE VAGINA THE
> VEINS THE ARTERIES THE VESSELS
> THE NERVES.
> —Wittig, 1976, 26

Other than the perceived violence enacted in the text, it is the list of body parts and functions that has provoked such a negative response from readers.[71] Crowder (1983, 121) notes that "even lesbian feminists" found this text disturbing, and she believes that this reaction stems from Wittig's subversive intention to "write the body." She explains that in doing so, Wittig has produced a work that both "uncovers deep ambiguity about the body in feminist ideology [and] attacks our 'feminine' revulsion at materiality" (121). Crowder points out the irony that although it is primarily women who are involved in the care of the body in society (for children or the elderly, as mothers or nurses, etc.), it is also women who "have interiorized disgust at the body" (121). Wittig's text, far from being simply a novelty, is so radically different from previous discourses on the female body that readers have reacted strongly; of course, that women have such a response is precisely because their subjectivity has been determined and controlled in advance by heteropatriarchy.[72]

As noted at the outset of this discussion, the list both begins and ends with the phrase "THE LESBIAN BODY," the only instances of this phrase in the book other than its title, thus suggesting that literally we have here the "the corps (corpus) lesbien" (Higgins 1976, 161). And like the lesbian subject *j/e*, the list is also broken into parts, scattered throughout the text at regular intervals, and thus both "piercing the book from part to part" and being fragmented in the process (Wittig 2005a, 46). However, as Higgins (1976, 161) points out, "it is impossible to say which of the two texts interrupts the other. The list resembles a continuous chant forming the back-

cal circles and Barth's understanding of the *imago Dei*, I suggest that this debate reveals not only a rejection of homosexuality by those holding the conservative position but a promotion of the ideology of the heterosexual nuclear family, with marriage and, most significantly, strong (nonpenetrated) masculinity at its center.

ground to the narrative paragraphs and flowing into the spaces between them." In this way, the text itself resembles the relationship between *j/e* and *tu* that we observe within the text; "an unending alternation between dismemberment and reconstitution, exclusion and inclusion, separation and relatedness … the intermingling of self and other, the presence of the other in the interstices of the divided self" (161).

The list enumerates a multitude of body parts, from the familiar (and either deemed acceptable within pornographic or romantic discourse, or unacceptable, as evidenced in the discourse of advertising) to those that we respond with aversion (as too private, too messy, too visceral), or those about which we are ignorant (particularly medical terms that are only known by the "experts").[73] By simply listing all these parts together one after the other, laying them open before the reader and ignoring any traditional hierarchical division between these parts, Wittig forcefully confronts her readers with a presentation of the body as a whole. Each body part/function is listed with the definite article, emphasizing its value and place within the body as a whole—no part is more or less desirable, important, or acceptable than any other part, and each part is needed for the body to be whole. Scanlon (1998, 86) also notes Wittig's use of the definite article, and states that this "makes the body parts both specific and general, for 'the' can refer to one specific body or can be a collective determiner for any body."

But Wittig also refuses any metaphorical celebration of the body. She explains that she chose "to talk about the body without metaphors … without sentimentality or romanticism…. This anatomical vocabulary is cold and distant and I used it as a tool to cut off the mass of texts devoted to love" (2005a, 46). Not only does Wittig refuse to engage the basic conventions of love poetry whereby certain parts of a women's body are described in terms of simile or metaphor—where eyes are like doves, lips like scarlet ribbon, and breasts like two fawns (Song 4:1–5), or where hair is like a forest, cheeks like two suns, and the gap between the breasts is like the Hellespont (Donne, "Love's Progress," lines 41, 48, 60)—Wittig's list functions to deconstruct traditional discourses of the body that segregate the various parts into particular categories. The anatomical (THE CHYLE THE CHYME ... THE PLEURA) is not usually placed beside that which is the focus in pornographic discourse (THE VAGINA THE BREASTS), and neither is usually placed beside the messy or the supposedly undesirable (THE SNOT ... THE WAX THE URINE THE FAECES ... THE FLATULENCE THE POUCHES) (Crowder 1983, 121).[74]

I suggest that it is on this point where the most significant contrast between Wittig's work and Gagnon's work is evident. While Gagnon's work is also bold in its frequent reference to anatomical descriptions, these are almost always genitally focused. Throughout his book, Gagnon (2001, 169, 181, 254, 364–65) constantly refers to the "fittedness of the penis and vagina" and the functionality of these body parts; the penis is an instrument for penetration, the vagina is a receptacle for the penis (139, 169, 181). As noted in the discussion of Gagnon, complementarity is clearly androcentric; the vagina was created *for* the penis, not the other way around. Such persistent genital focus with regard to sexual behavior results in an objectification of the body not dissimilar to pornography. Gagnon's explicit descriptions of sexual acts centered upon the genitals comes across as both clinical and far removed from the diverse expressions of love, sex, and desire that are part of human sexual experiences. Although Gagnon notes at one point that "kissing, caressing, and other forms of sexual contact" are permissible, and sexual intimacy does not always have to involve "phallic penetration," there is little else in his work to counter the implication that sexual intercourse primarily involves penile penetration of the "vaginal receptacle" (139, 365). Human beings are, in effect, reduced to their genitalia, and sexual function is centered upon "the primacy of penetration" (144).

By contrast, and in a deliberate effort to dismantle such androcentric and phallocentric understandings of the body and sexuality, Wittig presents us with "THE LESBIAN BODY," where "not only the breasts and genitals so dear to male writers, but the intestines, the muscles, the organs, the very bones themselves are invested with erotic power" (Crowder 1983, 122). Thus, rather than being the object of male desire, whose vagina is the receptacle designed for penetration by a penis, Wittig's lesbian body is a subject in her own right: "Inhabiting this *corps lesbien* is the person whose body is subject, not object ... and this self is not fetishized, but constructed, equally importantly, of all her organs, secretions, functions, and sensations" (Wenzel 1981, 281). The lesbian body therefore challenges the way in which heteropatriarchal ideologies have constructed sexual bodies (of both men and women), and in particular challenges the notion of the primacy of "phallic penetration."[75]

In *The Lesbian Body*, while the protagonists penetrate each other to the point of utter destruction ("Through m/y vagina and m/y uterus you insert yourself breaking the membrane up to m/y intestines"), the phallus has been displaced by the lesbian subject (Wittig 1976, 35; see also 56, 66, 74, 85). Shaktini (1982, 29) explores this aspect of Wittig's work, arguing that *Le corps lesbien* makes an important contribution to the feminist attack on "the semiological problem of 'phallogocentrism.'" She suggests that "Wittig relocates subjectivity outside the orbit of phallogocentrism," and that, even more powerfully, Wittig has lesbianized this, the most central of all heterosexual metaphors (33, 44). This is most evident, Shaktini argues, in poem 51, placed strategically near the center of the book, where Wittig reconfigures the Egyptian myth of Isis and "the ithyphallic god, Osiris" (32).[76] In the original myth, Osiris is killed and subsequently dismembered by his brother, who then scatters the fourteen pieces of his body throughout the land. Isis, the sister and wife of Osiris, searches for all the fragments in order to reconstruct Osiris, but she only finds thirteen pieces; his "male member" is missing (τὸ αἰδοῖον but also, in the same account, the phallus, ὁ φαλλός (Plutarch, *Is. Os.* 18 [358b, 365c]; Diodorus Siculus, *Bib. hist.* 1.22.6). Isis fashions one in order to restore him to life, and subsequently she conceives a son with the resurrected Osiris. In Wittig's retelling of the myth, "Isis the all-powerful" narrates the account as follows:

> The women lead m/e to your scattered fragments, there is an arm, there is a foot, the neck and head are together, your eyelids are closed, your detached ears are somewhere.... *I* pronounce a ban on the recording of your death so that the traitress responsible for your being torn to pieces may not be alerted. *I* announce that you are here alive though cut to pieces, *I* search hastily for your fragments in the mud ... *I* find your nose a part of your vulva your labia your clitoris, *I* find your ears one tibia then the other, *I* assemble you part by part, *I* reconstruct you ... *I* decree that you live as in the past Osiris m/y most cherished m/y most enfeebled *I* say that as in the past we shall succeed together in making the little girls who will come after us, then you m/y Osiris m/y most beautiful you smile at m/e undone exhausted. (1976, 78–79)

Wittig has completely lesbianized this myth. Not only have the figures in the story all become female, but deeper than this, the phallus has been completely displaced and so also has its social, political, and symbolic significance. But, central to Wittig's rejection of the valorization of the female, the phallus is not replaced by the vulva, womb, or even the clitoris. While these body parts are present in the story—given visibility when so often they are only seen when the female is reduced to these parts (as in pornography or when motherhood is emphasized as woman's greatest role)—no *one* body part is given more significance than another, but *all* parts are necessary for the reassembling of this broken body. Yet it is a reassembly that will continually be "undone" in order to highlight the instability of presenting any *one* body as the *only* body. K. Cope (1991, 88) explains, "Rather than a unified One, the lesbian body is only ever dispersed and vigilant, a body or bodies that you, or I, or they may not fix in any one particular shape."

One body that I am reminded of at this point is the body of Christ, about which Paul speaks in 1 Cor 12:12–27, not long after 1 Cor 11:2–16. Paul wants the Corinthians to view themselves as members of this body, and thus be unified in their diversity, as various parts of the one body. Understanding the rhetorical purpose of Paul's analogy at this point is a complex matter; Thiselton (2000, 990) reminds us, "Few terms have undergone so many twists and turns in the history of Pauline scholarship than *body* and *body of Christ*." But it is the sociopolitical aspect of this analogy that I wish to emphasize here (see Mitchell 1993, 159; Collins 1999, 458). The key aspect of this ancient analogy, according to Margaret Mitchell (1993, 158, 161), is its use to "combat factionalism" and thus promote "*concordia*." D. Martin (1995a, 39) also examines the Greco-Roman rhetoric of the body politic and suggests that the "ideological function" of such rhetoric needs to be considered, as the body politic (as with the human body) was seen as "a hierarchy, with different members (in this case, classes) assigned by Nature to positions in the body and to particular roles in the harmonious cooperation of the body's parts." Social disruption and agitation by those in lesser positions within society were viewed (by the elite) as unhealthy for the body as a whole, and thus rhetorical speeches of harmony (ὁμόνοια, "concord") were used to restore order and maintain the status quo (40–43). Here we return to Philo, as discussed in chapter 4, on the "head" and the "tail" and the way in which "the virtuous one" will "be the head of the human race and all the others like the limbs of the body which draw their life from the forces in the head and at the top" (*Rewards* 125). It is precisely this sort of rhetoric that some within evangelical circles use to maintain certain structures of authority within the church and home/family. By accepting their "natural" places within the created order, where the man is the "head" (and woman is the "tail"?) both men and women can function together in harmony, as different parts of a whole within a hierarchical framework.

But Wittig will have no part in this supposedly benevolent schema as it persists in maintaining women in a "naturally" subordinate position and men in a "naturally" dominant position. Rather, her presentation of the lesbian body invites rebellion and disorder, embracing that which is supposedly shameful and improper (Sedgwick 2003; Halperin and Traub 2009). On this issue of the equivalence between the physical body and the body politic, Chisholm makes some perceptive observations:

> It becomes natural for Western metaphysicians and political theorists to think of government in terms of body parts, organized to serve the needs of all members. Conversely it becomes necessary to rethink or re-imag(in)e the body in order to initiate political revolution. In the wake of a century of political revolutions, radical movements of the twentieth century concentrate their critique on the rhetoric of this Platonic body and all those discourses and practices that think about bodies and body politics in terms of unity, hierarchy, dominance, superior parts. (1993, 198)

Chisholm (1993, 198–99) goes on to examine the way in which the body politic in Western history can be considered a "phallocracy," and notes that in Wittig's work "we find no head, no phallus."[77] Of course, in Paul (and in "all those discourses and practices" of conservative evangelical scholarship we have considered), while we find frequent mention of a head (κεφαλή), we do not find mention of a phallus. But I suspect that Norman Brown's (1966, 132–34) observation regarding politics may be relevant here: "The penis is the head of the body."[78] Certainly, like the phallus, the head has become a male-only part of the anatomy in conservative evangelicalism. By contrast, Chisholm (1993, 199–200) suggests that *The Lesbian Body* offers a "counter-poetics" whereby "the categorical rigidity of classical physiology" is undermined and instead we are presented with "the unhierarchical, uncategorizable, heterogeneous lesbian body." Rather than a harmonious body, ruled by the head, the monstrous lesbian body "imag(in)es a wholly other libidinal and political economy" (201) in which every organ, muscle, limb, sense and function not only sit equally side by side (as in the list), but are also subject to rupture, destruction, dissection, and transformation (as in the poems).[79]

If "the Corinthian body" is considered, it is possible to argue that Paul finds it necessary to assert a rhetoric of the harmonious body precisely because the Corinthians were behaving so discordantly (Mitchell 1993, 161). Throughout the letter can be found the issue of divisions, quarrels, and possibly the development of factions (σχίσματα, ἔριδες, αἱρεσεις, 1 Cor 1:10–11; 3:3; 11:18–19; 12:25). Accordingly, it is possible to suggest that in Paul's thinking, the members of this particular body were not caring for one another and were being contentious and disruptive, with the result that the body of Christ was being divided (1:13), getting ill, and possibly even dying (11:29–30). As D. Martin (1995, 194) notes, "Paul focuses his argument on the fracturing of the church, the body of Christ. His solution to the problems surrounding the Lord's Supper is a social one: heal the fragmented body and restore unity.... The Strong at Corinth, by reinforcing social distinctions in the church, divide the church. They are quite literally, in Paul's view, 'killing' Christ by tearing apart his body." Paul's desire to see things restored to harmony and unity for the common good drives his use of this "body" rhetoric.

Some of these disruptive "body parts" are the men and women whom Paul addresses in 11:2–16. I have already argued that the men in particular may be likened to Wittig's lesbian figure—as contradictory, unthinkable figures, ignored or deemed hypothetical, viewed as effeminate and thus mislabeled as "homosexual"—and so perhaps these men (and women) are akin to rogue body parts in the Corinthian body, the body of Christ. As a result, given that "lesbianization produces a monstering not only of the text but also of the body" (Scanlon 1998, 78), we end up with a monstrous body of Christ akin to Sheffield's (2008, 238) "queer Chalcedic body," with its potential for encouraging a "polymorphous, transmutative gender performance."

Paradoxically, therefore, while the regulation of the individual body, as well as the wider body politic, as a heteropatriarchal organism may appear to create harmony and concord, only certain members of this system benefit, while other members suffer (contra 1 Cor 12:26). Freedom of movement and expression, while perhaps disruptive, may rather bring health and vitality to the body as a whole; that which is monstrous may in fact be that which is necessary for liberation and empowerment. Gagnon's strict insistence on genital anatomy as the primary indicator of God's design for the body, and phallic penetration as a central determiner for both "proper" sexual behavior (it must be heterosexual rather than same-sex) and "proper" gender expression (it must be done *to* women, who are thereby feminine, *by* men who are thereby masculine; men who are penetrated become effeminate, "something to be avoided at all cost" as Musonius Rufus reminds men) produces a rigidly constructed body that must be vigilantly maintained and protected from external influence lest it mutate into something monstrous. By contrast, Wittig's lesbian body undergoes dismemberment, fragmentation, and deconstruction, but also reconfiguration and transformation. Through these unending, multiple processes, *The Lesbian Body* not only challenges heteropatriarchal ideologies that have presented certain limited configurations of sex, gender, and sexuality as "natural" but also points to possibilities of being that extend beyond the "normal."

> *I* am the sovereign one, *I* thunder with m/y three voices the clamorous the serene the strident, but *I* immediately relinquish m/y indubitably hierarchical position at your arrival, *I* raise you from your kneeling posture ... may you lose the sense of morning and evening of the stupid duality with all that flows therefrom, may you conceive yourself as *I* at last see you over the greatest possible space ... may the black star crown you finally, giving you to sit at m/y side at the apogee of the figuration of lesbian love m/y most unknown. (Wittig 1976, 143)

Notes

1. Verses 14–15a belong with what some commentators describe as Paul's argument from "propriety" or "common sense" in vv. 13–15. Here Paul switches from a didactic style of theological argument (vv. 3–12) to one based on asking two rhetorical questions regarding both what is πρέπον ("proper") and also that which causes either ἀτιμία ("dishonor") or δόξα ("glory"), as determined through community discernment (ἐν ὑμῖν αὐτοῖς κρίνατε) (see Fee 1987, 524–26; Collins 1999, 413; Fitzmyer 2008, 408, 420).

2. As stated by Reverend Dennis Wiley, pastor of Convent Baptist Church, in the PBS television series *Religion and Ethics*, broadcast in 2004; cited by T. West 2007, 177. Wiley goes on to ask, "Why would God create someone of that orientation and then not allow them to have the same kind of opportunity for love, for relationships, for a healthy life as heterosexuals enjoy?"

3. Nowhere else does Paul refer to nature personified as a "teacher," although related terminology is found in Rom 1:26–27 and elsewhere in Romans (2:14, 27; 11:21–24). Paul also uses the phrase τοῖς φύσει in Gal 4:8 in describing "beings that *by* nature are not gods."

4. See D. Martin 1995a, 72–73; Schrage 1995, 521; Hays 1997, 189; Collins 1999, 397–99, 403, 413; Engberg-Pedersen 2000, 46; Thiselton 2000, 845; Keener 2005, 94.

5. Artemidorus's schema for interpreting dreams also reveals that what was viewed as "natural" or "unnatural" was clearly a constructed category. He categorizes

sexual acts as either in conformity with the law (κατὰ νόμον), contrary to the law (παρὰ νόμον), or contrary to nature (παρὰ φύσιν), and although he does not define these categories and at times certain acts appear under more than one heading, what is of central importance in determining the moral value of a particular act, according to Foucault's (1990b, 18). analysis of these categories, is "the social status of the 'other.'" As Foucault (28) wryly notes, Artemidorus's work is "a man's book that is addressed mainly to men in order to help them lead their lives as men."

6. Ellsworth's comment that man's headship is "just there" is a reminder of Barth's "It is just so" silencer, discussed in ch. 5.

7. This material is currently available from MacArthur's website: http://tinyurl. com/SBL0685m1. That this material is still influential is seen in the strength of his ministry (Grace to You); in 2006 MacArthur launched a telecast that is broadcast in many countries and is available on their website as a weekly video podcast: see http:// tinyurl.com/ SBL0685e. A GTY iPhone App is also now available: see http://tinyurl. com/SBL0685o1.

8. See J. Thompson 2003, 241, 250; Hiigel 2005, 32; Winter 2003a, 147; 2003b, 86; Keener 2005, 91–92; Hearon 2006, 609; Countryman 2007, 249–51.

9. See, e.g., Howard 1983, 37; MacArthur 1984, 257; Morris 1985, 149; Beardslee 1994, 105, 107; Garland 2003, 509; Gorman 2004, 265; Payne 2006, 15; MacArthur 2007, 70; cf. also Fitzmyer 2008, 417. Others who note that this is the behavior Paul is expecting but who do not necessarily advocate this as applicable for women today include Neyrey 1990, 132; Gundry-Volf 1997, 154; Winter 2003b, 79, 84–87, 91; A. Johnson 2004, 186; Keener 2005, 91; Countryman 2007, 249–51.

10. See Moffatt 1938, 151; Craig 1953, 124; Thrall 1965, 78; Morris 1985, 149; K. Wilson 1991, 445, 448, 455; Soards 1999, 223; J. Barclay 2001, 1126; Merkle 2006, 533; Fitzmyer 2008, 413, 420.

11. See Héring 1949, 90–91; Simon 1959, 111; Waltke 1978, 46; Howard 1983, 37; House 1988, 158; Peerbolte 2000, 78 n. 5, 92; Schreiner 2006a, 132, 137–38; MacArthur 2007, 70.

12. See Fitzmyer 2008, 413; see also F. Watson 2000b, 531 n. 15; 2000b, 52; Garland 2003, 510 n. 4; Crocker 2004, 153; Payne 2006, 10–11. This was also evident in Barth's (CD 3.4:177–78) description of the "tyrant" who takes "pleasure" in taking "advantage" of the woman, and the "rebellious woman" who is also "his pliable kitten."

13. For examples of the ideal "good woman," see MacArthur 1986. See also Barrett 2015. The notion of "biblical womanhood" can be seen in the Victorian notion of the woman as "the angel in the house" (Patmore 1992; Woolf 1966, 284–89; Wittig 1992e, 16; Countryman 2007, 249–50). For "God's princesses," see also the accompanying trend for sparkling pink "Princess Bibles" for girls (Walsh 2006; Holmes 2010). According to the blurb on Walsh's God's Little Princess Devotional Bible, this will "help girls blossom into the princesses they were always meant to be," by focusing on "virtues to create true beauty, such as honor, charity, compassion, sharing, truth [and] fairness." In such material Eve is usually presented as "God's first princess," a view that is a far cry from Tertullian's view of Eve and women (Cult. fem. 1.1.2). How women are to reconcile these conflicting images is uncertain; it is part of the ontological ambiguity women face in Christian contexts.

14. There is also a selection of Bibles aimed at boys. Some emphasize the idea of being a "warrior" for God, such as Walsh's *God's Mighty Warrior Devotional Bible* (2007). Although Eve is described as a princess, Adam is not described as a prince; rather, his "job" is to help God "rule over the earth" and "to take care of the world" (2007, 4). Other bibles for boys include Osborne's *2:52 Boys Bible: The Ultimate Manual* (2002), with the blurb: "Finally, a Bible just for boys! Discover gross and gory Bible stuff!" Drawing on Luke 2:52, the blurb also states: "This Bible helps boys become more like Jesus mentally, physically, spiritually, and socially—smarter, stronger, deeper, and cooler." I am not quite clear what it means to become more like Jesus "physically," and it seems hard to believe that a Bible full of "gross and gory" stuff is also the same Bible that girls will read learning to be graceful "princesses." I also find the idea that this is "finally" a Bible for the boys disturbing given the androcentric and chauvinistic history of almost every facet of the Bible's history, from its formation to its interpretation.

15. See Rom 13:12; 1 Cor 9:7, 24–27; 16:13; Eph 6:10–17; Phil 4:8; 1 Thess 5:8; Phlm 2; 2 Tim 2:3. Several scholars have recognized the way in which these portrayals of "biblical" femininity and masculinity are in fact infused with the Greco-Roman ideals (ideologies) that have shaped the New Testament writings (Moore and Anderson 2003; Conway 2008).

16. This point is illustrated by the comment from Ortlund (2006, 102), who is writing from a hierarchicalist viewpoint: "A man, just by virtue of his manhood, is called to lead for God. A woman, just by virtue of her womanhood, is called to help for God."

17. Curiously, Groothuis does not refer to 1 Cor 11:2–16 among the many texts she cites.

18. For Webb and others in the egalitarian camp, these views are often expressed in the form of an apologetic against the argument by the hierarchicalists that there is a "slippery slope" from egalitarianism to homosexuality as was seen in the discussion on C. Kroeger's views on homosexuality in ch. 4; see also Jones 2003, 13 n. 2.

19. Indeed, D. Martin and Gagnon have engaged in a series of debates on the issue of homosexuality and the interpretation of various scriptural passages, although their differing hermeneutical frameworks prevent any genuine communication, particularly as Gagnon appears to assume that all texts—be they biblical or e-mail—can be interpreted in the same way with regard to authorial intention. See, for example, the e-mail correspondence presented by Gagnon (2006a) on his website. Others who have also interacted substantially with Gagnon's work include Via 2003; Loader 2010, 15–28.

20. Of course, "nature's clues" are not always as clear as Gagnon would want them to be. Along with balding there are many other "natural" conditions that humans develop as they age (such as menopause or needing less sleep), but whether these conditions point to what is "natural" throughout all of one's life is doubtful. This illustrates not only Gagnon's faulty logic but also, more importantly, the complexity of a concept such as "nature" and the way in which it can be commandeered for a particular argument.

21. I have chosen to quote as an epigraph this poem from *Les Guérillères* partly

because it is the last poem in the book, and thus points forward to Wittig's subsequent book, *The Lesbian Body*, but also because the textual strategy that it presents is precisely the aim of the style I have chosen to utilize in this section, of writing "against texts," in the "margins, space" and to perhaps seek "action overthrow" (Wittig 2005a, 37–43).

22. Although Gagnon at times mentions texts outside the Protestant canon (such as the Wisdom of Solomon, Jubilees, and Sirach), he concentrates on Mosaic Judaism rather than Enochic Judaism; the former texts have a greater focus on the natural order with regard to sexual ethics and from which Paul may have drawn his theology (Loader 2007; D. Martin 2006, 53–54; Nissinen 1998, 107). Gagnon (2001, 292), however, specifically counters this Enochic context for Paul's thought.

23. Both W. Johnson (2006) and Rogers (2009) perceptively critique Gagnon's reading of Gen 1–3 and his understanding of complementarity as a biblical idea. Gagnon (2006b) responds to Rogers's book in an article on his website.

24. Others who mention the poetic nature of this work include J. Allen 1988, 113; Findlay 1989, 66; Chisholm 1993, 205; de Lauretis 2005, 58–59. Other scholars who note the link with the Song of Songs include Duffy 1990, 224–25; Chisholm 1993, 205; Scanlon 1998, 88–9; Ostrovsky 2005, 121. Fiona Black (2009, 14) has explored the grotesque body in the Song of Songs and notes that it is "provocative" to see *The Lesbian Body* "as a modern commentary on the Song of Songs."

25. Scanlon (1998, 75) states that while some critics refer to certain sections of the book as "poems," she finds this "problematic," as "the label again seems reductive and inaccurate" (although she does not explain why), and thus she prefers "prose segments," which she says are "discrete units of description." However, as noted above, she also acknowledges the "echoes" of the Song of Songs (89).

26. See also Wittig's remark in an interview concerning the different responses to *The Lesbian Body* in France and the United States; "les critiques français ont lu ce livre comme un poèm. Aux Etas-Unis, c'était le contraire" ("French critics read this book as a poem. In the United States, it was the opposite") (Devarrieux 1999, iii).

27. Gagnon (2001, 180) considers the argument that animals rarely engage in same-sex behavior as a "persuasive" aspect of an appeal to "nature" against homosexuality, but modern zoologists have observed a diverse range of means by which animals procreate and engage in sexual behavior (Bagemihil 1999; Zuk 2002; Sommer and Vasey 2006).

28. Whatling (1997, 239–40) also notes that, in personal correspondence, British lesbian feminist author and political activist Sheila Jeffreys admits she "can only bring herself to read *The Lesbian Body* 'minus the violence' which remains an 'unfortunate by product' of its message." However, as any reader would quickly discover, the text is saturated with violent images from the outset, making reading it "minus the violence" a near-impossible task.

29. This is also because Gagnon's focus is on behavior rather than orientation, due to his view that such behavior can be changed (420–29). This is also why he has come to prefer the term *homosex*; see the discussion in n. 3 of Gagnon 2005.

30. Linstrum (1988, 44) notes, "The word 'géhenne' can refer not only to infernal or purgatorial Gehenna, but also to the 'géhenne' of prison, of the place to which those who break with societal codes are expelled and in which they are then contained. This

prison is also the place of the incarceration of the insane, whose insanity prevents them from conforming to the order of society."

31. The island of Cytheras is traditionally associated with the birthplace of Venus, goddess of love. Wittig may have been influenced by the painting *L'embarquement pour Cythere* by Watteau (1717–1719) in the Louvre, which depicts aristocratic heterosexual couplings either departing from or embarking for the island, and she is thus transforming its meaning toward a lesbian point of view; this is a strategy Wittig utilizes throughout *The Lesbian Body* in order to challenge, disassemble, and rework the canonical discourses and myths of androcentric, dominant, Western culture, although I have not read any discussion on this in relation to "canonical" artworks. Wittig (2005a, 46) herself explains that she "borrowed and intertextualized" many texts, including the New Testament and Song of Songs, Homeric poems, and Baudelaire, for example. Ecarnot (2005, 185) notes that Wittig's writing is "sprinkled with quotations and rich in borrowed figures," which she then "parodies" and "travesties" with the result that "the myth of sexed identity as well as the claim to universality of the male subject are obliterated."

32. Marks (1979, 356) notes, in a somewhat resigned manner, "Sappho and her island Lesbos are omnipresent in literature about women loving women, whatever the gender or sexual preference of the writer and whether or not Sappho and her island are explicitly named." For more on the influence and importance of Sappho in literature in general, see Vanita 1996.

33. This one of Wittig's many allusions to the phrase ("The love that dare not speak its name") alluding to same-sex desire associated with the trials of Oscar Wilde; while on trial, Wilde was questioned about this phrase, which comes from the poem "Two Loves" by Lord Alfred Douglas (Holland 2003, 67–68; Wintermans 2007, 210–11, 284–85).

34. The term *protagonist* is the one Wittig (2005a, 47) chooses to describe the "I" and "you" in the text.

35. This dismissal of lesbianism has been a historically common approach; lesbianism has consistently been "underplayed … overlooked or trivialized" (Bennett 2006, 111). See also Vanita (1996, 5–6), who argues that "a determined Protestant bias" has led Marx, Freud, Lacan, Foucault, and most of their followers to overlook lesbianism and privilege "a heterosexual marriage-centered view of Western history and literature."

36. This notion of writing being likened to a "war machine" echoes the work of Deleuze and Guattari (Jardine 2007, 459).

37. Gagnon then goes on to cite a study whereby college students were randomly approached while walking across their campuses by members of the opposite sex and told the following statement: "Hi, I've been noticing you around town lately, and I find you very attractive. Would you go to bed with me?" Because 100 percent of the women gave an emphatic "No!" (and felt offended, insulted, and puzzled), while 75 percent of the men said "Yes!" (and felt flattered), Gagnon takes this as confirmation that men are more promiscuous than women. What Gagnon (and others, such as Buss 1994, 73; and Winston 2002) fails to take into account with such methodology is that for a woman such a random approach smacks of the predatory and potentially violent

sexual behavior of a stalker or rapist and says very little about female promiscuity (R. Clark and Hatfield 1989).

38. This reconfiguration of the subject (as multiple and fractured, passionate and violent, particular and yet universalizable) evokes Derrida's "genealogy of the subject" (Silberman 2007, 482–83).

39. Actually, a man wearing lipstick, pantyhose, and a pink dress is hardly descriptive of the "most bizarre forms" that some within the various LBGT communities choose to take (Halperin and Traub 2009).

40. Wink (2002, 33) also notes the "double standards" with which Gagnon chooses to critique certain aspects of same-sex behavior. Gagnon (2002) responds to Wink's comments on his website.

41. Chisholm (1993, 205) counts 109 poems, while K. Cope (1991, 86) suggests there are 110 poems. Shaktini (1982, 33 n. 12) notes two errors with the Avon publication; poem 16 is presented as if it were two poems, and poems 49 and 50 are presented as if they were one poem.

42. The word *lesbian* is used only as an adjective, not as a noun, and even then only very rarely (Shaktini 2005a, 156; Silberman 2007, 470).

43. Childs, cited in the acknowledgments of Gagnon's book and found (along with other similar positive comments) on Gagnon's website; see http://www.robgagnon.net/Reviews/homoblurbs.pdf. Contrary to these positive accounts of Gagnon's tone, D. Martin (2006, 28) states that Gagnon resorts to "a shaming logic" and "repeatedly insults gay men" (see also Countryman 2003, 191).

44. For a cogent rebuttal of Gagnon's interpretation of the Sodom story and the other Old Testament texts that Gagnon discusses, see J. E. Miller 2007.

45. Gagnon (2001, 302) concedes that Paul was chauvinistic at times but does not accept that he may have also been misogynistic.

46. As examples of the labels given by one socially dominant group to another group who are "different" and thus "other" (Ingebretsen 2001, 26).

47. For further discussion on the "transformation, transmutation, and transfiguration" of Wittig's figures, and thus also of traditional constructions of genre and gender in her book, see Ostrovsky 2005, 115, 121–24.

48. However, it is likely that those within evangelical communities who assess "others" (and themselves) in this way may argue that they are simply attempting to encourage behavior that conforms to their biblical interpretation of Christian ethics and morals.

49. Ingebretsen examines the views of several (extreme) right groups such as that led by Pastor Fred Phelps, founder of Westboro Baptist Church, in Topeka, Kansas. Their website is entitled "God Hates Fags" and states that "since 1955" their purpose has been "opposing the fag lifestyle of soul-damning, nation-destroying filth"; see their website, http://tinyurl.com/SBL0685j.

50. Russo (1986, 219) suggests that Bakhtin's portrayal of the female grotesque is "repressed and undeveloped," albeit "exuberant."

51. The notion that Christianity in the United States is a "man-based culture" most likely has a connection with Charles Kingsley's Victorian "muscular Christianity" (Hall 1994; Bederman 1995; Putney 2001). For a more recent manifestation of this

"man-based" Christianity, see the collection of essays in R. Williams (2001), and the discussion in Faludi (1999, 224–88).

52. Silberman (2007, 482) translates this even more succinctly as, "being passionate requires violence."

53. For more on the relationship between the works of Colette and Wittig's *The Lesbian Body*, see Marks 1979.

54. Vinz (1997, 169) uses this term (from Erich Fromm) to explain the motivation behind pronouncements of fundamentalist Jerry Falwell during the 1980s. Describing themes that I suggest are also familiar in Gagnon's arguments, Vinz states that Falwell employed the "rhetorical convention" of fear, such as portraying America as being on "the brink of disaster" and the potential assault and proselytization of "little children" by "deviates" (176). It is also noteworthy that Mel White, ghostwriter for Falwell, is gay; in his autobiography he discusses the "antihomosexual rhetoric" used by the religious right (1994, 17, 268). D. Wold (1998, 213–14) responds to White's book, suggesting rather that it is *his* rhetoric that is "inflammatory" and that White exercises "a spirit of vindictiveness against the so-called religious right."

55. This phrase comes from the title of one of Colette's novellas, *La retraite sentimentale* (see Colette 1974).

56. See also Gagnon's many online articles along these lines: see http://tinyurl. com/ SBL0685g.

57. The fierceness of the debate about sexuality within evangelicalism is not restricted to the US context; it has also created turmoil in the Church of England and the worldwide Anglican communion (Bates 2004).

58. This is precisely what happened with regard to the murder of Sophie Elliot by her ex-boyfriend Clayton Weatherston in Dunedin on 9 January 2008. He not only stabbed her 216 times, but also cut off her ears, nose, clumps of hair, parts of her genitals, and a nipple. He was convicted of her murder, and it was stated that he had engaged in a "persistent, focused, and determined attack … directed at disfiguring the body"; see Fuseworks Media 2009.

59. Each individual ought to be able to have the privilege of contributing to society through meaningful employment and thus ultimately being self-supportive, primarily meaning male heads of households of course, but even reformed criminals or the disabled, although preferably not women according to some conservative evangelical groups (Patterson 2006; Jepsen 2006).

60. This raises questions regarding the translation of *j/e* into English, for, as K. Cope (1991, 86) points out, "the single capital letter of the 'I' typographically reinforces the (false) sense of sovereignty of the 'I,' and makes it impossible to show the subject 'I,' riven and marked." She notes that it was Wittig who determined that the English "I" ought to be emphasized and marked by italicization, "rendering it foreign, different from the text over which it presides" (86). Shaktini (1982, 33, 41) presents the "I" as crossed with a line through it, although it is not clear from where she has derived this symbol, as at times she cites the translation by Le Vay, which uses the italicized "I." Scanlon (1998, 77) notes that it has been suggested that this crossed "I" with the line through it "would fittingly resemble a broken or cut phallus."

61. Higgins (1976, 163) observes that it is difficult to read aloud from the text

"without stumbling over the words split with a slash ... an impression of multiple starts and stops is created at the sentence level." She suggests that a "conflict between speech and silence pervades *Le Corps lesbien* and is one of its major themes" (1976, 163). Findlay (1989, 69) wonders if it might be "a chuckle," albeit one that Wittig keeps to herself.

62. Regarding the play on the word *bar*, Hart (1998, 217) explains that she asked Case what she meant by it, expecting a discussion on the concept of the bar (/) as a marker of division, but instead was (humorously?) told that it was a nightclub for lesbians.

63. See, for example, the anti–gay marriage organization National Organization for Marriage (NOM) with their "Gathering Storm" campaign http://tinyurl .com/SBL0685s or the pro-gay marriage organization, Marriage Equality USA, http:// tinyurl.com/SBL0685k. Other interested groups that have websites include, for the traditional stance: CBMW, American Family Association, Traditional Values Coalition, Family Research Council, Christian Coalition of America, Concerned Women for America, and Citizens for Community Values. On the liberal side of the debate see EqualMarriage.org, Gay and Lesbian Alliance for Marriage, National Gay and Lesbian Task Force, Soulforce, Freedom to Marry, and Love Makes a Family.

64. As noted in ch. 4 on κεφαλή, the issue of civil unions also caused considerable debate within the New Zealand context during 2004 and again with the Marriage Amendment Act in 2013. Nevertheless, given the different cultural contexts between these two countries, with their different histories of nationhood, the debate has not been so hotly contested here or elsewhere; for example, northern European countries legally recognized same-sex unions from 1989 (in Denmark) and the first legal same-sex marriages took place in the Netherlands in 2001 (Boele-Woelki and Fuchs 2003; Eskridge and Spedale 2006). For the history of this debate in Canada and the United States, see Pierceson 2005; Cantor et al. 2006; Rom 2007; Rayside 2007.

65. Wittig does this with the various pronouns in all her books; with *on* in *L'opoponax*, and *elles* in *Les guérillères* (Zerilli 1990, 161–68).

66. Rosenfeld (1984, 236)) contrasts Wittig's *j/e* with the masculine "egocentric *Je* of Descartes ... the Cartesian, uniform and self-centered subject." Rather than finding identity through a propensity for abstract reasoning and, I would add, through a relation to the feminine "other," Rosenfeld (236–37) suggests that "the split *j/e* of Wittig changes constantly and has no fixed identity," but also "acquires her identity as a sentient creature by uniting body and soul with another female," although "not as unified individuals, but organ to organ, bone to bone, nerve to nerve."

67. This may also remind us of the various portrayals of a female Christ that have emerged in the art world, including the sculptures by Edwina Sandys, *Christa* (1975), and James M. Murphy, *Christine on the Cross* (1984). For discussion on these see Moore 2001, 157; Clague 2005.

68. Ostrovsky, however, describes Christ's transformation as one of being "feminised," whereas lesbianization is a more accurate description of Wittig's process; Wittig is not replacing a masculine social/political/religious system with a feminine one, but she is transforming the system altogether.

69. Silberman (2007, 472) states that *J/e* and *tu* "never refer to proper names," and thus as "nameless" he finds them rendered "theoretical, even universalizable."

Although I still find his point a fair description of the figures within the text, they are in fact named once, as Latone and Niobe (Wittig 1976, 28). In addition, one of the "little monkeys" with "stiff pigtails" who sits between the protagonists—a child?—is also named, Chloë (1976, 30–31). I have yet to find any comment on these curious deviations within the text.

70. This concept is taken from Scanlon (1998, 92, 94).

71. Although some scholars describe these sections as individual lists (e.g., Scanlon 1998, 86), Wittig (2005a, 46) speaks of it as a singularity, "a primary layer ... a tool."

72. This issue is explored in Althaus-Reid and Isherwood 2008.

73. It is worth noting at this point that the translator of *The Lesbian Body*, Le Vay, was at the time of publication "an eminent practising anatomist and surgeon"; in her introduction to *The Lesbian Body*, Crosland (1976, vii) states that he pointed out that while "much poetic energy has been dedicated to the outside surface of the human body," nobody other than Wittig—"with the possible exception of certain contributors to the Old Testament" (presumably referring to the Song of Songs)—"has celebrated with such freedom the whole of the body ... everything that adds up to *life*."

74. Dworkin and MacKinnon (1988, 101) list the nine conditions of the ordinance of the city of Minneapolis for determining the nature of material that is pornographic (as opposed to erotic), the sixth of which is the exhibition of body parts, "including, but not limited to, vaginas, breasts, and buttocks ... such that women are reduced to those parts."

75. As for same-sex female intercourse, aside from a general indifference to the phenomenon, both ancient and contemporary discourse often centers on the issue of phallic penetration, be it at the level of popular culture or scholarly research, and visual or textual representation (Hallett 1989; Brooten 1996, 43–50; Butrica 2005). With regard to the proliferation of "girl-girl" sex in male heterosexual pornography, and the way in which this is portrayed so that penetration is an act reserved for either a male who (literally) enters the scene, or the male spectator, or the male reader/viewer of the scene (who is always present in any of these scenes), see the analysis of Jenefsky and Miller (1998). Wittig is one of the "many feminist theorists" cited by Jenefsky and Miller in their discussion of the presentation of both heterosexual penetrative sex and the highly sculptured female body as something "natural" (379). They argue, "An examination of the penetration shot in soft-core pornography offers insight into the regulation of gender in a heterosexual economy.... The rules of penetration stabilize phallic power and circumscribe gender identity; they are central to the preservation of the distinct social, political, and sexual categories known as 'men' and 'women.' And as many feminist theorists have argued, it is this differentiation that is the foundation of compulsory heterosexuality" (378).

76. Findlay (1989, 68–69) argues that this myth is the central organizing force of *The Lesbian Body*, as the thirteen fragments of Osiris's body "reappear in Wittig's text as the average of thirteen poems between each page of boldfaced, listed lesbian body parts" (see also Higgins 1976, 160–61; K. Cope 1991, 87–89).

77. The concept of "phallocracy" is derived from Norman Brown's (1966, 77, 129) critique of the body politic where he speaks of political power as phallic and the "tyranny of the genital" (see also Butler 1993, 57–91).

78. However, Chisholm (1966, 250) notes that despite his rejection of the state as phallocentric, Brown calls for a "polymorphous perversity," which, in fact, equals "penises everywhere." As she explains, "Brown insists that it is the male member that is in most need of liberation ... he advocates the free mobilization and deterritorialization of male sexuality ... a hom(m)osexual free-for-all" (1993, 200).

79. I have hinted at this view of the body earlier with the citation from McClure's (1966, 75) essay "Revolt," in which the "tail end of the beast" "vigorously shakes from itself the head end," and becomes "headless and self-decisive." Indeed, in many ways, McClure's essay is a similarly imaginative exploration to Wittig's of the "erotic and universal," of "flesh" and "beasts" (74).

Conclusion

When the apostle Paul learned of the various problems that were troubling the church in Corinth, not too long after he had left, he responded by sending them a letter. No doubt hoping to influence them on each of the issues he felt he needed to address, he employed a variety of rhetorical devices in order to persuade them of what was needed to resolve each problem and to restore a sense of unity to this somewhat fractured community. When he came to the matter of their behavior during public worship—some of them were doing something with their hair or head coverings that some others found inappropriate—this was a rather disconcerting issue but nothing that a short paragraph or two could not straighten out. At some point he would be visiting them in person, indeed he was hoping to spend the coming winter with them, so this letter would suffice in the meantime.

Little did Paul realize, of course, that this short section in a letter, so full of other apparently more serious issues, would influence the lives of men and women down through the centuries and across the world. Little did he realize that readers of this passage centuries later would find it so difficult to decipher that it would spawn countless academic theses, articles, and books. Traditional historical-critical approaches to this passage have attempted to determine the correct meaning of the words Paul used (such as κεφαλή), or the correct situation that occasioned this response (such as a "horror of homosexualism"), in order to make sense of this "notoriously difficult" passage. Yet for all the ink spilt attempting to discern what Paul meant by his various comments, the way this passage has consistently been used to bolster a heteropatriarchal model of gender and sexuality has seldom been examined.

Certainly much important feminist work on this passage has been done. Some of it has given a voice to the Corinthian women, so often otherwise dismissed as "problematic." Some of it has presented ways of reading this passage that emphasize a sense of mutuality and equality between the sexes, or at the very least challenged blatantly sexist interpretations and translations that in any other field would be thought preposterous. Other feminist work has acknowledged that Paul was indeed seeking to reinforce a hierarchical model of gender relationships in order to maintain the status quo; as a first-century, educated, Mediterranean male he would have seen nothing problematic in this.

But by appealing to both the creation accounts (Gen 1–2) and "nature" in his instructions, Paul drew on a powerful body of discourses in order to shape both the individual and the social bodies for which he felt responsible. Current readers of the text who insist that the same hierarchical ordering of relationships between men and women—or husbands and wives—be applied today in the home, church, and even, for some, the state, for the smooth functioning of society, often draw on the same body of discourses for support. However, they also have the added weight of being able to draw on this Pauline text, now no longer simply part of an occasional letter, but part of Scripture itself.

The materialist lesbianism of Wittig has demonstrated that rhetoric such as this conceals the political, economic, physical, and social subjugation of women by men. Presenting "the fact" that there are not only differences between the sexes but also that these are "natural," "biblical," and ordained by God is a powerful element in the operation of what Wittig (1992i, 27) calls "the straight mind." This is because these artificially constructed categories of supposed natural opposition are fundamental to the regime of heterosexuality. When these oppositional gender relations are also presented as "naturally" hierarchical, so that the male is seen as both the norm and also therefore "naturally" dominant, then this supports an androcentric, patriarchal, and heterosexual framework of both gendered and sexed being that can be described as heteropatriarchy. Even deeper, however, this framework is privileged as it is also integral to power relations within society and thus becomes indicative of what is "proper" regarding gendered and sexed behavior. It is also integral to a capitalist economic and political framework, and therefore an androcentric heteropatriarchal model of relations also tends to reify that which is white, Western, middle-class, and nuclear. The "straight mind" thus operates at every level of society. Yet this dominant ideological system is presented as so natural and "normal" that it gets taken for granted, as something "already there," and remains unchallenged. When it is also legitimated as the biblical model established by divine will, then its hegemony is virtually complete.

The goal of this project has been to both reveal and challenge these ideologies of gender and sexuality. In particular, I have sought to reveal the sex-gender ideologies that have informed Paul's arguments in 1 Cor 11:2–16 and also those that have informed recent and current interpretations of this passage. An engagement with queer theory has enabled such a critical investigation (or interrogation), as it is not only gender and sexuality but also politics and power that are implicated in a heteropatriarchal system. Queer theory contests and problematizes that which is posited as normative, exposing instabilities and injustices in a system that is presented as so stable and straightforward, so natural and normal, so biblical and God-ordained, that it should not be questioned. Part of the way queer theory challenges the "normal" is by presenting alternative models of gendered and sexed being. By engaging in experimental imaginings that stand outside the center and speak from the margins, queer theory troubles and subverts the "proper" model, revealing *all* models as ideologically constructed.

In order to do something "queer" with this passage, it was necessary to draw various lines of inquiry across it. The resultant intersections and collisions would thus create something potentially abject but also something able to expose and destabilize the normal. Wittig's materialist lesbianism and her theoretical lesbian figure (or signifier) provide an effective way of doing exactly that. Beginning with her call to systematically particularize the masculine gender in order to both highlight and correct the way in which men and the masculine are rendered invisible in an androcentric paradigm (1992c, 87), I focused on the Corinthian men, exploring the possibility that they were as involved as the women in the situation Paul was addressing. My main concern was not to determine the specific historical background to this situation but to reveal the ways in which scholars have allowed an androcentric ideology to affect the way they have read the text, with the result that the Corinthian women (and feminist exegesis) have been viewed as problematic but the Corinthian men (and a supposedly objective biblical scholarship) have been viewed as unproblematic. In addition, I explored the possibility that the Corinthian men were involved in "homosexuality," revealing a misunderstanding of first-century constructs of masculinity, so that what was most likely a "fear of effeminacy" was confused with a "horror of homosexualism."

As a corollary to her call to particularize that which has been deemed universal, Wittig also calls for that which has been deemed particular to be universalized. Consequently she seeks to bring the figure of the lesbian to the center, and challenges us to "lesbianize the heroes of love, lesbianize the symbols, lesbianize the gods and the goddesses, lesbianize Christ [and] lesbianize the men and the women" (1992c, 87; see also 2005a, 47). My intention to "lesbianize the men," by imagining the possibility that they might be (theoretical) lesbians, akin to Wittig's lesbian figure, also developed out of a desire to destabilize and displace that which has been dominant, namely Butler's reading of Wittig, the fiction of the phallus, and Boyarin's focus on the Corinthian women. In this way, that which has been subdominant—*re*readings of Wittig, the lesbian phallus, and the Corinthian men—have been able to emerge and demonstrate a form of resistance.

Because Wittig recognizes the power of language in the operation of the straight mind, she also challenges us to "attack the order of heterosexuality in texts" (1992g, 87; 2005a, 47) and "produce a political transformation of the key concepts" (1992a, 30). The second half of this book therefore focused on three sections of 1 Cor 11:2–16, all of which have as central the pairing of ὁ ἀνήρ and ἡ γυνή and historically and currently have been used to support heteropatriarchy; verse 3 with the word κεφαλή, verse 7 and the notion of the *imago Dei*, and verses 14–15a and the appeal to φύσις ("nature"). These verses have been central to much discussion in both ecclesial and academic settings regarding matters as diverse as gender roles in the family and the church, what it means to be the *imago Dei*, and issues of sexual orientation and same-sex marriage. Consequently, I have drawn on a range of material, intersecting various lines of inquiry *across* these verses in ways that would not typically be expected from a study of this passage but which would enable me to both reveal and challenge the ideologies of gender and sexuality as well as the politics and power relations that inform the ways in which this passage has been interpreted. From the Council of Biblical Manhood and Womanhood (CBMW) and Christians for Biblical Equality (CBE) to Barth's *Church Dogmatics*, and from ancient Stoic virtues to evangelical devotional books for (real) men and (godly) women—as well as devotional Bibles for (gross and gory) boys and (princess-like) girls—it became clear that while some diversity regarding models of gender exists, from the hierarchical and patriarchal to the egalitarian, all of these operate with a strong sense of the differences between the sexes and thus also with a heteronormative ideology of sexuality. This focus on the oppositional, and in most cases hierarchical, binary of "man and woman" has resulted in the dominance of an androcentric heteropatriarchal model of gendered and sexed being, which I have then destabilized through Wittig's theory and her lesbian figure.

The culmination of this dual strategy of exposing and challenging the ideological foundations behind these supposedly "natural" and

"God-ordained" models of gender and sexuality was seen in the final section of the last chapter with the juxtaposition of Gagnon's unnatural homosexual and Wittig's monstrous lesbian. By taking up Moore's (2007, 10) challenge to show how queer theory has the potential to shift discussions on homosexuality (and heterosexuality) into a "a radically different register," I have resisted and even transgressed the "normal" on several levels. In speaking from the subdominant position underneath the material on Gagnon, Wittig's monstrous lesbian—a figure on the outposts of what it means to be human—has physically moved to the top and center, destabilizing that which has been dominant and buttressed with powerful rhetoric, so that it is literally disempowered and forced off the page altogether. This is not to replace one hegemonic paradigm with another, however. Wittig's (1992e, 19–20) monstrous lesbian points to "a new personal and subjective definition for all humankind ... beyond the categories of sex" and is therefore multiple and open rather than (supposedly) unified and stable.

It is with a sense of thinking "beyond the categories of sex" that I conclude this book. There is still a "beyond" to reach. Part of this includes the concrete challenge to New Testament scholarship to show a greater awareness of the differences between first- and twenty-first-century frameworks for thinking about sex, gender, and sexuality. Part of this involves the more esoteric issue of exploring the notion of utopia (and dystopia) that has played at the fringes of this project and has already piqued the interest of some biblical scholars (R. Boer 1999). In addition, there are other texts, other symbols, other gods and goddesses to "lesbianize."

I would hope, then, that the "affair" between the New Testament and queer theory will not prove to have been just a "fling" that will soon end (always in tears) but, while never wanting to settle down, might be something that will flourish and be abjectly fruitful for a long time yet. The dominant heteropatriarchal paradigm will resist destabilization and rear its (beastly) head again. Wittig's lesbian will be dismembered and scattered, broken, and crucified, and yet remade and reborn again. As long as a text such as 1 Cor 11:2–16, with all its exegetical and contextual difficulties, its instabilities and ambiguities, is used to bolster a heteropatriarchal model of sexed and gendered being, then this can *only* be the beginning.

Appendix 1

Historical-Critical Research on 1 Corinthians 11:2–16

For those interested in 1 Cor 11:2–16, it can be useful to have a comprehensive overview of the state of historical-critical research on the various exegetical and historical elements of this text. This is partly because some studies tend to focus on one particular element and can unintentionally give the impression that other aspects of the text are uncontested. Even when multiple aspects of the text are addressed, the sheer quantity of issues that this text presents often means that many of these are overlooked or are subject to unexamined assumptions. It should be helpful, then, to have the bulk of these matters outlined in one place.

However, a thorough investigation of the material reveals a myriad of exegetical and historical possibilities for this passage. Such a myriad of possibilities ought to preclude the level of confidence that often accompanies work on this text, but as discussed in chapter 1, one of the underlying attributes of the historical-critical methodology is a positivism that seeks to render the passage clear and comprehensible. Multiple possibilities, lack of clarity, and unanswerable questions are qualities that do not sit comfortably within the historical-critical framework; a singular, clear, and correct explanation is generally the goal of such studies. One of the few points that is clear with regard to 1 Cor 11:2–16 is that virtually every aspect is contestable.

To begin with, some scholars question the integrity of 1 Corinthians as a whole (see the discussions in Schrage 1991, 63–71; M. de Boer 1994; Collins 1999, 10–14; Thiselton 2000, 36–41). Regarding 1 Cor 11:2–16 in particular, W. Walker (1975) proposed that the entire passage ought to be understood as a non-Pauline interpolation, constructed as three distinct pericopes. He stated that as far as he was able to determine, other than the suggestion by Johannes Weiss (1910) that verse 3 was an interpolation, "no one else has ever suggested this for the passage as a whole" (1975, 97

n. 14). Murphy-O'Connor (1976) challenged this suggestion. Lamar Cope (1978, 435–36) considered both W. Walker's and Murphy-O'Connor's positions, and he stated that W. Walker's hypothesis is "the best available," although the interpolation ought to be amended to 11:3–16. G. W. Trompf (1980, 197, 214) then noted that W. Walker's exegesis failed to persuade because he had "gone too far" by suggesting that the passage was made up of three distinct non-Pauline pericopes; otherwise, Trompf contended, the interpolation hypothesis (whether Pauline or not) must be considered a "real possibility."[1] W. Walker (1983) continued to argue for the non-Pauline interpolation of 1 Cor 11:3–16 (albeit now amended from 11:2–16) as well as the presence of three distinct pericopes. He acknowledged Cope's suggested amendment and the supportive arguments of M. Trompf and declared that "the case against Pauline authorship of 1 Cor 11:3–16 has now been cogently made, and I fully expect that this view will gain increasing acceptance" (109 n. 21). Murphy-O'Connor responded again (1986), particularly evaluating (and subsequently rejecting) the arguments put forward by Trompf. W. Walker (1987, 1988) continued to make his case more generally and also examined the specific issue of vocabulary in 1 Cor 11:3–16, concluding that his case for 1 Cor 11:3–16 as a non-Pauline interpolation was strengthened (1989, 82). More recently, Walker (2004) reiterated his hypothesis. The volume in which that essay appeared was subsequently given a negative review by none other than Murphy-O'Connor (2006), who critiqued the "fertile imaginations" of Walker and others writing on the topic of interpolations. Mount's (2005) reassertion of Walker's hypothesis was subsequently rejected by Penner and Vander Stichele (2005, 219 n. 15).[2]

This then brings us to the issue of which verses are actually under consideration. Those who view this passage as starting at verse 2 and ending at verse 16 are in the majority, but some prefer to start at verse 1, while a significant number prefer to begin at verse 3.[3]

While the majority of scholars argue (or assume) that the context is public worship, a few scholars view the context as private worship because of the otherwise (supposed) contradiction with 1 Cor 14:33b–36, which appears to silence women in church. Thus some understand the "praying and prophesying" of 11:4–5 to be something the women can do only in the privacy of their own homes (Simon 1959, 112). MacArthur (1984, 256–57; 2007, 71) maintained that the "praying and prophesying" is taking place "in public places rather than in the worship of the congregation," as women may not do so "in the meetings of the church where men are present." Some scholars accepted that the context is public worship but made the strained argument that Paul therefore does not want women to pray or prophesy in church at all (Synge 1953; N. Weeks 1972, 23, 26; 1988, 129–30). John Robbins (1985, 25–27, 35–39), for example, contended that 1 Cor 14:33b–36 precludes women speaking in worship and was harshly critical of those who allow 1 Cor 11 to control a reading of 1 Cor 14:33b–36. Gary Sanseri (1999, 29–36) stated unequivocally that Paul is taking the women to task not just because they were uncovered, but because they were prophesying in the first place. A few others (e.g., Grudem 1982, 239–55; 1987; 2000, 113–24, 183–92; Schreiner 2006b, 215–17) accepted that the context is one of public worship and that the Corinthian women were prophesying, but proceeded to argue that prophecy is therefore not authoritative (unlike teaching, for example) and that women also may not evaluate prophecy.

I addressed the issue of whether this passage is dealing with the behavior of the Corinthian women or with both the men and the women in chapter 2, so I will not deal with it here. But a key matter of debate concerns what the women (or men, or both the women and men) were doing with their heads. In particular, scholarship is divided on whether Paul is dealing with head coverings or hairstyles.

Many scholars think that Paul is addressing the matter of women's head coverings, although some of the details vary as to why this was an issue of concern. Barrett (1971, 251) suggested that by discussing head coverings Paul is "seeking to introduce into Greece an oriental custom" and not "combating a movement for the emancipation of women." Wire (1990, 130) argued that the issue arose as a result of the pneumatic women discarding their symbols of subordination as part of their new-found freedom in Christ. M. MacDonald (1990, 166; 2004, 157) similarly contended that the coverings represent symbols of subordination, but she also suggested that the women believed they had transcended sexual differentiation as a result. Others preferred to emphasize the clash of social values. Keener (2005, 92) noted that "upper-class women were far less likely to cover their heads" and that " 'naked' hair held different social connotations for different women" (see also D. Martin 1995a, 229–49; F. Watson 2000a, 42–47; Winter 2003b, 77–96; T. Martin 2004; Finney 2010). In Pentecostal circles, however, the notion of "covering" is often understood to be "spiritual" rather than physical (Carlé 1998, 40, 70–71). Nevertheless, neither Fee nor Powers addressed this issue; for both these Pentecostal scholars, the primary issue seems to be allowing women the spiritual authority to pray and prophesy in public worship (Fee 1987, 497 n. 22, 505, 508 n. 67; Powers 2001). Another group of scholars (e.g., Oster 1988; 1992; 1995, 260–64; Gill 1990, 1993) focused on the issue of men's head coverings, noting the Roman elite practice of *capite velato*; I also discussed this issue in more detail in chapter 2.

One of the first scholars to suggest that the issue concerned hairstyles rather than head coverings was Stefan Lösch (1947, 225–30), but his study caused little reaction at the time. It was Abel Isaksson's (1965, 165–86) study twenty years later on rituals surrounding hair and appearance for prophets and prophetesses in Christian worship, as based upon Jewish temple practices, that had more impact. Isaksson was followed by William Martin (1970, 233), who argued that it was "beyond reasonable doubt" that Paul was dealing with issues concerning hair length. James Hurley (1973, 195, 216) also considered the Jewish background of the passage, but contended that the issue was rather "the authority of husbands in relation to their wives as focused in the hair-style of wives at the worship service." Hurley (195 n. 13) referenced Isaksson only once, but both their studies have been viewed as significant in the development of this suggestion; Preston Massey (2007, 502–3) credited Isaksson and Hurley for being responsible for what he calls "this enduring controversy," stating, "Like a rock thrown into a pond sending ripples of water rolling to the banks, the IH [Isaksson-Hurley] theory has sent out is own constant waves."

Another significant development of this hairstyle idea, however, was the proposal by Murphy-O'Connor (1980, 490) that Paul was also addressing the behavior of the men and, as such, was concerned that their long hair was creating an association with "homosexuality," while the women were letting their hair down in an "unfeminine" way.[4] Given the issues that this raises regarding scholars' understandings of Greco-Roman sex-gender ideologies, I examined this proposal more closely in chapter 2.

Other hairstyle options have since followed. Preferring a Greco-Roman context and with a focus on the Corinthian women, Schüssler Fiorenza (1983, 227–28) proposed that "unbound ... dishevelled hair," which was characteristic of cultic practices associated with the "ecstatic worship" of Dionysus or Isis, had been adopted by the Corinthian women as a "mark of true prophetic behavior"; Paul was thus determined to "curb the pneumatic frenzy" of their worship by insisting that they "keep their hair bound up."[5] Gundry-Volf (1997, 154) emphasized "the problem of incurring shame through boundary-transgressing hairstyle[s]," although she also mentioned "unfeminine or unmasculine headdress" and "head-covering practices." Like Gundry-Volf, Hjort (2001, 65, 68) stressed the issue of gendered boundary crossing, suggesting that both men and women "have aspired to transvestism and the neutralization of the sexes by dressing and cutting their hair in accordance with the customs of the opposite sex." By contrast, Marlis von Gielen (1999, 222) emphasized that the issue involved short hair for women.

As one can see in this discussion of hairstyles, the history of scholarship on this passage, as for the letters to the Corinthians in general, has shifted from a focus on a primarily Jewish background to a recognition that Corinth was a Roman colony, albeit one with a Greek history. Consequently, while Barrett (1971, 249) spoke of "the practice of the devout and modest Jewess" with regard to head coverings, and Isaksson (1965, 161–62) focused on "Jewish sources … Jewish worship … Jewish tradition [and] Jewish religion" with regard to hairstyles for priests and prophets, scholars in the 1970s and 1980s focused primarily on the Greco-Roman world of the early Christians (Meeks 1974, 199–202; Schüssler Fiorenza 1983; C. Thompson 1988; Oster 1988, 1992, 1995; Gill 1990, 1993). Hjort (2001, 65) went so far as to say, with regard to Isaksson's study, "To assume a Jewish gender and marriage morality" background to this passage is "untenable." Nevertheless, not all scholars agree. James Thompson (2003, 240) stated that Paul's argument "would have functioned primarily within the context of Hellenistic Judaism" (see also B. Wold 2008, 286). But most scholars nowadays recognize the cosmopolitan nature of Corinth and consider what is called a Mediterranean context (Stuckenbruck 2001, 210 n. 15, 212; Payne 2006, 9–11; MacGregor 2009, 210; Calef 2009, 22–31; A. Johnson 2009, 53).

With regard to exegetical matters, I addressed in chapter 4 the intense nature of the debate over the interpretation of κεφαλή ("head") and the ideological issues that this entails. As for verse 10, which is perhaps the most confusing verse in the entire pericope,[6] the scope of the debate can be divided into issues surrounding the interpretation of the two phrases Paul used in this verse.

Regarding the first phrase, διὰ τοῦτο ὀφείλει ἡ γυνὴ ἐξουσίαν ἔχειν ἐπὶ τῆς κεφαλῆς ("because of this the woman ought to have authority on the head"), the debate has centered primarily on the word ἐξουσία for two reasons. First, given the parallelisms within the passage up to this point regarding the behavior of the men and the women (vv. 4 and 5), some scholars expected verse 10 (and possibly also vv. 11 and 12) to be the matching parallel statement for verse 7 (and thus also vv. 8 and 9) (see the discussion in Fee 1987, 513–15, 523–34; see also BeDuhn 1999, 308; Payne 2006, 13). Because Paul gave a reason why the men ought not to cover their heads, one might expect that he then gave a reason why the women ought to cover theirs. But instead, Paul stated that the woman "ought to have ἐξουσία on her head," and this unexpected statement has caused considerable confusion for scholars.

Second, in a passage that appears to argue for the authority (or priority or preeminence, or however one translates κεφαλή) of man over woman, some have found it difficult that the only clear mention in this passage of authority (or power, or however one translates ἐξουσία) is found here as something that the woman "ought to have." There are, therefore, several suggested solutions to this double difficulty. From Irenaeus onward, it was common to find a blatant substitution of κάλυμμα ("veil") for ἐξουσία (see the discussion in Winandy 1992, 621–22). Gerhard Kittel (1920, 17–25, 31) then proposed that ἐξουσία could be taken as the equivalent of an Aramaic word שלתוניה, meaning "veil" (see also Fitzmyer 1957–1958, 52–53). This is reflected in the RSV translation: "a woman ought to have a veil on her head." The NAB specifically footnotes the point that ἐξουσία "may possibly be due to mistranslation of an Aramaic word for 'veil.'" Most modern versions have rejected this specific translation, although many still persist in using the terminology of "covering."[7]

With regard to the "difficulty" involved in accepting that ἐξουσία was something the woman "ought to have," MacRory's (1915, 161–62) explanation at the outset of the twentieth century was fairly typical: because ἐξουσία means "power, authority, control," the woman therefore "ought to have on her head at public prayer a veil, as a sign of man's authority over her." Indeed, he added, "No better explanation than this has been found … if we might have expected the Apostle rather to say that she ought to have a sign of her own subjection (ὑποταγή …) than of man's authority, over her head … the context guards us against misunderstanding it of any authority but his" (161–62).[8] This unique attribution of a passive sense to the active meaning of "having authority" had already been rebuked by W. M. Ramsay (1907, 203) as "a preposterous idea which a Greek scholar would laugh at anywhere except in the New Testament, where (as they seem to think) Greek words may mean anything that commentators choose." Ramsay has continued to be cited on this issue, but the persistence of both this idea and the connection with a veil was strengthened by Werner Foerster's (1964; original 1949) article on ἐξουσία in which he reserved a special section for 1 Cor 11:10 and stated, "The only alternative is that the veil is a sign of woman's subordination to man.... The term ἐξουσία is used materially for the veil ... the veil signifies the dominion to which the woman is subject" (574). Again, many modern translations continue to perpetuate this understanding. The GNB is perhaps the most blatant: "a woman should have a covering over her head to show that she is under her husband's authority."[9]

In the same year that Foerster's article appeared in English, however, Morna Hooker (1964) published her groundbreaking article, "Authority on Her Head," in which she argued not only that Kittel's linguistic analysis was "too ingenious" but also that understanding ἐξουσία to mean "subjection" was "very strange" (413). While she still accepted the idea that Paul was contending that women be covered, Hooker (415–16) convincingly argued that ἐξουσία means the "authority" or "power" that is given to the woman in order to pray and prophesy. While Hooker's position has now been widely accepted, a few scholars still argue for the traditional understanding (Schreiner 2006a, 136; Merkle 2006, 537–38; Calef 2009, 37–38).[10] Gary Sanseri (1999, 141–45) contended not only for the traditional meaning of ἐξουσία but also for the current wearing of head coverings for women as a sign of their submission, and explained that his home church has now adopted the practice. Graeme Carlé (1998, 13, 70–71) proposed a Pentecostal view that the covering is "not a physical covering [but] a spiritual reality"; "in the face of an unavoidable spiritual warfare ... the man is to be the new 'covering' for the woman."[11]

The second aspect of this verse that has generated an enormous amount of scholarly speculation is the concluding phrase, διὰ τοὺς ἀγγέλους. Økland (2004, 183) is one of the few scholars who suggested that Paul's introduction of the angels at this point in his argument is "straightforward." Most have found this prepositional phrase a perplexing and awkward ending to the verse, and would agree with Hays (1997, 188) that it is "completely cryptic." The main interpretive options are as follows:

1. From the early church commentators onward, one possibility has been that οἱ ἀγγέλοι are human messengers or, more specifically, priests or bishops. While the latter options are generally disregarded now, the idea that οἱ ἀγγέλοι are human messengers still has a following. Murphy-O'Connor (1980, 496–97) initially viewed οἱ ἀγγέλοι as heavenly beings, but was subsequently convinced by Padgett's (1984, 81) argument that these are *female* messengers (Murphy-O'Connor 1988, 271–72; see also Winandy 1992, 628). More recently, Winter (2001, 136–37; 2003b, 89–91) suggested that οἱ ἀγγέλοι may have functioned as spies for the authorities.

2. Another possibility, originally proposed by Tertullian (*Cult. fem.* 1.2, 2.10; *Virg.* 1.7–12; 7.2), understands οἱ ἄγγελοι as lustful, fallen angels, akin to those in Gen 6:2 and 1 Enoch, despite the lack of negative references to ἄγγελοι in the New Testament. Many coupled this suggestion with a view of the veil as prophylactic or as functioning to promote modesty (Conzelmann 1975, 189; D. Martin 1995a, 229–49; Peerbolte 2000, 87–90; Stuckenbruck 2001, 227–33; T. Martin 2005, 268–69). Calef (2009, 38–39) saw this option as "far more likely" than any other, although she did not view οἱ ἄγγελοι as malevolent; Paul's concern is to warn about the dangers of cosmic disorder. Carlé (1998, 51–64) is the only one I am aware of who posited that the specific reference is to the enmity between Satan and the woman in Gen 3:14–16. Thiselton (2000, 841 n. 235), however, called this suggestion about fallen angels "idiosyncratic."

3. Perhaps the most common option is to view οἱ ἄγγελοι as good angels, either as those who are holy and present at the worship service, or as those who are guardians of the created order (Brooke 2003, 173–75; Økland 2004, 183–84; Fitzmyer 2008, 418–19). Fitzmyer's (1957–1958) study on the Qumran parallels has been especially influential here (see also Cadbury 1958).

4. Another option that has come to be frequently cited (although rarely followed) is BeDuhn's (1999, 308–13) suggestion that "Paul's outlandish anthropogony" led him to view the creation of woman—and thus a gendered and sexed humanity—as an act of οἱ ἄγγελοι. Linda Belleville (2003, 226 and n. 36) cited BeDuhn's "novel interpretation" approvingly, although she coupled this with Fitzmyer's suggestion.

I hope this overview of the historical and exegetical issues that are debated with regard to 1 Cor 11:2–16 will be helpful to the interested reader of this passage. I imagine that within historical-critical circles these issues will continue to be debated and the quest for the correct interpretation of key words and phrases and for the most likely scenario to explain Paul's argumentation and/or the Corinthians' behavior will inevitably continue. Such positivistic querying of this passage seems to do little more than confirm the "queer" nature of both the historical-critical project and this text.

Notes

1. Trompf (1980, 198 n. 7) also noted that it was Loisy (1935, 60–62) who had first suggested that 11:3–16 ought to be considered an interpolation.

2. An entirely different view proposed by Padgett (1984, 69–86) has had little support. He argued that the first part of this passage reflects the Corinthian position as outlined by Paul (vv. 3–7a), which Paul then proceeds to refute in vv. 7b–16. Shoemaker (1987) went even further, viewing vv. 3–9 as a Corinthian quote that Paul then refutes in vv. 10–16. For more on the merits or otherwise of these interpolation theories, see the discussions in Schrage 1995, 496–97; Witherington 1995, 231 n. 2; Peerbolte 2000, 82 n. 12; Stuckenbruck 2001, 206–8.

3. Start at verse 1: Bushnell 1923, lessons 29 and 32; Greig 1957–1958, 156–57; Key 1984, 143; Keener 1992, 17 (although he then proceeds to examine vv. 2–16); Christian 1999, 291. Start at verse 3: Moffatt 1938, 148; Boucher 1969, 50; Isaksson 1965, 155; Trompf 1980, 196; W. Walker 1983, 101; 1989, 75; Howard 1983, 32; Prior 1985, 179; Theissen 1987, 158; Powers 2001, 11; Bourne 2004, 80; Hays 2004, 143; Crocker 2004, 152; Mount 2005, 313.

4. Murphy-O'Connor (1980, 488 n. 27) refers to both Isaksson and Hurley but states that "their approach needs refinement." Murphy-O'Connor was critiqued by Delobel (1986) in particular, and Murphy-O'Connor (1988) responded.

5. Padgett (1984; 1986, 127–28) also argues for a Greek background to this issue regarding hair but strongly disagrees with Schüssler Fiorenza on many points.

6. It is very common to find scholars stating that this verse is particularly "puzzling" or "cryptic" (Beardslee 1994, 106; J. Barclay 2001, 1126; Garland 2003, 526; Calef 2009, 22). Others use similar phrases, such as "enigmatic" (Hooker 1964, 410; Fitzmyer 2008, 417), "obscure" (Barrett 1971, 253; Blomberg 1994, 212), "mysterious" (BeDuhn 1999, 295), "opaque" (S. Barton 2003, 1338), "baffling" (Byrne 1988, 33; Garland 2003, 526), and just simply "difficult" (R. Brown 1970, 352; W. Barclay 1975, 98). Corrington (1991, 226) perhaps summed up the situation well: "Paul appears to have dropped into this section of his argument quite a bombshell for later interpreters."

7. See LB, NIRV, GW, NLT, NJB, CEV, NAB, Amplified, and GNB.

8. See also Robertson and Plummer (1914, 232), who ask, "Why does Paul say 'authority' when he means 'subjection'?... For ἐξουσία we should expect ὑποταγή."

9. See also Phillips, LB, NJB, NIRV, GW, NLT, and Amplified, while both the CEV and NAB note this as a possible option.

10. Curiously, Calef cites Fitzmyer's 1957–1958 article, but a year before Calef's article was published, Fitzmyer (2008, 416) himself acknowledged, "Although I once followed Kittel's explanation ... I recognize today that that meaning of Greek *exousia* would scarcely have been understood by Paul's Corinthian readers."

11. For further detail, see the discussion in Thiselton (2000, 838–39), who concluded that the traditional viewpoint "was misconceived and misleading."

Works Cited

Primary Sources

Apuleius. 1989. *Metamorphoses*. Edited and translated by J. Arthur Hanson. 2 vols. LCL. Cambridge: Harvard University Press.

Aristotle. 1947a. *The Metaphysics*. Translated by Hugh Tredennick. 2 vols. LCL. 1933–1935. Repr., Cambridge: Harvard University Press.

———. 1947b. *The Nicomachean Ethics*. Translated by H. Rackham. LCL. 1926. Repr., Cambridge: Harvard University Press.

———. 1950. *The Politics*. Translated by H. Rackham. LCL. 1944. Repr., Cambridge: Harvard University Press.

———. 1953. *Generation of Animals*. Translated by A. L. Peck. LCL. 1943. Repr., Cambridge: Harvard University Press.

Aquinas, Thomas. 1964–1981. *Summa Theologiæ*. Translated by Edmund Hill et al. 61 vols. London: Blackfriars.

Diodorus Siculus. 1933–1967. *Library of History* [*Bibliotheca historica*]. Translated by C. H. Oldfather, C. L. Sherman, C. Bradford Welles, Russell M. Geer, and F. R. Walton. 12 vols. LCL. London: Heinemann.

Epictetus. 1946–1952. *Discourses*. Translated by W. A. Oldfather. 2 vols. LCL. 1926–1928. Repr., Cambridge: Harvard University Press.

Euripides. 1996. *Bacchae*. Translated by Richard Seaford. Warminster: Aris & Phillips.

Homer. 1995. *The Odyssey*. Translated by A. T. Murray. Revised by George E. Dimock. 2 vols. LCL. Cambridge: Harvard University Press.

Horace. 2004. *Odes and Epodes*. Edited and translated by Niall Rudd. LCL. Cambridge: Harvard University Press.

Horst, P. W. van der, ed. and trans. 1978. *The Sentences of Pseudo-Phocylides: With Introduction and Commentary*. SVTP 4. Leiden: Brill.

Juvenal. 1967. *The Sixteen Satires*. Translated by Peter Green. Harmondsworth: Penguin.

——. 2004. *The Satires*. Pages 128–511 in *Juvenal and Persius*. Edited and translated by Susanna Morton Braund. LCL. Cambridge: Harvard University Press.

Livy. 1919–1959. *History of Rome*. Translated by B. O. Foster, F. G. Moore, Evan T. Sage, and A. C. Schlesinger. 14 vols. LCL. Cambridge: Harvard University Press.

Lucian. 1913–1967. *Lucian*. Translated by A. M. Harmon, K. Kilburn, and M. D. MacLeod. 8 vols. LCL. Cambridge: Harvard University Press.

Lutz, Cora E. 1947. "Musonius Rufus, 'The Roman Socrates.'" *Yale Classical Studies* 10:3–147.

Philo. 1929–1953. *Philo*. Translated by G. H. Whitaker, F. H. Colson, and Ralph Marcus. 12 vols. LCL. Cambridge: Harvard University Press.

Philostratus. 1953. *The Life of Apollonius of Tyana*. Translated by F. C. Conybeare. 2 vols. LCL. 1912. Repr., London: Heinemann.

——. 2005. *The Life of Apollonius of Tyana*. Edited and translated by Christopher P. Jones. 2 vols. LCL. Cambridge: Harvard University Press.

Plutarch. 1927–2004. *Moralia*. Translated by F. C. Babbitt et al. 16 vols. LCL. Cambridge: Harvard University Press.

Sophocles. 1912–1913. *Sophocles*. Translated by F. Storr. 2 vols. LCL. London: Heinemann.

Virgil. 1999–2000. *Virgil*. Translated by H. Rushton Fairclough. Revised by G. P. Goold. Rev. ed. 2 vols. LCL. Cambridge: Harvard University Press.

Wilson, Walter T. 2005. *The Sentences of Pseudo-Phocylides*. Commentaries on Early Jewish Literature. Berlin: de Gruyter.

Secondary Literature

Abelove, Henry, Michèle Aina Barale, and David M. Halperin. 1993. "Introduction." Pages xv–xviii in *The Lesbian and Gay Studies Reader*. Edited by Henry Abelove, Michèle Aina Barale, and David M. Halperin. New York: Routledge.

Aichele, George, Peter Miscall, and Richard Walsh. 2009. "An Elephant in the Room: Historical-Critical and Postmodern Interpretations of the Bible." *JBL* 128:383–404.

Allen, Jeffner. 1988. "Poetic Politics: How the Amazons Took the Acropolis." *Hypatia* 3:107–22.

Allen, Jeffner, and Iris Marion Young. 1989. *The Thinking Muse: Feminism and Modern French Philosophy.* Bloomington: Indiana University Press.

Allen, Prudence. 1997. *The Concept of Woman: The Aristotelian Revolution 750 BC–AD 1250.* Grand Rapids: Eerdmans.

Althaus-Reid, Marcella. 2005. "From the Goddess to Queer Theology: The State We Are in Now." *Feminist Theology* 13:265–72.

Althaus-Reid, Marcella, and Lisa Isherwood, eds. 2008. *Controversies in Body Theology.* Controversies in Contextual Theology. London: SCM.

Amjad-Ali, Christine. 1995. "The Equality of Women: Form or Substance (1 Corinthians 11.2–16)." Pages 185–93 in *Voices from the Margin: Interpreting the Bible in the Third World.* Edited by R. S. Sugirtharajah. 2nd ed. Maryknoll, NY: Orbis.

Anderson, Janice Capel, and Stephen D. Moore. 2003. "Matthew and Masculinity." Pages 67–91 in *New Testament Masculinities.* Edited by Stephen D. Moore and Janice Capel Anderson. SemeiaSt 45. Atlanta: Society of Biblical Literature.

Anzaldúa, Gloria. 2009. "To(o) Queer the Writer—Loca, escritora y chicana." Pages 163–75 in *The Gloria Anzaldúa Reader.* Edited by AnaLouise Keating. Durham, NC: Duke University Press.

Arnold, Laura W., and Herbert F. Weisberg. 1996. "Parenthood, Family Values, and the 1992 Presidential Election." *American Politics Quarterly* 24:194–220.

Bagemihil, Bruce. 1999. *Biological Exuberance: Animal Homosexuality and Natural Diversity.* London: Profile.

Bailey, Derrick Sherwin. 1955. *Homosexuality and the Western Christian Tradition.* London: Longmans, Green.

Bakhtin, Mikhail. 1984. *Rabelais and His World.* Translated by Helene Iswolsky. Bloomington: Indiana University Press.

Balboa, Jaime R. 1998. "*Church Dogmatics*, Natural Theology, and the Slippery Slope of *Geschlecht*: A Constructivist-Gay Liberationist Reading of Barth." *JAAR* 66:771–89.

Barber, Stephen M., and David L. Clark. 2002. "Queer Moments: The Performative Temporalities of Eve Kosofsky Sedgwick." Pages 1–53 in *Regarding Sedgwick: Essays on Queer Culture and Critical Theory.* Edited by Stephen M. Barber and David L. Clark. New York: Routledge.

Barclay, John. 2001. "1 Corinthians." Pages 1108–33 in *The Oxford Bible Commentary.* Edited by John Barton and John Muddiman. Oxford: Oxford University Press.

Barclay, William. 1975. *The Letters to the Corinthians*. Rev. ed. Daily Study Bible. Edinburgh: Saint Andrew Press.

Barr, James. 2000. *History and Ideology in the Old Testament: Biblical Studies at the End of a Millennium*. Hensley Henson Lectures 1997. Oxford: Oxford University Press.

Barrett, C. K. 1971. *A Commentary on the First Epistle to the Corinthians*. 2nd ed. BNTC. London: Black.

Barrett, Matthew. 2015. "God's Design for Marriage: Celebrating the Beauty of Gender Roles in 1 Peter 3." Council on Biblical Manhood and Womanhood. http://tinyurl.com/SBL0685r.

Barth, Karl. 1932–1970. *Die kirchliche Dogmatik*. 4 vols. in 14. Zurich: EVZ.

———. 1936–1977. *Church Dogmatics*. Translated by G. T. Thomson et al. Edited by G. W. Bromiley and T. F. Torrance. 4 vols. in 14. Edinburgh: T&T Clark.

———. 1947–1951. *Die Lehre von der Schöpfung*. Vol. 3 of *Die kirchliche Dogmatik*. 4 parts. Zurich: EVZ.

———. 1968. *The Epistle to the Romans*. 6th ed. Translated by Edwyn C. Hoskyns. Oxford: Oxford University Press.

———. 2006. *Karl Barth–Willem Adolf Visser 't Hooft, Briefwechsel 1930–1968: Einschliesslich des Briefwechsels von Henriette Visser 't Hooft mit Karl Barth und Charlotte von Kirschbaum*. Karl Barth Gesamtausgabe 5, Briefe. Zurich: Theologischer Verlag.

Barton, Carlin. 1994. "All Things Beseem the Victor: Paradoxes of Masculinity in Early Imperial Rome." Pages 83–92 in *Gender Rhetorics: Postures of Dominance and Submission in History*. Edited by Richard C. Trexler. Medieval and Renaissance Texts and Studies 113. Binghamton, NY: Medieval and Renaissance Texts and Studies.

Barton, Stephen C. 2003. "1 Corinthians." Pages 1314–52 in *Eerdmans Commentary on the Bible*. Edited by James D. G. Dunn and John W. Rogerson. Grand Rapids: Eerdmans.

Bassler, Jouette M. 1998. "1 Corinthians." Pages 411–19 in *Women's Bible Commentary*. Edited by Carol A. Newsom and Sharon H. Ringe. Louisville: Westminster John Knox.

Bates, Stephen. 2004. *A Church at War: Anglicans and Homosexuality*. London: Tauris.

Battisti, Daniela Grazia. 1994. "The Rhetoric of Misogyny: Juvenal, Satire 6." PhD thesis. Rutgers University, New Brunswick, NJ.

Bauckham, Richard. 1998. *God Crucified: Monotheism and Christology in the New Testament.* Grand Rapids: Eerdmans.

———. 2008. *Jesus and the God of Israel: God Crucified and Other Studies on the New Testament's Christology of Divine Identity.* Grand Rapids: Eerdmans.

Bauer, J. Edgar. 2005. "*Mêmeté* and the Critique of Sexual Difference: On Monique Wittig's Deconstruction of the Symbolic Order and the Site of the Neuter." *CTHEORY*: http://tinyurl.com/SBL0685a.

Bauman, Whitney. 2009. "Religion, Nature, and Sexual Discourse." *Dialog* 48:6–7.

Beardslee, William A. 1994. *First Corinthians: A Commentary for Today.* St. Louis: Chalice.

Beauvoir, Simone de. 1984. *The Second Sex.* Translated by H. M. Parshley. 1953. Repr., Penguin Modern Classics. Harmondsworth: Penguin.

Bech, Henning. 1995. "Sexuality, Gender and Sociology." *Acta Sociologica* 38:187–92.

Beck, James R., and Craig L. Blomberg. 2005a. "Introduction." Pages 9–22 in *Two Views on Women in Ministry.* Edited by James R. Beck and Craig L. Blomberg. Counterpoints. Grand Rapids: Zondervan.

———, eds. 2005b. *Two Views on Women in Ministry.* Counterpoints. Grand Rapids: Zondervan.

Bedale, Stephen. 1954. "The Meaning of κεφαλή in the Pauline Epistles." *JTS* 5:211–15.

Bederman, Gail. 1995. *Manliness and Civilization: A Cultural History of Gender and Race in the United States, 1880–1917.* Women in Culture and Society. Chicago: University of Chicago Press.

BeDuhn, Jason David. 1999. " 'Because of the Angels': Unveiling Paul's Anthropology in 1 Corinthians 11." *JBL* 118:295–320.

Belleville, Linda L. 2003. "Κεφαλή and the Thorny Issue of Head Covering in 1 Corinthians 11:2–16." Pages 215–31 in *Paul and the Corinthians: Studies on a Community in Conflict: Essays in Honour of Margaret Thrall.* Edited by Trevor J. Burke and J. Keith Elliot. NovTSup 109. Leiden: Brill.

Bennett, Judith M. 2006. *History Matters: Patriarchy and the Challenge of Feminism.* Philadelphia: University of Pennsylvania Press.

Benveniste, Émile. 1971. *Problems in General Linguistics.* Translated by Mary E. Meek. Coral Gables, FL: University of Miami Press.

Bercovitch, Sacvan. 1975. *The Puritan Origins of the American Self.* New Haven: Yale University Press.

Berlant, Lauren, and Michael Warner. 1995. "What Does Queer Theory Teach Us about *X*?" *PMLA* 110:343–49.

———. 1998. "Sex in Public." *Critical Inquiry* 24:547–66.

Bible and Culture Collective. 1995. *The Postmodern Bible*. New Haven: Yale University Press.

Bilezikian, Gilbert. 2002. "I Believe in Male Headship." CBE International. http://tinyurl.com/SBL0685f1.

Bilezikian, Gilbert, W. Ward Gasque, Stanley N. Gundry, Gretchen Gaebelein Hull, Catherine Clark Kroeger, Jo Anne Lyon, and Roger Nicole. n.d. "Men, Women, and Biblical Equality." CBE International. http://tinyurl.com/SBL0685e1.

Birkett, Jennifer. 1996. "*Sophie Ménade*: The Writing of Monique Wittig." Pages 93–119 in *French Erotic Fiction: Women's Desiring, Writing 1880–1990*. Edited by Alex Hughes and Kate Ince. Berg French Studies. Oxford: Berg.

Bjork, Robert E., ed. 2010. *Oxford Dictionary of the Middle Ages*. Oxford: Oxford University Press.

Black, Fiona. 2009. *The Artifice of Love: Grotesque Bodies and the Song of Songs*. LHBOTS 392. London: T&T Clark.

Black, Mark C. 1993. "1 Cor. 11:2–16—a Re-investigation." Pages 191–218 in vol. 1 of *Essays on Women in Earliest Christianity*. Edited by Carroll D. Osburn. Joplin, MO: College Press.

Blattenberger, David E. 1997. *Rethinking 1 Corinthians 11:2–16 through Archeological and Moral-Rhetorical Analysis*. SBEC 36. Lewiston, NY: Mellen.

Blomberg, Craig L. 1994. *1 Corinthians*. NIV Application Commentary. Grand Rapids: Zondervan.

———. 2007. "Gender Roles in Marriage and Ministry: A Possible Relationship." Keynote paper presented at The Centre for the Theology of Gender Colloquium on "God and Gender: Evangelical Perspectives." Auckland, New Zealand.

Boele-Woelki, Katharina, and Angelika Fuchs, eds. 2003. *Legal Recognition of Same-Sex Couples in Europe*. European Family Law 1. Antwerp: Intersentia.

Boer, Martinus C. de. 1994. "The Composition of 1 Corinthians." *NTS* 40:229–45.

Boer, Roland. 1999. *Knockin' on Heaven's Door: The Bible and Popular Culture*. Biblical Limits. London: Routledge.

———. 2001. "Yahweh as Top: A Lost Targum." Pages 75–105 in *Queer Commentary and the Hebrew Bible*. Edited by Ken Stone. JSOTSup 334. Sheffield: Sheffield Academic.

Bohache, Thomas. 2000. "'To Cut or Not to Cut': Is Compulsory Heterosexuality a Prerequisite for Christianity?" Pages 227–39 in *Take Back the Word: A Queer Reading of the Bible*. Edited by Robert E. Goss and Mona West. Cleveland: Pilgrim.

Bonhoeffer, Dietrich. 1959. *Creation and Fall: A Theological Interpretation of Genesis 1–3*. Translated by John C. Fletcher. London: SCM.

Børresen, Kari Elisabeth. 1995a. "God's Image, Is Woman Excluded? Medieval Interpretation of Gen. 1, 27 and I Cor. 11,7." Pages 210–35 in *The Image of God: Gender Models in Judaeo-Christian Tradition*. Edited by Kari Elisabeth Børresen. 1991. Repr., Minneapolis: Fortress.

———. 1995b. "God's Image, Man's Image? Patristic Interpretation of Gen. 1, 27 and I Cor. 11, 7." Pages 187–209 in *The Image of God: Gender Models in Judaeo-Christian Tradition*. Edited by Kari Elisabeth Børresen. 1991. Repr., Minneapolis: Fortress.

Boston, Rob. 2006. "Religious Right Power Brokers: The Top Ten." *Church and State*. http://tinyurl.com/SBL0685q.

Boswell, John. 1980. *Christianity, Social Tolerance, and Homosexuality: Gay People in Western Europe from the Beginning of the Christian Era to the Fourteenth Century*. Chicago: University of Chicago Press.

———. 1997. "Concepts, Experience, and Sexuality." Pages 116–29, 484–90 in *Que(e)rying Religion: A Critical Anthology*. Edited by Gary David Comstock and Susan E. Henking. New York: Continuum.

Boucher, Madeleine. 1969. "Some Unexplored Parallels to 1 Cor 11,11–12 and Gal 3,28: The NT on the Role of Women." *CBQ* 31:50–58.

Bourcier, Marie-Hélène. 2005. "Wittig la Politique." Pages 187–97 in *On Monique Wittig: Theoretical, Political, and Literary Essays*. Edited by Namascar Shaktini. Urbana: University of Illinois Press.

Bourne, Ian. 2004. *Christian Lifestyle in the First and Twenty-First Centuries: A Commentary on 1 Corinthians*. Porirua, NZ: Parish Pastoral Productions.

Bourque, Dominique. 2005. "Dialogic Subversion in Monique Wittig's Fiction." Translated by Harriet Ellenberger. Pages 163–79 in *On Monique Wittig: Theoretical, Political, and Literary Essays*. Edited by Namascar Shaktini. Urbana: University of Illinois Press.

Boyarin, Daniel. 1990. "The Politics of Biblical Narratology: Reading the Bible like/as a Woman." *Diacritics* 20:31–42.

———. 1993a. *Carnal Israel: Reading Sex in Talmudic Culture.* The New Historicism: Studies in Cultural Poetics 25. Berkeley: University of California Press.

———. 1993b. "Paul and the Genealogy of Gender." Pages 13–41 in *A Feminist Companion to Paul.* Edited by Amy-Jill Levine with Marianne Blickenstaff. FCNTECW 6. London: T&T Clark.

———. 1994. *A Radical Jew: Paul and the Politics of Identity.* Contraversions 1. Berkeley: University of California Press.

———. 1995. *Galatians and Gender Trouble: Primal Androgyny and the First Century Origins of a Feminist Dilemma.* Colloquy 1. Berkeley: Center for Hermeneutical Studies.

———. 1997. *Unheroic Conduct: The Rise of Heterosexuality and the Invention of Jewish Man.* Contraversions. Berkeley: University of California Press.

———. 1998. "Gender." Pages 117–35 in *Critical Terms for Religious Studies.* Edited by Mark C. Taylor. Chicago: University of Chicago Press.

———. 2003. "On the History of the Early Phallus." Pages 3–44 in *Gender and Difference in the Middle Ages.* Edited by Sharon Farmer and Carol Braun Pasternack. Medieval Cultures 32. Minneapolis: University of Minnesota Press.

———. 2006. "Thinking with Virgins: Engendering Judaeo-Christian Difference." Pages 216–44 in *A Feminist Companion to the New Testament Apocrypha.* Edited by Amy-Jill Levine with Maria Mayo Robbins. FCNTECW 11. London: T&T Clark.

Braidotti, Rosi, with Judith Butler. 1994. "Feminism by Any Other Name." *Differences* 6.2–3:27–61.

Brauch, Manfred T. 1990. *Hard Sayings of Paul.* London: Hodder & Stoughton.

Braund, Susanna H. 1992. "Juvenal: Misogynist or Misogamist?" *JRS* 18:71–86.

———. 1995. "A Woman's Voice? Laronia's Role in Juvenal's *Satire* 2." Pages 207–19 in *Women in Antiquity: New Assessments.* Edited by Richard Hawley and Barbara Levick. London: Routledge.

Breen, Margaret Sönser, and Warren J. Blumenfeld, eds. 2005. *Butler Matters: Judith Butler's Impact on Feminist and Queer Studies.* Aldershot, UK: Ashgate.

Briscoe, Stuart. 2004. *Brave Enough to Follow: What Jesus Can Do When You Keep Your Eyes on Him.* Colorado Springs: Navpress.

Brooke, George. 2003. "Between Qumran and Corinth: Embroidered Allu-sions to Women's Authority." Pages 157–76 in *The Dead Sea Scrolls as Background to Postbiblical Judaism and Early Christianity: Papers from an International Conference at St. Andrews in 2001.* Edited by James R. Davila. STDJ 46. Leiden: Brill.

Brooten, Bernadette J. 1980. "Feminist Perspectives on New Testament Exegesis." Pages 55–61 in *Conflicting Ways of Interpreting the Bible.* Edited by Hans Küng and Jürgen Moltmann. Edinburgh: T&T Clark.

———. 1985. "Paul's Views on the Nature of Women and Female Homo-eroticism." Pages 61–87 in *Immaculate and Powerful: The Female in Sacred Image and Social Reality.* Edited by Clarissa W. Atkinson, Con-stance H. Buchanan, and Margaret R. Miles. Boston: Beacon.

———. 1988. "Response to 'Corinthian Veils and Gnostic Androgynes' by Dennis Ronald MacDonald." Pages 293–96 in *Images of the Feminine in Gnosticism.* Edited by Karen C. King. SAC. Philadelphia: Fortress.

———. 1996. *Love between Women: Early Christian Responses to Female Homoeroticism.* Chicago Series on Sexuality, History, and Society. Chicago: University of Chicago Press.

Brown, Norman O. 1966. *Love's Body.* New York: Random House.

Brown, Raymond. 1970. *Acts—1 Corinthians.* Broadman Bible Commen-tary 10. London: Marshall, Morgan & Scott.

Bruce, F. F. 1971. *First and Second Corinthians.* NCBC. London: Marshall, Morgan & Scott.

Burns, John Barclay. 2002. "Lot's Wife Looked Back: The Enduring Attrac-tions of Sodom for Biblical Commentators." *Journal of Religion and Society* 4:1–16.

Burrus, Virginia. 2000. *"Begotten, Not Made": Conceiving Manhood in Late Antiquity.* Figurae: Reading Medieval Culture. Stanford, CA: Stanford University Press.

———. 2006. "Radical Orthodoxy and the Heresiological Habit: Engaging Graham Ward's Christology." Pages 36–53 in *Interpreting the Postmod-ern: Responses to "Radical Orthodoxy."* Edited by Rosemary Radford Ruether and Marion Grau. New York: T&T Clark.

———. 2008. *Saving Shame: Martyrs, Saints, and Other Abject Subjects.* Divinations. Philadelphia: University of Pennsylvania Press.

Bushnell, Katherine C. 1923. *God's Word to Women: One Hundred Bible Studies on Woman's Place in the Divine Economy.* Moosewood, IL: God's Word to Women Press.

Buss, David M. 1994. *The Evolution of Desire: Strategies of Human Mating.* New York: Basic Books.

Butler, Judith. 1993. *Bodies That Matter: On the Discursive Limits of "Sex."* New York: Routledge.

———. 1994. "Against Proper Objects." *Differences* 6.2–3:1–26.

———. 1999. *Gender Trouble: Feminism and the Subversion of Identity.* 10th anniversary ed. New York: Routledge.

———. 2007. "Wittig's Materialist Practice: Universalizing a Minority Point of View." *GLQ* 13:519–33.

Butrica, James L. 2005. "Some Myths and Anomalies in the Study of Roman Sexuality." Pages 209–69 in *Same-Sex Desire and Love in Greco-Roman Antiquity and in the Classical Tradition of the West.* Edited by Beert C. Verstraete and Vernon Provencal. New York: Harrington Park.

Byrne, Brendan J. 1988. *Paul and the Christian Woman.* Collegeville, MN: Liturgical Press.

Cadbury, Henry J. 1958. "A Qumran Parallel to Paul." *HTR* 51:1–2.

Cahill, Sean. 2007. "The Anti-Gay Marriage Movement." Pages 155–91 in *The Politics of Same-Sex Marriage.* Edited by Craig A. Rimmerman and Clyde Wilcox. Chicago: University of Chicago Press.

Calef, Susan. 2009. "*Kephalē,* Coverings, and Cosmology: The Impenetrable 'Logic' of 1 Corinthians 11:2–16." Pages 21–44 in *Women, Gender, and Religion.* Edited by Susan Calef and Ronald A. Simkins. Journal of Religion and Society Sup 5. Omaha, NE: Creighton University Kripke Center.

Campbell, David C., and Carin Robinson. 2007. "Religious Coalitions for and against Gay Marriage: The Culture War Rages On." Pages 131–54 in *The Politics of Same-Sex Marriage.* Edited by Craig A. Rimmerman and Clyde Wilcox. Chicago: University of Chicago Press.

Cantor, Donald J., Elizabeth Cantor, James C. Black, and Campbell D. Barrett, eds. 2006. *Same-Sex Marriage: The Legal and Psychological Evolution in America.* Middletown, CT: Wesleyan University Press.

Carlé, Graeme. 1998. *Because of the Angels: Unveiling 1 Corinthians 11:2–16.* Paraparaumu Beach, NZ: Emmaus Road.

Carter, David. 2004. *Stonewall: The Riots that Sparked the Gay Revolution.* New York: St. Martin's.

Case, Sue-Ellen. 1989. "Towards a Butch-Femme Aesthetic." Pages 282–99 in *Making a Spectacle: Feminist Essays on Contemporary Women's Theatre.* Edited by Lynda Hart. Ann Arbor: University of Michigan Press.

"The Case for Gay Marriage." 2004. *The Economist,* 28 February, 9.

Castelli, Elizabeth A. 1991a. "'I Will Make Mary Male': Pieties of the Body and Gender Transformation of Christian Women in Late Antiquity." Pages 29–49 in *Body Guards: The Cultural Politics of Gender Ambiguity*. Edited by Julia Epstein and Kristina Straub. New York: Routledge.

———. 1991b. *Imitating Paul: A Discourse of Power*. Literary Currents in Biblical Interpretation. Louisville: Westminster John Knox.

———. 1994. "Heteroglossia, Hermeneutics, and History: A Review Essay of Recent Feminist Studies of Early Christianity." *JFSR* 10:73–98.

———. 1999. "Paul on Women and Gender." Pages 221–35 in *Women and Christian Origins*. Edited by Ross Shepard Kraemer and Mary Rose D'Angelo. New York: Oxford University Press.

———. 2004. "The *Ekklēsia* of Women and/as Utopian Space: Locating the Work of Elisabeth Schüssler Fiorenza in Feminist Utopian Thought." Pages 36–52 in *On the Cutting Edge: The Study of Women in Biblical Worlds: Essays in Honor of Elisabeth Schüssler Fiorenza*. Edited by Jane Schaberg, Alice Bach, and Esther Fuchs. New York: Continuum.

Castelli, Elizabeth A., David Halperin, Ann Pellegrini, Ken Stone, Deirdre Good, and Natalie Boymel Kampen. 1998. "Lesbian Historiography before the Name?" *GLQ* 4:557–606.

Cervin, Richard S. 1989. "Does Κεφαλή Mean 'Source' or 'Authority Over' in Greek Literature? A Rebuttal." *TJ* 10:85–112.

Chakkalakal, Pauline. 1997. "Paul and Women: A Critical Reflection." *Jeevadhara* 27:188–203.

Chambers, Ross. 2002. "Strategic Constructivism? Sedgwick's Ethics of Inversion." Pages 165–80 in *Regarding Sedgwick: Essays on Queer Culture and Critical Theory*. Edited by Stephen M. Barber and David L. Clark. New York: Routledge.

Chambers, Samuel, and Terrell Carver. 2008. *Judith Butler and Political Theory: Troubling Politics*. Abingdon, UK: Routledge.

Childs, James M. 2009. "Human Sexuality: A Manifold Discussion." *Dialog* 48:1–3.

Chisholm, Dianne. 1993. "Lesbianizing Love's Body: Interventionist Imag(in)ings of Monique Wittig." Pages 196–216 in *Reimagining Women: Representations of Women in Culture*. Edited by Shirley Neuman and Glennis Stephenson. Toronto: University of Toronto Press.

Christian, Ed. 1999. "Prophets under God's Authority: Headcoverings in 1 Corinthians 11.1–16." *Journal of the Adventist Theological Society* 10:291–95.

"Church to Debate Nature of Marriage." n.d. anglicantaonga.org.nz. http://tinyurl.com/SBL0685c1.

Clague, Julie. 2005. "Symbolism and the Power of Art: Female Representations of Christ Crucified." Pages 29–55 in *Bodies in Question: Gender, Religion, Text*. Edited by Darlene Bird and Yvonne Sherwood. Aldershot, UK: Ashgate.

Clark, Elizabeth, and Herbert Richardson, eds. 1977. *Women and Religion: A Feminist Sourcebook of Christian Thought*. New York: Harper & Row.

Clark, Gillian. 1982. "The Women at Corinth." *Theology* 85:256–62.

Clark, Gordon H. 1991. *First Corinthians: A Contemporary Commentary*. 2nd ed. Trinity Paper 29. Jefferson, MD: Trinity Foundation.

Clark, Russell, and Elaine Hatfield. 1989. "Gender Differences in Receptivity to Sexual Offers." *Journal of Psychology and Human Sexuality* 2:39–55.

Clines, David J. A. 2003. "Paul, the Invisible Man." Pages 181–92 in *New Testament Masculinities*. Edited by Stephen D. Moore and Janice Capel Anderson. SemeiaSt 45. Atlanta: Society of Biblical Literature.

Cobb, John B. 1983. "God and Feminism." Pages 75–91 in *Talking about God: Doing Theology in the Context of Modern Pluralism*. Edited by John B. Cobb and David Tracy. New York: Seabury.

Cohen, Cathy J. 1997. "Punks, Bulldaggers, and Welfare Queens: The Radical Potential of Queer Politics?" *GLQ* 3:437–65.

Cole, Edwin Louis. 1992. *On Becoming a Real Man*. Nashville: Nelson.

Coleman, Simon. 2005. "An Empire on a Hill? The Christian Right and the Right to be Christian in America." *Anthropological Quarterly* 78:653–71.

Colette. 1974. *Retreat from Love*. Translated by Margaret Crosland. London: Owen.

Collier, Diane M., and Deborah F. Sawyer. 1999. "From Isolation to Integration?" Pages 11–24 in *Is There a Future for Feminist Theology?* Edited by Deborah F. Sawyer and Diane M. Collier. STS 4. Sheffield: Sheffield Academic.

Collins, Raymond F. 1999. *First Corinthians*. SP. Collegeville, MN: Liturgical Press.

Comstock, Gary David. 1993. *Gay Theology without Apology*. Cleveland: Pilgrim.

Conway, Colleen M. 2008. *Behold the Man: Jesus and Greco-Roman Masculinity*. Oxford: Oxford University Press.

Conzelmann, Hans. 1975. *1 Corinthians: A Commentary on the First Epistle to the Corinthians*. Translated by James W. Leitch. Hermeneia. Philadelphia: Fortress.

Cooper, Sarah. 2000. *Relating to Queer Theory: Rereading Sexual Self-Definition with Irigaray, Kristeva, Wittig and Cixous*. Modern French Identities 3. Bern: Lang.

Cope, Karin. 1991. "Plastic Actions: Linguistic Strategies and *Le Corps lesbien*." *Hypatia* 6:74–96.

Cope, Lamar. 1978. "1 Cor 11:2–16: One Step Further." *JBL* 97:435–36.

Corrington, Gail Paterson. 1991. "The 'Headless Woman': Paul and the Language of the Body in 1 Cor 11:2–16." *PRSt* 18:223–31.

Countryman, L. William. 2003. Review of *The Bible and Homosexual Practice*, by Robert Gagnon. *ATR* 85:196–97.

———. 2007. *Dirt, Greed, and Sex: Sexual Ethics in the New Testament and Their Implications for Today*. Rev. ed. Minneapolis: Fortress.

Craig, Clarence Tucker. 1953. "The First Epistle to the Corinthians." Pages 32–62 in *Corinthians; Galatians; Ephesians*. Vol. 10 of *The Interpreter's Bible*: Edited by George Arthur Buttrick. New York: Abingdon-Cokesbury.

Crocker, Cornelia Cyss. 2004. *Reading 1 Corinthians in the Twenty-First Century*. New York: T&T Clark.

Crosland, Margaret. 1976. "Introduction." Pages v–viii in *The Lesbian Body*, by Monique Wittig. Translated by David Le Vay. New York: Avon.

Crowder, Diane Griffin. 1983. "Amazons and Mothers? Monique Wittig, Hélène Cixous and Theories of Women's Writing." *Contemporary Literature* 24:117–44.

———. 2005. "Universalizing Materialist Lesbianism." Pages 63–86 in *On Monique Wittig: Theoretical, Political, and Literary Essays*. Edited by Namascar Shaktini. Urbana: University of Illinois Press.

———. 2007. "From the Straight Mind to Queer Theory: Implications for Political Movement." *GLQ* 13:489–503.

Culbertson, Philip. 2008. "Eros and Liberation: New Ways of Thinking about Sex, Gender, and Sexuality." *New Zealand Journal of Counseling* 28:41–55.

Daly, Mary. 1973. *Beyond God the Father: Toward a Philosophy of Women's Liberation*. Boston: Beacon.

———. 1974. "The Qualitative Leap beyond Patriarchal Religion." *Quest* 1:29–32.

D'Angelo, Mary Rose. 1990. "Women Partners in the New Testament." *JSFR* 6:65–86.

———. 1995. "Veils, Virgins, and the Tongues of Men and Angels: Women's Heads in Early Christianity." Pages 131–64 in *Off with Her Head! The Denial of Women's Identity in Myth, Religion, and Culture*. Edited by Howard Eilberg-Schwartz and Wendy Doniger. Berkeley: University of California Press.

Davidson, James. 2007. *The Greeks and Greek Love: A Radical Reappraisal of Homosexuality in Ancient Greece*. London: Weidenfeld & Nicolson.

Dawes, Gregory. 1998. *The Body in Question: Metaphor and Meaning in the Interpretation of Ephesians 5:21–33*. BibInt 30. Leiden: Brill.

Dawson, Robert Dale. 2007. *The Resurrection in Karl Barth*. Barth Studies Series. Aldershot, UK: Ashgate.

DeConick, April. 2007. "How We Talk about Christology Matters." Pages 1–23 in *Israel's God and Rebecca's Children: Christology and Community in Early Judaism and Christianity; Essays in Honor of Larry Hurtado and Alan F. Segal*. Edited by David B. Capes, April D. DeConick, Helen K. Bond, and Troy Miller. Waco, TX: Baylor University Press.

D'Emilio, John. 1998. *Sexual Politics, Sexual Communities: The Making of a Homosexual Minority in the United States, 1940–1970*. 2nd ed. Chicago: University of Chicago Press.

Delobel, Joël. 1986. "1 Cor 11,2–16: Towards a Coherent Interpretation." Pages 369–89 in *L'Apôtre Paul: Personnalité, Style et Conception du Ministère*. Edited by A. Vanhoye. BETL 73. Leuven: Leuven University Press and Peeters.

Demirer, Derya Keskin, and Nicole Wilkinson Duran. 2004. "1 Corinthians 11 in Christian and Muslim Dialogue." Pages 451–54 in *Global Bible Commentary*. Edited by Daniel Patte. Nashville: Abingdon.

Denniston, J. D. 1954. *The Greek Particles*. 2nd ed. Oxford: Clarendon.

Devarrieux, Claire. 1999. "J'ai connu la guillotine: Interview with Monique Wittig." *Libération*, 17 June, iii.

Dodd, Brian. 1999. *Paul's Paradigmatic "I": Personal Example as Literary Strategy*. JSNTSup 177. Sheffield: Sheffield Academic.

Donadey, Anne, and Françoise Lionnet. 2007. "Feminisms, Genders, Sexualities." Pages 225–44 in *Introduction to Scholarship in Modern Languages and Literatures*. 3rd ed. Edited by David G. Nicholls. New York: Modern Language Association of America.

Doniger, Wendy. 1995. "'Put a Bag over Her Head': Beheading Mythological Women." Pages 15–31 in *Off with Her Head! The Denial of*

Women's Identity in Myth, Religion, and Culture. Edited by Howard Eilberg-Schwartz and Wendy Doniger. Berkeley: University of California Press.

Donne, John. 1992. *The Complete Poems*. E-book. Cambridge: Chadwyck-Healey.

Donovan, Josephine. 1990. "Animal Rights and Feminist Theory." *Signs* 15:350–75.

Dorrien, Gary. 2000. *The Barthian Revolt in Modern Theology: Theology without Weapons*. Louisville: Westminster John Knox.

Dover, K. J. 1978. *Greek Homosexuality*. London: Duckworth.

Dowling, Robin. 1994. "Headcoverings: An Exposition of 1 Corinthians 11:2–16." *Evangel* 12:37–40.

Doyle, Robert. 1987. "Created Male and Female: Sexuality, Personhood and the Image of God." Pages 43–56 in *Personhood, Sexuality and Christian Ministry*. Edited by B. G. Webb. Homebush West, Australia: Lancer.

Dreyfuss, Robert. 1999. "Holy War on Gays." *Rolling Stone*, 18 March, 38–41.

Duberman, Martin. 1994. *Stonewall*. New York: Plume.

Duffy, Jean H. 1990. "Monique Wittig." Pages 201–28 in *Beyond the Nouveau Roman: Essays on the Contemporary French Novel*. Edited by Michael Tilby. Berg French Studies. New York: Berg.

Duggan, Lisa. 1992. "Making It Perfectly Queer." *Socialist Review* 22:11–31.

Dunn, James D. G. 1989. *Christology in the Making: An Inquiry into the Origins of the Doctrine of Incarnation*. 2nd ed. London: SCM.

———. 1995. *1 Corinthians*. NTG. Sheffield: Sheffield Academic.

———. 2004. "Reconstructions of Corinthian Christianity and the Interpretation of 1 Corinthians." Pages 295–310 in *Christianity at Corinth: The Quest for the Pauline Church*. Edited by Edward Adams and David G. Horrell. Louisville: Westminster John Knox.

Dworkin, Andrea, and Catherine MacKinnon. 1988. *Pornography and Civil Rights: A New Day for Women's Equality*. Minneapolis: Organizing Against Pornography.

Ecarnot, Catherine Rognon. 2005. "Politics and Poetics of Travesty in Monique Wittig's Fiction." Pages 180–86 in *On Monique Wittig: Theoretical, Political, and Literary Essays*. Edited by Namascar Shaktini. Translated by Eileen Powis, Arthur Tang, and Namascar Shaktini. Urbana: University of Illinois Press.

Edelman, Lee. 1994. *Homographesis: Essays in Gay Literary and Cultural Theory*. New York: Routledge.

Edwards, Anne. 1989. "The Sex/Gender Distinction: Has It Outlived Its Usefulness?" *AFS* 10:1–12.

Ehrensperger, Kathy. 2004. *That We May Be Mutually Encouraged: Feminism and the New Perspective in Pauline Studies*. New York: T&T Clark.

Eilberg-Schwartz, Howard. 1995. "Introduction: The Spectacle of the Female Head." Pages 1–13 in *Off with Her Head! The Denial of Women's Identity in Myth, Religion, and Culture*. Edited by Howard Eilberg-Schwartz and Wendy Doniger. Berkeley: University of California Press.

Elliot, Elisabeth. 2006a. "The Essence of Femininity: A Personal Perspective." Pages 394–99 in *Recovering Biblical Manhood and Womanhood: A Response to Evangelical Feminism*. Edited by John Piper and Wayne Grudem. Wheaton, IL: Crossway. http://www.desiringgod.org/books/recovering-biblical-manhood-and-womanhood.

———. 2006. *The Mark of a Man: Following Christ's Example of Masculinity*. Grand Rapids: Revell.

Ellis, J. Edward. 2007. *Paul and Ancient Views of Sexual Desire: Paul's Sexual Ethics in 1 Thessalonians 4, 1 Corinthians 7 and Romans 1*. LNTS 354. London: T&T Clark.

Ellsworth, Roger. 1995. *Strengthening Christ's Church: The Message of 1 Corinthians*. Welwyn Commentary Series. Durham: Evangelical Press.

Engberg-Pedersen, Troels. 1991. "1 Corinthians 11:16 and the Character of Pauline Exhortation." *JBL* 110:679–89.

———. 2000. *Paul and the Stoics*. Louisville: Westminster John Knox.

Engels, Frederick. 1972. *The Origin of the Family, Private Property and the State: In the Light of the Researches of Lewis H. Morgan*. Translated by Alec West. London: Lawrence & Wishart.

Englebrecht, Penelope. 1990. "'Lifting Belly Is a Language': The Postmodern Lesbian Subject." *FS* 16:85–114.

Epps, Brad, and Jonathan Katz. 2007. "Monique Wittig's Materialist Utopia and Radical Critique." *GLQ* 13:423–54.

Eskridge, William N., and Darren R. Spedale. 2006. *Gay Marriage: For Better or for Worse? What We've Learned from the Evidence*. Oxford: Oxford University Press.

Evans, Ernest. 1930. *The Epistles of Paul the Apostle to the Corinthians*. Clarendon Bible 13. Oxford: Clarendon.

Evans, Mary. 1983. *Woman in the Bible*. Exeter: Paternoster.

Faludi, Susan. 1999. *Stiffed: The Betrayal of Modern Man*. London: Vintage.

Farnell, Lewis Richard. 1971. *The Cults of the Greek States*. 5 vols. 1896–1909. Repr., Chicago: Aegean.

Fatum, Lone. 1989. "Women, Symbolic Universe and Structures of Silence: Challenges and Possibilities in Androcentric Texts." *ST* 43:61–80.

———. 1995. "Image of God and Glory of Man: Women in the Pauline Congregations." Pages 50–133 in *The Image of God: Gender Models in Judaeo-Christian Tradition*. Edited by Kari Elisabeth Børresen. Minneapolis: Fortress.

———. 2005. "Christ Domesticated: The Household Theology of the Pastorals as Political Strategy." Pages 175–207 in *The Formation of the Early Church*. Edited by Jostein Ådna. WUNT 183. Tübingen: Mohr Siebeck.

Fee, Gordon. 1987. *The First Epistle to the Corinthians*. NICNT. Grand Rapids: Eerdmans.

Fessenden, Tracy, Nicholas F. Radel, and Magdalena J. Zaborowska, eds. 2001. *The Puritan Origins of American Sex: Religion, Sexuality, and National Identity in American Literature*. New York: Routledge.

Findlay, Heather. 1989. "Is There a Lesbian in This Text? Derrida, Wittig, and the Politics of the Three Women." Pages 59–69, 252–57 in *Coming to Terms: Feminism, Theory, Politics*. Edited by Elizabeth Weed. New York: Routledge.

Finney, Mark. 2010. "Honour, Head-coverings and Headship: 1 Corinthians 11.2–16 in Its Social Context." *JSNT* 33:31–58.

Fitzmyer, Joseph A. 1957–1958. "A Feature of Qumrân Angelology and the Angels of I Cor. xi. 10." *NTS* 4:48–58.

———. 1989. "Another Look at ΚΕΦΑΛΗ in 1 Corinthians 11.3." *NTS* 35:503–11.

———. 1993. "*Kephalē* in I Corinthians 11:3." *Int* 47:52–59.

———. 2008. *First Corinthians*. AB 32. New Haven: Yale University Press.

Foerster, Werner. 1964. "ἐξουσία." *TDNT* 2:560–75.

Foreman, K. J. 1962. *Romans, Corinthians*. Layman's Bible Commentaries. London: SCM.

Foster, Rachel Ann, and John P. Keating. 1992. "Research Note: Measuring Androcentrism in the Western God-Concept." *JSSR* 31:366–75.

Foucault, Michel. 1988. *The Care of the Self*. Vol. 3 of *The History of Sexuality*. Translated by Robert Hurley. New York: Vintage Books.

———. 1990a. *An Introduction*. Vol. 1 of *The History of Sexuality*. Translated by Robert Hurley. New York: Vintage Books.

———. 1990b. *The Use of Pleasure*. Vol. 2 of *The History of Sexuality*. Translated by Robert Hurley. New York: Vintage Books.

Foxhall, Lin, and John Salmon, eds. 1998a. *Thinking Men: Masculinity and Its Self-Representation in the Classical Tradition*. Leicester-Nottingham Studies in Ancient Society 7. London: Routledge.

———, eds. 1998b. *When Men Were Men: Masculinity, Power, and Identity in Classical Antiquity*. Leicester-Nottingham Studies in Ancient Society 8. London: Routledge.

Fredriksen, Paula. 2007. "Mandatory Retirement: Ideas in the Study of Christian Origins Whose Time Has Come to Go." Pages 25–38 in *Israel's God and Rebecca's Children: Christology and Community in Early Judaism and Christianity: Essays in Honor of Larry W. Hurtado and Alan F. Segal*. Edited by David B. Capes, April D. DeConick, Helen K. Bond, and Troy Miller. Waco, TX: Baylor University Press.

Freed, E. D. 2005. *The Morality of Paul's Converts*. London: Equinox.

Freeland, Cynthia A. ed. 1998. *Feminist Interpretations of Aristotle*. Re-Reading the Canon. University Park: Pennsylvania State University Press.

Fromm, Erich. 1941. *Escape from Freedom*. New York: Rinehart & Winston.

Frontisi-Ducroux, Françoise, and François Lissarrague. 1990. "From Ambiguity to Ambivalence: A Dionysiac Excursion through the 'Anakreontic' Vases." Translated by Robert Lamberton. Pages 211–56 in *Before Sexuality: The Construction of Erotic Experience in the Ancient Greek World*. Edited by David M. Halperin, John J. Winkler, and Froma I. Zeitlin. Princeton: Princeton University Press.

Fuchs, Esther. 2003. "Men in Biblical Feminist Scholarship." *JFSR* 19:93–114.

Fuseworks Media. 2009. "Trial Told of Sophie Elliott's Disfiguring Injuries." Voxy.co.nx. http://tinyurl.com/SBL0685r1.

Fuss, Diana. 1989. *Essentially Speaking: Feminism, Nature and Difference*. New York: Routledge.

Gagnon, Robert. 2001. *The Bible and Homosexual Practice: Texts and Hermeneutics*. Nashville: Abingdon.

———. 2002. "A Response to Walter Wink's *Christian Century* Review of *The Bible and Homosexual Practice*." RobGagnon.net. http://tinyurl.com/SBL0685p1.

Gagnon, Robert. 2005. "Why the Disagreement over the Biblical Witness on Homosexual Practice? A Response to David G. Myers and Letha

Dawson Scanzoni, *What God Has Joined Together?"* *Reformed Review* 59:19–130.

———. 2006a. "Dale Martin's Poststructuralist Persona and His Historical-Critical Real Self." RobGagnon.net. http://tinyurl.com/SBL0685g1.

———. 2006b. "Jack Rogers's Flawed Use of Analogical Reasoning in *Jesus, the Bible, and Homosexuality.*" RobGagnon.net. http://tinyurl.com/SBL0685h1.

———. 2009. "What Should Faithful Lutherans in the ELCA Do?" RobGagnon.net. http://tinyurl.com/SBL0685i1.

Garland, David E. 2003. *1 Corinthians.* BECNT. Grand Rapids: Baker Academic.

Garrison, Brenda. 2009. *Princess Unaware: Finding the Fabulous in Everyday.* Cincinnati: Standard.

Geytenbeek, A. C. van. 1962. *Musonius Rufus and Greek Diatribe.* Revised and translated by B. L. Hijmans. Wijsgerige Teksten en Studies 8. Assen: Van Gorcum.

Gielen, Marlis von. 1999. "Beten und Prophezeien mit unverhültem Kopf? Die Kontroverse zwischen Paulus und der korinthischen Gemeinde um die Wahrung der Geschlechtsrollensymbolik in 1 Kor 11,2–16." *ZNW* 90:220–49.

Gieschen, Charles A. 1998. *Angelomorphic Christology: Antecedents and Early Evidence.* AGJU 42. Leiden: Brill.

Gill, David W. J. 1990. "The Importance of Roman Portraiture for Head-Coverings in 1 Corinthians 11:2–16." *TynBul* 41:245–60.

———. 1993. "In Search of the Social Élite in the Corinthian Church." *TynBul* 44:323–37.

Glancy, Jennifer. 2004. "Boasting of Beatings (2 Corinthians 11:23–25)." *JBL* 123:99–135.

Gleason, Maud. 1990. "The Semiotics of Gender: Physiognomy and Self-Fashioning in the Second Century C.E." Pages 389–415 in *Before Sexuality: The Construction of Erotic Experience in the Ancient Greek World.* Edited by David M. Halperin, John J. Winkler, and Froma I. Zeitlin. Princeton: Princeton University Press.

Glen, J. S. 1965. *Pastoral Problems in First Corinthians.* London: Epworth.

Glick, Lesia. 2005. *Free to Be a Princess: Self-Esteem Bible Study for Women.* Greenville, SC: Destiny Publishing Group.

Godelier, Maurice. 1981. "The Origins of Male Domination." *New Left Review* 127, May–June, 3–17.

Gold, Barbara. 1998. "'The House I Live in Is Not My Own': Women's Bodies in Juvenal's *Satires*." *Arethusa* 31:369–86.

Goldman, Ruth. 1996. "Who Is That *Queer* Queer? Exploring Norms around Sexuality, Race, and Class in Queer Theory." Pages 169–82 in *Queer Studies: A Lesbian, Gay, Bisexual, and Transgender Anthology*. Edited by Brett Beemym and Mickey Eliason. New York: New York University Press.

Gorman, Michael. 2004. *Apostle of the Crucified Lord: A Theological Introduction to Paul and His Letters*. Grand Rapids: Eerdmans.

Goss, Robert. 1993. *Jesus ACTED UP: A Gay and Lesbian Manifesto*. San Francisco: HarperCollins.

———. 1999. "Queer Theologies as Transgressive Metaphors: New Paradigms for Hybrid Sexual Theologies." *T&S* 10:43–53.

———. 2002. *Queering Christ: Beyond Jesus ACTED UP*. Cleveland: Pilgrim.

Goss, Robert E., and Amy Adams Squire Strongheart, eds. 1997. *Our Families, Our Values: Snapshots of Queer Kinship*. Binghamton: Haworth.

Goss, Robert E., and Mona West. 2000a. "Introduction." Pages 3–9 in *Take Back the Word: A Queer Reading of the Bible*. Edited by Robert E. Goss and Mona West. Cleveland: Pilgrim.

———, eds. 2000b. *Take Back the Word: A Queer Reading of the Bible*. Cleveland: Pilgrim.

Gössmann, Elisabeth. 1999. "The Image of God and the Human Being in Women's Counter-Tradition." Pages 26–56 in *Is There a Future for Feminist Theology?* Edited by Deborah F. Sawyer and Diane M. Collier. STS 4. Sheffield: Sheffield Academic.

Goulder, Michael D. 2001. *Paul and the Competing Mission in Corinth*. Library of Pauline Studies. Peabody, MA: Hendrickson.

Green, Jesse. 1999. "Gays and Monsters." *New York Times Magazine*, 13 June, 13.

Greig, James C. G. 1957–1958. "Women's Hats: 1 Corinthians xi.1–16." *ExpTim* 69:156–57.

Grenz, Stanley J. 1998. *Welcoming but Not Affirming: An Evangelical Response to Homosexuality*. Louisville: Westminster John Knox.

Grimshaw, Mike. 2006. "Religion, Terror and the End of the Postmodern: Rethinking the Responses." *IJBS* 3: http://tinyurl.com/SBL0685j1.

Groothuis, Rebecca Merrill. 2004. "'Equal in Being, Unequal in Role': Exploring the Logic of Woman's Subordination." Pages 301–33 in *Discovering Biblical Equality: Complementarity without Hierarchy*. Edited by Ronald W. Pierce and Rebecca Merrill Groothuis. Downers Grove, IL: InterVarsity Press.

Groothuis, Rebecca Merrill, and Ronald W. Pierce. 2004. "Introduction." Pages 13–19 in *Discovering Biblical Equality: Complementarity without Hierarchy*. Edited by Ronald W. Pierce and Rebecca Merrill Groothuis. Downers Grove, IL: InterVarsity Press.

Gross, Larry P. 1993. *Contested Closets: The Politics and Ethics of Outing*. Minneapolis: University of Minnesota Press.

Grosz, Elizabeth. 1989. *Sexual Subversions: Three French Feminists*. St Leonards, Australia: Allen & Unwin.

Grudem, Wayne. 1982. *The Gift of Prophecy in 1 Corinthians*. Washington, DC: University Press of America.

———. 1985. "Does κεφαλή Mean 'Source' or 'Authority over' in Greek Literature? A Survey of 2,336 Examples." *TJ* 6:38–59.

———. 1987. "Prophecy—Yes, But Teaching—No: Paul's Consistent Advocacy of Women's Participation without Governing Authority." *JETS* 30:11–23.

———. 1990. "The Meaning of κεφαλή ('Head'): A Response to Recent Studies." *TJ* 11:3–72.

———. 2000. *The Gift of Prophecy in the New Testament and Today*. Rev. ed. Wheaton, IL: Crossway.

———. 2001. "The Meaning of κεφαλή ('Head'): An Evaluation of New Evidence, Real and Alleged." *JETS* 44:25–65.

———. 2004. *Evangelical Feminism and Biblical Truth: An Analysis of More Than One Hundred Disputed Questions*. Sisters, OR: Multnomah.

———. 2006a. *Countering the Claims of Evangelical Feminism*. Sisters, OR: Multnomah.

———. 2006b. *Evangelical Feminism: A New Path to Liberalism?* Wheaton, IL: Crossway.

Gruen, Lori. 1993. "Dismantling Oppression: An Analysis of the Connection between Woman and Animals." Pages 60–90 in *Ecofeminism: Women, Animals, Nature*. Edited by Greta C. Gaard. Philadelphia: Temple University Press.

Guest, Deryn. 2001. "Battling for the Bible: Academy, Church and the Gay Agenda." *T&S* 15:66–93.

———. 2005. *When Deborah Met Jael: Lesbian Biblical Hermeneutics*. London: SCM.

Guest, Deryn, Robert E. Goss, Mona West, and Thomas Bohache, eds. 2006. *The Queer Bible Commentary*. London: SCM.

Gundry, Robert H. 2010. *Commentary on the New Testament: Verse-by-Verse Explanations with a Literal Translation*. Peabody, MA: Hendrickson.

Gundry-Volf, Judith. 1997. "Gender and Creation in 1 Corinthians 11:2–16: A Study in Paul's Theological Method." Pages 151–71 in *Evangelium, Schriftauslegung, Kirche: Festschrift für Peter Stuhmacher zum 65. Geburtstag*. Edited by Jostein Ådna, Scot Hafeman, and Oscar Hofius. Göttingen: Vandenhoeck & Ruprecht.

Günther, Renate. 1998. "Are Lesbians Women? The Relationship between Lesbianism and Feminism in the Work of Luce Irigaray and Monique Wittig." Pages 73–90 in *Gay Signatures: Gay and Lesbian Theory, Fiction and Film in France, 1945–1995*. Edited by Owen Heathcote, Alex Hughes, and James S. Williams. Berg French Studies. Oxford: Berg.

Haacker, Klaus. 1994. "Exegetische Gesichtspunkte zum Thema Homosexualität." *TBei* 25:173–80.

Hahm, David E. 1977. *The Origins of Stoic Cosmology*. Columbus: Ohio State University Press.

Haines, Leah. 2004a. "Black Shirts Spark Anger." *The Dominion Post*, 24 August, A1, A4.

———. 2004b. "March Arouses Nazi Fears." *The Press*, 24 August, A3.

Hale, Jacob. 1996. "Are Lesbians Women?" *Hypatia* 11:94–121.

Hall, Donald E. 1994. "On the Unmaking and Making of Monsters: Christian Socialism, Muscular Christianity, and the Metaphorization of Class Conflict." Pages 45–65 in *Muscular Christianity: Embodying the Victorian Age*. Edited by Donald E. Hall. Cambridge Studies in Nineteenth Century Literature and Culture 2. Cambridge: Cambridge University Press.

Hallett, Judith P. 1988. "Roman Attitudes toward Sex." Pages 1265–78 in vol. 2 of *Civilizations of the Ancient Mediterranean: Greece and Rome*. Edited by Michael Grant and Rachel Kitzinger. 3 vols. New York: Scribner's Sons.

———. 1989. "Female Homoeroticism and the Denial of Roman Reality in Latin Literature." *Yale Journal of Criticism* 3:209–27.

Halperin, David M. 1990. *One Hundred Years of Homosexuality: And Other Essays on Greek Love*. New Ancient World. New York: Routledge.

———. 1995. *Saint Foucault: Towards a Gay Hagiography*. New York: Oxford University Press.

———. 2002a. "The First Homosexuality?" Pages 229–68 in *The Sleep of Reason: Erotic Experience and Sexual Ethics in Ancient Greece and*

Rome. Edited by Martha C. Nussbaum and Juha Sihvola. Chicago: University of Chicago Press.

———. 2002b. "Forgetting Foucault: Acts, Identities, and the History of Sexuality." Pages 21–54 in *The Sleep of Reason: Erotic Experience and Sexual Ethics in Ancient Greece and Rome.* Edited by Martha C. Nussbaum and Juha Sihvola. Chicago: University of Chicago Press.

———. 2002c. *How to Do the History of Homosexuality.* Chicago: University of Chicago Press.

Halperin, David M., and Valerie Traub. 2009. "Beyond Gay Pride." Pages 3–40 in *Gay Shame.* Edited by David M. Halperin and Valerie Traub. Chicago: University of Chicago Press.

Halperin, David M., John J. Winkler, and Froma I. Zeitlin, eds. 1990. *Before Sexuality: The Construction of Erotic Experience in the Ancient Greek World.* Princeton: Princeton University Press.

Handcock, Candice. 2000. "Redemptive TV Ministry." *Challenge Weekly,* 8 February, 1, 7.

Haraway, Donna J. 1988. "Situated Knowledges: The Science Question in Feminism and the Privilege of Partial Perspective." *FS* 14:575–99.

———. 2001. " 'Gender' for a Marxist Dictionary: The Sexual Politics of a Word." Pages 49–75 in *Women, Gender, and Religion: A Reader.* Edited by Elizabeth A. Castelli with Rosamond C. Rodman. New York: Palgrave.

Harrison, Beverley Wildung. 1985. *Making the Connections: Essays in Feminist Social Ethics.* Edited by Carol S. Robb. Boston: Beacon.

Harrison, Nonna Verna. 1994. "The Feminine Man in Late Antique Ascetic Piety." *USQR* 48.3–4:49–71.

Hart, Lynda. 1998. "Living under the Sign of the Cross: Some Speculations on Femme Femininity." Pages 214–23 in *Butch/Femme: Inside Lesbian Gender.* Edited by Sally Munt and Cherry Smyth. London: Cassell.

Hasian, M. A., and T. Parry-Evans. 1997. " 'A Stranger to Its Laws': Freedom, Civil Rights, and the Legal Ambiguity of *Romer V. Evans (1996).*" *Argumentation and Advocacy* 34:27–42.

Hayes, Susan. 1994. "Coming over All Queer." *New Statesman and Society,* 16 September, 14–15.

Hays, Richard B. 1986. "Relations Natural and Unnatural: A Response to John Boswell's Exegesis of Romans 1." *Journal of Religious Ethics* 14:184–215.

———. 1997. *First Corinthians.* IBC. Louisville: Westminster John Knox.

———. 2004. "Paul on the Relation between Men and Women." Pages 137–47 in *A Feminist Companion to Paul*. Edited by Amy-Jill Levine with Marianne Blickenstaff. FCNTECW 6. London: T&T Clark.

Heald, Cynthia. 1986. *Becoming a Woman of Excellence*. Colorado Springs: Navpress.

Hearon, Holly E. 2006. "1 and 2 Corinthians." Pages 606–23 in *The Queer Bible Commentary*. Edited by Deryn Guest, Robert E. Goss, Mona West, and Thomas Bohache. London: SCM.

Hegel, Georg Wilhelm Friedrich. 1975. *Lectures on the Philosophy of World History: Introduction, Reason in History*. Translated from the German edition of Johannes Hoffmeister by H. B. Nisbet. Cambridge Studies in the History and Theory of Politics. Cambridge: Cambridge University Press.

Heil, John Paul. 2005. *The Rhetorical Role of Scripture in 1 Corinthians*. SBLStBL 15. Atlanta: Society of Biblical Literature.

Heine, Susanne. 1987. *Women and Early Christianity: Are the Feminist Scholars Right?* Translated by John Bowden. London: SCM.

Henderson, Jeffrey. 1988. "Greek Attitudes toward Sex." Pages 1249–63 in vol. 2 of *Civilizations of the Ancient Mediterranean: Greece and Rome*. Edited by Michael Grant and Rachel Kitzinger. 3 vols. New York: Scribner's Sons.

Henderson, John. 1999. *Writing down Rome: Comedy, Satire, and Other Offences in Latin Poetry*. Oxford: Clarendon.

Hennessy, Rosemary. 1993. "Queer Theory: A Review of the *differences* Special Issue and Wittig's *The Straight Mind*." *Signs* 18:964–73.

Héring, Jean. 1949. *Première épître de saint Paul aux Corinthiens*. Commentaire du Nouveau Testament 7. Paris: Delachaux & Niestlé.

Hess, Richard S. 2004. "Equality with and without Innocence." Pages 79–95 in *Discovering Biblical Equality: Complementarity without Hierarchy*. Edited by Ronald W. Pierce and Rebecca Merrill Groothuis. Downers Grove, IL: InterVarsity Press.

Hewitt, Leah D. 1990. *Autobiographical Tightropes: Simone de Beauvoir, Nathalie Sarraute, Marguerite Duras, Monique Wittig, and Maryse Condé*. Lincoln: University of Nebraska Press.

Heyward, Carter. 1989. *Touching Our Strength: The Erotic as Power and the Love of God*. San Francisco: Harper & Row.

Higgins, Lynn. 1976. "Nouvelle Nouvelle Autobiographie: Monique Wittig's *Le Corps lesbien*." *Sub-Stance* 5:160–66.

Hiigel, John L. 2005. *Leadership in 1 Corinthians: A Case Study in Paul's Ecclesiology.* SBEC 57. Lewiston, NY: Mellen.

Hill, Lisa. 2001. "The First Wave of Feminism: Were the Stoics Feminist?" *History of Political Thought* 22:13–40.

Hjort, Birgitte Graakjær. 2001. "Gender Hierarchy or Religious Androgyny? Male-Female Interaction in the Corinthian Community—A Reading of 1 Cor. 11,2–16." *ST* 55:58–80.

Hoggard Creegan, Nicola, and Christine D. Pohl. 2005. *Living on the Boundaries: Evangelical Women, Feminism, and the Theological Academy.* Downers Grove, IL: InterVarsity Press.

Holland, Merlin. 2003. *Irish Peacock and Scarlet Marquess: The Real Trial of Oscar Wilde.* London: Fourth Estate.

Holmes, Andy. 2010. *My Princess Bible.* Carol Stream, IL: Tyndale House.

Hooker, Morna D. 1964. "Authority on Her Head: An Examination of I Cor. XI.10." *NTS* 10:410–16.

Horkheimer, Max, and Theodor W. Adorno. 2002. *Dialectic of Enlightenment: Philosophical Fragments.* Translated by Edmund Jephcott. Cultural Memory in the Present. Stanford, CA: Stanford University Press.

Hornsby, Teresa J. 2005. "The Gendered Sinner in Romans 1–7." Pages 143–66 in *Gender, Tradition, and Romans: Shared Ground, Uncertain Borders.* Edited by Cristina Grenholm and Daniel Patte. Romans through History and Cultures. New York: T&T Clark.

Horowitz, Maryanne Cline. 1976. "Aristotle and Woman." *Journal of the History of Biology* 9:183–213.

Horrell, David G. 1996. *The Social Ethos of the Corinthian Correspondence: Interests and Ideology from 1 Corinthians to 1 Clement.* SNTW. Edinburgh: T&T Clark.

Horrell, David G., and Edward Adams. 2004. "The Scholarly Quest for Paul's Church at Corinth: A Critical Survey." Pages 1–43 in *Christianity at Corinth: The Quest for the Pauline Church.* Edited by Edward Adams and David G. Horrell. Louisville: Westminster John Knox.

Horsley, Richard A. 1998. *1 Corinthians.* ANTC. Nashville: Abingdon.

———, ed. 2000. *Paul and Politics: Ekklesia, Israel, Imperium, Interpretation: Essays in Honor of Krister Stendahl.* Harrisburg, PA: Trinity Press International.

House, H. Wayne. 1988. "Should a Woman Prophesy or Preach before Men?" *BSac* 145:47–56.

Howard, J. Keir. 1983. "Neither Male nor Female: An Examination of the Status of Women in the New Testament." *EvQ* 55:31–42.

Huber, Lynn R. 2008. "Sexually Explicit? Re-reading Revelation's 144,000 Virgins as a Response to Roman Discourses." *Journal of Men, Masculinities and Spirituality* 2:3–28.

Huffer, Lynne. 2010. *Mad for Foucault: Rethinking the Foundations of Queer Theory*. Gender and Culture. New York: Columbia University Press.

Hughes, Alex. 2002. Review of *Relating to Queer Theory: Rereading Sexual Self-Definition with Irigaray, Kristeva, Wittig and Cixous*, by Sarah Cooper. *Modern Language Review* 97:991–92.

Humann, Roger J. 1981. "Exegesis Case Study: 1 Corinthians 11:2–16." *Consensus* 7:17–30.

Hurd, John C. 1983. *Origins of 1 Corinthians*. Macon, GA: Mercer University Press.

Hurley, James B. 1973. "Did Paul Require Veils or the Silence of Women? A Consideration of I Cor. 11:2–16 and I Cor. 14:33b–36." *WTJ* 35:190–220.

———. 1981. *Man and Woman in Biblical Perspective*. Contemporary Evangelical Perspectives. Grand Rapids: Academie Books.

Hurtado, Larry W. 2005. *How on Earth Did Jesus Become a God? Historical Questions about Earliest Devotion to Jesus*. Grand Rapids: Eerdmans.

Ince, Gwen. 2000. "Judge for Yourselves: Teasing out Some Knots in 1 Corinthians 11:2–16." *ABR* 48:59–71.

Ingebretsen, Edward J. 2001. *At Stake: Monsters and the Rhetoric of Fear in Public Culture*. Chicago: University of Chicago Press.

Irigaray, Luce. 1985. *This Sex Which Is Not One*. Translated by Catherine Porter with Carolyn Burke. Ithaca, NY: Cornell University Press.

———. 1991. "Questions to Emmanuel Levinas." Pages 178–89 in *The Irigaray Reader*. Edited by Margaret Whitford. Oxford: Basil Blackwell.

———. 1993. *An Ethics of Sexual Difference*. Translated by Carolyn Burke and Gillian Gill. Ithaca, NY: Cornell University Press.

Isaksson, Abel. 1965. *Marriage and Ministry in the New Temple: A Study with Special Reference to Mt. 19.13–12 [sic] and 1. Cor. 11.3–16*. ASNU 24. Lund: Gleerup.

Isherwood, Lisa. 2006. *The Power of Erotic Celibacy: Queering Heteropatriarchy*. Queering Theology. London: T&T Clark.

Ivarsson, Fredrik. 2007. "Vice Lists and Deviant Masculinity: The Rhetorical Function of 1 Corinthians 5:10–11 and 6:9–10." Pages 163–84 in *Mapping Gender in Ancient Religious Discourses*. Edited by Todd

Penner and Caroline Vander Stichele. BibInt 84. Atlanta: Society of Biblical Literature.

Jagger, Gill. 2008. *Judith Butler: Sexual Politics, Social Change and the Power of the Performative*. London: Routledge.

Jagose, Annamarie. 1996. *Queer Theory*. Dunedin, NZ: Otago University Press.

Jardine, Alice. 2007. "Thinking Wittig's Differences: 'Or, Failing That, Invent.'" *GLQ* 13:455–66.

Jardine, Alice A., and Paul Smith, eds. 1987. *Men in Feminism*. New York: Methuen.

Jeffreys, Sheila. 2003. *Unpacking Queer Politics: A Lesbian Feminist Perspective*. Cambridge: Polity.

Jenefsky, Cindy, and Diane Helene Miller. 1998. "Phallic Intrusion: Girl-Girl Sex in *Penthouse*." *Women's Study International Forum* 21:375–85.

Jennings, Theodore W., Jr. 2002. "YHWH as Erastes." Pages 36–74 in *Queer Commentary and the Hebrew Bible*. Edited by Ken Stone. JSOTSup 334. Sheffield: Sheffield Academic.

Jepsen, Dee. 2006. "Women in Society: The Challenge and the Call." Pages 388–93 in *Recovering Biblical Manhood and Womanhood: A Response to Evangelical Feminism*. Wheaton, IL: Crossway.

Jervis, L. Ann. 1993. "'But I Want You to Know …': Paul's Midrashic Intertextual Response to the Corinthian Worshipers (1 Cor 11:2–16)." *JBL* 112:231–46.

Jewett, Robert. 1979. "The Sexual Liberation of the Apostle Paul." JAARSup 47:55–87.

Jobling, David, Tina Pippin, and Ronald Schleifer. 2001. "Introduction: A Short Course in Postmodernism for Bible Readers." Pages 1–33 in *The Postmodern Bible Reader*. Edited by David Jobling, Tina Pippin, and Ronald Schleifer. Oxford: Blackwell.

Johnson, Alan F. 2004. *1 Corinthians*. InterVarsity Press New Testament Commentary Series. Downers Grove, IL: InterVarsity Press.

———. 2009. "A Review of the Scholarly Debate on the Meaning of 'Head' (κεφαλη) in Paul's Writings." *Ashland Theological Journal* 41:35–57.

Johnson, Nicole. 2003. *Keeping a Princess Heart: In a Not-So-Fairy-Tale World*. Nashville: Nelson.

Johnson, William Stacy. 2006. Review of *Jesus, The Bible, and Homosexuality: Explode the Myths, Heal the Church*, by Jack Rogers, and *The Bible and Homosexual Practice: Texts and Hermeneutics*, by Robert Gagnon. *ThTo* 63:386–94.

Jones, David W. 2003. "Egalitarianism and Homosexuality: Connected or Autonomous Ideologies?" *Journal for Biblical Manhood and Womanhood* 8:5–19.

Joy, Morny, Kathleen O'Grady, and Judith L. Poxon. 2002. "Introduction: French Feminisms and Religion." Pages 1–12 in *French Feminists on Religion: A Reader*. Edited by Morny Joy, Kathleen O'Grady, and Judith L. Poxon. London: Routledge.

Kader, Samuel. 1999. *Openly Gay, Openly Christian: How the Bible Really Is Gay Friendly*. San Francisco: Leyland.

Keener, Craig S. 1992. *Paul, Women, and Wives: Marriage and Women's Ministry in the Letters of Paul*. Peabody, MA: Hendrickson.

———. 2005. *1–2 Corinthians*. NCBC. Cambridge: Cambridge University Press.

Keuls, Eva C. 1985. *The Reign of the Phallus: Sexual Politics in Ancient Athens*. Berkeley: University of California Press.

Key, Daphne. 1984. "Women in the Church." Pages 141–52 in *The Role of Women*. Edited by Shirley Lees. When Christians Disagree. Leicester: InterVarsity Press.

Kirby, Vicki. 2006. *Judith Butler: Live Theory*. Live Theory. London: Continuum.

Kittel, Gerhard. 1920. *Rabbinica: Paulus im Talmud. Die "Macht" auf dem Haupte (1 Cor 11,10): Runde Zahlen*. Leipzig: Hinrichs.

Kittredge, Cynthia Briggs. 2000. "Corinthian Women Prophets and Paul's Argumentation in 1 Corinthians." Pages 103–9 in *Paul and Politics: Ekklesia, Israel, Imperium, Interpretation: Essays in Honor of Krister Stendahl*. Edited by Richard A. Horsley. Harrisburg, PA: Trinity Press International.

Kivisto, Peter. 1994. "The Rise or Fall of the Christian Right? Conflicting Reports from the Frontline." *Sociology of Religion* 55:223–27.

Klassen, William. 1984. "Musonius Rufus, Jesus, and Paul: Three First-Century Feminists." Pages 185–206 in *From Jesus to Paul: Studies in Honor of Francis Wright Beare*. Edited by P. Richardson and John C. Hurd. Waterloo, ON: Wilfrid Laurier University Press.

Klesse, Christian. 2007. *The Spectre of Promiscuity: Gay Male and Bisexual Non-monogamies and Polyamories*. Aldershot, UK: Ashgate.

Knust, Jennifer. 2006. *Abandoned to Lust: Sexual Slander and Ancient Christianity*. New York: Columbia University Press.

Köbler, Renata. 1989. *In the Shadow of Karl Barth: Charlotte von Kirschbaum*. Translated by Keith Crim. Louisville: Westminster.

Kraemer, Ross S. 1989. "Monastic Jewish Women in Greco-Roman Egypt: Philo Judaeus on the Therapeutrides." *Signs* 14:342–70.

Krauss, Rosalind E. 1997. "The Destiny of the Informé." Pages 235–52 in *Formless: A User's Guide*. Edited by Yve-Allain Bois and Rosalind E. Krauss. New York: Zone.

Kristeva, Julia. 1982. *Powers of Horror: An Essay on Abjection*. Translated by Leon S. Roudiez. New York: Columbia University Press.

Kroeger, Catherine Clark. 1987a. "The Apostle Paul and the Greco-Roman Cults of Women." *JETS* 30:25–38.

———. 1987b. "The Classical Concept of *Head* as 'Source.'" Pages 267–83 in *Equal to Serve: Women and Men Working Together Revealing the Gospel*. Edited by Gretchen Gabelein Hull. London: Scripture Union.

———. 1993. "Head." Pages 375–77 in *Dictionary of Paul and His Letters*. Edited by Gerald F. Hawthorne and Ralph P. Martin. Downers Grove, IL: InterVarsity Press.

———. 2004. "Does Belief in Women's Equality Lead to an Acceptance of Homosexual Practice?" *Priscilla Papers* 18.2:3–10.

———. 2006. "Toward an Understanding of Ancient Conceptions of 'Head.'" *Priscilla Papers* 20.3:4–8.

Kroeger, Richard, and Catherine Clark Kroeger. 1979. "St. Paul's Treatment of Misogyny, Gynephobia, and Sex Segregation in First Corinthians 11:2–6 [*sic*]." Pages 213–21 in vol. 2 of *Society of Biblical Literature 1979 Seminar Papers*. Edited by Paul J. Achtemeier. SBLSP 17. Missoula, MT: Scholars Press.

Lacan, Jacques. 1982. "The Meaning of the Phallus." Pages 74–85 in *Feminine Sexuality: Jacques Lacan and the école freudienne*. Edited by Juliet Mitchell and Jacqueline Rose. Translated by Jacqueline Rose. London: Macmillan.

Lakey, Michael J. 2010. *Image and Glory of God: 1 Corinthians 11:2–16 as a Case Study in Bible, Gender and Hermeneutics*. LNTS 418. London: T&T Clark.

Lambert, Christina D., and Sharon E. Robinson Kururpius. 2004. "Relationship of Gender Role Identity and Attitudes with Images of God." *American Journal of Pastoral Counseling* 7:55–75.

Laqueur, Thomas. 1990. *Making Sex: Body and Gender from the Greeks to Freud*. Cambridge: Harvard University Press.

Larson, Jennifer. 2004. "Paul's Masculinity." *JBL* 123:85–97.

Lauretis, Teresa de. 1988. "Sexual Indifference and Lesbian Representation." *Theatre Journal* 40:155–77.

———. 1991. "Queer Theory: Lesbian and Gay Sexualities: An Introduction." *Differences* 3:iii–xviii.

———. 1994. "Habit Changes." *Differences* 6.2–3:296–313.

———. 2005. "When Lesbians Were Not Women." Pages 51–62 in *On Monique Wittig: Theoretical, Political, and Literary Essays*. Edited by Namascar Shaktini. Urbana: University of Illinois Press.

Leipoldt, Johannes. 1954. *Die Frau in der antiken Welt und im Urchristentum*. Leipzig: Koehler & Amelang.

Leske, Adrian M. 1980. "Exegesis Case Study: 1 Corinthians 11:2–16." *Consensus* 6:11–17.

"Let Them Wed." 1996. *The Economist*, 6 January, 13–14.

Levine, Molly Myerowitz. 1995. "The Gendered Grammar of Ancient Mediterranean Hair." Pages 76–130 in *Off with Her Head! The Denial of Women's Identity in Myth, Religion, and Culture*. Edited by Howard Eilberg-Schwartz and Wendy Doniger. Berkeley: University of California Press.

L'Hoir, Francesca Santoro. 1992. *The Rhetoric of Gender Terms: "Man," "Woman," and the Portrayal of Character in Latin Prose*. Mnemosyne, Bibliotheca Classica Batava Sup 120. Leiden: Brill.

Linss, Wilhelm C. 1985. "St. Paul and Women." *Dialog* 24:36–40.

Linstrum, Cathy. 1988. "L'asile des femmes: Subjectivity and Femininity in Breton's *Nadja* and Wittig's *Le corps lesbien*." *Nottingham French Studies* 27:35–45.

Lissarrague, François. 1990. "The Sexual Life of Satyrs." Pages 53–81 in *Before Sexuality: The Construction of Erotic Experience in the Ancient Greek World*. Edited by David M. Halperin, John J. Winkler, and Froma I. Zeitlin. Princeton: Princeton University Press.

Lloyd, Genevieve. 1989. "Woman as Other: Sex, Gender and Subjectivity." *AFS* 10:13–22.

———. 1992. *The Man of Reason: "Male" and "Female" in Western Philosophy*. 2nd ed. London: Routledge.

Lloyd, Moya. 2007. *Judith Butler: From Norms to Politics*. Key Contemporary Thinkers. Cambridge: Polity.

Loader, William. 2007. *Enoch, Levi, and Jubilees on Sexuality: Attitudes towards Sexuality in the Early Enoch Literature, the Aramaic Levi Document, and the Book of Jubilees*. Attitudes towards Sexuality in Judaism and Christianity in the Hellenistic Greco-Roman Era. Grand Rapids: Eerdmans.

———. 2010. *Sexuality in the New Testament: Understanding the Key Texts.* London: SPCK.

Loisy, Alfred. 1935. *Remarques sur la littérature épistolaire du Nouveau Testament.* Paris: Émile Nourry.

Long, A. A. 2002. *Epictetus: A Stoic and Socratic Guide to Life.* Berkeley: University of California Press.

Loraux, Nicole. 1990. "Herakles: The Super Male and the Feminine." Translated by Robert Lamberton. Pages 21–35 in *Before Sexuality: The Construction of Erotic Experience in the Ancient Greek World.* Edited by David M. Halperin, John J. Winkler, and Froma I. Zeitlin. Princeton: Princeton University Press.

Lorde, Audre. 1983. "The Master's Tools Will Never Dismantle the Master's House: Comments at 'The Personal and the Political' Panel (Second Sex Conference, October 29, 1979)." Pages 98–101 in *This Bridge Called My Back: Writings by Radical Women of Color.* Edited by Cherríe Moraga and Gloria Anzaldúa. 2nd ed. New York: Kitchen Table/Women of Color Press.

Lösch, Stefan. 1947. "Christliche Frauen in Corinth (1 Cor. 11, 2–16)." *TQ* 127:216–61.

Loughlin, George. 2004. *Alien Sex: The Body and Desire in Cinema and Theology.* Challenges in Contemporary Theology. Oxford: Blackwell.

Lowe, Mary Elise. 2009. "Gay, Lesbian, and Queer Theologies: Origins, Contributions, and Challenges." *Dialog* 48:49–61.

Lowery, David K. 1986. "The Head Covering and the Lord's Supper in 1 Corinthians 11:2–34." *BSac* 143:155–63.

MacArthur, John. 1984. *1 Corinthians.* MacArthur NT Commentary. Chicago: Moody Press.

———. 1986. "God's High Calling for Women." Grace to You. http://tinyurl.com/SBL0685k1.

———. 2007. *1 Corinthians: Godly Solutions for Church Problems.* MacArthur Bible Studies. Nashville: Nelson.

MacCormack, Carol P. 1980. "Nature, Culture and Gender: A Critique." Pages 1–24 in *Nature, Culture, and Gender.* Edited by Carol P. MacCormack and Marilyn Strathern. Cambridge: Cambridge University Press.

MacDonald, Dennis Ronald. 1987. *There Is No Male and Female: The Fate of a Dominical Saying in Paul and Gnosticism.* HDR 20. Philadelphia: Fortress.

———. 1988. "Corinthian Veils and Gnostic Androgynes." Pages 276–92 in *Images of the Feminine in Gnosticism*. Edited by Karen C. King. Philadelphia: Fortress.

MacDonald, Margaret Y. 1990. "Women Holy in Body and Spirit: The Social Setting of 1 Corinthians 7." *NTS* 36:161–81.

———. 1999. "Reading Real Women through the Undisputed Letters of Paul." Pages 199–220 in *Women and Christian Origins*. Edited by Ross Shepard Kraemer and Mary Rose D'Angelo. New York: Oxford University Press.

———. 2004. "Virgins, Widows, and Wives: The Women of 1 Corinthians 7." Pages 148–68 in *A Feminist Companion to Paul*. Edited by Amy-Jill Levine with Marianne Blickenstaff. FCNTECW 6. London: T&T Clark.

MacGregor, Kirk R. 2009. "Is 1 Corinthians 11:2–16 a Prohibition of Homosexuality?" *BSac* 166:201–16.

MacHaffie, Barbara J. 1992. *Readings in Her Story: Women in Christian Tradition*. Minneapolis: Fortress.

MacKinnon, Catharine. 2006. *Are Women Human? And Other International Dialogues*. Cambridge: Harvard University Press.

MacRory, Joseph. 1915. *The Epistles of St. Paul to the Corinthians*. Dublin: Gill & Son.

Makumbe, John. 2010. "Man Is Head But Women Is Not Tail." *The Zimbabwean*, 16 April. http://tinyurl.com/SBL0685ll.

Marcus, Jane. 1982. "Storming the Toolshed." *Signs* 7:622–40.

Mare, W. H. 1976. *Romans, 1 Corinthians, 2 Corinthians, Galatians*. Vol. 10 of *The Expositor's Bible Commentary*. Edited by Frank E. Gaebelein. Grand Rapids: Zondervan.

Marks, Elaine. 1979. "Lesbian Intertextuality." Pages 353–77 in *Homosexualities and French Literature: Cultural Contexts/Critical Texts*. Edited by George Stambolian and Elaine Marks. Ithaca, NY: Cornell University Press.

Marmor, Judd. 1965. *Sexual Inversion: The Multiple Roots of Homosexuality*. New York: Basic Books.

Marshall, I. Howard. 2004. " 'For the Husband Is Head of the Wife': Paul's Use of Head and Body Language." Pages 165–77 in *The New Testament in Its First Century Setting: Essays on Context and Background in Honour of B. W. Winter on His 65th Birthday*. Edited by P. J. Williams, Andrew D. Clarke, Peter M. Head, and David Instone-Brewer. Grand Rapids: Eerdmans.

Martin, Biddy. 1994. "Sexualities without Genders and Other Queer Utopias." *Diacritics* 24.2–3:104–21.

Martin, Dale. 1995a. *The Corinthian Body*. New Haven: Yale University Press.

———. 1995b. "Heterosexism and the Interpretation of Romans 1:18–32." *BibInt* 3:332–55.

———. 2001. "Contradictions of Masculinity: Ascetic Inseminators and Menstruating Men in Greco-Roman Culture." Pages 81–108 in *Generation and Degeneration: Tropes of Reproduction in Literature and History from Antiquity to Early Modern Europe*. Edited by Valeria Finucci and Kevin Brownlee. Durham, NC: Duke University Press.

———. 2006. *Sex and the Single Savior: Gender and Sexuality in Biblical Interpretation*. Louisville: Westminster John Knox.

Martin, Troy. 2004. "Paul's Argument from Nature for the Veil in 1 Corinthians 11:13–15: A Testicle Instead of a Head Covering." *JBL* 123:75–84.

———. 2005. "Veiled Exhortations Regarding the Veil: Ethos as the Controlling Proof in Moral Persuasion (1 Cor 11:2–16)." Pages 255–73 in *Rhetoric, Ethic, and Moral Persuasion in Biblical Discourse: Essays from the 2002 Heidelberg Conference*. Edited by Thomas H. Olbricht and Anders Eriksson. ESEC 11. New York: T&T Clark.

Martin, William J. 1970. "1 Corinthians 11:2–16: An Interpretation." Pages 231–41 in *Apostolic History and the Gospel: Biblical and Historical Essays Presented to F. F. Bruce on His 60th Birthday*. Edited by W. Ward Gasque and Ralph P. Martin. Exeter: Paternoster.

Marx, Karl. 1904. *A Contribution to the Critique of Political Economy*. Translated by N. I. Stone. Chicago: Kerr.

———. 1970. *Critique of Hegel's "Philosophy of Right."* Translated by Annette Jolin and Joseph O'Malley. Edited by Joseph O'Malley. Cambridge Studies in the History and Theory of Politics. Cambridge: Cambridge University Press.

Marx, Karl, and Frederick Engels. 1939. *The German Ideology*. Edited by R. Pascal. London: Lawrence & Wishart.

Massey, Preston T. 2007. "The Meaning of κατακαλύπτω and κατὰ κεφαλῆς ἔχων in 1 Corinthians 11.2–16." *NTS* 53:502–23.

Matthews, Gareth B. 1986. "Gender and Essence in Aristotle." Pages 16–25 in *Women and Philosophy*. Edited by Janna L. Thompson. Australian Journal of Philosophy Sup 64. Bundoora, Australia: Australian Journal of Philosophy.

Mayman, Margaret. 2004. "Homophobia behind Opposition to Civil Unions." *Otago Daily Times*, 25 August, 11.

Mayordomo-Marín, Moisés. 2008. "Konstruktionen von Männlichkeit in der Antike und der paulinischen Korintherkorrespondenz." *EvT* 68:99–115.

McClure, Michael. 1966. *Meat Science Essays*. 2nd ed. San Francisco: City Lights Books.

McFague, Sally. 1987. *Models of God: Theology for an Ecological, Nuclear Age*. Philadelphia: Fortress.

McLaughlin, Eleanor. 2004. "Feminist Christologies: Re-dressing the Tradition." Pages 118–49 in *Reconstructing the Christ Symbol: Essays in Feminist Christology*. Edited by Maryanne Stevens. 1993. Repr., Eugene, OR: Wipf & Stock.

McMillen, Liz. 1997. "Judith Butler Revels in the Role of Troublemaker." *Chronicle of Higher Education* 43.37, A14–15.

Meeks, Wayne. 1974. "The Image of the Androgyne: Some Uses of a Symbol in Earliest Christianity." *HR* 13:165–208.

———. 1983. *The First Urban Christians: The Social World of the Apostle Paul*. New Haven: Yale University Press.

Meggitt, Justin. 1998. *Paul, Poverty and Survival*. SNTW. Edinburgh: T&T Clark.

Meier, John P. 1978. "On the Veiling of Hermeneutics (1 Cor 11:2–16)." *CBQ* 40:212–26.

Mercadante, Linda. 1978. "From Hierarchy to Equality: A Comparison of Past and Present Interpretations of 1 Cor 11: 2–16 in Relation to the Changing Status of Women in Society." Master's thesis. Regent College.

Merkle, Benjamin L. 2006. "Paul's Arguments from Creation in 1 Corinthians 11:8–9 and 1 Timothy 2:13–14: An Apparent Inconsistency Answered." *JETS* 49:527–48.

Meyers, Carol. 1988. *Discovering Eve: Ancient Israelite Women in Context*. Oxford: Oxford University Press.

Miller, J. David. 2009. "Translating Paul's Words about Women." *SCJ* 12:61–71.

Miller, James E. 1995. "The Practices of Romans 1:26: Homosexual or Heterosexual?" *NovT* 37:1–11.

———. 2007. "A Response to Robert Gagnon on 'The Old Testament and Homosexuality.'" *ZAW* 119:86–89.

Mills, Sara. 2003. *Michel Foucault*. Routledge Critical Thinkers. London: Routledge.

Mingo, Alberto de. 2004. "Saint Paul and Women." Translated by Sara Fernandez Cendon. *TD* 51:9–18.

Mitchell, Margaret. 1993. *Paul and the Rhetoric of Reconciliation: An Exegetical Investigation of the Language and Composition of 1 Corinthians*. Louisville: Westminster John Knox.

Moffatt, James. 1938. *The First Epistle of Paul to the Corinthians*. MNTC. London: Hodder & Stoughton.

Mollenkott, Virginia Ramey. 1983. *The Divine Feminine: The Biblical Imagery of God as Female*. New York: Crossroad.

Moloney, Francis J. 1984. *Woman First among the Faithful: A New Testament Study*. Blackburn, Australia: Dove Communications.

Moltmann, Jürgen. 1999. "Henriette Visser 'T Hooft and Karl Barth." *ThTo* 55:524–31.

Moore, Stephen D. 2001. *God's Beauty Parlor and Other Queer Spaces in and around the Bible*. Contraversions. Stanford, CA: Stanford University Press.

———. 2007. "A Modest Manifesto for New Testament Literary Criticism: How to Interface with a Literary Studies Field That Is Post-Literary, Post-Theoretical, and Post-Methodological." *BibInt* 15:1–25.

Moore, Stephen D., and Janice Capel Anderson, eds. 2003. *New Testament Masculinities*. SemeiaSt 45. Atlanta: Society of Biblical Literature.

Moore, Stephen D., and Yvonne Sherwood. 2011. *The Invention of the Biblical Scholar: A Critical Manifesto*. Minneapolis: Fortress.

Morris, Leon. 1985. *The First Epistle of Paul to the Corinthians: An Introduction and Commentary*. 2nd ed. TNTC. Grand Rapids: Eerdmans.

Morton, Donald. 1996. "Changing the Terms: (Virtual) Desire and (Actual) Reality." Pages 1–33 in *The Material Queer: A LesBiGay Cultural Studies Reader*. Edited by Donald Morton. Boulder, CO: Westview.

Mount, Christopher. 2005. "1 Corinthians 11:3–16: Spirit Possession and Authority in a Non-Pauline Interpolation." *JBL* 124:313–40.

Moxnes, Halvor. 2003. "Asceticism and Christian Identity in Antiquity: A Dialogue with Foucault and Paul." *JSNT* 26:3–29.

Muers, Rachel. 1999. "A Question of Two Answers: Difference and Determination in Barth and von Balthasar." *Heythrop Journal* 40:265–79.

Murnaghan, Sheila. 1988. "How a Woman Can Be More Like a Man: The Dialogue between Ischomachus and His Wife in Xenophon's *Oeconomicus*." *Helios* 15:9–22.

Murphy-O'Connor, Jerome. 1976. "The Non-Pauline Character of 1 Corinthians 11:2–16?" *JBL* 95:615–21.

———. 1980. "Sex and Logic in 1 Corinthians 11:2–16." *CBQ* 42:482–500.

———. 1982. *Becoming Human Together: The Pastoral Anthropology of St.
Paul*. Good News Studies. Wilmington, DE: Glazier.

———. 1986. "Interpolations in 1 Corinthians." *CBQ* 48:81–94.

———. 1988. "1 Corinthians 11:2–16 Once Again." *CBQ* 50:265–74.

———. 1996. *Paul: A Critical Life*. Oxford: Oxford University Press.

———. 1998. *1 Corinthians*. Doubleday Bible Commentary. New York:
Doubleday.

———. 2006. Review of *The Pauline Canon*, edited by Stanley E. Porter. *JTS*
57:677–79.

Myles, Robert J. 2010. "Dandy Discipleship: A Queering of Mark's Male
Disciples." *Journal of Men, Masculinities, and Spirituality* 4:66–81.

NASA. 2007a. "Pioneer-10 and Pioneer-11." nasa.gov. http://tinyurl.com/
SBL0685t.

———. 2007b. "The Pioneer Missions." nasa.gov. http://tinyurl.com/
SBL0685u.

Newman, Carey C. 1992. *Paul's Glory-Christology: Tradition and Rhetoric*.
NovTSup 69. Leiden: Brill.

Neyrey, Jerome H. 1990. *Paul, in Other Words: A Cultural Reading of His
Letters*. Louisville: Westminster John Knox.

Nietzsche, Friedrich W. 1984. *The Human, All Too Human: A Book for Free
Spirits*. Translated by Marion Faber and Stephen Lehmann. Lincoln:
University of Nebraska Press.

Nissinen, Martti. 1998. *Homoeroticism in the Biblical World: A Historical
Perspective*. Translated by Kirsi Stjerna. Minneapolis: Fortress.

Nordling, Cherith Fee. 2010. *Knowing God by Name: A Conversation
between Elizabeth A. Johnson and Karl Barth*. Issues in Systematic Theology 13. New York: Lang.

Nussbaum, Martha C. 2002. "The Incomplete Feminism of Musonius
Rufus, Platonist, Stoic, and Roman." Pages 283–326 in *The Sleep of
Reason: Erotic Experience and Sexual Ethics in Ancient Greece and
Rome*. Edited by Martha C. Nussbaum and Juha Sihvola. Chicago:
University of Chicago Press.

O'Hara, Ann, ed. 1995. *In the Embrace of God: Feminist Approaches to
Theological Anthropology*. Maryknoll, NY: Orbis.

Økland, Jorunn. 2002. "Feminist Reception of the New Testament: A
Critical Reception." Pages 131–56 in *The New Testament as Reception*.

Edited by Mogens Müller and Henrik Tronier. Copenhagen International Seminar 11; JSNTSup 230. London: Sheffield Academic.

———. 2004. *Women in Their Place: Paul and the Corinthian Discourse of Gender and Sanctuary Space.* JSNTSup 269. London: T&T Clark.

———. 2008. "Textual Reproduction as Surplus Value: Paul on Pleasing Christ and Spouses, in Light of Simone de Beauvoir." Pages 182–203 in *Marxist Feminist Criticism of the Bible.* Edited by Roland Boer and Jorunn Økland. Bible in the Modern World 14. Sheffield: Sheffield Phoenix.

Oliensis, Ellen. 1997. "The Erotics of *amicitia*: Readings in Tibullus, Propertius, and Horace." Pages 151–71 in *Roman Sexualities.* Edited by Judith P. Hallett and Marilyn B. Skinner. Princeton: Princeton University Press.

———. 2007. "Erotics and Gender." Pages 221–34 in *The Cambridge Companion to Horace.* Edited by Stephen Harrison. Cambridge: Cambridge University Press.

Olson, Gary A., and Lynn Worsham. 2000. "Changing the Subject: Judith Butler's Politics of Radical Resignification." *JAC* 20:727–65.

Olyan, Saul M. 1997. " 'And with a Male You Shall Not Lie the Lying Down of a Woman': On the Meaning and Significance of Leviticus 18:22 and 20:13." Pages 398–414, 513–24 in *Que(e)rying Religion: A Critical Anthology.* Edited by Gary David Comstock and Susan E. Henking. New York: Continuum.

Orr, William F., and James Arthur Walther. 1976. *1 Corinthians.* AB 32. Garden City, NY: Doubleday.

Ortlund, Raymond C. 2006. "Male-Female Equality and Male Headship: Genesis 1–3." Pages 95–112 in *Recovering Biblical Manhood and Womanhood: A Response to Evangelical Feminism.* 1991. Repr., Wheaton, IL: Crossway.

Ortner, Sherry. 1974. "Is Female to Male as Nature Is to Culture?" Pages 67–87 in *Woman, Culture, and Society.* Edited by Michelle Z. Rosaldo and Louise Lamphere. Stanford, CA: Stanford University Press.

Osborne, Rick. 2002. *2:52 Boys Bible: The Ultimate Manual.* New International Version. Grand Rapids: Zondervan.

Osiek, Carolyn. 1985. "The Feminist and the Bible: Hermeneutical Alternatives." Pages 93–105 in *Feminist Perspectives on Biblical Scholarship.* Edited by Adela Yarbro Collins. BSNA 10. Chico, CA: Scholars Press.

Osiek, Carolyn, and Margaret Y. MacDonald, with Janet H. Tulloch. 2006. *A Woman's Place: House Churches in Earliest Christianity.* Minneapolis: Fortress.

Oster, Richard E., Jr. 1988. "When Men Wore Veils to Worship: The Historical Context of 1 Corinthians 11.4." *NTS* 34: 481–505.

———. 1992. "Use, Misuse and Neglect of Archaeological Evidence in Some Modern Works on 1 Corinthians (1 Cor 7,1–5; 8,10; 11,2–16; 12,14–26)." *ZNW* 83:52–73.

———. 1995. *1 Corinthians.* College Press NIV Commentary. Joplin: College Press.

Ostrovsky, Erika. 2003. "Religion in the Fiction of Monique Wittig." Pages 191–202 in *Religion in French Feminist Thought: Critical Perspectives.* Edited by Morny Joy, Kathleen O'Grady, and Judith L. Poxon. London: Routledge.

———. 2005. "Transformation of Gender and Genre Paradigms in the Fiction of Monique Wittig." Pages 115–32 in *On Monique Wittig: Theoretical, Political, and Literary Essays.* Edited by Namascar Shaktini. Urbana: University of Illinois Press.

Padgett, Alan. 1984. "Paul on Women in the Church: The Contradictions of Coiffure in 1 Corinthians 11.2–16." *JSNT* 20:69–86.

———. 1986. "Feminism in First Corinthians: A Dialogue with Elisabeth Schüssler Fiorenza." *EvQ* 58:121–32.

Padgug, Robert. 1989. "Sexual Matters: Rethinking Sexuality in History." Pages 54–64 and 493–95 in *Hidden from History: Reclaiming the Gay and Lesbian Past.* Edited by Martin B. Duberman, Martha Vicinus, and George Chauncey. Penguin Social Sciences. New York: New American Library.

Pagels, Elaine. 1976. "What Became of God the Mother? Conflicting Images of God in Early Christianity." *Signs* 2:293–303.

Palin, Sarah. 2010. *America by Heart: Reflections on Family, Faith, and Flag.* New York: HarperCollins.

Papadópoulos, Stylianós G., Kōnstantios I. Mpelezos, and Sotērios S. Despotis, eds. 2009. *Apostolos Paulos kai Kórinthos: 1950 chronia apo Tē suggraphē tōn epistolōn pros Korinthious: ermēneia, theologia, istoria, ermēneias, philologia, philosophia, epochē: praktika, diethnous, epistēmonikou sunedriou (Kórinthos, 23–25 Septembrion 2007).* 2 vols. Athens: Ekdoseis Psychogios.

"Pathway to Same-Gender Blessings." n.d. anglicantaonga.org.nz. http://tinyurl.com/SBL0685d1.

Patmore, Coventry Kersey Dighton. 1992. *Poems*. 1906. Repr., Cambridge: Chadwyck-Healey.

Patterson, Dorothy. 2006. "The High Calling of Wife and Mother in Biblical Perspective." Pages 364–77 in *Recovering Biblical Manhood and Womanhood: A Response to Evangelical Feminism*. 1991. Repr., Wheaton, IL: Crossway.

Payne, Philip B. 2006. "Wild Hair and Gender Equality in 1 Corinthians 11:2–16." *Priscilla Papers* 20.3:9–18.

———. 2009. *Man and Woman, One in Christ: An Exegetical and Theological Study of Paul's Letters*. Grand Rapids: Zondervan.

Peerbolte, L. J. Lietaert. 2000. "Man, Woman, and the Angels in 1 Cor 11:2–16." Pages 76–92 in *The Creation of Man and Woman: Interpretations of the Biblical Narratives in Jewish and Christian Traditions*. Edited by Gerard P. Luttikhuizen. TBN 3. Leiden: Brill.

Peifer, Claude J. 1960. *The First and Second Epistles of St Paul to the Corinthians*. New Testament Reading Guide. Collegeville, MN: Liturgical Press.

Penelope, Julia. 1983. "Whose Past Are We Reclaiming?" *Common Lives/Lesbian Lives* 13:16–36.

Penner, Todd, and Caroline Vander Stichele. 2005. "Unveiling Paul: Gendering Ethos in 1 Corinthians 11:2–16." Pages 214–37 in *Rhetoric, Ethic, and Moral Persuasion in Biblical Discourse: Essays from the 2002 Heidelberg Conference*. Edited by Thomas H. Olbricht and Anders Eriksson. ESEC 11. New York: T&T Clark.

Perriman, A. C. 1994. "The Head of a Woman: The Meaning of κεφαλή in 1 Cor 11:3." *JTS* 45:602–22.

Philps-Townsley, Gillian. 1997. "All Things to All Men." Pages 114–21 in *The Vision New Zealand Congress 1997*. Edited by Bruce Patrick. Auckland, NZ: Vision NZ.

Phua, Richard Liong-Seng. 2005. *Idolatry and Authority: A Study of 1 Corinthians 8.1–11.1 in the Light of the Jewish Diaspora*. LNTS 299. London: T&T Clark.

Pierce, Ronald W. 2004. "Contemporary Evangelicals for Gender Equality." Pages 58–75 in *Discovering Biblical Equality: Complementarity without Hierarchy*. Edited by Ronald W. Pierce and Rebecca Merrill Groothuis. Downers Grove, IL: InterVarsity Press.

Pierceson, Jason. 2005. *Courts, Liberalism, and Rights: Gay Law and Politics in the United States and Canada*. Philadelphia: Temple University Press.

Piper, John. 2006. "A Vision of Biblical Complementarity: Manhood and Womanhood Defined According to the Bible." Pages 31–59 in *Recovering Biblical Manhood and Womanhood: A Response to Evangelical Feminism*. 1991. Repr., Wheaton, IL: Crossway.

Piper, John, and Wayne Grudem. 2006a. "Charity, Clarity, and Hope: The Controversy and the Cause of Christ." Pages 403–22 in *Recovering Biblical Manhood and Womanhood: A Response to Evangelical Feminism*. 1991. Repr., Wheaton, IL: Crossway.

———, eds. 2006b. *Recovering Biblical Manhood and Womanhood: A Response to Evangelical Feminism*. 1991. Repr., Wheaton, IL: Crossway.

Plaskow, Judith. 1993. "Anti-Judaism in Feminist Christian Interpretation." Pages 117–29 in *A Feminist Introduction*. Vol. 1 of *Searching the Scriptures*. Edited by Elisabeth Schüssler Fiorenza. New York: Crossroad.

Plumwood, Val. 1993. *Feminism and the Mastery of Nature*. London: Routledge.

Polaski, Sandra Hack. 2005. *A Feminist Introduction to Paul*. St. Louis: Chalice.

Popenoe, David. 1993. "American Family Decline, 1960–1990: A Review and Appraisal." *Journal of Marriage and the Family* 55:527–55.

Powers, Janet Everts. 2001. "Recovering a Woman's Head with Prophetic Authority: A Pentecostal Interpretation of 1 Corinthians 11.3–16." *Journal of Pentecostal Theology* 10:11–37.

Press, Howard. 1977. "The Existential Basis of Marxism." *Philosophy and Phenomenological Research* 37:331–44.

Preuss, Anthony. 1970. "Science and Philosophy in Aristotle's *Generation of Animals*." *Journal of the History of Biology* 3:1–52.

Prior, David. 1985. *The Message of 1 Corinthians: Life in the Local Church*. Bible Speaks Today. Leicester: InterVarsity Press.

Pritchard, Peter. 2008. *Manhood: Negotiating the Mind Fields*. Alachua: Bridge-Logos.

Punt, Jeremy. 2007. "Sex and Gender, and Liminality in Biblical Texts: Venturing into Postcolonial, Queer Biblical Interpretation." *Neotestamentica* 41:382–98.

Putney, Clifford. 2001. *Muscular Christianity: Manhood and Sports in Protestant America, 1880–1920*. Cambridge: Harvard University Press.

Quast, Kevin. 1994. *Reading the Corinthian Correspondence: An Introduction*. New York: Paulist Press.

Radcliffe, Timothy. 1990. "Paul and Sexual Identity: 1 Corinthians 11.2–

16." Pages 62–72 in *After Eve: Women, Theology and Christian Tradition*. Edited by Janet Martin Soskice. London: Collins.

Rae, Eleanor, and Bernice Marie-Daly. 1990. *Created in Her Image: Models of the Feminine Divine*. New York: Crossroad.

Ramsay, W. M. 1907. *The Cities of St. Paul: Their Influence on His Life and Thought: The Cities of Eastern Asia Minor*. Dale Memorial Lectures 1907. London: Hodder & Stoughton.

Rayside, David. 2007. "The United States in Comparative Context." Pages 341–64 in *The Politics of Same-Sex Marriage*. Edited by Craig Rimmerman and Clyde Wilcox. Chicago: University of Chicago Press.

Rees, Geoffrey. 2002. " 'In the Sight of God': Gender Complementarity and the Male Homosocial Signification of Male-Female Marriage." *T&S* 9:19–47.

Rehmann, Luzia Sutter. 2000. "German-Language Feminist Exegesis of the Pauline Letters: A Survey." *JSNT* 79:5–18.

Rekers, George A. 2006. "Psychological Foundations for Rearing Masculine Boys and Feminine Girls." Pages 294–311 in *Recovering Biblical Manhood and Womanhood: A Response to Evangelical Feminism*. 1991. Repr., Wheaton, IL: Crossway.

Rich, Adrienne. 1973. *Diving into the Wreck: Poems 1971–1972*. New York: Norton.

———. 1980. "Compulsory Heterosexuality and Lesbian Existence." *Signs* 5:631–60.

———. 1993. "Afterword [1986]." Pages 246–49 in *The Lesbian and Gay Studies Reader*. Edited by Henry Abelove, Michèle Aina Barale, and David M. Halperin. New York: Routledge.

Richlin, Amy. 1984. "Invective against Women in Roman Satire." *Arethusa* 17:67–80.

———. 1991. Review of *One Hundred Years of Homosexuality: And Other Essays on Greek Love*, by David M. Halperin. *Bryn Mawr Classical Review* 2:16–18.

———. 1993. "Not before Homosexuality: The Materiality of the *Cinaedus* and the Roman Law against Love between Men." *Journal of the History of Sexuality* 3:523–73.

Robbins, John W. 1985. *Feminism*. Part 1 of *Scripture Twisting in the Seminaries*. Jefferson, MD: Trinity Foundation.

Robertson, A. T. 1914. *A Grammar of the Greek New Testament in the Light of Historical Research*. London: Hodder & Stoughton.

Robertson, Archibald, and Alfred Plummer. 1914. *A Critical and Exegetical Commentary on the First Epistle of St Paul to the Corinthians*. ICC. Edinburgh: T&T Clark.

Rogers, Jack. 2007. "Presbyterian Guidelines for Biblical Interpretation: Their Origin and Application to Homosexuality." *BTB* 37:174–83.

———. 2009. *Jesus, The Bible, and Homosexuality: Explode the Myths, Heal the Church*. Rev. ed. Louisville: Westminster John Knox.

Roisman, Joseph. 2005. *The Rhetoric of Manhood: Masculinity in the Attic Orators*. Berkeley: University of California Press.

Rom, Mark Carl. 2007. "Introduction: The Politics of Same-Sex Marriage." Pages 1–38 in *The Politics of Same-Sex Marriage*. Edited by Craig Rimmerman and Clyde Wilcox. Chicago: University of Chicago Press.

Rosen, Ralph M., and Ineke Sluiter, eds. 2002. *Andreia: Studies in Manliness and Courage in Classical Antiquity*. Mnemosyne Bibliotheca Classica Batava Sup 238. Leiden: Brill.

Rosenfeld, Marthe. 1984. "The Linguistic Aspect of Sexual Conflict: Monique Wittig's *Le Corps lesbien*." *Mosaic: A Journal for the Comparative Study of Literature* 17:235–41.

Rowe, Arthur. 1991. "Hermeneutics and 'Hard Passages' in the NT on the Role of Women in the Church: Issues from Recent Literature." *Epworth Review* 18:82–88.

Rowlett, Lori. 2001. "Violent Femmes and S/M: Queering Samson and Delilah." Pages 106–15 in *Queer Commentary and the Hebrew Bible*. Edited by Ken Stone. JSOTSup 334. Sheffield: Sheffield Academic.

Rubin, Gayle. 1975. "The Traffic in Women: Notes on the 'Political Economy' of Sex." Pages 157–210 in *Toward an Anthropology of Women*. Edited by Rayna R. Reiter. New York: Monthly Review Press.

———. 1984. "Thinking Sex: Notes for a Radical Theory of the Politics of Sexuality." Pages 267–319 in *Pleasure and Danger: Exploring Female Sexuality*. Edited by Carole S. Vance. Boston: Routledge & Kegan Paul.

Ruether, Rosemary Radford. 1975. *New Woman, New Earth: Sexist Ideologies and Human Liberation*. Melbourne: Dove Communications.

———. 1983. *Sexism and God-Talk: Towards a Feminist Theology*. London: SCM.

———. 1995. "*Imago Dei*: Christian Tradition and Feminist Hermeneutics." Pages 267–91 in *The Image of God: Gender Models in Judaeo-Christian Tradition*. Edited by Kari Elisabeth Børresen. Minneapolis: Fortress.

Russo, Mary. 1986. "Female Grotesques: Carnival and Theory." Pages 213–29 in *Feminist Studies/Critical Studies*. Edited by Teresa de Lauretis. Bloomington: Indiana University Press.

Salih, Sara. 2002. *Judith Butler*. Routledge Critical Thinkers. London: Routledge.

Salomonsen, Jone. 2003. " 'Love of Same, Love of Other': Reading Feminist Anthropologies with Luce Irigaray and Karl Barth." *ST* 57:103–23.

Sanseri, Gary. 1999. *Covered or Uncovered: How 1 Corinthians 11:2–16 Applies to Worship and Leadership in the Church*. Milwaukee: Back Home Industries.

Sarup, Madan. 1993. *An Introductory Guide to Post-Structuralism and Postmodernism*. Athens, GA: University of Georgia Press.

Satlow, Michael L. 1995. *Tasting the Dish: Rabbinic Rhetorics of Sexuality*. BJS 303. Atlanta: Scholars Press.

Sawyer, Deborah. 2002. *God, Gender and the Bible*. Biblical Limits. London: Routledge.

Sayers, Dorothy. 1971. "The Human-Not-Quite-Human." Pages 37–47 in *Are Women Human? Astute and Witty Essays on the Role of Women in Society*. Grand Rapids: Eerdmans.

Scanlon, Julie. 1998. " 'XX+XX=XX': Monique Wittig's Reproduction of the Monstrous Lesbian." *Paroles gelées* 16:73–96.

Schaeffer, Ludwig F., Daniel P. Resnick, and George L. Netterville III, eds. 1970. *The Traditional World*. Vol. 1 of *The Shaping of Western Civilization*. New York: Holt, Rinehart & Winston.

Schaff, Philip, ed. 1919. *The Greek and Latin Creeds, with Translations*. Vol. 2 of *The Creeds of Christendom, with a History and Critical Notes*. New York: Harper & Row.

Schirrmacher, Thomas. 1993. *Paulus im Kampf gegen den Schleier: Eine alternative Auslesung von 1. Korinther 11,2–16*. Biblia et Symbiotica 4. Bonn: Verlag für Kultur und Wissenschaft.

Schleiermacher, Friedrich. 1860. *The Life of Schleiermacher: As Unfolded in His Autobiography and Letters*. Translated by Frederica Rowan. 2 vols. London: Smith, Elder.

Schneider, Laurel C. 2000. "Queer Theory." Pages 206–12 in *Handbook of Postmodern Biblical Interpretation*. Edited by A. K. M. Adam. St. Louis: Chalice.

Schor, Naomi. 1987. "Dreaming Dissymmetry: Barthes, Foucault, and Sexual Difference." Pages 98–110 in *Men in Feminism*. Edited by Alice Jardine and Paul Smith. New York: Methuen.

———. 1992. "Feminist and Gender Studies." Pages 262–87 in *Introduction to Scholarship in Modern Languages and Literatures*. Edited by Joseph Gibaldi. 2nd ed. New York: Modern Language Association of America.

———. 1995. "French Feminism Is a Universalism." *Differences* 7:15–47.

Schottroff, Luise. 1993. *Let the Oppressed Go Free: Feminist Perspectives on the New Testament*. Translated by Annemarie S. Kidder. Gender and the Biblical Tradition. Louisville: Westminster John Knox.

Schowalter, Daniel N., and Steven J. Frisen, eds. 2005. *Urban Religion in Roman Corinth: Interdisciplinary Approaches*. HTS 53. Cambridge: Harvard University Press.

———, eds. 2010. *Corinth in Context: Comparative Studies on Religion and Society*. NovTSup 134. Leiden: Brill.

Schrage, Wolfgang. 1991. *Der erste Brief an die Korinther: 1 Kor 1,1–6,11*. EKKNT 7.1. Zurich: Benziger.

———. 1995. *Der erste Brief an die Korinther: 1 Kor 6,12–11,16*. EKKNT 7.2. Zurich: Benziger.

Schreiner, Thomas R. 2006a. "Head Coverings, Prophecies and the Trinity: 1 Corinthians 11:2–16." Pages 124–39 in *Recovering Biblical Manhood and Womanhood: A Response to Evangelical Feminism*. 1991. Repr., Wheaton, IL: Crossway.

———. 2006b. "The Valuable Ministries of Women in the Context of Male Leadership: A Survey of Old and New Testament Examples and Teaching." Pages 209–24 in *Recovering Biblical Manhood and Womanhood: A Response to Evangelical Feminism*. 1991. Repr., Wheaton, IL: Crossway.

Schüssler Fiorenza, Elisabeth. 1978. "Women in the Pre-Pauline and Pauline Churches." *USQR* 33.3–4:153–66.

———. 1983. *In Memory of Her: A Feminist Theological Reconstruction of Christian Origins*. London: SCM.

———. 1984. *Bread Not Stone: The Challenge of Feminist Biblical Interpretation*. Boston: Beacon.

———. 1992. *But She Said: Feminist Practices of Biblical Interpretation*. Boston: Beacon.

Scroggs, Robin. 1972. "Paul and the Eschatological Woman." *JAAR* 40:283–303.

———. 1974. "Paul and the Eschatological Woman: Revisited." *JAAR* 42:532–37.

———. 1983. *The New Testament and Homosexuality: Contextual Background for Contemporary Debate*. Philadelphia: Fortress.

Sedgwick, Eve Kosofsky. 1990. *Epistemology of the Closet*. Berkeley: University of California Press.

———. 1992. *Between Men: English Literature and Male Homosocial Desire*. 2nd ed. New York: Columbia University Press.

———. 1994. *Tendencies*. London: Routledge.

———. 2003. *Touching Feeling: Affect, Pedagogy, Performativity*. Series Q. Durham, NC: Duke University Press.

Selinger, Suzanne. 1998. *Charlotte von Kirschbaum and Karl Barth: A Study in Biography and the History of Theology*. University Park: Pennsylvania State University Press.

Sellars, John. 2006. *Stoicism*. Ancient Philosophies. Berkeley: University of California Press.

Senack, Christine M. 1994. "Aristotle on the Woman's Soul. Pages 223–36 in *Engendering Origins: Critical Feminist Readings in Plato and Aristotle*. Edited by Bat-Ami Bar On. SUNY Series, Feminist Philosophy. Albany: State University of New York Press.

Shaktini, Namascar. 1982. "Displacing the Phallic Subject: Wittig's Lesbian Writing." *Signs* 8:29–44.

———. 1994. Review of *The Straight Mind and Other Essays*, by Monique Wittig. *Hypatia* 9:211–14.

———. 2005a. "The Critical Mind and *The Lesbian Body*." Pages 150–59 in *On Monique Wittig: Theoretical, Political, and Literary Essays*. Edited by Namascar Shaktini. Urbana: University of Illinois Press.

———, ed. 2005b. *On Monique Wittig: Theoretical, Political, and Literary Essays*. Urbana: University of Illinois Press.

Sheffield, Tricia. 2008. "Performing Jesus: A Queer Counternarrative of Embodied Transgression." *T&S* 14:233–58.

Shepherd, Sheri Rose. 2004. *His Princess: Love Letters from Your King*. New York: Multnomah.

Shirer, Priscilla Evans. 1999. *A Jewel in His Crown: Rediscovering Your Value as a Woman of Excellence*. Chicago: Moody Press.

Shoemaker, Thomas P. 1987. "Unveiling of Equality: 1 Corinthians 11:2–16." *BTB* 27:60–63.

Shorter Oxford English Dictionary on Historical Principles. 2002. Edited by Lesley Brown. 5th ed. 2 vols. Oxford: Oxford University Press.

Silberman, Seth Clark. 2007. "'I Have Access to Your Glottis': The Fleshy Syntax, Ethical Irony, and Queer Intimacy of Monique Wittig's *Le corps lesbien*." *GLQ* 13:467–87.

Silverman, Kaja. 1992. *Male Subjectivity at the Margins*. New York: Routledge.

Simon, W. G. H. 1959. *The First Epistle to the Corinthians*. Torch Bible Commentaries. London: SCM.

Simpson, Tony. 1992. "Real Men, Short Hair." Pages 261–64 in *Sport and Religion*. Edited by Shirl J. Hoffman. Champaign, IL: Human Kinetics.

Skinner, Marilyn B. 2005. *Sexuality in Greek and Roman Culture*. Ancient Cultures. Malden, MA: Blackwell.

Smith, Paul Julian. 1992. *Laws of Desire: Questions of Homosexuality in Spanish Writing and Film (1960–1990)*. Oxford: Clarendon.

Smyth, Cherry. 1992. *Lesbians Talk Queer Notions*. London: Scarlet.

Snyder, G. F. 1992. *First Corinthians: A Faith Community Commentary*. Macon, GA: Mercer University Press.

Soards, Marion L. 1999. *1 Corinthians*. NIBCNT. Peabody, MA: Hendrickson.

Sommer, Volker, and Paul L. Vasey. 2006. "Homosexual Behaviour in Animals: Topics, Hypotheses and Research Trajectories." Pages 3–42 in *Homosexual Behaviour in Animals: An Evolutionary Perspective*. Edited by Volker Sommer and Paul L. Vasey. Cambridge: Cambridge University Press.

Sonderegger, Katherine. 2000. "Barth and Feminism." Pages 258–73 in *The Cambridge Companion to Karl Barth*. Edited by John Webster. Cambridge: Cambridge University Press.

Soper, Kate. 2000. "Naturalized Woman and Feminized Nature." Pages 139–44 in *The Green Studies Reader: From Romanticism to Ecocriticism*. Edited by Laurence Coupe. London: Routledge.

Spargo, Tamsin. 1999. *Foucault and Queer Theory*. Postmodern Encounters. Cambridge: Icon/Totem.

Spelman, Elizabeth V. 1994. "Who's Who in the Polis." Pages 97–125 in *Engendering Origins: Critical Feminist Readings in Plato and Aristotle*. Edited by Bat-Ami Bar On. SUNY Series, Feminist Philosophy. Albany: State University of New York Press.

Spinelli, Simonetta. 2003. "Monique Wittig: Queer or Not Queer." *Labrys, etudes féministe* special issue. https://www.labrys.net.br/special/simonetta.htm.

Spivak, Gayatri Chakravorty. 1988. "Can the Subaltern Speak?" Pages 271–314 in *Marxism and the Interpretation of Culture*. Edited by Cary Nelson and Lawrence Grossberg. Urbana: University of Illinois Press.

———. 1993. *Outside in the Teaching Machine*. New York: Routledge.

Squeri, Lawrence. 2004. "When ET Calls: SETI Is Ready." *Journal of Popular Culture* 37:478–96.

Stanley, Alessandra. 1991. "Militants Back 'Queer,' Shoving 'Gay' the Way of 'Negro.'" *New York Times*, 6 April, 23–24.

Stone, Ken. 1997. "Biblical Interpretation as a Technology of the Self: Gay Men and the Ethics of Reading." *Semeia* 77:139–55.

———. 2000. "The Garden of Eden and the Heterosexual Contract." Pages 57–70 in *Take Back the Word: A Queer Reading of the Bible*. Edited by Robert E. Goss and Mona West. Cleveland: Pilgrim.

———. 2001a. "Homosexuality and the Bible or Queer Reading? A Response to Martti Nissinen." *T&S* 14:107–18.

———. 2001b. "Queer Commentary and Biblical Interpretation: An Introduction." Pages 11–34 in *Queer Commentary and the Hebrew Bible*. Edited by Ken Stone. JSOTSup 334. Sheffield: Sheffield Academic.

———, ed. 2001c. *Queer Commentary and the Hebrew Bible*. JSOTSup 334. Sheffield: Sheffield Academic.

———. 2003. Review of *God's Beauty Parlor: And Other Queer Spaces in and around the Bible*, by Stephen D. Moore. *JAAR* 71:706–8.

———. 2005. *Practicing Safer Texts: Food, Sex and Bible in Queer Perspective*. Queering Theology Series. London: T&T Clark.

Strongheart, Amy Adams Squire. 1997. "The Power to Choose: We're Here, We're Queer, and We Want to Get Hitched." Pages 79–96 in *Our Families, Our Values: Snapshots of Queer Kinship*. Edited by Robert E. Goss and Amy Adams Squire Strongheart. Binghamton: Haworth.

Stuart, Elizabeth. 2003. *Gay and Lesbian Theologies: Repetitions with Critical Difference*. Aldersho, UK: Ashgate.

Stuckenbruck, Loren T. 1995. *Angel Veneration and Christology: A Study in Early Judaism and in the Christology of the Apocalypse of John*. WUNT 2/70. Tübingen: Mohr.

———. 2001. "Why Should Women Cover Their Heads Because of the Angels? (1 Corinthians 11:10)." *SCJ* 4:205–34.

Sullivan, Kevin P. 2004. *Wrestling with Angels: A Study of the Relationship between Angels and Human in Ancient Jewish Literature and the New Testament*. AGJU 55. Leiden: Brill.

Sullivan, Nikki. 2003. *A Critical Introduction to Queer Theory*. Washington Square: New York University Press.

Swancutt, Diana M. 2003. "'The Disease of Effemination': The Charge of Effeminacy and the Verdict of God (Romans 1:18–2:16)." Pages 193–233 in *New Testament Masculinities*. Edited by Stephen D. Moore and

Janice Capel Anderson. SemeiaSt 45. Atlanta: Society of Biblical Literature.

———. 2006. "Sexing the Pauline Body of Christ: Scriptural Sex in the Context of the American Christian Culture War." Pages 65–98, 390–99 in *Toward a Theology of Eros: Transfiguring Passion at the Limits of Discipline*. Edited by Virginia Burrus and Catherine Keller. Transdisciplinary Theological Colloquia. New York: Fordham University Press.

———. 2010. "*Still* before Sexuality: 'Greek' Androgyny, the Roman Imperial Politics of Masculinity and the Roman Invention of the *Tribas*." Pages 11–61 in *Mapping Gender in Ancient Religious Discourses*. Edited by Todd Penner and Caroline Vander Stichele. BibInt 84. Atlanta: Society of Biblical Literature.

Swartley, Willard. 2002. "The Church and Homosexuality: Review Essay." *Mennonite Quarterly Review* 76:215–30.

Sykes, S. W. 1989. "Authority and Openness in the Church." Pages 69–86 in *Karl Barth: Centenary Essays*. Edited by S. W. Sykes. Cambridge: Cambridge University Press.

Synge, F. C. 1953. "Studies in Texts: 1 Cor 11.2–16." *Theology* 56:143.

Szesnat, Holger. 1994. "Greek 'Homosexuality': Whither the Debate?" *Akroterion* 39:46–63.

———. 1997. "Human Sexuality, History, and Culture: The Essentialist/ Social Constructionist Controversy and the Methodological Problem of Studying 'Sexuality' in the New Testament and Its World." *Scriptura* 62:335–61.

Tadlock, Barry L., C. Ann Gordon, and Elizabeth Popp. 2007. "Framing the Issue of Same-Sex Marriage: Traditional Values Versus Equal Rights." Pages 193–214 in *The Politics of Same-Sex Marriage*. Edited by Craig A. Rimmerman and Clyde Wilcox. Chicago: University of Chicago Press.

Talbert, C. H. 2002. *Reading Corinthians: A Literary and Theological Commentary*. Rev. ed. Reading the New Testament. Macon, GA: Smyth & Helwys.

Tamaki, Brian. 2006. *Bishop Brian Tamaki: More Than Meets the Eye*. Auckland, NZ: Tamaki Publications, Destiny Churches New Zealand.

Taylor, Gordon Rattray. 1957. *The Angel-Makers: A Study in the Psychological Origins of Historical Change, 1750–1850*. London: Heinemann.

Terry, Ralph Bruce. 1995. *A Discourse Analysis of 1 Corinthians*. Summer Institute of Linguistics and University of Texas at Arlington Publications in Linguistics 120. Dallas: Summer Institute of Linguistics/University of Texas at Arlington.

Theissen, Gerd. 1982. *The Social Setting of Pauline Christianity: Essays on Corinth.* Edited and translated by John H. Schütz. SNTW. Philadelphia: Fortress.

———. 1987. *Psychological Aspects of Pauline Theology.* Translated by John P. Galvin. Philadelphia: Fortress.

Thielicke, Helmut. 1964. *The Ethics of Sex.* Translated by John Doberstein. New York: Harper & Row.

Thiselton, Anthony C. 2000. *The First Epistle to the Corinthians.* NIGTC. Grand Rapids: Eerdmans.

Thompson, Cynthia L. 1988. "Hairstyles, Head-coverings, and St. Paul: Portraits from Roman Corinth." *BA* 51:99–115.

Thompson, Denise. 1989. "The 'Sex/Gender' Distinction: A Reconsideration." *AFS* 10:23–31.

Thompson, James W. 2003. "Creation, Shame and Nature in 1 Cor 1:2–16. The Background and Coherence of Paul's Argument." Pages 237–57 in *Early Christianity and Classical Culture: Comparative Studies in Honor of Abraham J. Malherbe.* Edited by John T. Fitzgerald, Thomas H. Olbricht, and L. Michael White. NovTSup 110. Leiden: Brill.

Thrall, Margaret E. 1965. *I and II Corinthians.* CBC. Cambridge: Cambridge University Press.

Thurman, Eric. 2010. "Novel Men: *Masculinity* and Empire in Mark's Gospel and Xenophon's *An Ephesian Tale.*" Pages 185–229 in *Mapping Gender in Ancient Religious Discourses.* Edited by Todd Penner and Caroline Vander Stichele. BibInt 84. Atlanta: Society of Biblical Literature.

Tischleder, Peter. 1923. *Wesen und Stellung der Frau nach der Lehre des heiligen Paulus: Eine ethisch-exegetische Untersuchung.* NTAbh 10.3–4. Münster in Westfalen: Aschendorff.

Tolbert, Mary Ann. 2000a. "Foreword: What Word Shall We Take Back?" Pages vii–xii in *Take Back the Word: A Queer Reading of the Bible.* Edited by Robert E. Goss and Mona West. Cleveland: Pilgrim.

———. 2000b. "Gender." Pages 99–105 in *Handbook of Postmodern Biblical Interpretation.* Edited by A. K. M. Adam. St. Louis: Chalice.

Townsley, Gillian. 2003. "'Searching for Ariadne's Thread': Some Reflections on 1 Corinthians 11:2–16." *Stimulus* 11:36–42.

———. 2006. "*Gender Trouble* in Corinth: Que(e)rying Constructs of

Gender in 1 Cor 11.2–16." *Bible and Critical Theory* 2:17.1–17.14. DOI: 10.2104/bc060017.

———. 2007. "Wittig's 'Lesbian' and the Corinthian Men: Problematising Categories of Gender in 1 Corinthians 11.2–16." *Hecate* 33:56–73

———. 2011. "*The Straight Mind* in Corinth: Problematizing Categories and Ideologies of Gender in 1 Corinthians 11:2–16." Pages 247–81 in *Bible Trouble: Queer Reading at the Boundaries of Biblical Scholarship*. Edited by Teresa J. Hornsby and Ken Stone. SemeiaSt 67. Atlanta: Society of Biblical Literature.

———. 2015. "'We're Here, We're Queer—Get Used To It!' Exclamations in the Margins (Euodia and Syntyche in Philippians 4.2)." Pages 95–113 in *Sexuality, Ideology, and the Bible: Antipodean Engagements*. Edited by Robert Myles and Caroline Blyth. Sheffield: Sheffield Phoenix.

Trebilco, Paul. 1990. "Women as Co-workers and Leaders in Paul's Letters." *Christian Brethren Research Fellowship Journal* 122:27–36.

Tress, Daryl McGowan. 1996. "The Metaphysical Science of Aristotle's *Generation of Animals* and Its Feminist Critics." Pages 31–50 in *Feminism and Ancient Philosophy*. Edited by Julie K. Ward. New York: Routledge.

Trible, Phyllis. 1984. *Texts of Terror: Literary-Feminist Readings of Biblical Narratives*. OBT. Philadelphia: Fortress.

———. 1989. "Bringing Miriam Out of the Shadows." *Bible Review* 5:14–25, 34.

Trompf, G. W. 1980. "On Attitudes Toward Women in Paul and Paulinist Literature: 1 Corinthians 11:3–16 and Its Context." *CBQ* 42:196–215.

Turcotte, Louise. 1992. "Foreword." Translated by Marlene Wildeman. Pages vii–xiii in *The Straight Mind and Other Essays*, by Monique Wittig. Boston: Beacon.

Turner, William B. 2000. *A Genealogy of Queer Theory*. Philadelphia: Temple University Press.

Tyler, Imogen. 2009. "Against Abjection." *Feminist Theory* 10:77–98.

Van Nortwick, Thomas. 2008. *Imagining Men: Ideals of Masculinity in Ancient Greek Culture*. Praeger Series on the Ancient World. Westport, CT: Praeger.

Van Seters, John. 2009. "A Response to G. Aichelle [*sic*], P. Miscall, and R. Walsh, 'An Elephant in the Room: Historical-Critical and Postmodern Interpretations of the Bible.'" *JHebS* 9:2–13.

Vander Broek, Lyle. 1985. "Women and the Church: Approaching Difficult Passages." *RefR* 38:225–31.

Vander Stichele, Caroline, and Todd Penner. 2005. "Paul and the Rhetoric of Gender." Pages 287–310 in *Her Master's Tools? Feminist and Postcolonial Engagements of Historical-Critical Discourse*. Edited by Caroline Vander Stichele and Todd Penner. GPBS 9. Atlanta: Society of Biblical Literature.

Vanita, Ruth. 1996. *Sappho and the Virgin Mary: Same-Sex Love and the English Literary Imagination*. New York: Columbia University Press.

Vejdovsky, Boris. 2001. "'Remember Me': The Wonders of an Invisible World—Sex, Patriarchy, and Paranoia in Early America." Pages 56–71 in *The Puritan Origins of American Sex: Religion, Sexuality, and National Identity in American Literature*. Edited by Tracy Fessenden, Nicholas F. Radel, and Magdalena J. Zaborowska. New York: Routledge.

Verdenius, W. J. 1980. "Notes on the Prologue of Euripides' *Bacchae*." *Mnemosyne* 33:1–16.

Veyne, Paul. 1978. "La famille at l'amour sous le haut-Empire romain." *Annales (ESC)* 33:35–63.

Via, Dan O. 2003. "Response to Robert A. J. Gagnon." Pages 1–39, 93–98 in *Homosexuality and the Bible: Two Views*. Edited by Dan O. Via and Robert Gagnon. Minneapolis: Fortress.

Vinz, Warren Lang. 1997. *Pulpit Politics: Faces of American Protestant Nationalism in the Twentieth Century*. Albany: State University of New York Press.

Visser 'T Hooft, Henriette. 1934. "Is There a Woman's Problem?" *Student World* 27:12–15.

———. 1962. "Co-humanity and the Covenant." *ThTo* 19:71–74.

———. 1981. "Unausweichliche Fragen." Pages 11–36 in *Eva, wo bist du? Frauen in internationalen Organisationen de Ökumene: Eine Dokumentation*. Edited by Gudrun Kaper, Henriette Visser 'T Hooft, and Mieke Scharffenorth-Korenhof. Gelnhausen: Burckhardthaus-Laetare.

Visser 'T Hooft, Willem A. 1982. *The Fatherhood of God in an Age of Emancipation*. Geneva: World Council of Churches.

Vorster, Johannes N. 2002. "Bodily Parts Vying for Power: Hierarchies and Bodies in Early Christianity." *Scriptura* 80:287–306.

Voss, Barbara L. 2000. "Feminisms, Queer Theories, and the Archaeological Study of Past Sexualities." *World Archaeology* 32:180–92.

Wald, Kenneth D., and Graham B. Glover. 2007. "Theological Perspectives on Gay Unions: The Uneasy Marriage of Religion and Politics." Pages

105–29 in *The Politics of Same-Sex Marriage*. Edited by Craig A. Rimmerman and Clyde Wilcox. Chicago: University of Chicago Press.

Walker, Michelle Boulous. 1998. *Philosophy and the Maternal Body: Reading Silence*. New York: Routledge.

Walker, William O. 1975. "1 Corinthians 11:2–16 and Paul's Views Regarding Women." *JBL* 94:94–110.

———. 1983. "The 'Theology of Woman's Place' and the 'Paulinist' Tradition." *Semeia* 28:101–12.

———.. 1987. "The Burden of Proof in Identifying Interpolations in the Pauline Letters." *NTS* 33:610–18.

———. 1988. "Text-Critical Evidence for Interpolations in the Letters of Paul." *CBQ* 50:622–31.

———. 1989. "The Vocabulary of 1 Corinthians 11.3–16: Pauline or Non-Pauline?" *JSNT* 35:75–88.

———. 2004. "Interpolations in the Pauline Letters." Pages 189–235 in *The Pauline Canon*. Edited by Stanley E. Porter. Pauline Studies 1. Leiden: Brill.

Walsh, Sheila. 2006. *God's Little Princess Devotional Bible*. Nashville: Nelson.

———. 2007. *God's Mighty Warrior Devotional Bible*. Nashville: Nelson.

Walters, Jonathan. 1993. " 'No More Than a Boy:' The Shifting Construction of Masculinity from Ancient Greece to the Middle Ages." *Gender and History* 5:20–33.

———. 1997. "Invading the Roman Body: Manliness and Impenetrability in Roman Thought." Pages 29–43 in *Roman Sexualities*. Edited by Judith P. Hallett and Marilyn B. Skinner. Princeton: Princeton University Press.

Waltke, Bruce K. 1978. "1 Corinthians 11:2–16: An Interpretation." *BSac* 135:46–57.

Ward, Graham. 1998. "The Erotics of Redemption—After Karl Barth." *T&S* 4:52–72.

Warner, Michael. 1991. "Introduction: Fear of a Queer Planet." *Social Text* 29:3–17.

———. 1993. "Introduction." Pages vii–xxxi in *Fear of a Queer Planet: Queer Politics and Social Theory*. Edited by Michael Warner (for the Social Text Collective). Cultural Politics 6. Minneapolis: University of Minnesota Press.

Watson, Francis. 2000a. *Agape, Eros, Gender: Towards a Pauline Sexual Ethic*. Cambridge: Cambridge University Press.

———. 2000b. "The Authority of the Voice: A Theological Reading of 1 Cor 11.2–16." *NTS* 46:520–36.

———. 2002. "Spaces Sacred and Profane: Stephen Moore, Sex and the Bible." *JSNT* 25:109–17.

Watson, Nigel. 1992. *The First Epistle to the Corinthians*. Epworth Commentaries. London: Epworth.

Webb, William J. 2001. *Slaves, Women and Homosexuals: Exploring the Hermeneutics of Cultural Analysis*. Downers Grove, IL: InterVarsity Press.

———. 2004a. "Balancing Paul's Original-Creation and Pro-Creation Arguments: 1 Corinthians 11:11–12 in Light of Modern Embryology." *WTJ* 66:275–89.

———. 2004b. "Gender Equality and Homosexuality." Pages 401–13 in *Discovering Biblical Equality: Complementarity without Hierarchy*. Edited by Ronald W. Pierce and Rebecca Merrill Groothuis. Downers Grove, IL: InterVarsity Press.

Webster, Alison. 1998. "Queer to Be Religious: Lesbian Adventures beyond the Christian/Post-Christian Dichotomy." *T&S* 4:27–39.

Weed, Elizabeth, and Naomi Schor, eds. 1997. *Feminism Meets Queer Theory*. Books from Differences. Bloomington: Indiana University Press.

Weedon, Chris. 1997. *Feminist Practice and Poststructuralist Theory*. 2nd ed. Oxford: Blackwell.

Weeks, Jeffrey. 1981. "Discourse, Desire and Sexual Deviance: Some Problems in a History of Homosexuality." Pages 76–111, 245–46 in *The Making of the Modern Homosexual*. Edited by Kenneth Plummer. London: Hutchinson.

———. 2002. "Sexuality and History Revisited." Pages 27–41 in *Sexualities in History: A Reader*. Edited by Kim M. Phillips and Barry Reay. New York: Routledge.

———. 2003. *Sexuality*. 2nd ed. Key Ideas. London: Routledge.

Weeks, Jeffrey, Brian Heaphy, and Catherine Donovan. 2001. *Same Sex Intimacies: Families of Choice and Other Life Experiments*. New York: Routledge.

Weeks, Noel. 1972. "Of Silence and Head Coverings." *WTJ* 35:21–27.

———. 1988. *The Sufficiency of Scripture*. Carlisle: Banner of Truth Trust.

Weiss, Johannes. 1910. *Der erste Korintherbrief*. KEK 5. Göttingen: Vandenhoeck & Ruprecht.

Welborn, Lawrence L. 1997. *Politics and Rhetoric in the Corinthian Epistles.* Macon, GA: Mercer University Press.

Wenzel, Hélène Vivienne. 1981. "The Text as Body/Politics: An Appreciation of Monique Wittig's Writings in Context." *FS* 7:264–87.

West, Mona. 1999. "Reading the Bible as Queer Americans: Social Location and the Hebrew Scriptures." *T&S* 10:28–42.

West, Traci C. "Naming the Problem: Black Clergy, U.S. Politics, and Marriage Equality." Pages 177–90 in *Our Family Values: Same-Sex Marriage and Religion.* Vol. 2 of *Defending Same-Sex Marriage.* Edited by Traci C. West. Westport, CT: Praeger, 2007.

Westboro Baptist Church. "God Hates Fags." http://tinyurl.com/SBL0685j.

Whatling, Clare. 1997. "Wittig's Monsters: Stretching the Lesbian Reader." *Textual Practice* 11:237–48.

White, Edward. 1999. *Marcel Proust: A Life.* Penguin Lives. New York: Viking Penguin.

White, Jerry. 1997. *Dangers Men Face: Overcoming the Five Greatest Threats to Living Life Well.* Colorado Springs: Navpress.

White, Mel. 1994. *Stranger at the Gate: To Be Gay and Christian in America.* New York: Simon & Schuster.

Wiegman, Robyn. 2007. "Un-remembering Monique Wittig." *GLQ* 13:505–18.

Williams, Craig A. 1999. *Roman Homosexuality: Ideologies of Masculinity in Classical Antiquity.* Ideologies of Desire. New York: Oxford University Press.

Williams, Rhys H., ed. 2001. *Promise Keepers and the New Masculinity: Private Lives and Public Morality.* Lanham, MD: Lexington Books, co-published with the Association for the Sociology of Religion.

Williams, Tony. 1996. *Hearths of Darkness: The Family in the American Horror Film.* London: Associated University Presses.

Wilson, Andrew P. 2006. "Stabat Maria: Marian Fragments and the Limits of *Masculinity.*" Pages 27–44 in *The Recycled Bible: Autobiography, Culture, and the Space Between.* Edited by Fiona Black. SemeiaSt 51. Atlanta: Society of Biblical Literature.

Wilson, Kenneth T. 1991. "Should Women Wear Headcoverings?" *BSac* 148:442–62.

Wilson, Nancy L. 1995. *Our Tribe: Queer Folks, God, Jesus, and the Bible.* San Francisco: HarperSanFrancisco.

Wilson-Kastner, Patricia. 1982. "Contemporary Feminism and Christian Doctrine of the Human." *Word and World* 2:234–42.

Winandy, J. 1992. "Un curieux *casus pendens:* 1 Corinthiens 11.10 et son interprétation." *NTS* 38:621–29.

Wink, Walter. 2002. "Sex and the Bible: To Hell with Gays?" *Christian Century* 119:32–34.

Winkler, John J. 1990. *The Constraints of Desire: The Anthropology of Sex and Gender in Ancient Greece.* New Ancient World. New York: Routledge.

Winston, Robert, producer. 2002. "Deepest Desires," program 2 of *Human Instinct*, BBC.

Winter, Bruce. 2001. *After Paul Left Corinth: The Influence of Secular Ethics and Social Change.* Grand Rapids: Eerdmans.

———. 2002. *Philo and Paul among the Sophists: Alexandrian and Corinthian Responses to a Julio-Claudian Movement.* 2nd ed. Grand Rapids: Eerdmans.

———. 2003a. "The 'Underlays' of Conflict and Compromise in 1 Corinthians." Pages 139–55 in *Paul and the Corinthians: Studies on a Community in Conflict: Essays in Honour of Margaret Thrall.* Edited by Trevor J. Burke and J. Keith Elliott. NovTSup 109. Leiden: Brill.

———. 2003b. *Roman Wives, Roman Widows: The Appearance of New Women and the Pauline Communities.* Grand Rapids: Eerdmans.

Wintermans, Caspar. 2007. *Alfred Douglas: A Poet's Life and His Finest Work.* London: Peter Owen.

Wire, Antoinette Clark. 1990. *The Corinthian Women Prophets: A Reconstruction through Paul's Rhetoric.* Minneapolis: Fortress.

Witherington, Ben, III. 1988. *Women in the Earliest Churches.* SNTSMS 59. Cambridge: Cambridge University Press.

———. 1995. *Conflict and Community in Corinth: A Socio-rhetorical Commentary on 1 and 2 Corinthians.* Grand Rapids: Eerdmans.

Wittig, Monique. 1971. *Les Guérillères.* Translated by David Le Vay. London: Peter Owen.

———. 1976. *The Lesbian Body.* Translated by David Le Vay. New York: Avon.

———. 1979. "Paradigm." Pages 114–21 in *Homosexualities and French Literature: Cultural Contexts/Critical Texts.* Edited by George Stambolian and Elaine Marks. Ithaca, NY: Cornell University Press.

———. 1992a. "The Category of Sex." Pages 1–8 in *The Straight Mind and Other Essays.* Boston: Beacon.

———. 1992b. "Homo Sum." Pages 46–58 in *The Straight Mind and Other Essays.* Boston: Beacon.

—. 1992c. "The Mark of Gender." Pages 76–89 in *The Straight Mind and Other Essays*. Boston: Beacon.

—. 1992d. "On the Social Contract." Pages 33–45 in *The Straight Mind and Other Essays*. Boston: Beacon.

—. 1992e. "One Is Not Born a Woman." Pages 9–20 in *The Straight Mind and Other Essays*. Boston: Beacon.

—. 1992f. "The Point of View: Universal or Particular." Pages 59–67 in *The Straight Mind and Other Essays*. Boston: Beacon.

—. 1992g. "Preface." Pages xiii–xvii in *The Straight Mind and Other Essays*. Boston: Beacon.

—. 1992h. "The Site of Action." Pages 90–100 in *The Straight Mind and Other Essays*. Boston: Beacon.

—. 1992i. "The Straight Mind." Pages 21–32 in *The Straight Mind and Other Essays*. Boston: Beacon.

—. 1992j. *The Straight Mind and Other Essays*. Boston: Beacon.

—. 1992k. "The Trojan Horse." Pages 68–75 in *The Straight Mind and Other Essays*. Boston: Beacon.

—. 2005a. "Some Remarks on *Les guérillères*." Pages 37–43 in *On Monique Wittig: Theoretical, Political, and Literary Essays*. Edited by Namascar Shaktini. Urbana: University of Illinois Press.

—. 2005b. "Some Remarks on *The Lesbian Body*." Pages 44–48 in *On Monique Wittig: Theoretical, Political, and Literary Essays*. Edited by Namascar Shaktini. Urbana: University of Illinois Press.

Wittman, Carl. 1972. "A Gay Manifesto." Pages 330–42 in *Out of the Closets: Voices of Gay Liberation*. Edited by Karla Jay and Allen Young. New York: Douglas.

Wold, Benjamin G. 2008. "Family Ethics in *4QInstruction* and the New Testament." *NovT* 50:286–300.

Wold, Donald J. 1998. *Out of Order: Homosexuality and the Ancient Near East*. Grand Rapids: Baker.

Wolfe, Susan J., and Julia Penelope. 1993. "Sexual Identity/Textual Politics: Lesbian {De Com} Positions." Pages 1–24 in *Sexual Practice/Textual Theory: Lesbian Cultural Criticism*. Edited by Susan J. Wolfe and Julia Penelope. Cambridge: Blackwell.

Woodman, A. J. 2002. "*Biformis Vates*: The *Odes*, Catullus and Greek Lyric." Pages 53–64 in *Traditions and Contexts in the Poetry of Horace*. Edited by Tony Woodman and Denis Feeney. New York: Cambridge University Press.

Woolf, Virginia. 1966. *Collected Essays*. Vol. 2. London: Hogarth.

Wright, N. T. 1991. *The Climax of the Covenant: Christ and the Law in Pauline Theology*. Edinburgh: T&T Clark.

Yeo, Khiok-khng. 1998. "Differentiation and Mutuality of Male-Female Relations in 1 Corinthians 11:2–16." *BR* 43:7–21.

Young, Audrey. 2004. "Family First Say the Men in Black." *The NZ Herald*, 24 August, A3.

Young, David. 2004. "Uncivil Union." *The Listener*. April 17–23:32–33.

Zeitlin, Froma I. 1990. "The Poetics of *Erōs*: Nature, Art, and Imitation in Longus' *Daphnis and Chloe*." Pages 417–64 in *Before Sexuality: The Construction of Erotic Experience in the Ancient Greek World*. Edited by David M. Halperin, John J. Winkler, and Froma I. Zeitlin. Princeton: Princeton University Press.

Zerilli, Linda M. G. 1990. "The Trojan Horse of Universalism: Language as a 'War Machine' in the Writings of Monique Wittig." *Social Text* 25–26:146–70.

———. 2005. "A New Grammar of Difference: Monique Wittig's Poetic Revolution." Pages 87–114 in *On Monique Wittig: Theoretical, Political, and Literary Essays*. Edited by Namascar Shaktini. Urbana: University of Illinois Press.

Zuk, Marlene. 2002. *Sexual Selections: What We Can and Can't Learn about Sex from Animals*. Berkeley: University of California Press.

Ancient Sources Index

Modern Authors Index

Subject Index

CPSIA information can be obtained
at www.ICGtesting.com
Printed in the USA
LVOW03s0408110717
540894LV00001B/3/P